THE SHUBERTS AND THEIR
PASSING SHOWS

BROADWAY LEGACIES

Geoffrey Block, Series Editor

Series Board

Dominic McHugh   Jeffrey Magee

Tim Carter   Carol J. Oja

Kim Kowalke   Larry Starr

Stephen Banfield, *emeritus*

THE SHUBERTS AND THEIR *PASSING SHOWS*

The Untold Tale of Ziegfeld's Rivals

JONAS WESTOVER

OXFORD
UNIVERSITY PRESS

OXFORD
UNIVERSITY PRESS

Oxford University Press is a department of the University of Oxford. It furthers
the University's objective of excellence in research, scholarship, and education
by publishing worldwide. Oxford is a registered trade mark of Oxford University
Press in the UK and certain other countries.

Published in the United States of America by Oxford University Press
198 Madison Avenue, New York, NY 10016, United States of America.

Library of Congress Cataloging-in-Publication Data
Names: Westover, Jonas, author.
Title: The Shuberts and their Passing Shows : the untold tale of Ziegfeld's
rivals / by Jonas Westover.
Description: New York : Oxford University Press, [2016] | Series: The
Broadway legacies series | Includes bibliographical references and index.
Identifiers: LCCN 2016008634| ISBN 9780190219239 (bound book : alk. paper) |
ISBN 9780190219260 (oxford scholarship online) | ISBN 9780190219277
(companion website)
Subjects: LCSH: Revues—United States—20th century—History and criticism. |
Shubert, Jacob J., 1878?–1963. | Shubert, Lee, 1873?–1953. | Shubert
Organization—History—20th century.
Classification: LCC ML1711.5 .W47 2016 | DDC 792.609747/1—dc23 LC record available
at http://lccn.loc.gov/2016008634
Hardcover 9780190219239
UPDF 9780190219246
EPUB 9780190219253
Oxford Scholarship Online 9780190219260
Companion Website 9780190219277

1 3 5 7 9 8 6 4 2
Printed by Sheridan Books, Inc., United States of America

TO JOHN GRAZIANO,

for opening the curtain in the first place,

and

TO PAUL CHAROSH,

for letting me hear their voices in so many ways.

CONTENTS

• • •

LIST OF FIGURES

• • •

*Images available on companion website

LIST OF TABLES

• • •

LIST OF MUSICAL EXAMPLES
• • •

A LIST OF *PASSING SHOW* PERSONAGES

• • •

Performers, Producers, Professionals, and Participants
Associated with the Revues

The Passing Show (PS) each person/act was involved in is mentioned
at the end of each entry.

P. DODD ACKERMAN (1876–1963): Scene designer and painter. Incredibly prolific designer, Ackerman was responsible for dozens of shows including *The Firefly* (1912) and *No, No, Nanette* (1925). He ran a studio in Brooklyn and employed a large number of theatrical builders and seamstresses. *PS 1915, 1916, 1917.*

ADELAIDE AND HUGHES: MARY ADELAIDE DICKEY (1884-1960) and JOHN J. HUGHES (ca. 1887-1920) were a dance duo active in vaudeville during the 1910s. They used a creative mixture of classical and popular styles. *PS 1912.*

FRED ALLEN (1894–1956): Comedian. Allen began in vaudeville, but went on to great success in many forms of entertainment, including on the Broadway stage, in movies, and television. *The Fred Allen Show* was the top-rated program on radio during the mid-1940s. *PS 1922.*

SAM ASH (1884–1951): Comedian and singer. A vaudevillian who made records early in his career, Ash appeared on Broadway throughout the 1920s, but went on to Hollywood in 1929, appearing in many serials. He was in over two hundred films, mostly playing bit parts. *PS 1922.*

FRED AND ADELE ASTAIRE: Fred (1899–1987) and Adele (1897–1981) were dancers and singers whose career began when they were small children and continued as a partnership into the 1920s, notably in *Lady Be Good* (1924) and *The Band Wagon* (1931). Adele quit performing after marriage in 1932, while Fred went on to become a central star of film musicals. *PS 1918.*

HAROLD ATTERIDGE (1887–1938): Writer, librettist, and lyricist. Born in Chicago, Atteridge wrote lyrics for several songs that found their way into Broadway shows, including *Madame Sherry* (1910). He moved to New York in 1910 and was soon after hired by the Shuberts. He wrote the book and lyrics to every edition of *The Passing Show* on Broadway. *PS 1912–1924, 1926, 1932.*

(GEORGE) WATSON BARRATT (1884–1962): Scene designer and artistic director. Trained as an illustrator, Barratt was hired by the Shuberts in 1918 and consequently was the principal scene designer for (reputedly) over three hundred of their productions. One of the most influential scene designers in Broadway's history, Barratt's early career was primarily his work on the Winter Garden revues. He was also an important patron and supporter of regional theater and art. *PS 1918–1919, 1922–1924, 1932.*

BILLIE BURKE (ZIEGFELD) (1884–1970): Actress. Burke came from a family of entertainers and began performing in 1903. She was successful on the stage, first in London, then New York, and eventually Hollywood (in films). Her most famous role was that of Glinda the Good Witch in *The Wizard of Oz* (1937). She perpetuated her husband (Florenz Ziegfeld's) name and show after he died through later productions. *PS 1934, 1936, 1943.*

HELEN CARRINGTON (1895–1963): Actress and singer. Began as a chorus girl in *The Passing Show* and eventually became a well-known comic and character actress. She was featured in *Plain Jane* (1924) and *Queen High* (1926) and remained on the stage into the 1930s, notably in *The Band Wagon* (1931). She also made films. *PS 1914, 1915, 1918.*

LINCOLN J. CARTER (1865–1926): Playwright, manager, builder, and inventor. The Chicago-based Carter had a remarkable career writing highly emotional melodramas from the late nineteenth century into the twentieth. His shows toured widely and were very popular. He was also known for his stage inventions and effects. *PS 1916.*

JOSÉ COLLINS (1887–1958): English singer and actress. The daughter of Lottie Collins, the singer known for "Ta-Ra-Ra-Boom-De-Ay," Collins starred in *The Merry Widow* by age 15 and was brought to America by the Shuberts in 1911 for *Vera Violetta.* She was known for an excellent soprano voice. *PS 1914.*

HOMER B. CONANT (1887–1927): Costume designer and illustrator. Conant was a Shubert employee during the 1910s and 1920s, providing many sketches for dozens of shows. During the same time, he also drew for many periodicals, including *The Broadside* and *Theatre Magazine. PS 1914–1917, 1919* (possibly more).

FRANCES DEMAREST (fl. 1910s): Singer and actress. Demarest was a success in vaudeville and on Broadway, with featured roles in several shows, including *Madame Sherry* (1910) and *The Royal Vagabond* (1919). *PS 1914, 1915, 1916.*

ERTÉ (1892–1990): Costume designer. Erté was a Russian artist partially responsible for the Art Deco style through his illustrations, costume work, stage designs, jewelry, and especially fashion. *PS 1922.*

FRANK FAY (1891–1961): Actor and comedian. A star in vaudeville by 1920, he also performed in a number of Broadway shows. He was the lead in *Harvey* (1944). Fay was also well known in Hollywood into the late 1940s, after which he became a writer for television. *PS 1918.*

HARRY FISHER (1868–1923): Comic actor in vaudeville and on Broadway. He was the "straight" man to George W. Monroe's overbearing female characters. The two were successes in such shows as *The Midnight Sons* (1909) and *The Sun Dodgers* (1912). *PS 1914, 1915.*

IRENE FRANKLIN (1876–1941): Actress, singer, lyricist, and comedian. Important female performer through songs like "Redhead" in vaudeville, she had several Broadway appearances before turning to film in the 1930s. *PS 1917.*

TRIXIE FRIGANZA (1870–1955): Boisterous comedic actress. Active in vaudeville and in numerous Broadway productions, her early successes include *The Prince of Pilsen* (1903) and the pre-*Follies* revue, *Higgeldy-Piggledy* (1905). She was also a noted suffragette. *PS 1912.*

BERNARD GRANVILLE (1886–1936): Actor, singer, dancer, publisher. Originally considered a rival to Jolson, Granville was successful in vaudeville and on Broadway. He was particularly known for replacing Vernon Castle in *Watch Your Step*. He had a movie career in his later years. *PS 1914.*

CHARLOTTE GREENWOOD (1890–1978): Comedian, dancer, and singer. Beginning as a chorus girl, the six-foot-tall dancer got noticed, going on to vaudeville and Broadway. She found great success as the "Letty" character in a number of musicals, including *So Long, Letty* (1929). She went on to star in television and movies, notably playing "Aunt Eller" in the film of *Oklahoma!* (1955). *PS 1912, 1913.*

"TEXAS" GUINAN (1885–1933): Actress, singer, speakeasy owner. Guinan began in vaudeville, and sang in several productions in 1909–1911. She was known for her vivacious, brash personality and appeared in several revues. During Prohibition she ran many speakeasies, where she acted as hostess and also put on revues of her own. *PS 1912.*

ERNEST (ERNIE) HARE (1883–1939): Singer. Active on Broadway through the 1910s, especially in revues, Hare began recording records in 1918 with great success, and eventually paired with Billy Jones to form the "Happiness Boys." They became two of the highest-paid performers on radio throughout the next two decades. *PS 1912, 1915.*

GEORGE HASSELL (1881–1937): British actor and comedian. Hassell was active in America after 1906, often in dramatic roles; he was in *The Girl from Brazil* (1916), after which he turned mainly to comedy. *PS 1918, 1922, 1923.*

PORTLAND HOFFA (1905–1990): Comedian and singer. Hoffa began in vaudeville, worked on Broadway in the 1920s, and then moved to radio with husband, Fred Allen. She was also active in television. *PS 1922.*

EUGENE HOWARD (1881–1965): Comedian and singer. The older brother in the Howard Brothers act, he was usually the "straight" man for his brother Willie, but he also took on many raucous comic roles. The two were considered the central stars of *The Passing Show* series and many of George White's *Scandals*. Eugene quit the act to become Willie's manager in 1940. *PS 1912, 1915, 1918, 1921, 1922.*

WILLIE HOWARD (1886–1943): Comedian and singer. The younger brother in the Howard Brothers act, Howard was considered among the first of the Jewish comedians to incorporate Yiddish humor and accents in the act. He was an important star on Broadway, especially in revues, appearing in Gershwin's *Girl Crazy* (1930). He also released recordings and starred in several short films. He appeared in the first *Passing Show* in 1912 and also the final version, in 1945/6, which played only in previews. *PS 1912, 1915, 1918, 1921, 1922, 1946.*

JOBYNA HOWLAND (1880–1936): Actress. Her career began in 1899, and she performed in many stage works, often comedies. Also active in movies, especially the Woolsey and Wheeler comedies, beginning with *The Cuckoos* (1930). *PS 1912.*

J.C. HUFFMAN (1869–1935): Director. Originally from Ohio, he performed as a child actor and singer before he was a director. Eventually he gained an international reputation and began working for the Shuberts as early as 1906. He was responsible for the direction of most of the Winter Garden revues, including *Artists and Models* and the *Greenwich Village Follies*, as well as many of the Shuberts' large-scale operettas. *PS 1914–1924, 1926*

ALEXIS KOSLOFF (ca. 1888–1983): Russian dancer and choreographer. Alexis followed Theodore to the United States after a high-profile career in Europe. He worked for the Shuberts for more than a decade. He also made films, but was based in New York, where he performed at the Metropolitan Opera and ran a dance studio. *PS 1915.*

THEODORE KOSLOFF (1882–1956): Russian dancer and choreographer. A member of Diaghilev's Ballet Russes, Kosloff came to America in 1912 and was instrumental in bringing high-quality dance to several venues, including the Winter Garden revues. He moved to Hollywood in 1917 to act and eventually run a dance studio. His wife, Maria Baldina, was a frequent dance partner and co-instructor. *PS 1912, 1915.*

The Lockfords: ZITA AND NARO LOCKFORD (formerly Lebateau) (fl. 1920s). Parisian acrobats and dancers. Their specialty was an "adagio" act. *PS 1922, 1924.*

JACK MASON (fl. 1910s–1940s): Choreographer, dancer, performer, and manager (not to be confused with the contemporary composer of the same name). Mason was active just after the turn of the century in both vaudeville and on the Broadway stage. His dancing partner was Lois Whitney. Mason choreographed some of the Winter Garden revues in the mid-1910s but also worked for several other producers. *PS 1914, 1915, 1918.*

ARTIE MEHLINGER (1886–1959): Vaudeville singer who toured widely as a part of Step, Mehlinger, and King during the 1910s, and he also teamed with singer George Meyer. The tenor wrote lyrics for several Tin Pan Alley songs, including "Hiawatha's Melody of Love," and he was strongly associated with others, such as "Carolina in the Morning." *PS 1913, 1914.*

EMILY MILES (1892–1947): Actress and singer. Miles began as a chorus girl, then became an understudy, and eventually took on a principal role in many *Passing Shows*. She retired in 1922 when she married Willie Howard. *PS 1914–1918, 1921, 1922.*

MARILYN(N) MILLER (1898–1936): Singer, dancer, and actress. Miller began performing as a child in vaudeville as part of her family's troupe and then moved onto the Broadway stage. Her star turns in shows such as *Sally* (1920), *Sunny* (1925), *Rosalie* (1928), and *As Thousands Cheer* (1933) brought her incredible popularity. She was also a Hollywood star, reprising her roles in *Sally* (1929) and *Sunny* (1930) in movies. *PS 1914, 1915.*

GEORGE W. MONROE (1857–1932): Female impersonator/comedian active in the 1880s until the 1910s. He was particularly known for his Irish matron character, "Aunt Bridget," in "The Doings of Mrs. Dooley" (1902) and other shows. He and Harry Fisher worked together in such shows as *The Midnight Sons* (1909) and *The Sun Dodgers* (1912). *PS 1914, 1915.*

NITA NALDI (1894–1961): Actress. Naldi began as a chorus girl, but she became nationally famous as a movie star after being featured in *Dr. Jekyll and Mr. Hyde* (1920) alongside John Barrymore. *PS 1918.*

NAZARRO TROUPE: Nat Nazarro Jr., J. Edward Nazarro, and Erman Nazarro, with more members possibly included in the overall troupe. Gymnasts and acrobats. Nat Jr. was a singer and dancer as well. Troupe: *PS 1914*. Nat Nazarro Jr.: *PS 1914, 1922, 1923.*

OSCAR RADIN (1874–1957): Conductor and composer. Russian by birth, Radin became a violinist in Pittsburgh, but soon turned to conducting. He worked in small companies until 1906, when he settled in New York and began working on Broadway until 1929. He began to compose scores for films after 1932, and conducted the music for several, including *Mad Love* (1935). Uncle of Oscar Levant, he was one of the most important musical theater conductors of his time. *PS 1912–1917, 1919.*

GEORGE AND DICK RATH (formerly George Meigs [dates unknown] and Wilbur Richard "Dick" Cameron [1894-1975]): Acrobats, singers. The duo was an adagio act that was active in vaudeville and on Broadway from the 1910s into the 1930s. They were at the center of a major lawsuit between Ziegfeld and the Shuberts in 1920. *PS 1919.*

FRANCIS RENAULT (ca. 1893–1955): Female impersonator, singer, and comedian. A "boy singer" in Gus Edwards' 1908 *School Days*, Renault performed in vaudeville. As an adult, Renault found great success as an impersonator with an expensive wardrobe and a beautiful falsetto voice. He opened his own club in Atlantic City in 1924, and eventually performed at the Metropolitan Opera and over forty times at Carnegie Hall. *PS 1922.*

BLANCHE RING (1871–1961): Vaudeville and Broadway performer, especially known for her "signature" songs, which included "I've Got Rings on My Fingers." Ring often invited audiences to sing along with her performances. She married Charles Winninger after appearing together in *The Yankee Girl* (1909). *PS 1919.*

ISABELLA RODRIGUEZ (dates unknown): Spanish dancer. Rodriguez danced in Europe, but fled in 1915 due to the war. Originally from Barcelona, she was known for her abilities with the castanets and was considered a specialist in Catalan styles. *PS 1918.*

SIGMUND ROMBERG (1887–1951): Composer. Romberg was born in Hungary but he moved to America in 1909. A central figure in the Shubert's creative team, Romberg wrote dozens of shows for the producers, including most of their Winter Garden revues and popular operettas of the 1920s, such as *Blossom Time* (1921), *The Student Prince* (1924), and *The Desert Song* (1926). *PS 1914, 1916–1918, 1923, 1924.*

CHARLES RUGGLES (1886–1970): Actor and comedian. Ruggles began working on the stage in 1905 and performed regularly until 1929. He appeared in many silent films during the 1910s and continued finding success in comedy movies up until his death. *PS 1918.*

FRANK SADDLER (1864–1921): Orchestrator. Saddler was an expert arranger, working in the Midwest for some time before moving to New York. His most famous collaborator was Jerome Kern. Saddler's students include many of the most important Broadway orchestrators from the 1920s and beyond, most notably Robert Russell Bennett. *PS 1912-1919.*

JEAN SCHWARTZ (1878–1956): Composer. Schwartz was a popular Tin Pan Alley composer and pianist. He had a vaudeville routine and was the designated accompanist for the Dolly Sisters. He was one of the most sought-after Broadway tunesmiths of his time, and eventually he wrote for film. *PS 1913, 1918, 1919, 1921, 1923, 1924.*

JACOB J. (J. J.) SHUBERT (c.1879–1963): Youngest of the Shubert Brothers he became deeply involved with overseeing productions after Sam's death. The Winter Garden revues, including *The Passing Shows*, were his projects.

LEVI (LEE) SHUBERT (c.1871–1953): Oldest of the Shubert Brothers, he was frequently responsible for the financial affairs of the firm.

SAM SHUBERT (c.1875–1905): The family of nine emigrated to Syracuse, New York, from Poland around 1881, and he was the first of the brothers to become involved in theater with a small onstage role. After various positions with theaters, he became a theater manager in 1897 and soon after was a tour manager before moving to New York City and establishing his family's business. He was killed in a train accident in 1905.

ETHEL SHUTTA (1896–1976): Actress and singer. Shutta began her career as part of her family's vaudeville show. Well-known as a Broadway performer, most notably in *Whoopee!* (1928), she also had a prolific career on radio, both with her husband, bandleader Geroge Olsen, and with Jack Benny. She made a remarkable comeback to the stage in Sondheim's *Follies* (1971). *PS 1922.*

ERNEST ROMAYNE "MA" SIMMONS (1865–1954): Costume supervisor. Simmons was one of the Shuberts' most trusted employees, performing an array of tasks. He worked for the firm from 1912 until just before 1950. Simmons was involved in some way with each of *The Passing Shows.*

COUNTESS THAMARA DE SWIRSKAYA (1888–1961): Russian dancer and pianist. Swirskaya studied in St. Petersburg and Paris, performed for Grieg, and had a successful career in both Europe and America, traveling between the two on multiple occasions. She appeared on film, on Broadway, in vaudeville, and with the Metropolitan Opera. Her first American national tour was in 1910, complete with a dancing troupe and orchestra. She continued to perform throughout the 1920s as a dancer and settled in Los Angeles, playing piano into the 1950s. *PS 1916.*

FRANK D. THOMAS (fl. 1905–1920): Scene designer and inventor. Designed "effects" that made use of film as early as 1913 at the Winter Garden. *PS 1913, 1914.*

TRADO TWINS: FRANK (1904–1980) AND PETER (1904–1969) TRADO were actually twin brothers who worked as a comedy duo active in vaudeville and eventually in films. *P.S 1922, 1923.*

NED WAYBURN (1874–1942): Dance instructor, director, and choreographer. Wayburn was one of the primary figures in the development of dance during the early twentieth century, running a school for chorus girls and staging his own revues. He was an important force in the early Winter Garden revues. *PS 1912, 1913.*

CHARLES WINNINGER (1884–1969): Actor in vaudeville, Broadway, and eventually a well-known film presence in movies. He played "Cap'n Andy" in *Show Boat* (1927). He married Blanche Ring after they appeared together in *The Yankee Girl* (1909). *PS 1919.*

ED WYNN (1886–1966): Comic actor active in vaudeville, on Broadway, on film, and also television. Wynne was a major star of revues, especially in his own shows in the 1920s and 1930s. *PS 1916.*

FLORENZ ZIEGFELD, JR. (1867–1932): Theater producer and impresario. His father ran the Trocadero Club in Chicago, immersing Ziegfeld in the world of entertainment at a young age. Best remembered for his series of revues begun in 1907 called the *Follies*, he also produced a number of other key shows, including *Show Boat* (1927). The Shubert brothers negotiated the rights to the *Follies* property after Ziegfeld's death.

FOREWORD

• • •

In contrast to plot-driven musical comedies and operettas, the perennially popular revue genre from the 1890s to about 1930 featured skits, songs, dances, stylish sets, and female pulchritude within a looser narrative, albeit often constructed within a unified thematic framework. In 1912, the producers and brothers Lee and J. J. Shubert launched an annual series of revues called *The Passing Show*, a name borrowed from the revue (then designated "review"), which begat the form in 1894. From 1912 to 1924, with the exception of 1920, the Shuberts' *Passing Shows* became the reliable annual rival of Florenz Ziegfeld's *Ziegfeld Follies* (1911–1925, 1927, and 1931), formerly more simply and less-indulgently designated as the *Follies* (1907–1910). *The Shuberts and Their Passing Shows: The Untold Tale of Ziegfeld's Rivals*, the pioneering new Broadway Legacies volume by Jonas Westover, the young but distinguished scholar of the revue genre, "challenges the notion that Ziegfeld and his *Follies* were the only important revues of the era" and offers a comprehensive rediscovery of a major series of shows that unfortunately has been largely "passed" over by history.

From the beginning, the Shubert brothers' consistently successful series of *Passing Shows* provided a worthy alternative to those of their local rival and arguably served as an unrivaled repository for present and future stars and both rising and established talents. The first edition not only included a score by Louis Hirsch but also interpolated Irving Berlin's early hit "Everybody's Doing It Now" to accompany stage action and another Berlin song, "The Ragtime Jockey Man," for Willie Howard, who would gain more lasting fame for his role as Gieber Goldfarb in the Gershwins' *Girl Crazy* in 1930. Following Hirsch and Berlin's opening gambit, the ever-present Sigmund Romberg became the Shuberts' main "house" composer for well over half the remaining revues (1914, 1916–1919, and 1923–1924), enhanced by proven interpolated popular songs by lesser-known composers. Audiences at one of these Romberg shows, *The Passing Show of 1916*, also witnessed the first George Gershwin song to be performed on the Broadway stage. Most of the lasting songs, however, were not composed by Romberg or Gershwin, but several fondly remembered songs offered by composers now largely forgotten, most notably Tony Jackson's "Pretty Baby" from the 1916 edition (credited to composer Egbert Van Alstyne and lyricist Gus Kahn), and two perennial hits from 1918, Lee S. Roberts's "Smiles" and John Kellette's "I'm Forever Blowing Bubbles."

In addition to Willie Howard and his brother Eugene, the central stars of numerous *Passing Shows* who deserve and receive a chapter of their own in this volume, Westover introduces readers to Marilynn (later Marilyn) Miller, the future star of Jerome Kern's *Sally* (1920) and *Sunny* (1925), as a fifteen-year-old talent who lit up the Broadway stage in *The Passing Show of 1914*. We also meet the phenomenal new brother-and-sister dance team of Adele and Fred Astaire in 1918, *Show Boat*'s future Cap'n Andy, Charles Winninger, in 1916 and 1919, and in the 1916 edition Ed Wynn, the future star of Rodgers and Hart's *Simple Simon* (1930), the voice of the Mad Hatter in Walt Disney's *Alice in Wonderland* (1951) and Uncle Albert in the Disney version of *Mary Poppins* (1964). The 1922 edition featured the young Ethel Shutta, who in her seventies could still stop a show when she belted Stephen Sondheim's "Broadway Baby" in another *Follies* nearly fifty years later in 1971. The final *Passing Show* edition of 1924 offers yet another fascinating historical footnote since it led to the discovery of Joan Crawford, one of the forty-five carefully chosen girls in the chorus, reduced from the eighty members who graced the stage when the series began its long run in 1912.

In *The Shuberts and Their Passing Shows* Westover, who has published articles on *The Passing Shows* and other early revues, guest edited a special issue on the revue in *Studies in Musical Theatre*, and contributed 406 articles on diverse topics in the second edition of *The Grove Dictionary of American Music*, follows his award-winning dissertation at CUNY on *The Passing Show of 1914* with new research that examines the legacy of all *The Passing Shows*. After a chapter on the genesis of the revue genre, Westover moves on to individual chapters on the many stars in *The Passing Shows* firmament, including the Howard brothers, female and male choruses and the early career of chorus girl Joan Crawford, the songs and their acclaimed orchestrations by Frank Saddler and Robert Russell Bennett, and the role of dance and scenic design. The two chapters on *The Passing Show of 1914* explore the interplay of character, dialogue, and song, and engage the meanings behind a wide range of parodied material within their social contexts.

The rivalry between the Shuberts and Ziegfeld recalls the story of another Schubert, the nineteenth-century composer Franz Schubert, whose life and music was set to the hit musical *Blossom Time*, produced by the Shubert brothers in 1921. Just as Franz Schubert's story seems incomplete without at least acknowledging his more famous contemporary, Ludwig van Beethoven, it seems nearly impossible to tell the story of the Broadway Shuberts and their *Passing Shows* without taking into account what their neighbor and rival Ziegfeld was up to. For this reason, the final chapters generously document, analyze, and clarify the often acrimonious and litigious personal and professional feud between the Shubert brothers and Ziegfeld as it moved "from neutral to spiteful." Readers will also learn about the ironic twists that befell *The Passing Show* after the death of Ziegfeld in 1932 and the subsequent rise of the Ziegfeld Myth for which the Shuberts, who produced later editions of the *Ziegfeld Follies*, played a conspicuous part.

Thanks to Jonas Westover's *The Shuberts and Their Passing Shows: The Untold Tale of Ziegfeld's Rivals*, readers of this rigorously researched and copiously illustrated history will gain a vivid and vicarious understanding of a series of revues that, while seemingly ephemeral, served as a fertile breeding ground of talent and ideas and a Broadway legacy that was anything but a passing one.

Geoffrey Block
Series Editor, Broadway Legacies

ACKNOWLEDGMENTS

• • •

I have many people to thank for their encouragement and support throughout this project. The first would have to be John Graziano, who, as I mentioned in the Dedication, was the first to suggest diving into this era and (specifically) thinking in more depth about the revue as a genre. John and Roberta Graziano were steadfast supporters of my work and consistently offered suggestions and help with the project, a gift for which I will be forever grateful.

I also want to thank Paul Charosh, whose knowledge of the music of this era was essential to my understanding the context for many of the references. He was one of the few people who knew many of the individuals that I encountered for the first time as part of my research. Our daily conversations about performers such as Irene Franklin and Victor Herbert gave me a much broader perspective on the entire cultural milieu, which repeatedly helped remind me that I needed to approach the material on its own terms rather than through my own distant lens. He is also one of the kindest people I have ever known and a true friend.

The Shubert Archive was almost a miracle to me, both in the materials it housed, and also concerning kindness of the staff. My primary contact there was Mark Swartz, who answered my questions and provided materials with swiftness and thoughtfulness, and I am deeply thankful for his enthusiasm and encouragement. He also put up with my ramblings concerning new finds and new ideas, and I must also appreciate him for that. Maryann Chach and Sylvia Wang were also helpful and patient with me, and I cannot thank them enough for their aid. The Shubert Archive also kindly provided me with the permission to use materials from virtually every part of their vast collection, including scripts, lyrics, music, advertising materials, and a seemingly unending ream of personal communications between the Shuberts themselves, their staff, and the hundreds that were a part of their cultural milieu.

I wish to thank Geoffrey Block and the unidentified readers for Oxford, all of whom made incredibly useful suggestions as to the overall shape of the final product and concerning many of the details. Norm Hirschy has been an excellent guide down the road of my first book, always willing to field my frequent questions. David Grayson gave me helpful feedback on some of the chapters. The community of musical theater scholars has been very generous with their time and attention. This has been particularly true of those involved with the Society of American Music, where I have given multiple papers at conferences, inundating my colleagues with *Passing Show* research. I wish to especially thank Tom Riis, Ryan Bunch, Trudi Vorp Wright, Ben Sears, Brad Connors, Gillian Rodger, Michael Pisani, Sarah Schmalenberger, Tim Brooks, Anna Wheeler Gentry, Dominic McHugh, Dominic Symonds, Dan Shore, Meg Farrell, and Jennifer Jones Wilson for their suggestions, willingness to listen, and discussions concerning the topic. Richard C. Norton provided some important information about songs. I also want to thank Grant Hayter-Menzies for generously sharing documents from Charlotte Greenwood's unpublished memoirs that helped bring to life the experience of a newly hired cast member.

I must thank Bob Kosovsky at the Performing Arts Department of the New York Public Library as well. Bob helped orient me to the very large world of non-catalogued resources that the library holds. Martha Hayes at the Theater Museum of Repetoire Americana in Mount Pleasant, Iowa, was generous with her time and introduced me to their collection of Lincoln J. Carter materials. The Museum is a remarkable jewel of American theatrical resources that deserves greater attention.

This journey has included many surprises along the way, including many unusual finds in unusual places. One of these was Grapefruit Moon Gallery, a virtual store that specializes in popular art and illustration of the early twentieth century. I was thrilled to discover that one of the Gallery's locations was in Minneapolis, and one of the owners, Sarajane Blum, was kind enough to provide me with digital scans of the store's remarkable collection of chorus girl photographs. I must also extend my thanks to many eBay sellers who were willing to make photocopies of music and documents for me that otherwise would have been impossible to acquire.

Finally, I have to thank my friends and family. My parents, Bonnie and Allan Westover, have been a part of this journey since the day I left the Shubert Archive for the first time and called to tell them I was nearly hysterical with excitement about this new material. They both have been constant sources of encouragement; I cannot thank them enough. My mother went above and beyond the call of duty, proofreading each chapter through numerous drafts. I must also thank friends who have been with me through the whole process of the book, including Jane Wilson, Brok Kretzmann, and Tony Lee. A special thanks to the Monday night post-orchestra crew, which included Stephen Decker, Allen Teyvel, Chaise Loper, D.J. Kieley, Mac Boeck, and Loren Keller; without their help, I might have fallen victim to the mediocre and quit before the book was completed. And lastly, to the voiceless ghosts whose music we will never hear—I hope this is only the beginning.

ABOUT THE COMPANION WEBSITE

• • •

www.oup.com/us/thepassingshows

Oxford has created a Web site to accompany *The Shuberts and Their Passing Shows: The Untold Tale of Ziegfeld's Rivals*. Due to the large number of available figures, many images that help illuminate the text are provided here. The reader is encouraged to consult this resource in conjunction with the monograph. Online examples are indicated in the text with Oxford's symbol ⊙.

THE SHUBERTS AND THEIR
PASSING SHOWS

INTRODUCTION

• • •

The discovery of *The Passing Show* was, for me, much like Indiana Jones finding the Ark of the Covenant. I had heard of the Shubert Archive from my advisor, John Graziano, while I was taking courses at the Graduate Center of the City University of New York. Although I had already decided on a dissertation topic, he mentioned that there was much work to be done on the revue, and that the Shuberts had produced multiple annual shows. It was worth a look, I thought, and I decided to peruse the materials for the earliest of their annuals. I made an appointment to visit the Archive to see what types of documents had survived, and when I saw how many boxes of letters, scripts, and production notes were extant, I became excited. But when I asked to see the music, the archivists were surprised. I was told that no one had ever asked to see the music, or at least not in their memory. When I returned the following day, I was greeted by five large packages, wrapped in archival paper and tied together with string. Knowing that the scores and parts for many shows from before the 1920s were lost, I could only guess as to what these overflowing bundles represented. We cut the string and unwrapped the packages, and I stood there in awe. Sitting before me were dozens of songs, mostly written by Louis A. Hirsch, complete with partiturs, piano/vocal music, and the individual instrumental parts for almost every song from *The Passing Show of 1912*. As I looked at the name on the partiturs, I was astonished to see Frank Saddler's signature appear again and again. I knew Saddler from his work with Jerome Kern, but I knew almost nothing about what he actually *did*. And here, sitting in these boxes, were dozens of examples of his orchestrations. I think I disturbed the archivists a bit, because as I made my way through the music, I intermittently laughed to myself, shocked at the remarkable treasure trove of materials I was able to sift through. Riding home on the subway, I kept on shaking my head in wonder at what I had spent the day looking at. I knew then that I had an entirely new project and, like it or not, this was going to become my new dissertation topic. It was not so much a choice as a calling; I honestly felt that I had a responsibility to tell the stories of these creators, artists, and entertainers, many of who have fallen into obscurity through no fault of their own, but rather through the passage of time. I knew this was a tale I had to tell.

I first set about choosing a show to focus on. By working with a single revue, I could examine the process of its creation, assess the individual elements within the show, and do a reconstruction (as much as possible) of an entire revue. The result of this was my dissertation, "A Study and Reconstruction of *The Passing Show of 1914*: The American Musical Revue and its Development in the Early Twentieth Century" (CUNY Graduate Center, 2010). The show was nearly complete (only missing a single song); it was the first full show written by Sigmund Romberg; and it was also the debut of Marilyn(n) Miller.[1] Saddler did many of the orchestrations, and there were wonderful contributions by people who were unknown today but incredibly famous in their time. I held a read-through (and sing-through) of the show, and I was pleased to see that my small but interested audience enjoyed the experience.

In 2014, I had the pleasure of conducting a centennial performance of some of the music, and I knew without a doubt that there was much more to be said about these revues.

Starting in 1912, the Shubert brothers produced an extravagant series of revues called *The Passing Shows*. Each year, a new edition would be crafted, featuring new musical styles, the latest dance fads, and some of the biggest stars of the day. Including dozens of chorus women and men, these revues were hits both in New York's Winter Garden Theater and also on tour. This book examines these shows in depth, with a look at their creators and content. Challenging the notion that Ziegfeld and his *Follies* were the only important revues of the era, this work details the remarkable efforts put forth by a whole host of incredible personalities. Some chapters of this book—notably the first, second, and fourth—consider the enormous cadre of people involved with the shows. The third chapter reconstructs the early history of the Howard Brothers and examines their contributions to the revues. But the middle chapters—five through seven—examine the content of the shows themselves. Finally, the last two chapters cover the intriguing story of the relationship between the Shuberts and Ziegfeld, told using in-house memos, personal letters, and documents packed away for a century. When Ziegfeld died, the Shuberts were part of shaping their former rival's legacy, in part using the amazing theatrical machine they had developed for their own revues. Fred and Adele Astaire, George Gershwin, Joan Crawford, and Ed Wynn are among the stars still remembered today who were a part of the series, but they performed alongside many others who have fallen out of the limelight. This book brings those stars, their songs, and stories back to life, making the Broadway of the 1910s and 1920s seem like yesterday.

When it came to sources, I chose to include almost everything I could find, from magazine articles to personal letters. With the advent of digital searching, I was able to find a host of articles that would have eluded me otherwise. I will be eternally grateful to Thomas M. Tryniski and his Old Fulton Postcards site (http://www.fultonhistory.com), which is one of the largest collections of newspapers that is digitally searchable and includes not only the *New York Clipper* and the *New York Dramatic Mirror*, but also many smaller papers that can be incredibly useful. The one paper I deliberately chose to veer away from was the *New York Review*, which was created mainly by the press agents for the Shuberts. It is nearly impossible to tell which items are fabrications and which are real, and I felt that rather than tease out the truth from something that was unreliable, it would be best to avoid it entirely. The only use I make of it in the book is to include a review of the *Follies of 1914* accompanied by a private letter to J. J. Shubert that also gives the honest perspective of the writer. A comparative analysis of the *Review* and its contemporary papers awaits; the inner politics of reviewers and the Shuberts is far too complicated to examine without context (their relationship with Alexander Woollcott, whom they famous banned from their shows, is a prime example).

The transatlantic component of *The Passing Show* should also be addressed. The Shuberts were connected to a number of theaters overseas (especially in London and Paris), but there were major concerns about having rights secured there, for shows, music, and ideas. J. J. and Lee corresponded frequently about having shows stolen by unscrupulous producers in England, and it is clear that they struggled with global legal issues. Despite some suggestion to the contrary, there seems to be no truth to rumors that *The Passing Shows* that took place in London had any connection to the American originals. There were a few British editions—most notably in 1914 and 1915 (with music by Herman Finck and lyrics by Arthur Wimperis)—but they did not have any relationship to the revues of the Shuberts.

I offer many suggestions for future topics throughout this text, and it is my sincere hope that others will begin to explore these paths. The world of musical theater between 1900 and 1920 is complicated and rich, and there are hundreds of fascinating personalities who participated; I can only see a bright future for the study and recovery of some of this wonderful material. Scores, scripts, and a bevy of supporting materials can be found that will bring these shows to life, and it is just a matter of putting forth the effort to piece it all together. I identify venues where some of the documents are located in order to inspire inquiring souls to begin their research. The stories of many of the people, places, and things mentioned in this book await further study, and I look forward to having a much larger and more nuanced understanding of what Broadway was before the post-WWII musicals that now define it.

NOTE

1. Miller dropped the second "n" from her first name later in her career. However, since she used the double "n" during her years in *The Passing Show* series, this is the form of the name I will use.

1

A TWELVE-HOUR SHOW SQUEEZED
INTO THREE

• • •

THE CREATIVE FORCES BEHIND
THE PASSING SHOWS

From the producers to the wig-makers, the number of contributors to the enormous Winter Garden revues was remarkable. Lee and J. J. Shubert's flagship annual revue, *The Passing Show*, was only one of several productions put on by the brothers, and this meant that a virtual army was required to keep their theatrical machine running smoothly. As employers, the Messrs. Shubert provided steady work for some of the most important creative forces at the beginning of the twentieth century, with many theatrical figures spending the whole of their careers as steadfast—and incredibly busy—members of the Shubert production staff. In all of their myriad entertainments, nowhere was this consistent connection with creative talent more apparent than with the Winter Garden revues.

When the Shubert brothers began regularly producing revues in 1911, it probably came as no surprise to anyone familiar with the world of theater; the family—Sam, J. J., and Lee—and their organization were fundamental to the development of Broadway and American theater. As a cultural force, they determined many aspects of what constituted the Great White Way. Not only did they produce events, but they also owned and operated a plethora of theaters nationwide, a combination that put them in a position to shape much of what Americans saw onstage. All three brothers began working at the turn of the twentieth century, and a few of the Shuberts were still personally involved with productions until the 1960s. Some of the greatest successes (and failures) on Broadway can be ascribed to this notable family and their staff, with their stories represented among the most incredible and important tales in New York's theatrical history. The vast legacy of the Shuberts has been well documented in a survey of theaters (and the shows they housed) still held by the Shubert Organization.[1] Of all their accomplishments, however, one story that remains to be told is that of the revues housed at the Winter Garden Theater during its earliest years. And among these productions, none was more central to the Shuberts' success in this genre than *The Passing Show*.

The portrayal of the Shuberts and their revues is complex, with some writers extoling the virtues of the brothers, while others suggest they were nothing but cruel, hard-nosed businessmen.[2] The latter comes into play in full force in the few books written about the history of the revue. Gerald Bordman claims that the format was perfected by Ziegfeld with an artistic flair and then copied by the Shuberts, who he calls "Broadway's most notorious copycats."[3] This statement is surprising, however, because Bordman also notes that several revues took place between 1907 and 1911, when the Shuberts "pounced" on the format—this included *The Gay White Way* (1907), *The Merry-Go-Round* (1908), *The Mimic World* (1908), *The Merry Whirl* (1910), and *Up and Down Broadway* (1910).[4] According to this account, the Shuberts were waiting until they saw a profit-making, tried-and-true formula in Ziegfeld's creation, but the fact is that of these five shows, three of them, *The Gay White Way*, *The Mimic World*, and *Up and Down Broadway* were produced, in whole or in part, by the Shuberts themselves. The time for the revue had come, and it did not take a half-decade of popular *Follies* to convince the Shuberts to go ahead with their own series.

The roots of the revue reach back into the nineteenth century even before the Shuberts or Ziegfeld were born. By the 1850s, minstrel shows included multiple forms of entertainment, and the following two decades saw many performances in New York City that combined unusual assortments of acts at colorful locations like Tony Pastor's and Fox's Old Bowery Theater. For example, P. T. Barnum's American Museum featured a production of *Aphrosia, or, The Spirit of Beauty*, on March 14, 1864, but the bill also included a Tyrolean whistler, William B. Harison (a comic singer who improvised lyrics and songs), and Ned, the Learned Musical Seal.[5] The "Free and Easy," the concert saloons, and the variety halls all made use of a multiplicity of talent during this era. It was in this milieu that one of the earliest works that called itself a "revue" took place: *The Dramatic Review of 1868*, by John Brougham, played during January and February of 1869.[6] It was referred to as a burlesque in the "Parisian style" that made use of songs, pantomime, comedy, and even a transformation scene—all elements that would become part of *The Passing Shows*. The production only ran for three weeks, but it was one of many intermittent theatrical attempts at developing the formula that would define the genre by the end of the century.

Two performers, though, were essential to the rise of the revue, both onstage and behind it as producers. Joe Weber and Lew Fields were active during the last quarter of the nineteenth century, and their careers follow the chronology of the developing revue almost exactly, with Fields acting as one of the catalysts for the Shubert-driven series. Weber and Fields began their collaboration as children in 1877, and they specialized in dialect acts borrowed from the minstrel show.[7] They performed in cheap theaters on the Bowery, such as Turn Hall. After performing together for years, they eventually purchased and ran the Weber and Fields Broadway Music Hall in 1896. The shows they produced there included theatrical burlesques tied together by thin plots that also comprised a wide array of comedians, dancers, and other acts. By 1904, the duo separated, although they remained in the business, with Fields leaving the location to perform on his own. Fields became closely connected with the Shuberts in 1905–1906, when he allied himself with the brothers against the Syndicate, the name commonly used to describe the massive Theatrical Trust held by Marc Klaw and Abe

Erlanger. The Syndicate's hold on the entertainment world during the turn of the century was powerful, and Fields found them incredibly difficult to work with in the industry. Eventually, the producer became more attracted by the Shuberts, who were determined to break up the Trust and forge their own theatrical niche. By the end of the 1905–1906 season, Fields had signed a deal with Lee Shubert, with both men hoping to further their own ends by making an alliance.[8] This connection was a key step toward making a Shubert revue a reality, and there is no doubt that Fields's influence (professionally and personally) was essential for encouraging the creation of *The Passing Show* series.

The formative times for the revue were also the years during which Sam Shubert—the eldest of the brothers—began and solidified his theatrical career.[9] Starting with an onstage role in *May Blossom*, Sam was willing to do anything to be a part of the theater, working his way up to manager of Syracuse's Bastable Theatre by 1897. J. J. and Lee followed in his footsteps, taking management jobs in upstate New York regional theaters. Sam's first great opportunity came when he ran the national tour for Charles Hoyt's *A Stranger in New York*. By 1900, the three brothers moved to New York City, and it only took them a short time before they were managing, leasing, and eventually producing theatrical events. The three worked tirelessly to build their business, but they were constantly thwarted by Klaw and Erlanger's Syndicate. The situation between the Shuberts and the Syndicate reached its climax when, in 1905, Sam Shubert took a train for Pittsburgh to battle the latter in court. Sam wanted to challenge the monopolists' right to refuse to lease him a theater. The eldest brother was the driving force behind the Shubert family's success, and he would not abide by the Syndicate's shady legal machinations. Sadly, the train he was on crashed and Sam was killed. The result of this accident was that beating and breaking up the Syndicate became as much of a personal matter as a business one for both of the younger siblings. The family persevered, staging a successful tour for actress Sarah Bernhardt the following season, partially using the fifty theaters they now had as part of their own network. As Lee and J. J. expanded their theatrical interests over the course of the next decade, they opened their own theaters and eventually developed their own film company and vaudeville circuit.[10]

Given the remarkable rise to prominence the Shuberts enjoyed during these developmental years, they became more strongly associated with the varied facets of theatrical life, encountering the proto-revue through most of the ventures they undertook. Whether they were hiring a new set designer, a dance coach, or a prominent star, there was almost no way they could have avoided connections with the developing genre. Memos and telegrams in the Shubert Archive make it clear they also frequently sent agents to Europe to watch for anything that would attract an audience. Tours were also fundamental to shaping the Shuberts' interests, especially tying the family to Chicago, the midwestern hub for vaudeville and the place where many New York shows had extended runs (oftentimes even longer than their Broadway engagements). This connection helped to develop ties to Charles Frohman and David Belasco, but they were not the only theatrical leaders the Shuberts would have encountered there. Ziegfeld himself had lived in the Windy City, helping his father with the management and promotion of the Trocadero Club before he himself went to Europe to discover new acts.

Fig. 1.1. *Cover for sheet music selections from* The Passing Show *(1894).*
Author's Collection.

The revival of the revue in the 1890s came just as the Shuberts, Weber and Fields, and Ziegfeld were beginning their theatrical careers, and it was in this period that the revue became a standardized genre. The first production to make use of the title in this era was *The Passing Show* by Sydney Rosenfeld and Ludwig Englander, which opened on May 12, 1894 (see Figure 1.1). Although the nineteenth-century predecessors had used non-narrative components, this was the first production to regularly use the term *revue* (or *review*) in its description, although it was also referred to as a *topical extravaganza* elsewhere in the program. The entertainment was very popular; it had a lengthy seven-month run on Broadway and an even more extensive national tour. The producer, George Lederer, based *The Passing Show* partly on English and (primarily) French models, also linking it to earlier forms, such as burlesque, the extravaganza, and the variety show.[11] The show combined timely references with spectacular scenery and a parade of young chorus girls, and many of the songs made mention of other shows or events. The name "passing show" referred to the dizzying movement of the world paraded before the eyes of anyone in a fixed position, an excellent title choice for a show that used seemingly unrelated events that moved on and off a stage. The popularity of *The Passing Show* was enough to spawn imitators, and in doing so, the revue found its theatrical footing. Similar productions followed, both in New York and on the road, including *Oriental America* (1895), *Higgledy-Piggledy* (1904), and *Mamzelle Champagne* (1906). In these shows, there was no overriding structure that could be identified as a revue; the genre itself did not yet exist, though it soon would be defined when the *Follies* began. Ziegfeld, too, combined nineteenth-century American theatrical entertainments with French models. He wanted the production to seem new, however, so when he opened his new rooftop show in 1907, he borrowed the name "Follies" from a column written by the production's author, Harry B. Smith, called "Follies of the Day."[12]

The genesis of the revue and the beginning of the theatrical careers for those who became producers during the teens and twenties meant that they were part of a shared milieu—one that encouraged the development of the revue on a number of fronts. For the Shuberts, however, the revue was also tied inexorably to the largest real estate concern of their early years: the massive, luxurious Winter Garden Theater. To inaugurate the newly built venue, the revue *La Belle Paree* opened on March 20, 1911, along with a companion piece, *Bow Sing*.[13] As Lee Davis points out, the show had two important components that made it stand out: it contained a large collection of songs by Jerome Kern and it was the first Broadway appearance of Al Jolson. But despite those favorable attributes, Davis, like many authors before him, continually referenced the relationship to Ziegfeld:

> *La Belle Paree* had some of the trappings of a Ziegfeld show: girls in elaborate and usually pink costumes, opulent sets and strutting showgirls. What it didn't have was the Ziegfeld touch: the distinctive eye of the master, the willingness to spend thousands of dollars upon one scene, to dress his girls in real furs and real diamonds because, as he put it, "it makes them feel like royalty," to outfit a drugstore scene with real French perfume, to have an unerring eye for beauty, a tin ear for music, and hardly any noticeable sense of humor.[14]

The bias toward Ziegfeld's revues seems to seep through the prose of many authors at every step, glorifying Ziegfeld, and at the same time vilifying the Shuberts—something that I discuss in more depth in chapter 8. The result, according to these critics, was that the choices the Shuberts made about their own productions were based on imitation and not invention. But what is not mentioned is that even before *The Passing Show of 1912* opened, the earlier Winter Garden revues had been well received.

Both *The Revue of Revues* (opened on September 27, 1911) and *The Whirl of Society* (opened on February 12, 1912) had a fair number of performances (55 and 136, respectively), and these two shows established the Fall and Spring Revue pattern that the Winter Garden would maintain almost every year until 1923, when *The Dancing Girl* became the first plot-driven musical to hold the spring position. Table 1.1 lists the shows that were part of this pattern.[15] With the exception of *Sinbad* and *Robinson*

Table 1.1 Fall, Spring, and Summer Revues at the Winter Garden Theater.

Theater Season	Fall Revue	Winter/Spring Revue	Summer Revue
1911–1912	The Revue of Revues	The Whirl of Society	The Passing Show of 1912
1912–1913	From Broadway to Paris	None	The Passing Show of 1913
1913–1914	The Pleasure Seekers	The Whirl of the World	The Passing Show of 1914
1914–1915	Dancing Around	Maid In America	The Passing Show of 1915
1915–1916	A World of Pleasure	Robinson Crusoe, Jr.*	The Passing Show of 1916
1916–1917	The Show of Wonders	None	The Passing Show of 1917
1917–1918	Doing Our Bit	Sinbad*	The Passing Show of 1918
1918–1919	Sinbad*	Monte Cristo, Jr.*	Monte Cristo, Jr.* Held Over
1919–1920	The Passing Show of 1919	The Passing Show of 1919 Held Over	Cinderella on Broadway
1920–1921	Broadway Brevities of 1920	The Passing Show of 1921	The Whirl of New York
1921–1922	None	Make It Snappy	Spice of 1922
1922–1923	The Passing Show of 1922	The Dancing Girl**	The Passing Show of 1923

* A musical with revue elements
** Not a revue

Crusoe, Jr.—Al Jolson vehicles where the plot would halt for a significant portion of an act to allow Jolson to come out and sing his favorite songs—and *Monte Cristo, Jr.*, called an "extravaganza" with "several vaudeville turns thrown in," almost every production at the Winter Garden during these years was a revue.[16] The Winter Garden Theater was synonymous with the revue for more than a decade after the house opened its doors.

It seems probable that because the Shuberts staged revues throughout the year at the Winter Garden, it was not a surprise that they chose to continue making money with this large theater even after the traditional theater season had come to a close. The *Follies* was the main summer attraction in New York (although it was not the only show playing), and what Ziegfeld's show did most effectively, from a financial standpoint, was to prove that an annual market for a show during the hot summer months could be maintained. This astute fiscal decision was part of what led to the inauguration of *The Passing Show* series in 1912 and maintained its viability into the 1920s.[17]

But more importantly for the Shuberts was the building of the Winter Garden Theater. Everything about it was monumental in size, and it is clear from the earliest documents that the producers had high hopes for what the location would offer audiences. The stage itself was one of the largest in New York, outmatched only by the Hippodrome, allowing for an extravagant setting and lots of performers, making it ideal for the genre in these early years. The building had been built originally to house the American Horse Exchange and was therefore full of large open spaces. When the Shuberts leased the property from William Vanderbilt, they immediately went about making changes to turn the space into a theater. William Albert Swasey was the architect hired to transform the massive building into a theater with only a single balcony. Swasey "covered the ceiling in sky blue canvas and trimmed both ceiling and walls with latticework. The overall color scheme was ivory and gold. Garlands and leaves entwined the box fronts and proscenium arch. The curtain was constructed of heavy rose-pink plush; the floors were covered with red Pompeian tile; and the wall spaces were decorated with Pompeian pottery, statuary, shrubs, and flower boxes.[18] This grand interior was intended to display a level of opulence that would have easily matched the over-the-top nature of the revues that graced the stage at the time. It was a risk creating a theater so far north (on Broadway and Fiftieth Street) where nothing but apartments, saloons, and trolley car garages lay. Lee was told that anything beyond Forty-Fifth Street was simply out of reach of audiences. However, the magnificence of the theater and the quality of the shows were a big enough draw to keep audiences coming. This enormous structure, boasting 1,750 seats, was one of the largest of the theaters on Broadway in 1911, and it is no surprise that it was here that the Shuberts put on their most opulent revues. As the Archive states, "between 1906 and 1943 the Shubert brothers produced a staggering 104 revues. At their most basic, these shows featured lots of scantily clad chorus girls, popular songs, and colorful sets and costumes. At their best, they represented the height of wit, glamour, and sophistication."[19] The theater can be seen in a postcard in Figure 1.2, in which *The Passing Show of 1916* is advertised atop the building.

It is essential to realize that the Winter Garden shows always had a life beyond Broadway, just like many of the other theatrical productions mounted by the Shuberts. For example, *The Whirl of the World*, the spring revue that preceded *The Passing Show of 1914*, was sent on the road only a short time before the summer revue was to open. In May of 1914, the *New York Times* reported the following:

"The Whirl of the World" will bring its New York run at the Winter Garden to a close Wednesday evening. The following day the production will be taken to Chicago, where it will open for a Summer run. The Winter Garden will remain dark for a week and a half, when it reopens on June 6 with "The Passing Show of 1914."[20]

Fig. 1.2. Postcard featuring the Winter Garden Theater, 1916. Author's Collection.

The Shuberts, following in the footsteps of many nineteenth-century impresarios, knew that New York was not the only city where an elaborate production was profitable, and it is clear that they felt that their spring revue could continue to thrive elsewhere.[21] However, New York was the home of the Winter Garden, and it is there that the Shuberts opened their new series of revues in 1912.

Stories of long-term collaborators exist across the spectrum of Broadway, with pairs such as Comden and Green, Lerner and Loewe, and Kander and Ebb spanning the decades. Relationships between producers and their employees are less frequently legendary, but some connections, such as Joseph Urban's work for Ziegfeld, do receive some attention. Of all the connections between producers and their staff, however, there are few associations in the history of Broadway that match the remarkable career of Harold Atteridge during his quarter-century tenure within the Shubert offices. Atteridge was an all-purpose writer, responsible for the lyrics and the books of every edition of *The Passing Show* from its inception in 1912 until 1924; those revues he did not work on (after 1926) simply did not make it to Broadway.[22] But what is so astonishing beyond this fact is that he was the man responsible for almost every Winter Garden revue, including most of the shows in Table 1.1 and beyond, with substantial contributions to editions of other revue series for the Shuberts, *Artists and Models* and the *Greenwich Village Follies*. Atteridge was so well respected, he was even hired by the competition to write the book for the *Follies* of 1927. Atteridge had a gift to move swiftly from one idea to the next, always searching for new concepts, jokes, or turns of phrase. He was not always concerned with producing the highest quality of lyrics—some of the songs he wrote were clunky to say the least—but he had his share of hits, and many of his sketches demonstrate a breezy, pun-filled, playful sense of humor akin to the early vaudeville scripts that survive for Burns and Allen or the Marx Brothers.

In an article from the *New York Times*, Atteridge provides perhaps the most concise description of the flow of events for the genesis of a revue.[23]

Writing a Winter Garden revue involves many details and this work is unlike that of the librettist who writes a straight musical comedy . . . It must be remembered that there are more principals for whom parts and songs numbers must be arranged, and that, due to the nature of travesties indulged in, constant revisions are necessary up until the very week before the premiere.

Seven or eight weeks ahead I have a private conference with J. J. Shubert, who engages the cast and chorus, plans the scenery and lighting effects, and superintends the production, and together we map out a skeleton idea of the forthcoming revue. Then we scout about for a promising composer, and I begin writing a series of lyrics to be used. In the average Winter Garden offering about thirty-five numbers are written, and ten songs from this list are eliminated before the premiere.

Rehearsals of the principals start at least four weeks in advance, the chorus beginning a fortnight earlier under the supervision of a dancing director. As soon as rehearsals are progressing the weeding out process begins. Certain lines must be eliminated and scenes built up; new entertainers are engaged and special parts must be written for them; a turn in the Mexican situation, politics, woman suffrage, eugenics, or any other much-discussed current topic, necessitates a re-arrangement of certain travesty material.

I attend every rehearsal and am always on hand to follow out suggestions from whoever happens to be staging the production. At the first dress rehearsal, and there are usually three or four because the Winter Garden productions open in New York without a preliminary tryout, the show is of at least five hours duration.

The weak spots are bolstered up, certain song numbers that lack the necessary dash and spirit are eliminated, and the entire programme routine condensed and rearranged. The length is gradually cut down for the opening night.

I do most of my writing between the hours of midnight and 5 a.m. I write in long hand under an electric desk lamp, and always alone. Most of the comedy dialogue that I write for the Winter Garden revues I observe in everyday life—on the Subway, in restaurants, on the street, in hotel lobbies, at church, in barber shops, in business offices, and most any place where ordinary people are to be seen. During the day I watch persons and at night I write about them.

It usually takes me from thirty minutes to an hour to write the finished lyrics for a song. I read all the newspapers every day and this affords me a field of current information. The Winter Garden revues, especially the annual "Passing Show," is a résumé of theatrical, business, and political topics of the past season set to song, dance, and laughter.

This rich document provides a window into the step-by-step process by which a "Winter Garden revue" was developed under the tutelage of both Atteridge, who was central to its creation, and J. J. Shubert. It is not a mistake that Atteridge is said to have created the *book* for these musicals because, as mentioned earlier, there was indeed a storyline that bound together the various characters and events in the revue. This article points out that the creation of the show, primarily under Atteridge's supervision, was a process of writing an excess of material that was then reworked for length. As a lyricist, Atteridge worked closely with the composer(s) as numbers were being written and, since Atteridge himself came up with the ideas for the grand finales and many of the transformation scenes, he must have worked with whoever was staging the scene to make it work with the songs (thematically), and fall in line with Shubert's expectations. Atteridge was the main creative force behind *The Passing Show*, from working on the script alone (with his electric lamp) to sitting in on rehearsals as the show took shape. He could dash off lyrics for a new song if the moment required and could adjust a scene to highlight different performers as needed. "Rapid-fire" seems a perfect term to describe a man in the midst of a business where the "Now" was the most important element. Atteridge was extremely busy, and he had to work at top speed to satisfy the Shuberts' demands, all the while working on every element of their enormous musical production machine. His writing process and his approach to organizing a revue is discussed in more depth in chapter 6.

The other Shubert mainstay who contributed to nearly every edition of *The Passing Show* was director, J. C. Huffman. The programs credit Huffman with "staging" the revue, which meant that he was responsible for the blocking and flow of the scenes. However, Huffman was also particularly interested in lighting. This is made clear in part of a written testimonial for the director on his one-hundredth show for the Shuberts, *Marching By* (1932):

> Mr. Huffman is an authority on stage lighting and in kindred matters. His monographs upon technical stage subjects have been much used as textbooks at Columbia, Harvard, and other universities, where there are courses in stagecraft. This genius of the stage contends that just as lights can be blended to produce desired effects, so can actors, acting, and scenic values be blended. He works according to this theory.[24]

Originally from Bowling Green, Ohio, Huffman became well known at the Alvin Theater in Pittsburgh, and from there he made his way to New York City. In an unusual turn of events, he was not engaged by the Shuberts there but was approached in Berlin, where he had an appointment at the Volkstheater.[25] He began working for the Shuberts circa 1906, with his first directorial credit as *The Shulamite*. He continued working for the brothers for nearly thirty years, until retiring after 1932. Although there appears to have been several rough patches, including in 1911 when a "stormy scene" ensued, the rumors that he was paid an astonishing $1,000 weekly to direct all the Winter Garden shows would suggest that he found a comfortable position (at least in one regard) for the remainder of his career.[26] It is not surprising that few documents remain that help to trace Huffman's contributions to the series, since he was probably not involved in the production until Atteridge, J. J., and the composer(s) had decided on the main components of the show. However, the final product retained a consistency of vision under a single director over the years.

In an article similar to the one penned by Atteridge, Huffman wrote a piece for the *New York American* in which he described his approach as a director for revues.[27] Huffman's central point in "Revue Proves Hardest Test of Craftsmanship on Stage" was that there was no formulaic system that one can use for the genre, noting that a keen sensitivity to the public's needs, and especially "a psychological setting of pace" was essential for making the show flow smoothly. "I presume that the casual reader of this will come to the conclusion that staging a big Broadway revue is not as intricate as [a book show]," he said. "Really, it is more so." He advised that one should neither copy hits from other people nor rely on one's own past successes, saying that the fickleness of audiences should never be overestimated. He then takes the reader through the way in which they made decisions for the *Greenwich Village Follies* of 1928, especially noting the many changes the production staff had to make before the show opened in New York City.

Huffman's article, like Atteridge's before him, is one of the few documents available from Shubert staff that provides insight into the inner workings of these monster musicals. Both authors of these articles were incredibly adept at moving at astonishing speeds, first in the conference room, later in rehearsals, and then again on the road with the revues before they opened in New York City. For the first three *Passing Shows*, rehearsals happened in the area around New York; when *The Passing Show of 1914* brought the cast together for rehearsals, it was "in the Hudson Grove, near the Jersey side of the Edgewater Ferry landing."[28] The earliest mention of a "tryout" in Atlantic City, where many shows held what would eventually be called previews, was in 1913 (though there are notices that suggest this might have begun on a limited basis on an earlier date; future tryout locations included Chicago, Detroit, and Cincinnati). The brief item demonstrates exactly the process mentioned by the creators in that "the curtain was rung up at an early hour and the new show was still under way at midnight."[29] Perhaps the most important element that the director and writer impress on the reader is that the creation of a revue is not a simple matter that is thrown together in a casual manner with no sense of structure. In fact, for both of them, it was harder than the average musical comedy with a straightforward narrative. Huffman's insightful comment about the dangers of repetition and the pitfalls of copying one's past successes is perhaps the most critical statement of all. Great care and effort was put forth (and not to mention a great deal of money) to ensure that each *Passing Show* offered something new and vibrant for audiences. These shows had a significant run in New York, but they also toured most of the same cities each year. Even though some elements might become traditional, such as the Act I Finale transformation scene (discussed in more depth in chapter 5), it could never be a simple rehash of the year before. Beyond self-mimicry, Atteridge and Huffman would also have been careful to make sure that the content they included was new and impressive.[30] Invention and surprise were the key means of bringing in the same crowd on an annual basis, and Atteridge and Huffman gave them something fresh every year.

The director for the first two installments of *The Passing Show* deserves mention, although he did not continue after 1913. Ned Wayburn was perhaps the most important figure in popular dance during this era, and he ran a school that educated young women in the proper methods to become a chorus girl. It was the Wayburn School (and later his dance method handbooks and records) that funneled chorus girls to the Broadway stage, especially for the Shuberts and Ziegfeld. The first several Winter Garden revues, including *From Broadway to Paris* and *The Honeymoon Express*, were directed and choreographed by Wayburn, and so it was not a surprise that he would also be asked to be intricately involved in the development of the annual summer show. From the large-scale numbers devised by Wayburn, it seems clear that he was an important predecessor to the human-geometric stylings of Busby Berkeley. Wayburn's relationship to the Shuberts soured after his efforts on *The Honeymoon Express*, but their connection seems to have improved enough that Marilynn Miller was sent to the school at the expense of the producers only one year later.[31]

When Wayburn left the series in 1914, Jack Mason was hired as the new choreographer. Mason later shared these duties with Allan K. Foster. Both dancers been active on Broadway and in vaudeville since the turn of the century as performers and as choreographers, but it is unclear when their respective connections with the Shuberts began. The joint positions continued into the 1920s, and they seem to have taken turns working on the Fall and Spring Winter Garden revues and *The Passing Show*. The two were in the employ of the Shuberts for years, working with the brothers into the early 1930s. It is probable that they had a close working relationship since they were given the all-important (and challenging) task of working with the chorus girls throughout many revues. However, both men also coached the dancers for many operettas of the 1920s, and thus demonstrated the flexibility to work with different styles.

Part of successfully building a revue was to hire a composer who could match the frantic pace for the development of a *Passing Show* while still creating good tunes. A number of songwriters were brought on over time to give the series its sound. The first was Louis Hirsch, a young man who was often engaged by the Shuberts. A regular contributor to early revues, he later wrote for Ziegfeld's *Follies* as well as for *The Greenwich Village Follies*, and it was he who provided the bulk of the music for *The Passing Show of 1912*.[32] It may be that Hirsch, who received a paltry twenty-five dollars a week for his score, ended up becoming involved in the formation ASCAP (the American Society of Composers, Authors, and Publishers) two years later, due in part to the small fee he received for his work on this show.

Hirsch used multiple styles, from uptempo ragtime songs to slow ballads, offering a new musical flavor for each new scene. Many of the songs are topical, and one can see in both Hirsch's music and Atteridge's lyrics a connection between this revue and the productions it burlesques. One scene involved Andrew Carnegie and characters meant to parody David Belasco and Teddy Roosevelt (renamed "The Strenuous Citizen"). The song they sing, "Carnegie" (also called "Handy Andy," see Figure 5.2), plays on the different ways to pronounce Carnegie's name, his political ties, and his odd penchant for philanthropy: "I want to give all of my cash away / So take it pray, don't let it stay / I'll send you a library P.D.Q. / Or give a medal to you."

"Pirates and the Quaker Girl" combines characters from two different shows—not surprisingly, *The Quaker Girl* and the *Pirates of Penzance*—and uses musical material from the latter show. However, the song has new lyrics and even uses new musical material, thus employing new and old elements simultaneously: "If you don't go, I will bawl / I won't be your wife at all. / I know you Pirate of Old Penzance; / You only fight in a song and dance."

"The Policeman's Song" also uses the *Pirates of Penzance* as a musical basis on which it can burlesque with new lyrics: "We're policemen that you know (Taran-ta-ra) / From the old Casino Show (etc.) / But we're only actor men (etc.) / For we've made a change again."

Most of the references to other shows are more textual than musical, but the script calls for brief musical interpolations of several famous works, including Rimsky-Korsakov's *Scheherezade*, the "Anvil Chorus" (from Verdi's *Il trovatore*), and the "Flower Song" from Bizet's *Carmen*. At only a cursory glance, the rest of the music uses simple syncopation for ragtime numbers and contrasts this with lilting, romantic melodies.[33] One song, "The Wedding Glide," is a duet that makes use of both of these musical styles; it was particularly popular and recorded by Shirley Kellogg, who sang it in the show.[34]

Beginning with *The Passing Show of 1914*, an important composer was hired as the central musical contributor. The show may have been the first full score Sigmund Romberg wrote for the Shuberts (he had contributed interpolations earlier), but it was certainly not his last. Romberg's tenure with the producers lasted even longer than Atteridge and Huffman, stretching from the small number of songs he contributed to *The Whirl of the World* in 1914 to *My Romance* in 1948, only three years before his death.[35] Working with a wide range of musical styles, Romberg composed some of the most successful operettas of the twentieth century, including *Blossom Time* (1921), *The Student Prince* (1924), and *The Desert Song* (1926), as well as more traditional musical comedies, such as *Poor Little Ritz Girl* (1920) and *Up in Central Park* (1945). He was also responsible for the music, in whole or in part, for many Winter Garden revues. By the time rehearsals were to begin for the 1914 *Passing Show*, Romberg and Atteridge must have become well acquainted, and the two men would continue working together on nearly thirty productions until their last collaboration, *Artists and Models of 1925*. A fanciful telling of their first meeting can be found in Romberg's quasi-biography, *Deep in My Heart*:

> The following morning Romberg was introduced to Atteridge, who was one of the cleverest authors and lyricists on Broadway. The young composer fought to hide his awe of this man, with his imposing reputation. Atteridge put him at ease immediately, treating him as though he were an established composer. They discussed means of working together and finally Sigmund broached a question which had worried him since the preceding day. "Would it be possible, Mr. Atteridge, for me to write the music before the lyrics are written? Only because my knowledge of the English language is not yet perfect." He asked the favor with some trepidation. The prestige of Atteridge was such that he was entitled to the privilege of writing his part first and then having the composer shape the music to fit his words. But the lyricist, with great courtesy, agreed to write the words to suit the music.[36]

The reason Romberg was so concerned about language was that he had only recently moved to the United States from Vienna, where he had initiated a musical career after leaving his home in Hungary. On his arrival, he immediately began absorbing as much of New York's musical culture as he could, and the resulting songs secured him a position with the Shuberts. As principal composer for *The Passing Show*, he wrote music for the 1914, 1916, 1917, 1918, 1923, and 1924 editions.

As the series progressed through the years, the number of songs assigned to a single composer decreased, with more musicians responsible for sharing the burden of providing the melodies. Jean Schwartz and Albert W. Brown shared the duties for *The Passing Show of 1913*, with most numbers attributed to both men and a smaller percentage written by one or the other. Schwartz returned several times, and received sole credit for the 1919 edition. The most extensive lineup of composers in the early years was for 1915, when three tunesmiths—Leo Edwards, W. F. Peters, and J. Leubrie Hill—wrote the various songs and dances. When the score for *The Passing Show of 1915* was published by Schirmer as a "complete" revue (it was the only score from the series to be published as a whole), the composer listed was Edwards, who had written most of the pieces, and Peters and Hill were included as providing "additional numbers." However, the Broadway program did not identify which numbers were by whom, and thus the audience would never know the difference (although this was clarified in the published score). When Romberg was the featured composer, however, he usually did most of the work himself. For example, he wrote most of the 1914 show, but a few songs were provided by Harry Carroll, a regular contributor to Shubert productions during the teens. Otto Motzan worked with Romberg in 1916 and 1917, while Jean Schwartz was the secondary composer for the 1918, 1923 and 1924 editions. The last few shows—1926, 1932, 1934, and 1945/1946—used music by four or more composers, without a central guiding force.

The Passing Show of 1912 set up a pattern for the remainder of the series when it brought in music in another way also. The revue included at least two song interpolations, meaning that these were songs not written by the main songwriters, but they were instead imported from an outside source. This practice was common for both musical comedies as well as revues, and so it would not have surprised the audience to find "Ragtime Jockey Man" (words and music by Irving Berlin) and "The Philadelphia Drag" (music by Harold Orlob and lyrics by Atteridge) in the list of musical numbers.[37] Both artists were given credit in the program for the "outside" song, which was often the case. A notable exception to this rule was in *The Passing Show of 1916*. The show included a song called "How to Make a Pretty Girl," or "How to Make a Pretty Face" as it was known during the tour. The credit, according to the program, went solely to Sigmund Romberg, who wrote the bulk of the score. However, when the song was published by Schirmer later that year, the title was changed to "The Making of a Girl," and credit was shared with a new name to the Broadway stage—George Gershwin (see Figure 1.3). This was Gershwin's first song for the Great White Way, and since it toured most of America, it was probably the first of his songs that received national attention. The young pianist first played a different song for E. R. Simmons, a prominent Shubert employee, and it was Simmons who sent him to meet Romberg.[38] In an interview in 1920, Gershwin recalled that it made "quite a hit," and it was "on the strength of this that Mr. Askins [a manager for whom he had been a rehearsal pianist] offered to introduce me to Max Dreyfuss, the head of T. B. Harms and Francis, Day, and Hunter, the publishers."[39]

Andy Razaf (as A. P. Razafkevifo, a misprint of his surname, Razafkeriefo) had his first song, "Baltimo'," performed in *The Passing Show of 1913* as an interpolation. The cover depicts the trim and tuxedoed figure of Artie Mehlinger, whose name is splashed across the bottom of the page as if he wrote the song, but this "sensational song hit" was a major achievement for Razaf, who wrote both the words and the music and was, at the time, just seventeen years old and working as an elevator operator. Razaf remembered meeting the show's conductor, Oscar Radin, and showing

Fig. 1.3. *"The Making of a Girl" sheet music cover. Author's Collection.*

him the music, but it was Mehlinger who responded most enthusiastically, "taking one look at the music and having it played over again on the spot."[40] Razaf's biographer, Barry Singer, notes that Razaf, who was black, saw the acceptance of the song as "magnificently promising," despite the knowledge that only white men were writing for Broadway at the time. This may not have been entirely true—Noble Sissle and Eubie Blake had a song called "That Peach-a-reen-a-Phil-a-peen-o Dance" that was included in *The Passing Show of 1917*—but it was relatively uncommon. Working as a Tin Pan Alley writer, however, was now an option, and Razaf's remarkable career, with the production of lyrics for an estimated eight hundred songs, began in the halls of the Winter Garden.[41]

Razaf and Gershwin's success stories were not the only ones for composers in *The Passing Show* series, or, for that matter, many of the revues. The case for these two aspiring songwriters involved the beginning of their careers, but an interpolation could come from anywhere, frequently giving well-established composers like Harry von Tilzer yet another hit. A host of other composers and lyricists wrote interpolations during the run of *The Passing Show*, including Clarence Gaskill, Isham Jones, and Earl Carroll, whose *Vanities* revue series would eventually be competition. There are numerous examples of already-published songs being adopted by someone performing in a *Passing Show*, most often a star. Willie and Eugene Howard, for example, can be seen on the cover of "June Moon," a song by Joe Lyons and Frank Magine (lyrics) and Charley Straight (music).[42] The music had been published by the Broadway Music Corporation earlier in 1921, and the first edition, which was widely distributed, used the same cover, but without the brothers' picture or any mention of *The Passing Show of 1921*. "I'm Forever Blowing Bubbles," an interpolation for the tour of the 1918 edition, was given an entirely new cover after it was featured by Helen Carrington (and some "Bubble Girls"), providing co-authors Jaan Kenbrovin and John William Kellette with an unexpected boost for a song that had been written without the show in mind.

Even members of the cast could benefit from having their own songs placed in the show. Muriel Window, a minor star in *The Passing Show of 1914*, sang "The Brazilian Max-Cheese" (a play on the name of a dance called the "maxixe") at some point during the tour of the show. She had written the lyrics herself and the music had been composed by Ernesto Nazareth. Additionally, some songs seem to have been interpolated and could not, for whatever reason, include the words "Passing Show" on their cover. "She Taught Me to Dance the Fandango" (1915) by John T. Murray and "Why Do They Make Girls Like You?" (1916) with lyrics by Joe Goodwin and music by the prolific Al Piantadosi both mention that the songs were successes at the Winter Garden, but neither mentions the revue.[43] The best selling sheet music from any *Passing Show* was also an interpolation. "Goodbye Broadway, Hello France" (words by C. Francis Reisner and Benny Davis and music by Billy Baskette) was an addition to the finale of the 1917 production early in the Broadway run and was a smash hit.[44] There were several pieces of music included during the ballet sections, too, but these were chosen by performers and not commissioned specifically for the revues (this is discussed in more depth in chapter 5).

The result for the composers and lyricists of interpolations was the one certainty that no other entertainment medium of the period could provide: guaranteed exposure. Before the advent of radio, songs near the turn of the century relied primarily on vaudeville for their dissemination. If a composer was lucky, a gifted performer would become attached to a tune and would travel widely with it, sometimes singing it multiple times during a single night if it was a hit. Charles Hamm's remarkable study of Irving Berlin's "Alexander's Ragtime Band" shows that the song followed this pattern, with singer Emma Carus "intruducing" [*sic*] it to an array of audiences in 1911 before the number went, in more modern terms, viral, and was taken up by other vaudevillians within weeks.[45] On the surface, it would seem that sheet music and recordings would be a good way to judge a song's efficacy, but neither outlet—especially records—was a reliable way to get a song across without performed support.[46] The most important place to present a song was in the theater, and when a song made it into *The Passing Show*, it guaranteed the authors audiences throughout the Northeast and most of the Midwest. Often playing in Shubert-owned houses, thousands of theatergoers would hear numbers by these young songwriters. As the composer sat in New York, the great rolling tour would spread their words and music across the country in the most lavish way possible, with many people buying a ticket simply because it was an event they attended every year.

The way these audiences heard the music was important too. The art of the orchestrator has only received attention in recent years, with many of the musicians who fulfilled this role remaining in obscurity for decades.[47] The Shuberts hired several men to turn the composer's music into a full score for the pit orchestra, but the one who worked most diligently on *The Passing Show* series was Frank Saddler. Saddler's reputation as the most important person in the development of Broadway orchestration was solidified through his more well-known work with composer Jerome Kern and his mentorship of Robert Russell Bennett, who became the featured "man for the job" after 1927. Bennett wrote several articles praising Saddler's work for small orchestras of fifteen to eighteen musicians, mentioning his skill with creating unique percussive effects and creatively assigning melodic fragments through the orchestra.[48] What has only recently been discussed has been Saddler's abilities with a full-scale pit orchestra, which in the case of *The Passing Shows* was at least twenty-three players and possibly more if the string sections were expanded.[49] No matter which composer was hired, Saddler was the Shubert's principal orchestrator during the 1910s, preparing his partiturs (the full orchestration without vocal parts) with great care and clarity. He would then send the pages to a copyist agency that would prepare the parts for members of the pit. Saddler was not the only person who worked for the Shuberts in this capacity. Sol P. Levy (who eventually made his way to Hollywood), William Schulz, and Hilding Anderson, were among others who contributed orchestrations. Allan K. Foster, the dancer, also provided several orchestrations. Once the Shuberts hired someone, they often fulfilled multiple roles over the years based on individual skill sets. But, much like with other long-term artists who were associated with the revue series, it was the sound developed by Saddler that would be the signature musical arrangement for these Winter Garden shows.

Another musical force found on programs year after year was the man at the podium, Oscar Radin. As musical director (the term applied to the conductor of the pit), he was in charge of organizing the musicians and doing what a good conductor does—being ready for anything. Huffman and Radin had known each other in their younger days, and when Huffman was hired at the Winter Garden, Radin was retained, as well.[50] The Shuberts thought a great deal of the conductor, and they weren't alone; even his orchestras loved the man and presented him with a gold watch as a gift.[51] Radin was the conductor at the Winter Garden during each of the revues during the teens, and he was the conductor for all *The Passing Shows* until he began working with Ziegfeld in *The Midnight Rounders of 1920*, after which he was involved with several editions of the *Follies*. Contrary to legends about the relationship between talent and producers, these non-Shubert jobs did not mean the musician was at odds with his former employers; Radin returned to conduct *The Passing Show of 1926* and many other Shubert productions. Additionally, Radin acted as a composer when it was required for plays with music that were produced by the Shuberts.[52] In his career as a conductor, Radin appears to have been a baton-wielding maestro and not a violin-wielding one, which had been the tradition in the past.[53] If there were any questions as to Radin's direct involvement with the creation of a show, a brief note on the front page of the overture for *The Passing Show of 1914* shows that Saddler and Radin interacted through the scores, which suggests that Radin may have looked at the scores before they were given to the copyists. Figure 1.4 shows Saddler's note to the conductor, complete with his treble-clef "S" signature.

Saddler's suggestion to Radin concerning a lengthening procedure for the Overture reads as follows: "Oscar, If you want repeat choruses on any of these—insert the 1st ending before my modulation—making my connections 2nd ending. Saddler." Radin probably surveyed the arrangement by looking at Saddler's full scores during rehearsals. It is certain that the conductor would have felt competent to consider orchestrations at length since he, too, provided orchestrations to many Broadway productions. Similar to the situation with the orchestrators, several other conductors are mentioned during later years, including Clarence Rogerson (1918), Alfred Goodman (1921 and 1923),[54] Fred Walz (1922), and Tom Jones (1932). However, if Radin was available, he was the Shuberts' first choice.

Another central figure and regular member of the creative team was (George) Watson Barratt, whose Broadway career began with the Shuberts in 1918. Originally a prolific illustrator for such notable magazines as the *Saturday Evening Post*, Barratt became the driving force for the look of many of the Winter Garden revues, starting with *Sinbad* and then *The Passing Show of 1918*. Not only was he the designer for nearly every iteration of the series after this, but he was also the visionary behind the elaborate sets of almost all of Romberg's operettas (produced by the Shuberts) throughout the 1920s and 1930s. He is credited with having produced over three hundred shows for the producers and over one thousand during his career, and

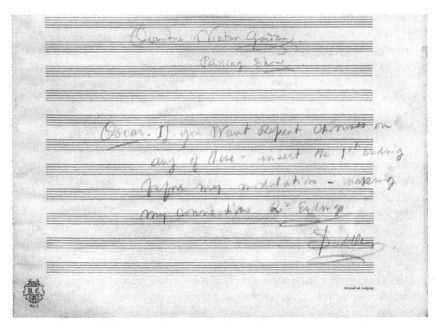

Fig. 1.4. Title page for The Passing Show of 1914 *overture manuscript.*
Shubert Archive.

for years, he was one of the most sought-after designers in the country.[55] With the unusually large Winter Garden stage, Barratt was given ample space to create the ever-changing range of sets needed for these shows. From luscious harems to modern movie studios and Roman amphitheaters, Barratt worked closely with Atteridge to craft the exotic and the spectacular sights that people expected for large-scale revues. The foreign settings of both revues and operettas gave the designer opportunities to explore the décor, colors, and architecture of places such as Cuzco, Cordoba, Vienna, and Berlin. To be as up to date on recent trends as possible, he was frequently sent by the Shuberts across the United States and Europe to see the most modern productions and become ready to adapt his own style when necessary.[56] Barratt's work was highly praised by critics, but, as with almost all his contemporaries, his extraordinary output deserves closer inspection.[57]

Another contributor to the scenic world of *The Passing Show* was P. Dodd Ackerman, one of the most active set designers and scene painters during these years. Ackerman had set up his business as early as 1909, and over the next two decades, his workshop would produce the sets for hundreds of Broadway shows and, beginning in the fall of 1919, countless vaudeville acts.[58] He was even the go-to designer for many movies shot in New York. A profile published in the *Dramatic Mirror* listed his main employees and also mentioned the large number of other people working for him at his Brooklyn plant, with men doing the carpentry and painting and women providing the sewing.[59] Drapes, decorations, scenery, cycloramas, props, and so much more were available, and Ackerman was also responsible for creating sets that could easily be stored and transported, an essential element for any show that went on the road.[60] As with many areas of production, a few other designers who worked for the Shuberts created set pieces when necessary, such as Rollo Wayne's contributions in 1922 and 1932.

In certain cases, the creator of an effect or a scene is given special mention in the program, probably due to contractual obligation, for the phantasmagorical showpiece they developed. The *Passing Show of 1913* featured two specialty sets, "The Capitol Steps" and "Tango Square," both of which were conceived and manufactured by George Williams.[61] Called "The Charge of the U. S. Cavalry," the spectacular finale to Act I of *The Passing Show of 1916* was "invented and built by Lincoln J. Carter."

According to the *New York Press*, the "realistic battle scene" featured "a line of khaki-clad men on wooden horses which plunged realistically. Behind the riders were row upon row of soldiers and the whole effect was of a great mass of men rushing pell-mell into battle. You caught the glint of sabres and the acrid smell of powder. That scene had the audience tingling."[62]

The moment was one of the night's highlights, and the inventor received mention wherever the show traveled, probably because the Shuberts realized that Carter's name—he was a major theatrical figure—helped sell tickets.

Although Ackerman had his own studio, Barratt usually relied mainly on other Shubert staff to transform his ideas into reality. In a collaborative effort such as musical theater, he sometimes was personally responsible for lighting, props, costuming, and other elements.[63] But generally, the tasks were doled out to others. In several cases, the program merely states that the "Winter Garden Property Co." or the "Winter Garden Electrical Department" was responsible for the work in these areas. However, the person in charge was just as often mentioned. For example, James (J. H.) Surridge was the head of set construction for the 1912, 1913, 1914, and 1916 editions.[64] This position was taken over by Edward Margolies for the 1921 show.[65] For 1915 and 1917–1919, however, the programs did not specify who took this position, and many of the in-house memos did not clarify who was in charge of what portion of the work. Set painters such as the Young Brothers (John H. and Louis) were regular employees, beginning with their work for the 1912 revue. Robert Law did the work the following year, and both (along with William Rising) were engaged for *The Passing Show of 1914*. By 1922, United Scenic Studios ("under the direction of Earnest Schlageter") was responsible for the construction. Those in charge of stage props and lighting seemed to change regularly, too, though a few names, like Nick Kronyak and "The New York Calcium Light Company" are mentioned for some years and not others. An interesting change seems to come in the program of 1917, when many of these less glamorous contributors are simply left off the program entirely. The trend to include fewer credits continues in later years, with some positions being frequently left out of the programs into the 1920s.[66]

One area where attributions were always made, though, was for costuming. Almost every man in the show wore a tuxedo as his standard costume, meaning that it was usually the outfit worn if no special character was intended and was certainly used for each of the chorus men. Throughout the entire series, the Shuberts got these clothes from the Ford Uniform Company.[67] Shoes for the show were also purchased at the same location year after year; I. Miller was the company the producers chose during almost all of *The Passing Shows*. It was no surprise, since Israel Miller was the principal shoemaker for all of Broadway beginning at the turn of the century and for the next thirty years, when the store and its line expanded significantly.[68] A detailed promotional image of Charlotte Greenwood shows her carefully crafted shoes, probably created with the detailed instructions of the designer for the 1912 show, Melville Ellis.

The issue of costume design touches on the very nature of collaborative work, and although several names appear alongside the "costumes designed by" line in the program, this area of production was not nearly as straightforward as one might expect. The source of the gowns was clear, with both stars and girls in specific scenes wearing the work of well-known dressmakers such as Dancrey (1913), Joseph (1914), Faibisy (1916), and others. One of the more famous designers to work for the series was Erté, who provided concepts for portions of *The Passing Show of 1922*. As one of the architects of the Art Deco style, Erté was an avowed modernist, and he was particularly interested in putting this into practice with chorus girl costumes. According to the program, Erté did the designs, handing them off to Max Weldy, who supervised their production and tailored each outfit to specific performers.

The designer for *The Passing Show of 1917* was probably Homer Conant, who provided drawings for a majority of the outlandish outfits worn by the chorus. Conant worked extensively for the Shuberts during the 1910s, sketching designs for most of the stars as well as the chorus members. Some of his more imaginative images for 1917 included women dressed as postage stamps for "Won't You Send a Letter to

Fig. 1.5. "Champagne Girl" Grace Keeshon from The Passing Show of 1917.
Courtesy of Grapefruit Moon Gallery.

Me?" and as butterflies for "My Yokohama Girl." This was the beginning of an important trend; instead of portraying women performing an action or a job (such as the
Baseball Girls in the 1915 edition), the women transformed into something else. In
one of the final production numbers, they became dancing champagne flutes during
the song, "The Girl Who Drinks Champagne" (see Figure 1.5). The scene was a duet
between Franklyn Batie and Yvette Rugel, with Conant's glassware showgirls dancing and singing behind them.

So many individuals were involved with creating the costumes within the
Shubert studios that the credit is not accurate in the programs. Melville Ellis was
credited with the costume designs for *The Passing Show of 1914*, but several of the
extant costume sketches are actually by Conant. The same designer was given credit
for the 1916 edition, but only for some of the dresses, with "additional" garments
by Mme. Kahn. In all probability, designers worked scene by scene on an individual
basis that was determined by what was needed when. For example, items crafted
for *The Passing Show of 1919* were completed in different locations, according to sur-
viving documents, and thus the complicated work that went into crafting the "oriental" costumes for the King Solomon scene would have been a group effort (see
Figure 1.6). Since the show hurtled forward at such a magnificent rate, little time
would have been given for the entire shop to complete its job, and efficacy was more
important than a unified approach to a show.[69]

Fig. 1.6. *The Court of King Solomon scene*, The Passing Show of 1919.
Author's Collection.

Most advertisements for *The Passing Shows* proclaimed that the revues were "under the direct supervision" of the brothers themselves, but just how true was this? The role the Shuberts played in the development of their shows has been a source of contention in the past, but the documents available in the Shubert Archive tell a rich story of involvement from almost every conceivable angle. Cables, telegrams, and memos remain extant for each Winter Garden revue, and the story told through these interactions demonstrates that J. J. and Lee were integral to creating the shows. The true driving force, however, was J. J., who felt that the Winter Garden shows were his personal projects. Former director of the Shubert Archive, Brooks McNamara, suggests that Lee wanted to become associated with high-quality drama, while J. J. cultivated musical theater.[70] Fields's biographers echo this notion, but they state that the financial agreement with Fields was Lee's attempt to undermine J. J.'s interests, giving the seasoned professional musicals and leaving J. J. out of the loop entirely.[71] Lee probably had hoped to offer the Winter Garden to Fields while the theater was being built, but the actor–producer (who was more interested in the actual shows than their financial element) was too deeply in debt to his new partners, and tried to make up what he owed by performing endlessly. Fields went on tour with *Up and Down Broadway* during the summer of 1910, and it was then that J. J. took control over the Winter Garden, changing the layout of the building and reconfiguring the project. With a new project under his watch, J. J. was not going to passively stand by as the shows were created without his input.

Fields's biographers also ask a question that is worth repeating: "So why didn't the Shuberts simply hire Lew Fields to produce the *Passing Show*?"[72] Their answer is that J. J. probably wanted to keep control of the theater and the project for himself. But further than that, I suggest, is that they knew they could use the talent behind Fields to achieve the same ends. Wayburn had worked closely with Fields on *The Mimic World* (1908), which the Shuberts had coproduced with Fields. The collaboration between Wayburn and Fields continued through eleven productions until 1912, and there is little doubt that the elder entertainer shared much of his knowledge and skill with the younger choreographer. With Fields's illness and J. J.'s growing prominence, it is likely that placing Wayburn in the director's chair meant the first *Passing Show* could carry some traces of Fields's handiwork while simultaneously offering Wayburn a greater range of creative freedom.

While J. J. was the central figure behind the production of *The Passing Shows*, the extant documents demonstrate that both he and Lee were involved in supervision. The brothers sent and received comments about everything from casting, costume-making, talent scouting, musical choices, and prop building. For example, a memo from Lee to J. J., dated June 12, 1912, includes directions to ask a scout in France about buying a complete "harem scene, and see what [they] will let us have it for."[73] Notes sent to Jake Flamm (the property manager) and to John Young (scene painter) during the preparations for *The Passing Show of 1914* show J. J. worried about items arriving at the stage in time for rehearsals and double-checking on the location of "little foot stools" as well as the fountain for the Omar Khayyam scene.[74]

Hiring performers was one of the main concerns for the brothers, but given the remarkable reach of their theatrical world by 1911, they had no trouble finding high-quality, top-tier talent for revues. Multiple drafts exist for each edition of *The Passing Show*, offering an in-depth study for the relatively quick development of each show, with J. J. meticulously working out the cost for the myriad stars, dancers, and comedic teams; it is fascinating to watch as names are crossed off, salary amounts changed, and notes on possible replacements are suggested in margins. In the end, every participant had to be given the Shubert seal of approval. McNamara interviewed J. J.'s son John, who said that the brothers never fought over financial affairs, but that their differing tastes sometimes created havoc when it came to putting on show.[75] McNamara also indicates that over time, Lee became less involved with the day-to-day production affairs and became more focused on the business itself, letting J. J. run most of the artistic elements. The memos support this assertion, with almost all of the detail-oriented suggestions for revues in the 1920s coming from J. J.'s desk. Relying on his excellent staff and overseeing it all, J. J. watched carefully as each show was staged, set in motion, and toured across America.

The relationship of Mason and Foster (the choreographers) was a perfect example of the key to the tremendous success of the impressively vast Shubert theatrical machine. In both dance professionals, the brothers had competent, proven employees that could succeed in multiple capacities if necessary. Since both could work with chorus girls effectively and understood the needs of the Winter Garden Theater intricately, they could manage the tasks the Shuberts assigned them quickly and receive raves for their work. In developing a network of creative collaborators who knew each other well and could successfully and repeatedly create a show that impressed the critics and brought in audiences, J. J. and Lee built a theatrical model with a built-in flexibility that no other producers could match. This meant they always had a way of creating a show that maintained a certain level of formulaic consistency while, at the same time, it could be developed by at least one other artist working for the team. This certainly seems true in the case of composers, too. Romberg could be hired for a *Passing Show* while Schwartz could be moved to the Fall revue without causing a significant break in the quality and speed necessary for the creation of these shows. By keeping a cadre of highly professional staff that could be interchangeable when necessary, the Shuberts could move effortlessly between their flagship summer series and the other shows they produced during the year. A steady stream of entertainment available to audiences both on Broadway and through the touring versions of these shows meant there was always something to look forward to from this remarkable team of creators.

Beyond the services the Shuberts used for some of their shows, the two exceptions to this pattern were Harold Atteridge and J. C. Huffman. Atteridge was the point person for the organization of the shows as they developed, and he worked tirelessly to forge each revue from the myriad components of the theatrical world, undoubtedly helping to choose talent and then writing the lyrics and scripts each person would perform. But beyond his creative contributions, it is likely that Atteridge was the glue that held the production staff together, frequently reporting to J. J. Atteridge must have had to develop strong relationships with dozens, if not hundreds, of people involved with the shows, keeping the machine running smoothly despite the difficulties that arose, as they often do in creative endeavors, with each individual personality.[76] Considering the breakneck swiftness of the process for each show, he must have been a calm figure at the center of the great Shubert/Winter Garden revue production storm. Huffman, on the other hand, became the force for development once a show went into rehearsals. He put the pieces together on the stage itself, working diligently with the conductor, the choreographer, and the performers to find the right balance and tempo for the show. Atteridge was present at these rehearsals, too, and must have aided Huffman in the process, though he was probably keenly aware (due in part to his temper) that Huffman was the one in charge at this point in the creation of the revue. Although they may not have admitted it, the Shuberts could never have produced their annual series without Atteridge and Huffman, both devoting untold hours of their lives to the creation of these revues. With these two supervising the daily grind of the theatrical staff, the magnificent *Passing Shows* lit up stages everywhere, night after night, with their multifaceted stars.

1. Maryann Chach, Reagan Fletcher, Mark E. Swartz, and Sylvia Wang, *The Shuberts Present: 100 Years of American Theater* (New York: Harry N. Abrams, 2001), Shubert Archive.

2. Almost every autobiography written by someone in the theater during the first half of the twentieth century mentions a connection to the Shuberts, with most of the statements (written after Lee and J. J.'s deaths) positive. Fred Astaire, Fred Allen, and Charlotte Greenwood (all cited elsewhere in this book) are positive in their depictions of the brothers. Recent authors covering a wide range of Broadway history offer their own images, with Larry Stempel's *Showtime: A History of the Broadway Musical Theater* (New York: Norton, 2010) and Mark N. Grant's *The Rise and Fall of the Broadway Musical* (Boston: Northeastern University Press, 2004) retaining positive depictions of the brothers. The central contributor to shaping the Shuberts' negative reputation is Foster Hirsch's book, *The Boys from Syracuse: The Shuberts' Theatrical Empire* (Carbondale and Edwardsville: Southern Illinois University Press, 1998). The book is built mainly on notes from personal interviews between Howard Teichmann (a former employee) and John Shubert (J. J.'s son) near the end of the son's life in the 1950s. However, much that is contained in the book is unsubstantiated, and since none of the participants are alive to clarify or refute the statements, much of the content is merely hearsay. Especially questionable are the sexual tales related about everybody from Al Jolson to the Shuberts themselves.

3. Gerald Bordman, *American Musical Revue: From the Passing Show to Sugar Babies* (New York and Oxford: Oxford University Press, 1985), 52–53. Bordman's book and the two others listed subsequently are the most extensive overviews of the revue as a genre, and they are all highly critical of the Shubert series. These include Robert Baral, *Revue: A Nostalgic Reprise of the Great Broadway Period* (New York: Fleet Publishing, 1962); and Lee Davis, *Scandals and Follies: The Rise and Fall of the Great Broadway Revue* (New York: Limelight Editions, 2000).

4. Bordman, *American Musical Revue*, 52.

5. This information was obtained from the Music in Gotham website and database (http://www.musicingotham.org), accessed December 1, 2015. This ongoing project covers musical events in New York City from 1862–1875, and much of the data are available through the searchable website. *Aphrosia* was originally titled *Satanas, or The Spirit of Beauty*, by Joseph Stirling Coyne (1859).

6. "Events," *New York Times*, February 15, 1869, 7. See also Gillian Rodger and Jonas Westover, "American Revue," in *Encyclopedia of Popular Music of the World*, vol. 6: *Genres*, edited by John Shepherd (London: Continuum Press, 2013).

7. See Armond Fields and L. Marc Fields, *From the Bowery to Broadway: Lew Fields and the Roots of American Popular Theater* (New York and Oxford: Oxford University Press, 1993) for a thorough examination of the pair's careers.

8. A. Fields and L. M. Fields, *From the Bowery to Broadway*, 222–24. More on the Shubert–Fields relationship is discussed in chap. 8.

9. Jonas Westover, "Shubert (family)," *The Grove Dictionary of American Music*, 2nd ed., edited by Charles Hiroshi Garrett (New York: Oxford University Press, 2013).

10. A. Fields and L. M. Fields, *From the Bowery to Broadway*, 222.

11. See Raymond Mander and Joe Mitchenson, *Revue: A Story in Pictures* (New York: Taplinger, 1971); and Jacques Damase, *Les Folies du Music Hall: A History of the Music-Hall in Paris* (London and New York: Spring Books, 1962) for a discussion of British and French works from the nineteenth century.

12. Cynthia Brideson and Sara Brideson, *Ziegfeld and His Follies: A Biography of Broadway's Greatest Producer* (Lexington: University Press of Kentucky, 2015), 73.

13. Chach et al., *The Shuberts Present*, Shubert Archive, 268.

14. Davis, *Scandals and Follies*, 98.

15. It is worth mentioning that in several instances, revues were also staged in between the fall and spring, depending on either the number of performances during the fall and/ or the touring schedule of the fall show.

16. Bordman, *American Musical Theatre*, 338.

17. More on why *The Passing Show* came to be can be found in chap. 8.

18. Chach et al., *The Shuberts Present*, Shubert Archive, 267–68.

19. Chach et al., *The Shuberts Present*, Shubert Archive, 287.

20. "Whirl of World Ends Wednesday," *New York Times*, May 24, 1914, X5.

21. Almost no research has been produced about the revues cited in Table 1.1, with little known about them other than that many were star vehicles for Al Jolson. A detailed analysis of these shows might help to explain how the various series of annual revues were different from those that were seen regularly on Broadway. Much of the materials for these shows—including the original orchestrations, parts, and scripts—are extant and are available for study at the Shubert Archive in New York City. Further research in this area would greatly enrich the context of musical theater during this era, as well as deepen our knowledge of the history of the revue.

22. It is important to mention that a second playwright, George Bronson-Howard (1883–1922), was the co-author for *The Passing Show of 1912*, but that was his only contribution to the series. Documents in the Archive do not clarify which elements came from Atteridge and which ones Bronson-Howard contributed. Bronson-Howard lived a fascinating life as a writer and was active as a newspaper man, novelist, playwright and, eventually, as a screenwriter for silent films.

23. "Harold Atteridge, A Rapid-Fire Librettist." *New York Times*, June 14, 1914, X8.

24. Vince McKnight, "Marching By," [Press release], Shubert Archive, J. C. Huffman Folder, ca. 1932.

25. Ibid.

26. "Shuberts Reengage Huffman." *Variety*, July 15, 1911, 4. In truth, it seems Huffman continued to have moments where he walked out on rehearsals in fits of rage. An article in *Variety* from 1920 announced Huffman's "official" break with the organization, which must have been resolved somehow despite the news item. See "Huffman Quits as Shubert Manager," *Variety*, June 11, 1920, 13. No doubt the pressures of continually being in charge of enormous productions were significant, and in all probability these were only a few of the emotionally charged moments for the director and producer.

27. J. C. Huffman, "Revue Proves Hardest Test of Craftsmanship on Stage," *New York American*, June 10, 1928, M-5.

28. "Theatrical Notes," *New York Times*, May 26 1914, 11.

29. "Atlantic City First," *Variety*, July 5, 1913, 10.

30. More about the relationship between the *Follies* and *The Passing Shows* is discussed in chap. 8.

31. For an excellent study of Wayburn's influence on dance, see Barbara Stratyner, *Ned Wayburn and the Dance Routine: From Vaudeville to the Ziegfeld Follies*, Studies in Dance History, No. 13. (Madison, WI: The Society of Dance History Scholars, 1996). This small but excellent book is essential for those studying the period of the 1910s–1920s on Broadway, and it also points to many places where more work could be pursued regarding Wayburn's specific work on individual shows.

32. Jonas Westover, "Louis Hirsch," *The Grove Dictionary of American Music*, 2nd ed., edited by Charles Hiroshi Garrett (New York: Oxford University Press, 2013).

33. One reviewer remarked, "As for the music, it is all syncopated, which is merely a fancy word for the popular type of 'rag.' There was every imaginable rag ever known, with the possible exception of the dishrag." "Dame Nature on View at Shubert," Shubert Archive, *PS 1912* show files.

34. A contemporary recording of "The Wedding Glide" (with Ada Jones and Billy Murray) is available at the Library of Congress' National Jukebox Digital Archive. The Kellogg recording can be found on the CD *Music from the New York Stage (1890–1920)*: vol. 2 (Pearl, GEMM CD 9054).

35. The finest study of Romberg's life and his music is William A. Everett, *Sigmund Romberg* (New Haven: Yale, 2007).

36. Elliot Arnold, *Deep in My Heart* (New York: Duell, Sloan, and Pierce, 1949), 211–13. While *Deep in My Heart* may present a fictitious unfolding of the events of Romberg's life, complete with novel-like dialogue, the facts themselves align with Atteridge's description of how the Winter Garden revues were put together.

37. Brian Drutman, "The Birth of the Passing Show" in *The Passing Show: The Newsletter of the Shubert Archives*, vol. 11, no.1 (Summer 1987), 1–3.

38. For how this song fit into Gershwin's career, see Edward Jablonski, *Gershwin: A Biography* (New York: Doubleday, 1988), 20–21.

39. Gordon Whyte, "Musical Comedy Notes," *Billboard*, March 13, 1920, 26. Gershwin claims the show as "the *Passing Show of 1917*," but he was one year off. This error has been repeated in many sources, possibly stemming from the error in this article.

40. Barry Singer, *Black and Blue: The Life and Lyrics of Andy Razaf* (New York: Schirmer, 1992), 31.

41. Ibid., 33.

42. The song title would eventually become the name of a comedic play from 1929 by George S. Kaufman and Ring Lardner about two young rubes whose mediocre Tin Pan Alley song becomes a hit despite its quality. "June Moon" songs became the butt of jokes for years to come, and it is possible from the sappy lyrics that the Howard Brothers realized this even in 1921 and may have performed the song as an over-the-top love duet between the two of them. As comedians, they would not have chosen a song like this for its sentimental charm.

43. It is difficult to say why this might be, especially since "Fandango" was published by Bernard Granville, who himself starred in *The Passing Show of 1914*. The Goodwin/Piantadosi song was published by Shapiro, Bernstein, and Co., which had published many *Passing Show* songs in the past. Unfortunately, most details concerning the publication of Tin Pan Alley songs are lost due to the lack of extant documents.

44. The song was published by Feist and was put in place sometime in August. By the end of September, it was being sung by others, including Charles Martin, who performed it throughout the South with the Barnum and Bailey Circus. See "Barnum and Bailey Show Now Invading South," *Billboard*, September 29, 1917, 26.

45. Charles Hamm, *Irving Berlin: Songs From the Melting Pot—The Formative Years (1907–1914)* (New York and Oxford: Oxford University Press, 1997), chap. 3.

46. One of the great mysteries of early recorded sound is why some people chose to make records and others did not. Sometimes major stars would never be recorded, and often songs that were hits by one star would be recorded by church vocalists who may never have even heard the original performance. The "Gems" series that was released on Victor between 1910 and 1930 is one of the most important sources for contemporary recordings of musical theater songs, but it never featured original artists, using instead whatever local singers were present at the time. This topic is discussed in more detail in chapt. 5.

47. The most extensive guide to the post–*Show Boat* era is Steve Suskin's *The Sound of Broadway Music: A Book of Orchestrators and Orchestrations* (New York and Oxford: Oxford, 2009).

48. George J. Ferencz, ed., *"The Broadway Sound": The Autobiography and Selected Essays of Robert Russell Bennett* (Rochester, NY: University of Rochester Press, 1999).

49. Jonas Westover, "Orchestrations for *The Passing Show of 1914*: An Analysis of the Techniques of Frank Saddler and Sol Levy," in *Music, American Made: Essays in Honor of John Graziano*, edited by John Koegel (Sterling Heights, MI: Harmonie Park Press, 2011).

50. Huffman and Radin had known each other in their younger days, and when Huffman was hired at the Winter Garden, Radin was retained as well. This brief biography of Radin tells of his youth: "Oscar Radin was born in the somewhat unpronounceable city of Byelsk-Grodno, Russia. When his family moved to the land of the free and the brave they settled down in Pittsburgh. There Radin Sr. decided to lay aside a portion of his hard-earned income to pay for the musical education of his son, who had expressed a desire to become acquainted with the intricacies of the violin. When Oscar Radin had completed his studies, he obtained a position as second violinist at the theater housing the Pittsburgh Stock Company. He was with this orchestra less than a month when he evolved the idea of giving the customers excerpts from contemporary operettas instead of the customary cut-and-dried popular songs. Curiously enough, the director of the theater was J. C. Huffman . . . Mr. Huffman became interested and suggested that Radin try the plan, which he did with success. All this occurred some twenty-five years ago, and when Mr. Huffman was engaged by the Shuberts the following season, he informed them of Radin, who was sent for and placed in charge of one of the their orchestras." See "Al Jolson's Conductor," *New York Times*, December 18, 1927, X2.

51. See "New Features for Winter Garden," *New York Times*, April 15 1911, 11.

52. "Shuberts to Stage 'Turandot' Dec. 31" *New York Times*, December 19, 1912, 15. Concerning *Turandot* (the play), it says, "The piece is staged by J. C. Huffman, and incidental music is being written by Oscar Radin."

53. Many conductors for theatrical productions in the nineteenth and early twentieth centuries played violin instead of using a baton while standing in front of the orchestra. An image of Radin from an untitled section of *New York Tribune* on conductors (March 4, 1917, 4) clearly shows a baton in his hand. For the tours, however, several of the fist violin parts are also marked "Leader," which strongly suggests these conductors may have also played violin.

54. Goodman was also a composer, and provided much of the score for *The Passing Show of 1922*.

55. "Watson Barratt, Designer, 78, Dies," *New York Times*, July 8, 1962, 65.

56. "'Night in Spain' at the Majestic," *Brooklyn Standard Union*, January 9, 1927, 10. Barratt also had a prominent international reputation; his sets for the thirty-seven scenes of *Gay Paree of 1927* were used by request for the International Exposition for the Arts of the Stage in Paris to demonstrate the various arts of the world. See "In New York Town," *The Wave, Rockaway Beach*, December 9, 1926, 2.

57. Some of his papers are housed at the Special Collections of the University of Wisconsin at Madison.

58. "Vaudeville Volleys," *New York Dramatic Mirror*, August 7, 1919, 1213.

59. "The Ackerman Studios," *New York Dramatic Mirror*, July 29, 1919, 1174.

60. "New Scenic Equipment to Meet New Conditions," *Variety*, September 28, 1917, 12.

61. Ned Wayburn took credit for the "Capitol Steps," according to Stratyner, but the program identifies Williams as the designer. Like so many scenes in musical theater, the truth was more along the lines of collaboration.

62. "New Revue Opens in Winter Garden," *New York Press*, June 23, 1916, 5. Carter was a prolific author, manager, and inventor of stage equipment, and his shows toured successfully throughout the country. He was based in Chicago and was one of the most successful entertainers from the 1890s until World War I. A collection of his papers is at The Theatre Museum of Repertoire Americana in Mount Pleasant, Iowa.

63. For the Romberg operetta *Blossom Time* (1921), based on a fictional account of the life and music of Franz Schubert, Barratt studied the milieu of 1820s Vienna in great detail. He himself reproduced a number of paintings that had once belonged to Schubert, as well as works that had influenced the composer. See "Attractions to Be Soon in Playhouses," *Binghamton Press*, September 12, 1925, 8.

64. It is unclear, but it may be that this J. H. Surridge is the same man who, during the 1880s, was part of a minstrel team with Edwin French and later a manager for other minstrel troupes.

65. Margolies was an established theatrical builder by 1908. He was the head of Margolies Construction Company, which was hired many times to renovate or build newly constructed theaters throughout the United States, including on Broadway. He was specifically hired by the Shuberts to design and construct their theaters. See "To Add New House to List," *New York Dramatic Mirror*, August 7, 1919, 1205.

66. In several cases, attributions were made for very specific items used during the shows that were provided by outside companies. For example, Sohmer Pianos received credit each year for being the "piano of choice," probably through an arrangement with the manufacturer. Other items, including cigarettes, gramophones, wigs, and even drinking water, were identified with other companies in the programs.

67. The company, a major supplier of men's theatrical formal wear as well as "historically accurate" military outfits and clothes for ushers, was located at 204 West Forty-Third Street.

68. Christopher Gray, "A Little Jewel Box of a Shoe Store," *The New York Times*, February 10, 2008, RE6. The store was located at the corner of Broadway and Forty-Sixth Street.

69. See Chach et al., *The Shuberts Present*, Shubert Archive, 155–69, for several costume sketches and designs from the Winter Garden revues, including several items from *The Passing Shows*. Also included are comments concerning many of the specific costume and set designers.

70. Brooks McNamara, *The Shuberts of Broadway* (New York: Oxford University Press, 1990), 80.

71. Fields and Fields, *From the Bowery to Broadway*, 223.

72. Fields and Fields, *From the Bowery to Broadway*, 316.

73. See Shubert Archive, *PS 1912* show files.

74. Jonas Westover, "Putting It Together: The Creative Team and Players of *The Passing Show of 1914*," *The Passing Show*, vol. 29 (2010–2011).

75. McNamara, *The Shuberts of Broadway*, 40–41. Hirsch's *Boys from Syracuse* disputes that the statement concerns financial decisions, but my own study in the archive gave no evidence of that.

76. The types of difficulties that arose during the New York run of *The Passing Shows* is hard to ascertain, since most in-house issues were usually not reported to the press. The touring shows, however, can be followed more closely. J. J. required his tour managers to send a telegram after the performance of every show on a daily basis. Reading through only one or two months of these communications is enough to demonstrate the extreme complexities of keeping the show going: broken limbs, problems with police, unhappiness with other staff, complaints about pay, and the desire for more time onstage are but a few of the concerns the tour managers reported.

2

A MATCHLESS MÉLANGE OF
MIRTH AND MELODY

• • •

THE STARS OF *THE PASSING SHOWS*

In March, following a performance of *The Passing Show of 1921*, the Winter Garden Theater celebrated its tenth anniversary with a huge event, "the first of its kind ever attempted in New York."[1] Dozens of performers who had at one time graced the stage of the large theater were asked to appear, and several dancers, singers, and comedians accepted the invitation. White Studios created an amazing image for the occasion, with the Howard Brothers and Al Jolson as Winter Garden centerpieces (see Figure 2.1).

This list of 195 stars acts as a who's who of the entertainment world during the 1910s, and over two dozen people returned to sing numbers from past Winter Garden shows and be entertained by host Willie Howard. The event was a tribute to the theater, but it was also a reminder to the theater community that the Shuberts represented one of the most successful production firms in the country.

In the beginning of their careers, the Shuberts were very clever in the way they put together the necessary components for success. Brooks McNamara tells of the struggles at the Herald Square Theater in 1894, noting that when the brothers took on the lease, the owners were insistent that the new managers honor each production that had already been agreed upon before the season began. This made choosing their own shows nearly impossible, and even when they could secure a good play, it was often difficult to fill the seats. Within a short time, however, it was clear to Sam that hiring a star was exactly what could help keep an otherwise floundering show afloat. This was precisely what he did as their business expanded. The stock company that was housed at Herald Square was headed by Richard Mansfield, an English actor and one of the most recognized celebrities in the world by 1900. Three years later, Sam convinced Mansfield to star in their production of *Old Heidelberg* (the source play for *The Student Prince*) at the Lyric Theater. This move was seen as an astonishing feat by the press. The *New York Times* proclaimed, "The building of the [Lyric Theater] is the latest and perhaps greatest venture of the Shubert firm. That these two brothers, neither of them more than twenty-seven years old, could have climbed so far up after only nine years of experience in the business of theatrical managers

Fig. 2.1. Winter Garden anniversary photograph, 1921. Shubert Archive.

seems little short of remarkable."[2] To Lee Shubert, however, it was Sam's ability to secure Mansfield's contract that was the impressive achievement; Lee said that Sam's "direct convincing manner . . . inspired confidence that he knew his business and was able to carry out successfully anything that he undertook. A dozen older, established managers in New York would have jumped at the opportunity to secure Richard Mansfield for their theaters, and here was a boy not yet twenty years of age who had won this difficult, exacting, and opinionated star over at the first contact."[3]

Sam's ease with people, his passion for the theater, and his zest for business were essential to setting the tone for the success of the firm, and it very well may have been the primary reason for the creation of the Shubert empire. With the sudden death of their exceptional brother in 1905, both Lee and J. J. struggled to keep a grip on the family's fortunes. There is no question that the two younger Shuberts paid careful attention to the lessons learned by Sam's experiences, and one thing Sam knew as well as any media mogul today was that the right star could sell anything.

In general, revues were *the* place to find the top talent of the day collected together in one colossal production. Audiences were treated to stars stemming from three general areas: experts in dance, first-rate singers of Tin Pan Alley–style songs, and uproarious comedians. To be sure, there were many other acts included, but these usually featured lesser-known (and, therefore, lesser-paid) entertainers who specialized in one category or another, such as female impersonators, acrobatic troupes, and dialect singers. Rounding out the cast were the dozens of chorus girls, dancing girls, and chorus boys, each hoping a featured act would suddenly leave and present them with an unexpected chance for stardom. And, sometimes, it *did* happen. This remarkable mix of talent allowed revues to be unlike other musical entertainments of the day, especially the operetta and the musical comedy, because the flexibility of the show's structure could easily complement whatever collection of stars the producers could weave together.

It is not surprising, then, that vaudeville was the central clearing house for many stars of *The Passing Shows*. As stated earlier, by its very nature, the revue was one of the top achievements for a vaudevillian.[4] The salary was often better, the engagement more regular, and the traveling less frequent (with longer stays in some locations), all enticing components for vaudeville stars. The Shuberts and their employees were constantly on the lookout for engaging talents and personalities, and in many cases, they were found in vaudeville houses across the globe. This chapter highlights the careers of only some of the entertainers the Shuberts hired for *The Passing Show* series, examining the multiple ways they were located, their roles and experiences with the productions, and the effect the revues had for many of these stars' careers.

The headliner for the first *Passing Show* (1912) was Trixie Friganza, a tremendous success in American and British vaudeville circuits, as well as in musical comedies. By this time, she was one of the most sought-after comediennes in show business, and there is no doubt the Shuberts saw her as the central draw for this revue. Friganza had been onstage since the late 1880s, both in variety and vaudeville, but she also had repeated triumphs on the early Broadway stage. She was a popular comedic actress, known for her loud, witty personality. She frequently made the jump between New York and London, as well as touring extensively in the United States. By the time the Shuberts engaged her for *The Passing Show of 1912*, she could command a high fee, and she received the top salary for a single performer at $300 a week, according to accounts for the revue.[5] Friganza earned her pay; she appeared in numerous scenes in as varied roles as "Keokuk," "Julia Scream," "Nancy Sykes" (from *Oliver Twist*), and for a brief moment as "Salome." When the show toured, she was given at least one scene where she appeared as herself. This is probably because she was adored by the press, as is evident in this review from the *New York Morning Sun*:

> Trixie, fair and fat and fascinating, and magnetic to her finger tips, was the bright particular star in the galaxy of funmakers, dancers, and pantomimsts. Her voice and smile would win the most adamantine to applause, and whether she tries to sing with her mirth-provoking silvery voice, or posed as a dancer in pink gauze skirts, the audience loved her dearly and welcomed her with joy.[6]

The script is full of the kind of groan-worthy jokes that Atteridge specialized in. While dressed as Keokuk, the Indian chief, she is asked by Andrew Carnegie (Clarence Harvey) if she will dance the dance of the seven veils.[7] Her response: "I can't. The other six veils are in the laundry." As a singer, she delivered Hirsch's "All the World Is Madly Prancing" with a chorus and a dancing couple; "You Never Could Tell We Were Married" as a solo; and she was part of the "Metropolitan Squawk-tette," a quartet that parodied opera. She was lauded throughout the run of *The Passing Show of 1912*, but she quickly took advantage of a return to vaudeville when the tour came to a close in the spring of the following year. Frank Cullen reports the following:

> Her vaudeville salary was more than she earned on Broadway, and the work was less tiring with two acts a day that ran roughly 25 minutes each . . . A roly-poly, rollicking *nut* comedian and impersonator, her presence on any vaudeville stage promised fun and [a] strong box office.[8]

Even with positive reviews in the Winter Garden production, Friganza did not hesitate to return to vaudeville. This reflexive relationship between Broadway and vaudeville provided exciting opportunities for performers throughout the late nineteenth and early twentieth centuries, and a person at the top of the field could forge a solid career by alternating circuits and venues.

The majority of performers who were center attractions for *The Passing Shows* enjoyed similar flexibility. Blanche Ring and her husband Charles Winninger were engaged for *The Passing Show of 1919* at the top of the bill. Ring had first been employed by the Shuberts in *The Gay White Way* (1907), and she was the kind of known quantity that would surely draw a crowd to the Winter Garden. Winninger had been in various circuits since he was nine years old, but he was not nearly as popular as his wife during his early career. The couple was known for (among other talents) their excellent skills at mimicking other performers, and they were given roles as Giometti, the Florentine Poet (played by Ring), and Lionel Neri (played by Winninger, a burlesque on Barrymore's performance) in *The Passing Show*. Together, they made an astonishing $1,000 a week and were the draws the Shuberts hoped they would be. An unnamed critic in *Billboard* was impressed, saying Winninger's Neri showed "marvelous versatility," while "Miss Ring, with the radiance of her personality and the cleverness of her art would lift any show to a quality of superiority."[9] Even though the show was praised overall, the critic admitted that "a paucity of comedy material is noticeable in the performance as a whole."[10] For this reviewer, it was the quality of the stars that made *The Passing Show of 1919* a successful production.

One aspect of Ring's performances that captured the heart of her audiences was her invitation for them to sing along during the chorus, something they often did. In a review of one of her engagements at the Colonial Theater, the *New York Dramatic Mirror*'s Reid reports "her breezy and infectious personality swept across the foot-lights and won her a big hand. As customary, she saved her best song, 'All in Favor Say Aye,' for accompaniment by the audience. The gallery was loudly obliging."[11] It would have been nearly impossible for Ring to invite the tremendous Winter Garden audience to participate in this kind of communal activity and that may have been one of the reasons she was not as effective in the revue. In place of this routine, she and Winninger, along with a crop of "Skating Beauties" sang "Summertime in the Winter Garden." The lyrics praise the wondrous young women of the chorus:

> It's always summer time at the Winter Garden
> For that's one garden where pretty flowers always grew
> There's dainty violets and blushing mignonettes
> And there are daisies and daisies never tell you knew
> There are tulips breathing love and passion
> There are song birds making music fill the air
> It's always summer time at the Winter Garden
> And you are welcome to take your little girlie there.

While no more or less inspired than the average Atteridge lyric, the song seems a poor fit for a comedic married couple to present, especially when the audience would expect a more intimate approach from Ring. It is not surprising then that it was in the revue's dialogue that the actress could draw more attention to herself as an indi-vidual and, probably, as a more effective presence.

A number of high-profile comedians were hired over the years to keep audiences amused, and for them, well-written jokes were essential. One of the most prominent was Ed Wynn, the featured actor for the 1916 edition. Wynn was highly sought after by producers and managers for many types of entertainment, and he was also quite intel-ligent, trying to do whatever was necessary to ensure the best deals for himself. For example, when he was hired for *The Passing Show of 1916*, he had already been engaged as a headliner at the Hippodrome in London. The manager there, Albert de Courville, was excited to have Wynn as part of the cast, but since he made the deal with Wynn through an agent, de Courville was not able to personally sign the contract. Wynn used this as a loophole to get out of the contract and sign with the Shuberts.[12] Three years later, Wynn would again demonstrate his business savvy and interest in securing the best possible position for performers when he became a central figure in the Actor's Equity strike against management.

Once the Shuberts had Wynn, Atteridge provided him with several major scenes in the production. Billed as "himself" in each appearance, Wynn dispensed with characters and instead played the "perfect fool," a title he would eventually embrace. One reviewer summed up the scene that received the most attention, with Wynn fill-ing various roles concerning automobiles (see Figure 2.2): "[Wynn] has made a great hit. His garage scene is said to be screamingly comic delight burlesquing, as it does,

Fig. 2.2. Ed Wynn in the garage scene, The Passing Show of 1916.
Author's Collection.

all the mad, wild things that go in the sale of a second hand car, the patching up of a crippled car, [and] the sale of gasoline."[13] In the scene, the star also succeeds in selling a car to a blind man, with the joke being that the auto in question is a horrible wreck.

SCENE VI: Auto Scene.
(As curtain rises on a garage scene, a man enters pulling a Ford with a rope. A woman is pushing the car.)
(Wynn discovered working on car L. Bus[iness] of explosive, etc.)
WOMAN: Here's a garage.
MAN: I hope this will cure you of taking trading stamps. (Man cranks car). It's no use, it won't go.
WYNN: Maybe if you put a new needle in, it might play.
MAN: Play? I'm trying to get the darn thing to go.

WYNN: Oh, let me try. (Goes to work bench, returns to car with large saw, hatchet, and feather, gets under car and chops and saws.) Now try it. (Man cranks and loud noise comes from hood.) Sounds a little better. Hand me that feather. (Tickles spokes and other parts of car.) That's no good; oh, wait. (Fright business). You can't even frighten it. (Wynn gets under car again and then gets out and laughs).

MAN: What's the matter?

WYNN: There's no motor in it.

MAN: No motor? But I just drove it 200 yards!

WYNN: You didn't drive—you skidded. (Bus. of hammer, saw, feather, etc.) (Tickles woman accidentally.)

WOMAN: How dare you?

WYNN: I beg your pardon, I won't charge you for that. (After alarm clock bus., man concealed on upstage side of auto pushes car off.) Now there's a scene that didn't mean much, but from now on it's laugh after laugh. [Scene continues, with Wynn selling gasoline via an eyedropper and selling a car to a blind man.]

Wynn's final dialogue about the scene fits into the way his whole part was conceived; the "meta" approach of his character was used throughout the show. While Atteridge is listed as the writer of the book, Wynn's own statements suggest that the creation of his material was more a collaboration than a passive acceptance of previously written lines.

> The high price of gasoline is no joke, yet in the garage scene in "The Passing Show," when I sell it in an eyedropper it gets a terrific howl. Many of these things come by accident, pure and simple. They [Atteridge?] never thought of putting in the eyedropper. It just happened. All of my ad lib matter came about in the same fashion. In other words, my part is one which grows with the staging of the show. I feel my way very carefully and listen to all advice, but that does not mean that I take it."[14]

When the revue opened in June, the reviewers lauded Wynn's escapes and his nutty humor, even if they had seen it in show after show (and would continue seeing it for years to come). The *New York Times* said that while Wynn was virtually the same as he was in the *Follies of 1915*, "his pseudo-impromptu prattle is always entertaining, and any revue is better for his hanging around ... His garage scene is amusing."[15] Some critics were not as excited; Wynn was even called an "insufferable bore" by the *Brooklyn Daily Eagle*.[16] But the comedian stayed with the show during its tour, receiving high praise in numerous cities.

Wynn is one of the few headlining stars of *The Passing Show* series whose name remains familiar to twenty-first century audiences. While this may be more a result of his brief but memorable role of Uncle Albert in Disney's *Mary Poppins* (1964), the truth is that many of the important entertainers of the day have been long forgotten. One comedy duo that was immensely popular in the first two decades of the 1900s was that of George W. Monroe and Harry Fisher. The two men had been active on Broadway since the 1880s, and eventually performed together as a team. In

The Passing Show of 1914, Fisher was given the villain role (using the term loosely) of Baron von Criquet. The Baron was expected to deliver witty dialogue rather than do any strenuous dancing or singing. Monroe was not featured in the songs or dances either, but instead he was responsible for a great deal of dialogue. It was the high-quality comedy banter between the two that audiences enjoyed, but Monroe was the bigger draw. It is not surprising then that both "funmakers" were also engaged for *The Passing Show of 1915*.

Monroe was a professional female impersonator, lauded for his ability to behave in a loud, boisterous manner that would not have befit a proper lady of the day. Monroe's character in *The Passing Show of 1914* was named Little Buttercup, Queen of the Movies, sending up a combination of the Gilbert and Sullivan character from *H.M.S. Pinafore* (Little Buttercup) as well as that of Celia Gill, the actress who saves the film industry, a burlesque on the musical entitled *Queen of the Movies* (1914). Monroe had actually been doing the same shtick since the 1880s, perfecting his act for years: "George Monroe did almost exactly what he has been doing on the stage for the last decade or more in a very clever way," noted a reviewer in 1900.[17]

In *The Passing Show of 1915*, Monroe and Fisher returned to the Winter Garden triumphant. Not only had they continued with the company throughout the United States tour, concluding in the late spring, they appeared in vaudeville whenever the opportunity arose. Although they had several amusing moments together, most notably the end of the second scene, Fisher was seen as an interchangeable "straight man" by the Shuberts, who went so far as to leave his name off the list of stars in advertisements and publicity programs. However, the two pros knew how to make the best of their time together onstage. In one of Atteridge's best sketches, Monroe plays Lily, who is in search of the "Song of Songs" (Figure 2.3). This would have been uproariously funny in 1915 because the main character in Edward Sheldon's play of the previous season, *Song of Songs*, featured a young woman named Lily who is convinced to model nude for a sculptor with whom she later falls in love. The visual incongruity between the play's Lily and Monroe's Lily (who carries both a piano roll and a "big piece of bologna") would have been irresistible.

Fisher takes on the character of Senator Calkins, the overbearing older man Lily is forced to marry in the source play. Here, the joke is that she is actually "No. 4" on the list of wives; Calkins is a "Mormon polygamist." When he asks her what she's carrying, she tells him: "It's the Song of Songs. My father decomposed it. He had a sweetheart in Greece. It's a sort of greasy song. It's the story of my life. When my true love comes to me, I'm going to hold him gently and peacefully in my arms, if I have to slug him in the ear." He then invites her to move in with him in his Atlantic City home, where "several mules and a nice automobile truck" await her. The pun-filled, silly dialogue continues as the other three wives dance on stage. The reviewer for the *Dramatic Mirror* provides a colorful description of a later scene involving the two actors:

> Harry Fisher, with his dog-like bark and high pitched voice, was a genial polyga-mist who lured George Monroe as [Heinrich] Sudermann's pitiable heroine into a matrimonial alliance. While their love was ripening into a condition approaching disaster because the nuptial chamber had not twin but quadruplet beds, Eugene Howard as R. G., the mysterious detective of "Under Cover" was attempting to

Fig. 2.3. *George W. Monroe as Lily,* The Passing Show of 1915.
Author's Collection.

find the smuggled jewels which his brother, Willie, as a pestiferous orphan, was concealing upon various innocent people.[18]

Significant research has been done on transvestitism in the theater, the result demonstrating that Monroe's specialty act was not necessarily connected to gay culture of the time, but rather an accepted part of stage fare, known by the 1890s as the "dame" role.[19] Other actors, such as George K. Fortescue, portrayed a variety of over-the-top female roles for a number of years at the end of the nineteenth and the beginning of the twentieth century. Julian Eltinge's style of female impersonation, however, was also common in both vaudeville and on Broadway. It involved meticulous recreation of every aspect of a woman, from clothing and makeup to body movements and interactions with men. Eltinge's act was a matter of parody in *The Passing Show of 1914,* but the series itself included some of these "serious" impersonators during the

1920s. The most prominent were Francis Renault and Barbette (an acrobat who later appeared in *Jumbo*), both well-known artists before the Shuberts hired them.

Renault had been a sensation in vaudeville for at least twelve years before finding a place at the Winter Garden in *The Passing Show of 1922*. Born Antonio Auriemma, Renault is a good example of an entertainer whose Broadway credits do not give an accurate sense of just how active he was on various stages; although he appeared only once in a major Broadway house, he had been in vaudeville since he was a child. Renault's act consisted of impersonating a woman through several means, most notably with his voice and through an extraordinary display of fabulous and ostentatious clothing.[20] As a boy, he had been lauded for his wonderful soprano range, apparently making him a favorite of Ida McKinley, the former first lady. As an adult, Renault managed to keep singing in this high range using a remarkable falsetto, scoring him the comment by a critic that "his vocal attainments are of the high-class variety."[21] In fact, during an appearance at the Colonial Theater, one reviewer said, "Renault's best asset is his voice," which was strong enough to seem a match for a "real" woman's tessitura.[22] In several instances, those who saw the act were impressed by Renault's ability as a mimic (most notably of Lillian Russell) and as a satirist. He also was known for using elaborate stage settings that included a cyclorama that projected swirling colors throughout the theater.[23] For many, however, it was the stunning garments Renault wore that caused a sensation. When he began to receive attention in the late 1910s, he billed himself in *Dramatic Mirror* ads as "The Parisian Fashion Plate," and frequently boasted about his $5,000 (eventually $50,000) wardrobe. The Shuberts were interested enough in Renault to sign him to their vaudeville circuit, bring him on stage for *The Passing Show*, and then send him back into vaudeville, where he was a headliner throughout the 1920s.

As a member of the second-tier stars of the 1922 revue, Renault was assigned scattered moments in the show, using only a few of the many skills he possessed. He was part of a trio of singers in "My Diamond Girls," joining Sam Ash and Mlle. Alcorn—this was his only chance to display his voice as a soloist.[24] His "starring" moment came at the end of the first act, however, as a dancer. Playing the part of the "slave," Renault acted the part of a doomed servant who could only escape execution by beating other combatants in a life-or-death battle. The queen, played by Olive Alcorn, demanded a fight, but she was so overcome with the brute strength of the slave that they locked together for a dance that was both passionate and risqué. Called "the most daring" dance in the show, the "Ballet Les Conquerants" was thrilling for audiences. "Few more suggestive dances have been attempted . . . and none of rarer excellence by the principals, nor with setting half so lavish," gushed one critic.[25] To any audience member well acquainted with Renault's act, the shock was not so much the sexually charged dance but, probably, the fact that he appeared as a man! One can only wonder what spurred this choice by the show's creators, especially given the great accomplishment of Renault's vaudeville turn, which gave the glamorous impersonator an over-the-top, starring position as the pinnacle of womanly beauty. It may have been concern about Renault's (overly?) convincing femininity, or it may have been the desire to balance out the seriousness of the "Diamond Girl" personality with an aggressively masculine personae. Whatever the case, Renault seems to have stayed with the revue only while it was in New York, returning to his former act in February of 1923, resuming his role as a vaudeville diva.[26]

As with many of the high-profile stars mentioned here, the Shuberts were relentless in their pursuit of the hottest talent of the day. Friganza, Wynn, Ring, Renault—and so many others—were performers who were secured by the Shuberts directly out of the vaudeville circuits. Some of these acts were famous in their own right, but just as many were little-known troupes, specialty artists, or comedy duos. The Shubert Archive contains letters or telegrams from agents trying to interest the brothers in the collection of entertainers they had available. In a letter from Harry Weber, a large list of potential attractions were touted, with the manager politely suggesting, "I thought possibly there might be something in this list that would interest you for your Spring or Summer Productions."[27] His impressive list of acts makes for an exciting version of the show that never happened, but the standouts of Lady Duff Gordon, Stella Mayhew, and especially the "4 Marx Brothers" never found their way to a Winter Garden *Passing Show*.

At other times, the Shuberts relied on their own eyes and ears in the field for suggestions. Melville Ellis and Harry Pilcer, both performers themselves, were trusted to be responsible for spotting and approaching possible upcoming acts. Ellis wrote to J. J. concerning Adelaide and Hughes, the featured dancers of the 1912 *Passing Show*, noting "their run is the best [Pilcer] has ever seen."[28] But a majority of the time, a general awareness of the goings-on of the entire entertainment industry seems to have been enough of a priority for the brothers that they attended events themselves hoping to find the stars of the future.

If the act somehow matched whatever criteria the Shuberts were looking for, the traditional agent-to-agent negotiations took place, and if successful, the performers would find themselves on one of the most prominent stages in the country. Additionally, the prospect of the national tour meant that they would receive extensive national exposure. Atteridge, however, seems to have tried to match the level of the performers with their proper place on the bill. For example, the duo of Freeman and Dunham were assigned prominent yet mid-level roles in *The Passing Show of 1914*. The two had been popular in the two-a-day vaudeville shows, but they were frequently paired with other acts; during the teens, they regularly traveled with "The Fifteen Honey Girls" rather than appear alone.[29] Both men could sing and dance, and they were given several different parts in the 1914 edition that capitalized on these skills. The Nat Nazarro Troupe of "equilibrists" (acrobats) was another act that had its followers outside of Broadway, but it was included in several of *The Passing Show* editions. Three of the family members—Nat Nazarro, Jr., J. Edward Nazarro, and Erman Nazarro—were featured in the calisthenics scene in the 1914 edition, while Nat Jr. continued on in the 1922 and 1923 editions as a singer and dancer. Known for their remarkable agility and gymnastic feats, the Nazarro troupe brought an original flavor to the show that few other acts could have offered. The 1923 and 1924 editions included the Trado Twins (Frank and Peter), two brothers who specialized in the vaudeville triple threat: singing, dancing, and comedy. Brief parts were crafted by Atteridge for dozens of hopefuls over the years, but only a few found that they were suddenly celebrities.

The most glittering star to emerge from the vaudeville ranks, traipse through the Winter Garden curtains, and glide into fame was undoubtedly Marilyn(n) Miller. Today, Miller is only remembered by a small number of devotees, but in her day, she was one of the most important stars of stage and screen. After her debut in the 1914 installment of *The Passing Show*, Miller would continue to appear in shows at the Winter Garden, including the 1915 version of the annual revue as well as *The Show of Wonders* (1916). Eventually, Miller would join forces with Ziegfeld and become one of the most famous performers of her generation, known for her singing, dancing, acting, and gift for impersonation. Her early death due to an infection from a botched nasal surgery (as well as her growing alcoholism) cut her career short, but she was enough of a star to become the woman a young Norma Jean Mortensen would model herself after, both as a performer and in name, when she adopted the moniker Marilyn Monroe. The parallels between the two were so pronounced that Miller's biography by Warren G. Harris is entitled *The Other Marilyn*.[30]

Harris recounts Miller's experiences in London, where she was dancing and singing with her family in a vaudeville troupe called the Five Columbians. After being fined in Chicago for including an underage performer in 1911, the troupe went to Europe, where the rules regarding children on the stage were less strict. It was here that she was seen by Lee Shubert and eventually recruited to become part of the cast for *The Passing Show of 1914*. In an article published just before the show opened, Miller's appearance in New York was probably "buzzed-up" by the Shuberts themselves, who felt they had a marketable star in the fifteen-year-old young woman. The article is included in its entirety below, providing a window into the ways in which the Shubert marketing machine worked to support a future star that virtually nobody in show business would have known at the time.

MARILYNN MILLER REACHES NEW YORK VIA LONDON
This Girl from Dayton, Ohio, Had to Dance Abroad Before She Could Get Recognition In New York
One of the most fascinating ingénues to have her name flashed across Broadway this season is Marilynn Miller, one of the principals in "The Passing Show of 1914," the new Winter Garden Summer musical revue. Miss Miller has a role that requires plenty of exerting ballet and eccentric dancing, and she also carries a lilting song number that is certain to prove popular during the warm weather.
About six weeks ago, when abroad, Lee Shubert was invited to attend one of the evening parties at the Lotus Club, one of the supper clubs that flourish after the lights are dimmed at midnight in the London cafés. Mr. Shubert accepted the courtesy and enjoyed the novel form of entertainment at this English rendezvous with considerable interest. Marilynn Miller was at the time a feature on the program, and after watching her perform, Mr. Shubert immediately extended an offer for an extended engagement in this country. Her father, Caro Miller, who manages her business affairs, accepted.
This is Miss Miller's first appearance in New York, but she has been dancing gaily behind the footlights ever since the age of five. She was born in Dayton,

Ohio, and has two older sisters, formerly of the vaudeville stage, who are living in Chicago. When a little tot and wearing short dresses, Marilynn wanted a bunch of luscious California grapes that reposed in a glass dish just out of her reach on an old-fashioned sideboard in the dining room. No one was in the room to hand her the grapes, so, being possessed with a youthful spirit of ingenuity, she raised right up and stood on her toes. Mother Miller, happening in at that moment, hesitated in surprise, tiptoed out, and, flushed with hopes for professional activities as a stage mummer, she sent for the manager of the town opera house post haste.

When the manager arrived, Mrs. Miller escorted him into the dining room. Marilyn was just finished the bunch of grapes and was chuckling gleefully over her achievement. After much coaxing the youngster was persuaded to walk about on her bare toes and perform a series of childish gyrations.

The manager was elated, and immediately suggested that the child be coached for a stage dancing act. She was engaged for a week at the opera house, and from then on her popularity jumped by creditable degrees up the thermometer to success. With her father, Caro Miller, she has appeared throughout the Middle West and the South, and also played extensively in vaudeville abroad.

Miss Miller is still very young, but she is in no respects what might be termed as a "youthful prodigy." She has attained her success by years of constant, steady work and diligent practice. She is slim in appearance, but athletic and graceful in body poise.

She has learned to dance chiefly by watching the evolutions of well-known terpsichorean artists in London, Paris, and Berlin. Some of her eccentric steps are exceedingly difficult, and her ballet movements show skill and suppleness. Being a clever fencer, she spends considerable time every day handling the foils, and this exercise has improved her artistic dance motions immensely.[31]

This article is interesting in several ways, not the least of which is the fictional story about the grapes and the local opera house manager. In fact, Miller was from a performing family, and her mother, Ada Reynolds, was active on the stage long before her children were born. Because of her family's travels, young Marilyn was sent to live with extended relations in Memphis, Tennessee.[32] It was probably very common to have the types of stories in this article developed by agents in order to give a context for the emergence of a performer's talent—the same publicity machine still operates today. Some details are certainly true, including Caro Miller's connection with the Shuberts stemming from Lee's visit to the Lotus Club, where Marilynn was signed for the upcoming Winter Garden revue. Most important, however, the article stresses her physical prowess as a dancer, especially one who is classically trained but has the ability to do popular styles as well. Whatever the source of the amusing anecdote, there is no question that when *The Passing Show of 1914* finished its tour in the spring of 1915, Miller had become a sensation across the country.

Miller performed in a wide range of numbers over the course of her two years with the Winter Garden Company. First of all, Miller was hired to be the *prima ballerina* for the ballet sections of each revue, demonstrating her prowess in classical styles. Another part of Miller's performance in this musical was as an "eccentric" dancer, a term frequently used to describe any hoofer who used unusual steps in their routine, such as bending the knees inwards or feigning a fall.[33] In the second act of the 1914 show, Miller was part of a group of four that both sang and danced dressed in "Mardi Gras costumes," according to the script. The song, entitled "Good Old Levee Days," was modeled after the "coon songs" of the 1890s and early 1900s that recalled an antebellum South that never truly existed; "Levee Days" describes a world where the "darkies" and "pickaninnies" danced and sang while they "piled that cotton high." These songs were still frequent in shows of the time, from "Lovey Joe" in the Ziegfeld *Follies of 1910* to "All Aboard for Dixie Land" in *High Jinks* (1914).[34] Although other performers used the technique, no blackface was used as Miller and the others danced and sang about the "good old days." Though the choreography for the song is no longer extant, the poses and footwear for each character in the photos match the flavor of the ragtime syncopations in the music, suggesting a dance done in a popular style.[35] Here, Miller was expected to dance in a way that showed something distinctly different than her ballet skills would have demonstrated.

Miller was also an effective mimic and actress. In 1915, she portrayed contemporary star Clifton Crawford, while Julian Eltinge and others were convincingly imitated the previous year. Her speaking part was vastly expanded for *The Passing Show of 1915*, and she joked and cajoled her way through the whole revue as "First Love" (see Figure 2.4). Called a "host on her own" by one critic, Miller could hold the attention of the entire fifteen hundred–seat theater with charm and effervescence.[36] Critics overwhelmingly praised her poise, beauty, and abilities, with several pointing out that every time she took the stage she was greeted by thunderous applause. With the strong foundation and experience that she gained while working as part of the cast for two seasons, Miller was well situated to go confidently forward in a career that would take her far beyond the theaters of Broadway.

Like Miller, several *Passing Show* players were recruited from Europe. The vibrant world of live entertainment in London was a very rich source for the Shuberts, and it provided many top talents of the day, even if they were originally from the States. The most prominent English performer to lead a *Passing Show* was José Collins. By the time José appeared on Broadway, she was already famous in England, where she had been performing since the tender age of eleven. José's sweet soprano voice and her good looks brought her fame at an early age, and she was brought to America by the Shuberts to play a lead in *Vera Violetta* (1911), the show that catapulted a blackfaced Al Jolson to stardom. Her fame was such that she was hired by Florenz Ziegfeld to be one of the headliners of the *Follies of 1913*, where she sang the song, "Isle D'Amour," with music by Leo Edwards and lyrics by Earl Carroll. After the show closed on Broadway in September of 1913, Collins continued to perform with the revue, staying with the touring production until it concluded in the spring.[37] Even though she encountered some hostility in Canada when she apparently waved the British flag more vigorously than the American one (the angry party was actually made up of the American chorus girls in the show), she was successful enough to merit a starring role in the Shubert brothers' next musical, *The Passing Show of 1914*. Playing the ingénue, Kitty Mackay, she was the highest paid person in the show at $500 per week, but she had to work for her pay; Collins sang five songs in the revue and appeared in many scenes as both a dancer and delivering lots of dialogue.

Fig. 2.4. Marilynn Miller as "Youth" and Willie Howard as "Charlie Chaplin,"
The Passing Show of 1915. *Author's Collection.*

Choosing to stay in America after the show was over in New York, she played in vaudeville and then starred in Lew Fields's *Suzi* (1914). Collins's charm, her ease with audiences, and her remarkable singing voice made her a perfect central figure in the revue and, according to critics, one of the primary reasons for the show's success.

George Hassell, the English comedian, was a central player in the Shuberts' revue series, not just for one season, but for many. He was a fixture of the later *Passing Shows*, appearing first in 1918, and subsequently returning for the editions of 1922 and 1923. The Shuberts did not need to acquire Hassell overseas; he came to the United States in 1905 and joined John Craig's stock company at the Castle Square Theater in Boston. In an interview in 1916, Hassell lamented the fact that he had become so strongly associated with musical comedy, pointing to the well-received "serious" roles he had taken on over the years. A "fun-maker" in *The Girl from Brazil*

(1916), he played Herr Torkel, a doltish Swedish moneylender, a part which he proudly claims he played "in a wholly Shakespearean manner."[38] Hassell was much sought after during the teens and was very well established as a comedian by the time he was engaged by the Winter Garden Company. Over his years treading the boards for the Shuberts, he became Victor Gates (1918), a poor "sap" and other roles in 1922, and finally himself in the 1923 show. In an interview with the *New York Sun*, he attributed his decision to stick with comedy to two things: a conversation with his wife and his dwindling bank account.[39] However, he also felt that his girth was helpful to his achievements: "The public believes a fat man can be funny. I mapped out a routine of mock seriousness . . . that would prove 'sure fire' even if the lines were not . . . I was a fat servant in *The Girl from Brazil*, a fat 'Tweedlepunch' in the revival of *Florodora*, and now in the new *Passing Show*, I am a fat auctioneer, a fat playgoer, [and] a fat actor."[40] Barnett Parker and James Watts, both mentioned in the article as comedians in *The Passing Show of 1923*, were among the dozens of English performers who were hired by the Shuberts.

Paris was another location where excellent performers could be found, and the Shuberts almost always had an agent searching for gems among the throngs. Melville Ellis, mentioned earlier, was in Paris during the spring of 1912, and his reports to the Shuberts over time included a long list of which performers should be hired and which avoided.[41] Fred Allen mentions that J. J. Shubert undertook the search for excellent European talent on his own each spring.[42] Each *Passing Show* included numerous dancers, experts in both popular styles and classical techniques, and many of these acts were not only French, but usually Parisian. One imported act was the Lockfords, an "acrobatic pair from the wilds of Paris who are nothing short of marvelous."[43] Zita Lockford and her brother, Naro, were dancers unlike anything seen in New York during the early 1920s, at least according to the fanfare they received. Originally a featured attraction at the Folies Bergeres, the Shuberts hired them for *The Passing Show of 1922* and they returned for the 1924 edition.[44] Known as an "adagio" act, they incorporated balancing specialties with novel movements—a type of performance that remains popular in companies such as *Cirque du Soliel* in the twenty-first century. In the 1922 revue, they were one of the star attractions, ending Act I with a riveting "Ballet of Siam." The elaborately staged sequence was too much for some, with the *New York Tribune* dismissing it as a "pretentious exotic ballet of Siamese extraction."[45] This negative impression, however, was rare in the press surrounding the show, especially on tour; one critic hailed the Lockfords as "vigorous" and "amazing," saying the pair was "the one outstanding feature of [*The Passing Show of 1922*]."[46] It appears that the siblings decided to add a new feature to the show a month after the September 1922 opening, perhaps to keep the performance interesting for repeat showgoers. An announcement was made in late November that the two had added a segment called "Impressions of New York": "[It] is composed of two movements, according to Zita Lockford—'rush . . . whizz.'"[47] Naro's starring moment in the revues came in 1924, when the "Gold, Silver, and Green" production number earned him high marks for his "astonishing acrobatic dance."[48] The result of their hard work in the Winter Garden shows meant that the Lockfords earned a door into vaudeville in North America and were able to make a name for themselves internationally. Many of the lucky European performers found that an engagement with the Shuberts brought them opportunities that might never be possible otherwise, including work in other Broadway shows, more touring productions, circuses, and the new burgeoning medium sweeping the country—the movies.

An important change for performers in *The Passing Show* series came in 1920, when the Shuberts created their own vaudeville circuit, challenging the powerful Keith United Booking Office that, at the time, had an iron grip on the industry. Not only did this move allow the brothers to use the theaters they had built across the country during the day (as opposed to the larger shows only using the building at night), but it funneled talent into their own shows in a more direct manner. The venture only lasted until 1924, but it brought a slew of acts through the doors and opened competition in a field where competition was fierce. In some cases, this circuit allowed entertainers, managers, and the Shuberts themselves unprecedented flexibility in terms of processing and placing acts in the most profitable circumstances. Several future stars benefitted, but none left a more compelling story behind than Fred Allen, whose appearance in *The Passing Show of 1922* was a pivotal moment in his career, his personal life, and his rise to fame.

Allen was one out of many celebrities who directly attributed the Shuberts and *The Passing Shows* with a solid leap forward as a performer. From humble beginnings in Boston to the height of his fame as hosting the top-rated radio program of the mid-1940s, *The Fred Allen Show*, the comedian found success in almost every major entertainment medium of the early twentieth century, with roles in movies and a continuing presence on television until his death in 1956. Allen wrote extensively about his time with the Shuberts and, specifically, about what his experience in the 1922 show was like. In one of his many memoirs, *Much Ado about Me* (1956), Allen provides a lengthy account of the entire process of moving out of the Keith vaudeville circuit, into the Shubert one, and the move to the Winter Garden.[49] His story is both vivid and entertaining, reflecting the excitement that Allen as a twenty-eight-year-old just finding his voice and enjoying his "break" must have felt. Originally brought on as a part of a company surrounding and supporting Nora Bayes ("a great artist and a wonderful woman"), Allen acknowledges the importance of developing assurance by working with entertainers who already had mastered their acts: "Shubert vaudeville . . . [let me play] on the bill with big-name performers like Lew Fields, Nora Bayes, William and Gordon Dooley, Nan Halperin, Bonita and Lew Hearn, and Stan Stanley and entertaining better audiences gave me confidence. I had been able to polish my act and improve the quality of my comedy," he explains.[50] Allen takes the reader through his manager's happiness at negotiating a deal with J. J. Shubert, a tense (but hilarious) meeting with Atteridge, the daily rehearsals at the Century Theater, and a nerve-wracking grilling by J. J. before the show took its final shape. His story of the Atlantic City previews tells how the stage crew had not yet finished the sets and lighting before the curtain went up on the 8:30 p.m. opening that ran for five hours. Perhaps the most enlightening component of his chapter, however, is the discussion of how Allen crafted and reshaped his own comedic monologues.

Instead of taking on a character as part of the thin plot, Allen supplied his comedy in front of the curtain in what was referred to as "in one," meaning that his bit allowed for a complete scene change on the rest of the stage. He was not alone; Wynn, Friganza, Miller, the Howard Brothers, and so many more took on this chore many times over the series. Allen's "in one" occurred three times throughout the revue—first as a type of "MC" discussing the show and doing a Will Rogers impersonation; second with the "Old Joke Cemetery," where the too-oft-told bits go to die; and last with some amusing jabs at Prohibition and a long letter from his fictional, New Rochelle–based mother. The backdrop used for the cemetery was Allen's own idea, and to convince Shubert to use it, he paid for its creation by the hand of comic-strip artist (and former vaudevillian) Mark Leddy, whose *Winnie Winkle* was a major hit in contemporary papers. Some of the jokes he included were "It Is Easier to Say a Mouthful Than to Get One," "The Church Is on Fire; Holy Smoke," and "Lost, a Ford—Lizzie, Come Home—All Is Forgiven." The ringer, though, was a punch line still used in the comedy of Jackie Mason later in the century: "Under the arched entrance to the cemetery a sign read THIS IS A ONE WAY STREET; a hearse, passing under the arch, was labeled: 'Who Is That Lady in the Hearse? That Is No Lady—That Is My Wife.'"[51] As the revue played at the Winter Garden and as it toured the country, Allen's narrative talks of reworking jokes and adding new lines, always trying to judge what audiences reacted to and how quickly they caught on to his humor.

The touring production was fundamental to the success of a revue in the way that a multi-year run on Broadway is in the post-2000 musical theater culture. It was the most assured way of garnering large audiences in the major cities of the East and Midwest, and, if the show did well, it went as far west as California. After all, people knew they were receiving an enormous kaleidoscope of talent when they saw a touring *Passing Show*, and aspiring acts did not have to desperately hope that their show would stand out in each venue. For Allen, a return to Boston as part of the Winter Garden Company signaled his return "as a local boy who had made good."[52] He wasn't kidding, either. A small note in *Library Life*, the staff bulletin of the Boston Public Library, includes this entry: "John F. Sullivan, whose stage name is Fred Allen, is one of the stars of 'The Passing Show of 1922' now at the Shubert Theater. 'Johnny,' as he was known to the older members of the evening force, was an entertainer par excellence even in the years, from 1908 to 1914, when he was employed in the Library."[53]

Chicago, however, was one place Allen was thrilled to arrive; this was the one city where the company would stay for six months to a year. While there, Allen says, he "became very friendly with Ethel Shutta and her husband, Walter Batchelor [the stage manager] . . . When we saw that our notices were good . . . many of the married couples, as well as groups of chorus girls, moved into furnished apartments where they could enjoy home cooking and a change from hotel life."[54] Through visiting Shutta and Batchelor ("a fine cook"), the comedian befriended Portland Hoffa, a chorus girl and close friend of Shutta. Their friendship blossomed into romance and they were married in 1927, while Hoffa was performing in George White's *Scandals* of 1926.

One final comment about Allen's *Passing Show* appearance gives insight into the way the Shuberts dealt with their stars (or employees, as they undoubtedly thought of them). When the 1922 tour veered toward California, the Shuberts cut Allen from the show as an unnecessary expense. They had already cut every featured name (including Renault, Hassell, Sam Ash, the Fooshee sisters, and many others) with the exception of the Howards—the "official" stars. It was standard practice to put talented chorus members in place of the higher paid attractions when the tour began, so it was not a surprise that Allen, whose only companions in the final Midwest portion of the show were the Lockfords, was told to return to New York for a new assignment. When Allen told the road manager that the "Old Joke Cemetery" back-drop was his property, he was ignored, and he was ignored again when he left a note for J. J. informing the producer that the curtain belonged to him but could be rented for fifty dollars weekly if they chose to keep it. Allen had to file a legal injunction to get the curtain back, which he eventually did, but not before J. J. sent in a photog-rapher to snap a shot of it so that a copy could be made. However, the photo was taken in poor light, and when the film was developed, the jokes could not be read. One can imagine Allen grinning when he explains, "J. J. had been thwarted. Justice had triumphed."[55] This led to a few months of difficult relations between J. J. and Fred, but when a spot opened in *The Greenwich Village Follies* in the spring of 1924, Allen was one of the first to be hired for a starring spot. Business was business, and however difficult the Shuberts may have been in terms of salary or contract terms, they recognized talent when they saw it, and even a legal dispute that verged on the personal was not enough to end a partnership that could give both managers and employees a profitable future.

For many hopefuls in show business, the future was always uncertain. Even *if* they were noticed, and even *if* the production they were part of was good, and even *if* they got good reviews, they might not find better deals waiting for them at the end of a show's run. Of the many *Passing Show* players, only a few found their niche so quickly after the revue ended. When conditions were right, though, entertainers like Miller could bask in their success and look forward to more opportunities. This was the case for Charlotte Greenwood, who made her Broadway debut as a featured per-former with *The Passing Shows of 1912* and 1913. Within only three years, she would become the titular character of *So Long, Letty* (1916) and its sequels. For Greenwood, it all began with a nervous meeting with J. J. and Lee Shubert.[56]

Greenwood's first break came when she was hired by the ubiquitous and stern cho-reographer, Ned Wayburn, for the chorus of *The White Cat* (1905). Over the next few years, through work in other musical comedies and in vaudeville, she gained more confidence in herself as a performer. Still, the dissolution of her "Two Girls and a Piano" act left her unhappy and at loose ends until she was contacted by the Shubert brothers in the spring of 1912. When they made it clear they liked her work and her specialties—the "Camel Walk" and a song entitled "The Kangaroo Hop"—she tear-fully accepted the job. She recalled, "I walked back to my hotel on eggs and indulged myself in a good cry. At last I had come to the end of the long road toward success. The Holy Grail of Broadway acclaim was finally at my fingertips."[57] She started work-ing on the parts they assigned her during weeks of run-throughs in small rehearsal halls spread throughout New York. Eventually, the Shuberts called for a general rehearsal that brought the whole ensemble together at the Winter Garden. There, Charlotte soaked up the excitement of the enormous production, especially enjoy-ing working with other players. "The veterans were kind to the youngsters, as vet-erans in the theater invariably are, and we were one large, happy family . . . I was as happy as a lark."[58] She was especially thrilled to be sharing the stage with so many entertainers she had admired for years, including Friganza, Ernest Hare, and Jobyna Howland. While in rehearsals, Wayburn, who had treated her roughly in the past, yelled at Greenwood repeatedly, forcing the twenty-two-year-old to sing louder and louder, insisting that if she can be seen and not heard, she should not be onstage at all. She suffered through these moments of humiliation and came out stronger than ever, thanking Wayburn even as she outshouted him in his own theater; doubtless, the difficulty of filling the enormous Winter Garden with one's voice without microphones was a challenge for any performer.

In the end, her determination led to (generally) rave notices from the critics for her exuberant turns in the show. Many critics mentioned her lanky frame—"[she] must be the tallest dancer on stage and also have the longest arms"—but she also was praised for her singing and the quality of her portions of the revue.[59] A writer for the *Clipper* said she "went big" and "sang and danced herself into popularity," while in the *Morning Sun* it was reported that she "dances amiably."[60] Not every mention was positive, however. The dance move she became associated with was a particular type of leg lift, and she apparently used the technique too many times for one reviewer. Channing Pollock, the critic for *Green Book Magazine*, was not kind to any of *The Passing Show* entertainers, but this was probably because he was aligned with Ziegfeld. Grant and Greenwood, "smack of the two-a-day [vaudeville]," he proclaimed, and "Miss Greenwood's principal asset seems to be the ability to lift her foot to the level of her head without bending her knee, a grotesque performance she repeats several dozen times in the course of the evening."[61] The truth, probably much to Pollock's dismay, was that the revue was *meant* to feel like an upper-class vaudeville show, and it was certainly no secret that many of the stars were also prominent in such circuits. Greenwood's brand of humor, through physical, spoken, and sung means, was infectious for many, and she was engaged for the next year's *Passing Show* in July.[62] She only stayed with *The Passing Show of 1913* for a few weeks, hoping to be engaged by a more highbrow production. "Mr. J. J." gave her a release, but it was not a serious drama she was hired for; Greenwood was cast in the *Tik Tok Man of Oz* as Queen Ann Soforth, "the ambitious Amazon set on conquering the world," a comedic role that led to further comedies and greater fame.[63] Greenwood's role as Aunt Eller in the movie *Oklahoma!* (1955) still evidences the spark of humor the actress demonstrated throughout her career.

Stardom was certainly in store for one of the most recognizable acts of *The Passing Show of 1918*: vaudeville veterans and Broadway newcomers Fred and Adele Astaire. The brother and sister team began dancing in 1904, when Adele was eight and Fred was only five, and they performed in several circuits over the next decade, always studying new dance styles and incorporating them into their act. By the time they were booked into the New York City–based houses in 1916, they were receiving greater and greater attention, with Adele frequently being singled out as the more gifted (and more charming) of the siblings. The following year, their stay in the Big Apple had attracted the attention of the Shuberts. When Lee met with the two, he offered them a spot in an open-air show, *The Nine O'Clock Revue*, as well as spots in the upcoming *Passing Show*. The Forty-Fourth Street Roof Theater's *Nine O'Clock Revue* was a burlesque-based show starring T. Roy Barnes (who had had a prominent role in *The Passing Show of 1914*). Soon the production's start time moved to 8:30 p.m., so the title was changed to *Over the Top*, with Ed Wynn replacing Barnes. Although the production did not receive high praise, the Astaires did, and by the time they began rehearsing for the Winter Garden show several months later, they had made a last-ing impression on the theater-going crowd. One admirer was Charles Dillingham, another producer, who signed them for *Apple Blossoms* after they were done with their yearlong Shubert contract. Fred relates, "Mr. Lee was kind and understanding about it" and states that he only had a few interactions with J. J.[64]

This edition of *The Passing Show* was wartime entertainment, taking place in the summer of 1918 at the height of American fighting in World War I. The eighteen-year-old Fred was lucky not to be drafted, but he did participate in the war effort at home; he and Adele's scene at the top of the second act, called "Birdland" in the program, was a patriotic aviator production number called "Twit Twit Twit." The song was a nod to "Knit, Knit, Knit," which had appeared in the Fred Stone vehicle, *Jack O'Lantern*, earlier in the year; the lyrics of the original speak of women knit-ting "comfies" (sweaters) for American soldiers across the Atlantic.[65] Adele had the role of "Miss Robin," Fred was "Chanticleer," and they danced with eighteen chorus girls made up to look like big and small birds (ten and eight girls, respectively). Astaire biographer Peter Levinson bemoans the mediocre quality of this material, but lyricist Atteridge and songwriters Sigmund Romberg and Jean Schwartz actu-ally created a clever mix between the expected revue fare and an appeal to "do your bit" (*Doing Our Bit* was also a successful 1917 Winter Garden revue); since the first half of the show ended with an air raid on London, this would have been a gentle reminder that America's boys were in Europe too.[66] Both Astaires wore "snow owl" outfits, according to the costume plot of the show, and though Fred remembers hating the costume, at least one critic found it a "prettily conceived thing, with the show girls topping off the bit with a raiment of colored feathers."[67] Birds from all across the land are called "because they need you over there / to do your share up in the air. / So put your fighting feather on / and fly across the deep blue sea." The song is in a gentle B-flat major with a slower rhythm in the verse alternating with an energized patter rhythm in the chorus. Given the skills of the Astaires and the well-rehearsed chorus members, "Twit Twit Twit" was probably not nearly as wretched as Levinson made it out to be. In fact, every moment the siblings appeared in the production, they seemed to generate a sensation among the press. The advertisement taken out in *Variety* boasts praise for both brother and sister, with special attention given to Fred as one of the "dancing waiters" in Child's Restaurant; from the description of this frantic predecessor to the famous *Hello, Dolly!* number, Astaire's movement was more in the "eccentric dancer" cat-egory than any standard popular style (▶Figure 2.5).

According to Fred Astaire's autobiography, it is clear—even forty years later—that the future movie star felt his experiences with this revue ushered he and his sister's careers into a higher bracket. Sharing "the famous Dressing Room 18" with many of the other principals, including Sammy White, Lou Clayton, Charles Ruggles, Frank Fay, David Dreyer, George Hassell, Roger Davis, and Edward Basse, Astaire developed friendly connections with many well-established veterans at the top of their fame, important networking that would help his career immensely. Although Willie and Eugene Howard "didn't dress there, [they] spent most of their time with us. It was like a club. Crap games, bets on horses [and] fights . . . The Howard Brothers would count me in on their talks, too, and that made me feel pretty big."[68]

Fred felt that he learned many lessons as part of such an important show, including one day in Detroit where he slept through call time and almost missed the performance. With the good notices he received and the camaraderie he built with the other featured entertainers, it was no surprise that Astaire was given an opportunity every small bit-player hoped for as a member of a *Passing Show*; when the show went on tour and some of the more expensive, top-billed stars were dropped from the cast, the Shuberts always put a lesser paid performer in their place. When Frank Fay was sent elsewhere, Astaire took over his many roles in the show, resulting in several speaking parts, even more singing, and national exposure. "That tour took us to all the big cities [that were] sold out everywhere in advance," remembers the dancer.[69] In the end, *The Passing Show of 1918* was a key moment in the career of the Astaires. Fred summed it up best: "Our general education and Broadway experience were well furthered by this engagement. It was a prominent showcase, and brought its performers to the notice of the show world."[70]

One final type of performer that was included in *The Passing Show* star category was the replacement. But, unlike the situation with Astaire, not all featured roles were taken by second-tier performers, but were reworked for new cast members. The most prominent replacement star was Texas Guinan, who joined the cast of *The Passing Show of 1912* at some point during the tour (probably late in the Chicago run). She sang several songs, including "The Wedding Glide" with Bernard Thornton.[71] Guinan is remembered as the most notable owner of speakeasies during Prohibition, but she was active on the stage before she owned one. Finding her voice in vaudeville as "The Lone Star," the singer became known in the Midwest before moving to New York in 1906. Within three years, she was starring in several touring productions, including *The Gay Musician* (1909) and *The Kissing Girl* (1910). Revues became her specialty; she was included with the Howard Brothers in the touring cast of *The Whirl of the World* in 1915 before making appearances in several revues of the 1920s. She was not only known for her charm and electric wit, but also for her brash behavior; during *The Passing Show of 1912* engagement in Winnipeg, Guinan outraged the "British feminine conscious by riding cross-saddle."[72] Guinan was able to make good use of her fame to profit, and an advertisement from September 1913 shows that she wrote a book on weight loss, proclaiming "Texas Guinan, Star of the 'Passing Show' Company, Offers Her Own Marvelous New Treatment to Fat Folks."[73] The caption under her picture read "Miss Texas Guinan, God's Masterpiece and the most fascinating actress in America." Although neither her weight loss method nor her performance skills were her crowning achievements, Guinan used the opportunities afforded her through *The Passing Show* to become an important New York personality.

Tales of having reached, or being within reach, of the "Holy Grail of Broadway acclaim" could be written for every edition of *The Passing Show* series in its initial annual run (1912–1924), as well as into the next two decades, during the transformation of the series and the incorporation of the *Follies* into the Shubert empire upon Ziegfeld's death. As the tenth anniversary picture of the Winter Garden demonstrates, many more individual histories are yet to be told, from the martial misadventures of Frances White and Frank Fay to the antics of De Wolf Hopper and the Avon Comedy Four. For established stars and new acts, this series of revues signified the attainment of something important in their careers. It may have been an exciting interruption in an otherwise vaudeville-centered life, a high-paying gig that took the central star across the United States, or a stepping stone to fame in a variety of media, but whatever the case, being cast in a *Passing Show* was a reason to celebrate. Personal stories, critic's reviews, and archival documents demonstrate the many ways these shows represented success for dozens, if not hundreds, of entertainers.

But beyond a mere laudatory celebration of this series, these tales suggest other avenues to consider for early Broadway studies. The reflexive relationship between Broadway (frequently thought of as the bastard stepchild to legitimate theater) and vaudeville (which has been seen as the awkward second cousin to Broadway) points to a complicated web of entertainment structures that resist simple analyses, or even a straightforward understanding of performance careers. There were many options for every player, and, as in Frances Renault's case, sometimes vaudeville and nightclubs were more attractive choices. However, for Fred and Adele Astaire, their *Passing Show* tenure took them out of the two-a-day circuits forever. Charlotte Greenwood and Fred Allen would become stars of radio, film, and television, but their Broadway and vaudeville roots were always acknowledged. Unlike the post–World War II theatrical world, where expectations for what constituted stardom encompassed a different array of media with its own accepted hierarchies, the 1910s and 1920s seem to have offered a set of less value-charged options for entertainers. Stepping foot onto the Winter Garden stage, and then onto the myriad theaters on the tour that followed, could and did change the lives of so many for the better.

NOTES

1. "Winter Garden Anniversary," *New York Sun*, March 2, 1921, 14, and "Winter Garden Celebrates Tenth Anniversary This Evening," *New York Sun*, March 21, 1921, 16.

2. "Week's Playhouse Bills," *New York Times*, October 11, 1903, 11.

3. Brooks McNamara, *The Shuberts of Broadway* (New York and Oxford: Oxford University Press, 1990), 11.

4. Numerous articles on what constitutes success in vaudeville were written during the late nineteenth and early twentieth century, and there is no solid consensus for what the "top" was. For some, it was playing the Palace Theater in New York, while for others, it was transatlantic fame. But just as often, the chance to appear in *The Passing Show*, the *Follies*, or any of the myriad post-1919 revues seems to have been the pinnacle. Most likely, a combination of all of these events represented the hopes of many performers.

5. The Howard Brothers received $400 total, while the orchestra (with at least twenty-five members) received $800 per week. See Shubert Archive, *PS 1912* show files.

6. "Fun in 'Passing Show,'" *New York Morning Sun*, Undated, in Shubert Archive Clipping File.

7. Tropes on *Salome* were common in this period, both onstage and in song. Larry Hamberlin provides a first-rate analysis of the musical exoticism in chapter 4 of *Tin Pan Opera: Operatic Novelty Songs in the Ragtime Era* (New York and Oxford: Oxford University Press, 2011), chap. 4: Visions of Salome.

8. Frank Cullen, *Vaudeville, Old and New: An Encyclopedia of Variety Performers in America*, VI, 417.

9. "Musical Comedy Productions," *Billboard*, November 8, 1919, 24.

10. Ibid.

11. Reid, "Blanche Ring at the Colonial," *New York Dramatic Mirror*, May 27, 1919, 841.

12. "Wynn with Shuberts," *Variety*, April 7, 1916.

13. "At the Teck—'The Passing Show of 1916,'" *Buffalo Evening News*, October 21, 1916, 4.

14. "Ed Wynn's Different Models of Humor," *New York Sun*, July 2, 1916, 2.

15. "'The Passing Show' is a Lively One," *New York Times*, June 23, 1916, 9.

16. "Settings Feature 'The Passing Show,'" *Brooklyn Daily Eagle*, June 23, 1916, 9.

17. "George W. Monroe at the Grand Opera House," *New York Times*, September 23, 1902, 9. The article also includes an interesting comment on the way that this particular musical manipulates elements of different genres, perhaps suggesting the same type of complicated genre issues that would arise in the early revue: "The makers of the Monroe offering have done another rash thing. They have dared to introduce a plot into the farce.... In fact, the plot of the farce was in evidence throughout the evening—just like the plot in the common or garden play of Broadway—and it was quite a plot, at that."

18. "The Passing Show of 1915," *New York Dramatic Mirror*, June 2, 1915, 8. Heinrich Suderman's play *Die indische Lilie* ("The Indian Lily," 1911) was translated into English by L. Lewisohn and published the same year in the United States.

19. Laurence Senelick, "Transvestitism 2" in *Encyclopedia of Homosexuality*, edited by Wayne R. Dynes (New York: Garland Publishing, 1990), 1317.

20. For *School Days*, Renault was billed as "Webster Aurimenia." Misspellings of his last name seem to have continued into some of his other vaudeville appearances, including a photo credit on the sheet music cover of Irving Berlin's "At the Devil's Ball," until he took on the new stage moniker.

21. H. W. M., "Show Reviews—At the Alhambra," *New York Clipper*, August 18, 1920, 10.

22. C. C., "Show Reviews—At the Colonial," *New York Clipper*, March 14, 1923, 9.

23. W. V., "Francis Renault," *New York Clipper*, July 7, 1920, 12. "The stage setting, of Chinese effect, is of purple and green with a big cyclorama taking in a large part of the stage ... On each side of the stage, far back, are tall stands at the top of which are four blue lights. The backdrop divides down the middle, showing a staircase, and down this Renault makes his first appearance. Clad in a gorgeous black and gold gown, he sang his first song."

24. Robert Baral suggests that this number contained sparklers and nudity, but since none of the reviews mention what would have certainly attracted attention, it is unclear where this notion was generated. See Baral, *Revue*, 114 (chap. 1, n. 3). It is not certain, but likely, that Renault appeared as a woman for this song.

25. "'Passing Show of 1922' Scenic Wonder," *Evening Telegram*, September 21, 1922, 3.

26. "About You! And You!," *New York Clipper*, February 21, 1923, 15. It may have been that Renault was gay and was reluctant—or the Shuberts were reluctant—to have the dance as part of the touring show. Several rumors surrounding Renault's relationships with men, including Cary Grant, can be found in books about homosexual stars, but, as is frequently the case, the evidence is unclear. This does not mean the rumors are false; it merely references a culture of conduct that was wisely secretive and private, and it is therefore challenging to prove.

27. Letter from Harry Weber to J. J. and L. Shubert, April 17, 1918, Shubert Archive, *PS 1918* show file.

28. Letter from Melville Ellis to J. J. Shubert, June 3, 1912, Shubert Archive, *PS 1912* show file.

29. "Frank Tinney Again in Vaudeville," *New York Times*, January 7, 1913, 11.

30. Warren G. Harris, *The Other Marilyn* (New York: Arbor House, 1985). In the book's first chapter, Harris compares several facts that tie the two women: "Not until Marilyn Monroe died, sixteen years after she assumed her new name, could the eerie parallels between the two Marilyns be noticed. Marilyn Monroe also had three unsuccessful marriages—including one in which her name actually became Marilyn Miller—and her last years were a similar study in decline. At her passing, Marilyn Monroe was thirty-six, a year younger than Marilyn Miller when she died," 15.

31. "Marilynn Miller Reaches New York Via London," *New York Times*, June 21, 1914, X9. The same story is repeated in "She Likes Grapes," *New York Dramatic Mirror*, July 1, 1914, inside cover. Another article, published in Philadelphia just before Miller appeared with the show on tour, strives to achieve the same goal. See "Premiere Danseuse at 16," *Philadelphia Evening Ledger*, September 30, 1914, 9.

32. Harris includes many details of Miller's life that seem just as apocryphal as the grape story. For example, Harris suggests an African American boy who carried coal into her house during her time in Memphis was one of the earliest inspirations for her dancing. Harris (p. 20) tells us that Marilynn herself claimed this, but since there are no citations in the book, it is unknown where (or if) she made this statement.

33. Barbara Stratyner includes a good discussion of how eccentric dancing worked and what it was used for onstage in the chapter on "Individual Specialty Acts" in *Ned Wayburn and the Dance Routine: From Vaudeville to the Ziegfeld Follies* (Madison, WI: A-R Editions, 1996), 33–50.

34. "Lovey Joe" was written by Will Marion Cook (lyrics) and Joe Jordan (music), both African American, and performed in blackface in the *Follies* by Fanny Brice. See Jerome Charyn, *Gangsters and Gold Diggers: Old New York, the Jazz Age, and the Birth of Broadway* (Emeryville, CA: Thunder's Mouth Press, 2003), 174. "All Aboard for Dixie Land" was by George L. Cobb (music) and Jack Yellen (lyrics). Blackface would have been very common for these numbers, especially at the Winter Garden, where Al Jolson performed regularly throughout the teens to great acclaim. The technique was also used in many *Passing Shows*. It is unclear why, then, "Levee Days" was not performed this way.

35. Keysheets for *The Passing Show of 1914* are available through the New York Public Library's Digital Archive and can be seen online.

36. "Passing Show of 1915 Premier," *Billboard*, June 12, 1915, 4.

37. The date the tour ended is not entirely clear, but Collins's return to the vaudeville stage is mentioned in the "Vaudeville" section of the *New York Dramatic Mirror*, April 29, 1914, 19. She appeared at the Palace with Robert Evett beginning on the evening of April 20. The unnamed reviewer says, "Of one thing we're sure, no one on the musical stage is more appealing, both optically and earfully, than Miss Collins."

38. Louis R. Reid, "Serious Role His Aim," *New York Dramatic Mirror*, October 7, 1916, 5.

39. "Four Comics of 'Passing Show,'" *New York Sun*, June 28, 1923, 16.

40. Ibid.

41. Letter from Harry Weber to J. J. and L. Shubert, April 17, 1918, Shubert Archive, *PS 1918* show file.

42. Allen, *Much Ado about Me*, 280.

43. W. A., "Attractive Chorus in the New Passing Show," *The Tech*, March 25, 1925, 2.

44. The two had been working together since they were young and were the children of an unnamed famous Parisian actress. Their family name was Lebateau, but they "Americanized" their names to be better remembered in the States. See "News and Gossip of the Orpheum Circuit," *Vaudeville News*, February 12, 1927, 7.

45. B. F., "Winter Garden Show Rich in Ballet and Extravaganza," *New York Tribune*, September 21, 1922, 10.

46. "In Brooklyn Theaters," *Brooklyn Daily Eagle*, December 5, 1922, 14.

47. "Lockfords Have New Dance," *Billboard*, November 26, 1921, 14.

48. "New Winter Garden Revue Appeases Eye," *New York Times*, September 4, 1924, 13.

49. Allen, *Much Ado about Me*, chap. 15.

50. Ibid., 234–35.

51. Ibid., 266.

52. Ibid., 271.

53. "News Notes," *Library Life*, January 15, 1923, unpaginated.

54. Allen, *Much Ado about Me*, 274–75.

55. Ibid., 277–78.

56. A first-rate account of the comedienne's life can be found in Grant Hayter-Menzies, *Charlotte Greenwood: The Life and Career of the Comic Star of Vaudeville, Radio, and Film* (Jefferson, NC: McFarland and Co., 2007). I wish to sincerely thank Mr. Hayter-Menzies for supplying me with the portions of Greenwood's unpublished memoir, *Never Too Tall*, that concern her relationship to the Shuberts and her involvement in the two *Passing Shows*.

57. Hayter-Menzies, *Charlotte Greenwood: The Life and Career*, 51. While I do not wish to diminish Greenwood's emotional reaction to her meeting with the Shuberts, an alternative version of this story was presented to the *New York Sun* in an interview with Sydney Grant. He takes credit for encouraging her to leave vaudeville, and like Greenwood, he was hired as a second-tier star in *The Passing Show of 1912*. According to Grant, it was he who suggested that the Shuberts see Greenwood perform and says they "were signed at the same time." See "A New Funny Woman," *New York Sun*, February 9, 1913, 8. I feel this joint hiring is probably the more accurate story of what happened based on an in-office cost memo, which lists Grant and Greenwood together in the list of payees. Also, they are listed as "partners" in the review of the show in *Variety*. Together, they received $400 a week, the same as the Howard Brothers. See J. J. Shubert, memo to Lee Shubert, June 20, 1912, Shubert Archive, P. S. 1912 show file.

58. Greenwood, *Not Too Tall*, chap. 5, unpaginated.

59. "Lively Summer Fun in the Winter Garden," *New York Sun*, July 23, 1912, 9.

60. "Winter Garden Reopens," *New York Clipper*, August 3, 1912, 6, and "Fun in 'Passing Show,'" *New York Morning Sun*, Undated, Shubert Archive, PS 1912 show file.

61. Channing Pollock, "The Winter Garden," *Green Book Magazine*, October 1912, 636.

62. Greenwood and Grant did not continue with the show on tour, probably because of the high cost of keeping them in the program. Fred Allen's memoir includes an extensive explanation of how stars moved in and out of *Passing Shows* depending on the run of the tour and the needs of the stars in New York.

63. Hayter-Menzies, *Charlotte Greenwood*, 60.

64. Fred Astaire, *Steps in Time* (New York: Harper Collins, 1959 and 1981), 62.

65. Thanks to Paul Charosh for pointing out this connection.

66. Peter Levinson, *Puttin' On the Ritz: Fred Astaire and the Fine Art of Panache* (New York: St. Martin's Press, 2009), 25.

67. For the costume plot, see Shubert Archive, P. S. 1918 show file. For the review, see Ibee, "The Passing Show," *Variety*, July 1918, 13. Baral incorrectly says the two were "decked out as young chicks." See Baral, *Revue*, 111.

68. Astaire, *Steps in Time*, 64–68.

69. Ibid., 68.

70. Ibid., 67.

71. "On the Rialto," *New York Dramatic Mirror*, June 10, 1914, 8.

72. "Miss Texas Guinan," *New York Dramatic Mirror*, October 8, 1913, 16.

73. "Advertisement," *New York Sun*, September 7, 1913, 13.

3

THE HEBREW MESSENGER BOY
AND THE THESPIAN

• • •

THE HOWARD BROTHERS

Despite the remarkable talents that so many other entertainers brought to the Winter Garden stage, there was little question in the minds of most theatergoers that the central stars of *The Passing Show* series were the Howard Brothers. They stayed with the show throughout the entire engagement, from previews to the end of the tour, and it was their name that loomed large in almost every advertisement. Appearing in the first edition in 1912, Eugene and Willie Howard went on to headline five of the twelve annual shows. And, in the end, it was a Howard who saw the final curtain of both *The Passing Show* and the large-scale revue, closing both a show and an era simultaneously.

From the outset, the Shuberts thought of the series as a collection of star performers rather than a vehicle for a single personality. The documents for the genesis of *The Passing Show of 1912* make it clear that many performers were considered for the cast, and the possible A-list entertainers changed drastically over the three months of preparation for the revue. By June 20th, 1912, a memo from J. J. Shubert provides the costs for the show, and, as mentioned in chapter 2, Trixie Friganza was the highest paid cast member at $300 a week. The Howards (together, as an act) received $400 per week, equaling the cost of two other teams: Adelaide and Hughes, and Grant and Greenwood.[1] Most of the announcements for the show also place the Howards among the lower list of the featured performers. There was no way the Shuberts could have known how popular the comedic team would be with audiences and the resulting impact the Howards would have on the soon-to-be annual revue. The relationship between the series and the duo gradually developed, coming from years of successful shows and their much-loved national tours.

Eugene was the older brother and, based on correspondence between the team and producers, he was the one responsible for voicing the business decisions the two Howards made. Willie was the scrappy younger sibling, often taking chances both onstage, as the deliverer of jokes to Eugene's straight man, and off, such as a stint he made in the 1910s as a professional boxer. Perhaps because of his longer and more successful career, there are more stories of Willie's youth than there are of Eugene's, but nonetheless, it is clear that they both shared an avid love of the theater and of performing, beginning in childhood.

The story of the Howard Brothers' beginnings closely aligns with the tales of Irving Berlin, George Gershwin, Eddie Cantor, and so many other performers whose roots lay in European or Russian Jewish communities. Eugene was born on July 7, 1881, in Neustadt, Germany. His given name was Isadore (or Isidore) Levkovitz, and he was the oldest son of Rabbi Leopold Levkovitz and his wife, Mathilda. The family included two more sons, Sam and William, and three daughters, Rachel, Cecelia, and Minnie.[2] Most of the family was born in Germany, with William greeting the world on April 13, 1886, but the two youngest daughters were native New Yorkers. The family home was listed at 340 West 121st Street in 1900 and at 2296 Seventh Avenue in 1910, both in Harlem.

Singing was a skill that all the siblings possessed, according to the brothers, and all six children could regularly be heard as singers at their father's synagogue. It was Isadore who first became associated with the stage, however, when he received a role in the chorus for *The Belle of New York* in 1897.[3] The sixteen-year-old was renamed "Eugene Howard" by the stage manager, and he toured with the show for many months before returning to New York. The younger Levkowitzes were entranced by Isidore's success and decided that they, too, wanted to become stage stars. Even though Willie originally chose to use the same Anglicized moniker as his brother, he was persuaded by Eugene to drop it in favor of his real first name so that the elder brother could make good use of the new title. The first mention of the two boys performing together is in 1900 in the *New York Dramatic Mirror*, when it was announced that Edwin E. Allen was introducing a new vaudeville act starring himself, using songs by Eugene Howard, featuring Morris Shay on the violin, and including songs by "Master Willie Lefkowitz [sic]."[4] Shortly afterwards, the name "Master Willie Howard" was used when the boy's father signed a contract with the music publisher Witmark in 1901.[5] Willie's job required him to dash from school in Harlem to Proctor's 125th Street Theater by 3:15 p.m. (only a few blocks from home), when he would begin work as a "water boy." Although he did hand out glasses of water to patrons at the theater, Howard was also required to sing popular songs while doing so. For five dollars a week, Willie sang numbers such as "Pretty Mollie Shannon," "When You Were Sweet Sixteen," "Sadie, You Won't Say Nay," and "Because." According to Witmark, a good water boy did not just perform the song, but also encouraged the audience to join in during the refrains, sometimes acting as a "plant" within the audience; this practice was already several years old by the time Willie was doing it. Any means of repeating a song was an important step toward selling the tune through both performance and sheet music. Willie was well liked at the theater, and was sometimes even featured in events outside Proctor's. On a cold night in January of 1902, for example, Willie received special mention as one of the performers during a banquet for two thousand *New York Telegram* newsboys that took place at the Lenox Lyceum.[6] That same year, Howard accompanied Anna Held as she sang in the aisles during intermission of her shows. Their performing chemistry was strong enough that, according to Willie, he was included in the touring production of *The Little Duchess*. By the time they reached Washington, DC, Willie's voice broke, and (again, according to Willie) Florenz Ziegfeld himself fired the youth.[7] Willie then turned from relying mostly on his vocal talents to perfecting and performing impersonations, especially of Jewish comedians Joe Welch and Sam Bernard.

Eugene had been busy during these early years performing onstage, taking work where he could find it, from appearing on vaudeville bills to plugging songs, just like his younger brother. When Willie's contract was canceled, Eugene saw an opportunity. Incorporating their brother Sam into the act, Eugene rechristened himself "Harry Lee" and for a short time, the three performed as the Lee Brothers. Sam quit the act to work in burlesque, and his place was taken by a youth named Tom Dunne, and they changed the act's name to the "Messenger Boys' Trio." Howard, Dunne, and Howard found particular fame at the Orpheum Theatre circuit between 1902 and 1906, performing skits, doing impersonations, and especially performing songs. They weren't an immediate hit; a reviewer in 1904 said the "young men have fairly good voices and introduce just enough comedy to make their act a good one" but suggested they needed more practice to get noticed.[8] They improved quickly, however, and the group soon began touring from New York to San Francisco, receiving acclaim almost every place they stopped. It is particularly interesting that their movements can often be traced by watching the reports made in the *New York Clipper* by M. Witmark and Sons, with whom they continued a relationship beyond Willie's initial hiring. As the Messenger Boys' Trio would move from one location to the next, Witmark published those songs that the trio found most pleasing to the crowds. For example, both "Sweet Adeline" and "Nellie Dean" were hits in California, and Witmark's statements in the "Music and Song" section of the *Clipper* encouraged other performers to consider these sheets for their own appearances.[9]

One important aspect of their performance was that the Messenger Boys incorporated what was called "Hebrew" comedy into their act. In the nineteenth century and into the twentieth, the Hebrew character was one of four well-known dialect types found in both comedy and song, with the others being Southern Black, German ("Dutch"), and Irish.[10] A contemporary advertisement for Bob Manchester's Cracker Jacks entices customers to come and see a show that would have included all four of the ethnic/racial stereotyped groups (see Figure 3.1). The Hebrew character was a peddler with a shabby coat and a long, false beard.

The characters in the Messenger Boys were meant to be Jewish and use several aspects of the "type," including a partially Yiddish dialect and comedy that included commentary on an array of Jewish cultural topics. Comedy about tailors and other stereotypically Jewish professions would be mixed with stories about family, commerce, and entertainment. Later descriptions of the Messenger Boys' Trio frequently include a note that Willie Howard—the youngest of the three actors—was trying a "new" kind of Hebrew comedy, one that focused on a young man without the expected props of the topcoat and beard. Many reviewers called this turn the "younger Hebrew," and were impressed with Willie's skill in developing the characterization. The "smooth face" was, to some, more realistic and more inviting than the "grotesque beard that had come to be regarded as an essential to the part."[11] *Variety* followed their performances closely during March and April of 1906, reporting any new changes made at Hurtig & Seamon's, where the new character was introduced.[12] Somewhere during these early months in the spring, the two Howard Brothers quit the Messenger Boys' Trio, leaving Dunne the act, but no actors. Dunne tried to find

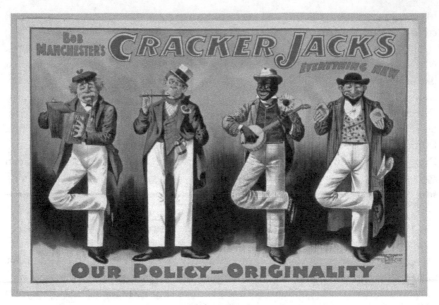

Fig. 3.1. The four dialect types: German ("Dutch"), Irish, Black, and Hebrew. Author's Collection.

another impersonator to do the work Willie had been so gifted at, but by August of 1906, it was clear the new lineup did not satisfy audiences. Things were different for the Howard Brothers, though. By mid-May, Willie Howard knew his "young Hebrew" was a hit, as *Variety* reported:

> Howard and Howard were the hit of the bill if judgment may be based on the volume of applause that greeted them. The younger member of the partnership is decidedly entertaining in his Hebrew dialect work. His comedy is uncommonly clever and he displays judgment beyond his years in the degree of restraint which he exercises. He does not overdo at any point. The audience demanded every parody he knew.[13]

Even in the early days of the act, Willie was the star player. Eugene had a strong voice, said reviewers, and he "fills his part in the contract" by wearing "an English walking suit of proper cut." Perhaps unfairly, they concluded that "very little else is required of him that could not as well be done by a phonograph."[14] Singing ballads such as "When the Bloom is on the Heather" and often performing on the piano, Eugene had a solid voice and was a reliable performer, and other critics were far more amenable to his style and his abilities.

For the next four years, the Howards continued to travel widely as a pair, receiving strong notices in places such as Des Moines, Iowa, and Denver, Colorado. One wonders what gentile audiences must have made of these comedians, especially given the relative lack of Jewish communities outside large urban areas during this era. Willie performed several songs, including "Thomashevsky" and the "Yiddish Rag," that made no secret about the character he was portraying; Boris Thomashevsky was one

HOWARD AND HOWARD.

Fig. 3.2. The Howard Brothers, 1908. Bert Levy cartoon from Variety.

of the most important figures in Yiddish American Theater at the time.[15] Although these audiences may not have understood every nuance of the pair's humor, the duo was warmly received throughout the country. Even in the face of possible confusion with another set of Howard Brothers—Andrew and James, who told jokes but primarily played (and juggled!) banjos—Eugene and Willie found an audience and maintained a regular presence on the stage. In 1908, their manager, Ed S. Keller, announced that the two were embarking on a European tour as part of the Orpheum Circuit, and he also indicated that they expected to be a part of a musical comedy on Broadway when they returned.[16] An evocative cartoon from *Variety* depicted the brothers, with Willie in costume as the messenger boy, complete with the cigar that exploded during the bit (see Figure 3.2).

Despite the hope that they would find guaranteed entry into a Broadway theater with the completion of this tour, the brothers instead remained in vaudeville. By 1909, however, they received top billing, meaning they were the penultimate act. One reviewer described a night at Hammerstein's with the duo: "It was next to closing when the boys appeared. They ripped the house wide open, beating every other number on the program by a mile or more. As a Hebrew, there is nobody with anything on Willie."[17]

As the act continued into the next decade, the Howard Brothers solidified their original routine, but also added new turns to keep audiences coming to see them.

The title they started out with in 1904—"The Messenger Boy and the Thespian"—stayed with them for several years. One wonders if this was an original sketch or borrowed, since an announcement in 1900 that included both Howard boys also listed a duo named Maddox and Wayne, with the latter pair performing an act with this title.[18] Whoever originated the bit, it became the Howard Brothers' signature until 1910. The turn included several unconnected jokes, structured like a late-night talk show monologue. Willie, who spoke with a Yiddish-inspired accent, delivered the punch lines. It is interesting that Eugene's lines did not employ this affect, probably as a way of emphasizing the ethnicity of Willie's character. Interspersed throughout were musical moments—some comic, some serious, and some meant for novelty. One musical turn was described by reviewers as an interplay between a mimicked violin (Willie) and a mimicked cello (Eugene) that was both creative and funny.[19] Several of the songs mentioned earlier would be included in between the comedy, and near the end, Eugene would usually perform from the piano and Willie would employ the exploding cigar. They changed their material on multiple occasions, especially after they went on tour. Part of returning as headliners to the same vaudeville houses meant that new tunes and fresh gags (usually called "modern" comedy) could be incorporated into the older framework. If performers changed their material too much or tried to entirely reinvent themselves, audiences (at least according to the trade papers) were generally not receptive to the seeing a performer in an unfamiliar context. The challenge, then, was to construct a format that presented ever-changing components within a recognizable context, something the Howard Brothers were able to do rather quickly. This was particularly important in an entertainment world where imitators sprung up like weeds, stealing material and therefore spoiling opportunities for the original creator. An advertisement for the brothers from 1906 proclaims not only "Yes, We Are Really Brothers," but also that they are the originators of the act (see ▶Figure 3.3, the Howard Brothers advertisement in *Variety*, 1906).

Thankfully, the duo made a Vitaphone short sound film in 1926, offering today's audiences a chance to experience a truncated version of their routine. Here, it is called "Between Acts at the Opera." By this time, Willie had taken on a new character that was a "named" version of the Hebrew messenger boy, now called "Sammy." There are indications that Sammy was a moniker used by several acts to describe the wise-cracking Jewish jokester that Willie had originated, but whatever the case, he was using the name Sammy Meyers (accompanied with the descriptor "an orphan boy") by *The Passing Show of 1915*. In the short, Willie stands with his shoulders slumped in an oversized top hat with an exaggerated look that almost says "oh, well," complete with heightened eyebrows and his mouth drawn down. Eugene smiles pleasantly most of the time, except on occasions where he has to chide his silly companion. The most impressive part of the short is the vocal performance by the two, imitating opera stars such as "Al McGluck" (Alma Gluck). There was no question that both men had excellent singing voices with large ranges and could perform many styles effectively and without hesitation, making them far more versatile than several of their contemporaries. Willie would continue to appear in other short features throughout the next two decades (including the hilarious *Tyrone Shapiro, the Bronx Caballero*), but this is the only routine of the brothers that survives on film.[20]

During this period of success as a duo, much attention was paid to the fresh approach that the Howards took toward the Hebrew character. In this discussion, older comedians were referenced, especially those who had been popular in the two decades before the turn of the century. One article pointed to Sam Bernard, another Jewish comedian, mentioning that in 1911, he could ask for $4,000 a week for a "single turn."[21] Bernard's agent claimed that the Hebrew was a rather new type of act, but the anonymous writer noted that this was not the case, listing the most important performers of the "Hebrew" type active in the world of variety (which preceded vaudeville). The list included Will H. Fox, Billy Lester (of Lester and Allen), the Rogers Brothers, Weber and Fields, the Weston Brothers, Wood (of Wood and Shepherd), Lottie Collins (the mother of José Collins), and Dave Howard (of Howard and Thompson, "the first 'double Jew' turn ever"). Although the beard and coat could not have been the only style of the Hebrew character in this era, it must have been prevalent enough that when Willie Howard embodied the younger character, the effect was immediate and positive. Much of this reaction seems to stem from the sense that Howard was more of a *character* than a *caricature*. Not unlike blacks wearing blackface, even when performers were Jewish themselves, many of them (such as Lew Fields) continued the exaggerated portrayal non-Jews would espouse. A letter of complaint was sent to one of the Bowery theaters that featured *The Grass Widows*, a production that had Dutch, Irish, and Hebrew impersonators as part of its olio. The dissenting note was published in the *New York Morning Telegraph*: "Dear sir Manager [:] As you have comedian on the stage making fun of the Jews [.] your hole [sic] business is from the jews [.] the irish spend 10¢ but the jews spent $1.00."[22] The author finishes by requesting that the Irish become the new butt of the comedy. The reviewer for the paper says that this is an old complaint, but points out that "these kicks are few" and that this protest will "probably not abolish the Hebrew comedian." Willie Howard's take on this type of offending, dialect-speaking, ethnic stereotype was more nuanced and decidedly less crude. Abandoning the older type achieved numerous goals simultaneously, including offering greater flexibility to Howard as a performer, banishing the previous style to an old-fashioned, poorly-costumed past, and humanizing the character enough so that a variety of emotions (including empathy) could be connected to the performer. In one impressive—and bold—gesture, the new Howard Brothers act transformed the Hebrew comedian into a recognizable (and un-false-bearded) face, paving the way for Fanny Brice, Eddie Cantor, and scores of other top-grossing stars of the teens.

As the brothers continued to be lauded in vaudeville, they began to look for opportunities in musical comedy. With a new act during 1910, calling themselves "The Hebrew Porter and the Salesman," they completed a full swing through the Orpheum Circuit again, scoring triumphs across the West Coast. After the turn of the year, a change seems to have taken place in their goals; by 1911, they must have been serious about seeking steady employment outside of vaudeville because the two announced interest in possible theatrical runs. The first of these appears in February, when a headline in *Variety* read "Hebrew Comedians as Stars," suggesting the Howard Brothers were "likely" to find a position in musical comedy.[23] This missive was issued from Chicago, but it is probable that New York was where they wanted to land. By May, the two were playing the Colonial Theater, when a reviewer predicted a bright future for the Howards:

> Howard and Howard were called back from their dressing rooms. Not any of the "pet acts" playing four and five times a season has anything on these brothers. For solid laughter and applause coming from all parts of the house their reception could not be beaten. They do just enough, don't "steal" any bows, or make "speeches." They do their work, are a big success, and move away not to return until another season passes. Wise boys, those Howards. They are practically a new act to New York every season for the past five years.[24]

With first-rate reviews and a precise deployment of their material in New York, the act would have been a good bet for the Shuberts, who had inaugurated the Winter Garden revues the same season.

That the revue format had been implemented was the first of two key elements for the Howards' success. The second was the beginning of the Sunday night concerts. Starting on December 10, 1911, the Shuberts used the Winter Garden as an oversized vaudeville hall. This was a shrewd decision in many ways. First of all, they already had a large number of performers working for them at that very theater. Since each of these players' contracts had a "non-competition" clause, it meant that they could not appear at another theater even if they wanted to. This Sunday night endeavor, then, gave acts the opportunity to continue making money. It was also, cleverly, an opportunity for the Shubert creative team to try out new material with the performers they already had. This meant that not only could new music and sketches be introduced, but also that pieces that were heard in the current productions could be sharpened, reworked, or encored during the evening. Since popular songs were not encored during the three-hour-long revues, this was one way an audience might hear their favorite numbers again. It was also a good way of rehearsing outside of the traditional confines of the show. The Shuberts were pleased at the turnout for the first night's performance, with the Garden drawing "capacity, with the overflow filling all the 'Sunday' houses in the vicinity."[25] Early in February, Al Jolson, who had dazzled audiences in *Vera Violetta* (the first Winter Garden revue), joined the Sunday cast as the central performer.

The Howard Brothers made their first appearance on the Winter Garden stage not long afterwards, on March 10, 1912. As they had been in vaudeville, the pair was a sensation, but they had no time to revel in their success. The two had been hired by Hammerstein's to top the bill the following Monday night, but when it was discovered they had played the Winter Garden, their engagement was immediately canceled.[26] William Hammerstein had engaged all of his acts through the United Booking Office, and in the past, the non-competition clause in that contract had kept these performers from working at other vaudeville houses. However, the Winter Garden had not implemented its new format until midway through the season, and although Hammerstein claimed to have told his performers that they were not to appear for the Shuberts, many of them had done just that. The problem was that there were not enough separate acts yet to fill a bill, which at this time required at least ten to fifteen "turns." The Shuberts sought new talent, inviting many new performers to join the Sunday shows. Scores of hopefuls accepted the offer, but the defection of the

Howards was the last straw for United, who made it clear that they only supported Hammerstein. For the Howards, though, this was the contract they had been searching for. They were signed for two years as Shubert-exclusives at $1,000 per a week, with Willie Howard becoming one of the end men "opposite Al Jolson," while "Gene Howard [assisted] Billie Taylor [becoming] the second interlocutor of the first minstrel part."[27] This contract represented the biggest boost in their careers and changed the fortunes for both men for the rest of their lives.

They continued to perform at the Sunday night shows for the next few months, but by the late spring, the format for the presentation changed, dropping the minstrel show and adopting a more free-flowing, vaudeville-like pattern. Once they were under contract for the Shuberts, it was only natural that they would become involved in a regular production, and the next Winter Garden revue was only then taking shape. Even in very early drafts of *The Passing Show of 1912*, there was a place for these prominent vaudevillians, and as Bronson-Howard and Atteridge developed their threadbare plot, the skills of the Howard Brothers were incorporated into the revue. The show opened on July 22, 1912, and it was an immediate hit. The principals all received positive notices and audiences flocked to the production. Willie did several impersonations, including one of David Warfield, the star of *The Return of Peter Grimm*, a major hit of the season. Eugene, in the same scene, took on the guise of David Belasco, the famous producer and author of the play. The two were also required to sing. Willie was the first to be featured, performing a song by Irving Berlin called "Ragtime Jockey Man" as a soloist, backed up by a chorus of the "smaller" chorus girls; one review said they were "rewarded with much applause," while another said Willie "put it over" effectively.[28]

The younger Howard then performed "The Bacchanal Rag" as a duet with Anna Wheaton, and in the second act, he was part of a quartet in "The Metropolitan Squawk-tette," along with Eugene, Trixie Friganza, and Ernest Hare. For these numbers, the vocal parts were much like the operatic parodies the brothers had done in vaudeville, and they demonstrated their singing skills, showing off the robust style and impressive range they possessed. The most extensive review of their turn in the show noted that they both performed admirably, with Eugene indulging in a "wider scope than he has heretofore attempted, getting away well with everything he [attempts]." Willie, though, was destined for stardom; "Probably as versatile a player as there is in musical comedy," the reviewer continued, Willie "surprise[s] the audience with the range of his ability."[29] The first act concluded with something that would become a staple of the later *Passing Shows*: a duet between the brothers. Early in the run, they performed "Cohen's Yiddisha Band," but they later replaced the song with "My Dixie Daisy." Their years together in vaudeville served them well, and whenever the two appeared with a song together over the next decade, audiences went wild. As a result, their performances of either original numbers or interpolations were the most commonly produced pieces of sheet music from these revues, and their star power could turn a mediocre melody into a significant success.

As the show went on tour in the fall, the Howards joined the cast in a large, cross-country adventure. They were certainly used to extensive traveling, but it must have been a relief to deal with a fixed group of fellow performers rather than a constantly shifting array of new acts in each city. A long-term engagement in Chicago during the early months of 1913 also promised more stability than most vaudeville stops would afford, and, much like Charlotte Greenwood and Fred Allen's recollections about this location, the Howards must have appreciated the predictability the revue afforded. However, this brief interlude was only a short respite from what would be a remarkable tour; although one might expect the Howards to return to New York to prepare for the next *Passing Show*, the 1912 production traveled until December of 1913. This did not mean the show as it had appeared at the Winter Garden was the same one onstage in Brooklyn at this late date. In fact, reports indicate that even by October of 1912, the show had "new specialties constantly added," making it "an almost totally different production from its first performance."[30] As the revue transformed, material seems to have moved in and out of use over time, with old sketches returning as cast members shifted. By these final performances, the top principals remained, including Friganza and Hare, but reviews indicate it had become Willie's show. The *Brooklyn Daily Eagle* called Howard "the host," noting that he "proves himself an intelligent and versatile singer, dancer, imitator, and comedian."[31] From the description of Willie's performance, it is clear that he was doing some of the same bits that he had done in the past, but that he had also incorporated new material into the revue. Frequent memos between the Shuberts and the tour manager, Henry Lehmann, make it clear that these new components were usually suggested by J. J. himself, but on other occasions, they were new songs written by or discovered by cast members. The *Daily Eagle* review mentions several new elements to Willie's performance, including imitations of singer Jack Norworth and a "'Yiddisher Glide.'"[32] The Shuberts were probably thrilled to read the comment that Howard was "frankly a whole show in himself," knowing that they had a star who had the potential to rival Jolson.

This success did not mean that Eugene and Willie were above sharpening their work. One of the most insightful documents concerning this tour is a set of extensive notes written by Ned Wayburn about three performances of *The Passing Show of 1912* in Philadelphia on May 28–30, 1913.[33] Many of the comments would appear familiar to any musical theater production today, such as "too much volume from orchestra during solos" or "[you] *must* give the numbers a chance to draw 'applause' at their climaxes" (instead of removing pauses). Other critiques are specific to this show, though, and make it clear that Wayburn's original directions in New York were the result of a specific vision that was diluted over the multiple months on tour. For example, a lighting effect that was used during the premiere was a quick drop on the lights when a thief was discovered in a box. Wayburn insisted this had to be reinstated because, if the revue was going to parody the original, it had to use the lights exactly the way that they had appeared in the burlesqued play. Also, there were many indications that the lighting, sets, props, and costumes needed serious attention if they were to carry the Shubert name. Near the end of his assessment, Wayburn stated, "No effect can be gotten from 'dirty,' 'ragged,' 'faded,' 'ill-fitting' costumes—and *filthy* shoes."

Both of the Howards received attention from Wayburn during this extensive series of notes, providing insight into the challenges that a lone act would have faced when incorporated into a revue. The first issue for Willie was that he "slight[ed] the lyric" of both "The Ragtime Jockey-Man" and the Act I finale. Given Howard's performance style of asides and offhand remarks, it is not surprising he would have continued this approach in his singing. Also, there were times that singers did not produce enough sound to fill the hall. Wayburn noticed this in the singing of "The Bacchanal Rag," saying "Mr. Howard and Miss Brunelle [need] to try for 'harmony' effect on close—in 'bit'—using full volume of their voices. Mr. Howard demonstrates that *he* can do this with telling effect in his individual specialties." Eugene was only mentioned a couple of times by name, but only because of a new costume Wayburn felt was inappropriate. Finally, Willie's exits were an issue. Wayburn wrote, "Mr. Howard to bow if audience insists—as nothing is to be gained by his 'fighting' the audience as they are left with that impression and none other, and it reflects to his discredit and he is criticized as having a bad case of 'ego' or 'self-esteem,' which the writer knows cannot be said of him." The notes also speak to some of the difficulties the Howards had transitioning from a self-contained vaudeville team to a part of a much larger ensemble that involved a full orchestra, chorus, and many other players. Although to some these may sound like harsh words, they were probably quite helpful to the brothers to get a sense of what was expected of them in the more grandiose world of the revue.

Before leaving the subject of Wayburn's notes, I think some of Wayburn's feelings about what had happened to "The Metropolitan Squawk-tette" during the tour were also interesting. Outside of problems with costumes, the whole feel of the number had become diminished by the performers' attitudes and their actions. His comments here and elsewhere speak to a lackadaisical treatment by the performers that surely came from doing the number nightly for nearly a year:

> The Exit of the Quartette is "amateurish" and not an improvement on the original *clean-cut* one, and the Quartette is not the genuine hit that it was at the New York opening because it is not taken *seriously* and sung "*sincerely*" without any effort to be funny, which is so "obvious." One of the oldest tricks to get a laugh—is employing the musicians to make "discords." This, like 'the old flag' and a *certain kind* of "fall" —never fail—but such nauseating devices do not belong in a "Passing Show of 1912," but in a "PASSÉ SHOW OF A.D. 12."

The insistence on not overdoing the comedy ("hamming it up") is a consistent complaint in the vaudeville reviews, and, as mentioned earlier, it is one thing the Howards seemed to avoid, which made audiences appreciate them. However, like most performers, the brothers needed some reminding to keep their act fresh and appropriate for their venues, and clearly Wayburn was happy to oblige. That the director wanted this revue to be of a higher caliber than vaudeville is also clear here, and his insistence on a degree of professionalism he found lacking in "lower houses" demonstrates the high expectations the large-scale revue was held to in its early years.

The tour finished in mid-December of 1913, but the brothers had been rehearsing for an upcoming show in January, *The Whirl of the World.* This meant that by the time that *The Passing Show of 1914* was in preparation, they were preparing to tour with the earlier production. However, when their duties with this smaller show were completed, they joined Marilynn Miller in the 1915 edition of the annual summer show. Tours for the later *Passing Shows* were usually shorter than the first, probably because the Shuberts realized by then that there would be a regular pattern for

Winter Garden productions. This is exactly the kind of remarkable positioning that the Howards knew they were getting when the signed a contract with the producers. The ability to shuffle stars into and out of their offerings was one of the strongest elements of the Shubert theatrical machine, and what it meant was that as long as an entertainer was part of the team, they would have a place on the stage. It was an exciting engagement, and, much like the elation Charlotte Greenwood remembered feeling when J. J. and Lee hired her, the Howards must have understood the opportunities that the future held for them. They had become nationally recognized stars, and for the next two decades performed on the most prestigious stages across the country. And, although they primarily worked for the Shuberts, one or both of the brothers worked for a small collection of the most important producers in America, including George White, Irving Caesar, Alexander Aarons and Vinton Freedley, and Bobby Connolly.

Atteridge's script for *The Passing Show of 1915* includes extensive scenes of dialogue between the Howards that must have stemmed from or would eventually become part of the brothers' vaudeville routine. As Ed Wynn mentioned in his interview for the 1916 edition, it was not unusual for the performers to help develop the comedy they would deliver. It is interesting, for example, that a portion of Eugene and Willie's banter for their 1926 Vitaphone short was used in the opening for the second act of the 1915 show, suggesting Atteridge had little to do with the writing for this scene. The back-and-forth banter was called "sidewalk talk" in the trade papers, and this was the Howards' signature. It is likely that these jokes were those that worked well enough to still get laughs eleven years later, and some of them may have been even older than that. However, even an extended vaudeville sequence with the brothers could not have sustained an entire revue of this size, and other scenes between the Howards were probably more of a collaboration between the two and the larger creative team. One of the reasons for this idea is a small note in a memo from E. R. Simmons to J. J. Shubert during preparations for *The Passing Show of 1918*.[34] Simmons, while brainstorming ideas for the upcoming revue, suggested a Wagner-themed scene where Eugene could play Siegfried (with a ukulele instead of a horn) and "Billie" could be "Mime," the dwarf. He concludes by writing that this type of directed satire would "get them away from the Hebrew comedy." It is unclear exactly what Simmons meant by this remark. It could be that Willie's tendency to use Jewish culture as a backdrop for some jokes was partially the reason for this statement, but it might also be that it was the style of the Howard Brothers' vaudeville act that was more at issue. When the two of them performed alone, there was no thrust to the comedy, and it easily moved from one idea to the next without direction. Placing the dialogue within a larger context may have been the concern. But, whatever the case, Simmons makes it clear that some type of "scenario" was useful in urging the Howards into new comedic territory.

An excellent example of this situation can be found in one of the last scenes from *The Passing Show of 1915*, where Willie and Eugene combined the characters for the show with Aesop's story of "Androcles and the Lion" (which had also been a successful play at Wallack's that same season). The complete scene is included in Appendix 1 and a photo of the moment can be seen in Figure 3.4. The section is a conversation between Sammy (an orphan boy), played by Willie, and R. J. (a detective), Eugene.[35]

Fig. 3.4. *Willie and Eugene Howard as Androcles and a Roman Centurion,*
The Passing Show of 1915. Author's Collection.

The two characters are involved with a madcap chase for stolen pearls, and R. J. has asked Sammy to perform in a movie, which is how they end up in a scenario that is otherwise completely unrelated to the plot. The moment captures exactly the kind of banter that had characterized the vaudeville routine, with Eugene presenting an idea that gets a wise crack response from Willie. The scene starts with something general—a joke playing with the phrase "moving pictures." Eugene then begins to set up the scene, interrupted by Willie with comments about being eaten by a lion, which he then turns into a pun involving another of the past season's shows (*Inside the Lines* by Earl Derr Biggers). As Eugene continues to construct the scene through dialogue, Willie humorously conflates the beast with his wife. As the tension builds with the clear indication that Willie will have to face the lion alone, each actor is given more solo dialogue until finally, Willie has an extended speech filled with specific instructions for stage "business." And, to finish the scene, they again return to a single punch line for a finale. The timing of the scene was excellent and received several positive comments in the reviews. What is even more impressive is that it managed to incorporate some "Hebrew" humor (a comment about non-Jewish tailors) as well as a joke about another unrelated playwright (Shaw). The scene was short, full of several clear places for laughter, and was expertly timed. Other scenes of the 1915 show also incorporate this pattern, but those that used more characters were often less taut in their joke delivery and timing. Instead, scenes between vaudeville partners (such as Monroe and Fisher or the two Howards) were usually stronger than the more open-ended moments that included multiple cast members onstage at the same time. In these larger scenes, Atteridge could not rely on the specific charms of a previously polished vaudeville routine and had to work from scratch on the comedy, which naturally would not come across as effectively.

However popular the Howards were, they were still part of a larger ensemble and were still new enough that they took second place to George W. Monroe in advertisements for *The Passing Show of 1915*. Although it did not last as long as the tour for the 1912 edition, the 1915 show was touring at the same time that *The Passing Show of 1916* was in rehearsals. Thus, George W. Monroe, the Howard Brothers, and Marilynn Miller (the four principal stars) were shifted to the Fall Winter Garden Revue, *The Show of Wonders*. It would not be until the summer of 1918 that the Howards returned to *The Passing Show* series, but this time, they received top billing. When they returned in 1921 and 1922, they had become the stars that embodied the series in the eyes of the Shuberts and the public.

As the Winter Garden revues changed shape in the late teens and early twenties, shows would sometimes be held over in New York or no new revue would be introduced at all, and this had a great impact on *The Passing Shows*. The first time there was a disruption of the annual revue was in the latter part of 1919, when the 1920 show was being organized. Part of this new direction for the Shuberts was that they had acquired a new property—a smaller revue called *The Greenwich Village Follies*, which offered opportunities to try out fresh material. Additionally, they debuted a new series that could have become an annual show—*Spice of 1922*—but it was never repeated. However, the most important element of the new decade was that it saw an explosion in revues, and no doubt this caused the Shuberts to rethink the role of *The Passing Show* series in their offerings. Using the Howards as a *sure thing*, the team provided consistency for a series that was starting to see a wider range of competition beyond Ziegfeld's annual and Cohan's intermittent revues.

This star position gave the Howards the chance to feature several songs, and, as mentioned earlier, a bevy of sheets were printed that proudly displayed the two brothers on the cover. It also meant that many new songs were written specifically for the two to perform. However, one piece of the musical puzzle that is not clear from either the published sheet music or the piano/vocal parts in the Shubert Archive is just how, exactly, the two sang many of these songs together. Without exception, there is no written harmonization for two male voices, which suggests that the Howards must have improvised or personally developed vocal harmonies themselves. Unfortunately, as they did not record these songs, the musical nuances they included to "bring a song over" are lost to history. An examination of the many numbers they performed, however, offers at least a glimpse into what was written for them and what was chosen by them to become part of *The Passing Shows*. These songs can be seen in Table 3.1, where a few trends become clear.

The first of these trends is that nearly all the songs sung by the Howards were done as duets between the brothers, with the exception that Willie was sometimes given the spotlight. Eugene's only solo number was in 1915, and for whatever reason, he did not take such a position again. The second thread is that they were comfortable replacing songs as the show progressed, either on tour or even during the initial run at the Winter Garden. This happened when the song was done only by the brothers (without chorus) and was not tied to the action onstage. Thus, they took the chance to switch out songs during the moments when they were doing an "in one,"

Table 3.1. Songs Performed by Willie and Eugene Howard in *The Passing Shows*.

Show	Song Title	Composer(s)	Lyricist(s)	Performer(s)	O/I
PS 1912	"Ragtime Jockey Man"	I. Berlin	I. Berlin	WH, C	I
PS 1912	"The Bacchanal Rag"	L. Hirsch	H. Atteridge	A. Wheaton, WH, C	O
PS 1912	"Cohen's Yiddisha Band"	Harry Piani	Ballard MacDonald	WH, EH	I
PS 1912	"Metropolitan Squawk-tette"	L. Hirsch	H. Atteridge	WH, EH, T. Friganza, E. Hare	O
PS 1912 (t)	"Mr. Pagliacci"	L. Hirsch	H. Atteridge	WH, EH	O
PS 1912 (r)	"My Dixie Daisy"	Christiné	Schuyler Greene	WH, EH	I
PS 1912 (r)	"The Yiddisha Rag"	Joseph H. McKeon, Harry Piani, W. Raymond Walker		WH	I
PS 1915 (r)	"Broadway Sam"	L. Edwards	B. Merrill	WH	O
PS 1915	"My Trilby Maid"	Bobby Jones, Will Morrissey, H. Atteridge		EH, C	O
PS 1915	"Isle D'Amour"	L. Edwards	Earl Carroll	WH, EH	I
PS 1915	"The Shakespearean Rag"	L. Edwards	H. Atteridge	WH, EH	O
PS 1915 (r)	"Rosie Rosenblott"	Sam Lewis	George Meyer	WH	I
PS 1915 (r)	"We Want a Mighty Navy"	Charles Elbert	Howard Wesley	WH, EH	I
PS 1918	"That Soothing Serenade"	Harry DeCosta	H. DeCosta	WH, EH	I
PS 1918	"The Galli Curci Rag"	S. Romberg	H. Atteridge	WH, EH, V. Englefield	O
PS 1918	"Boots"	S. Romberg	H. Atteridge	WH, EH	O
PS 1918	"Messenger Boy"	S. Romberg	H. Atteridge	WH	O

(Continued)

Table 3.1. (Continued)

Show	Song Title	Composer(s)	Lyricist(s)	Performer(s)	O/I
PS 1918 (r)	"Venetian Moon"	Phil Goldberg, Frank Magine	Gus Kahn	WH, EH	I
PS 1918 (r)	"Dreaming of a Sweet To-Morrow"	Phil Goldberg, Frank Magine	Howard Brothers	WH, EH	I
PS 1921	"June Moon"	Frank Magine, Charley Straight	Joe Lyons	WH, EH	?
PS 1921	"When Caruso Comes to Town"	Abner Silver	Alex Gerber	WH, EH	?
PS 1921	"When Shall We Meet Again?"	Richard Whiting	Richard Egan	WH, EH	?
PS 1921	"Michigan"	Malvin Franklin	Alex Gerber	WH, EH	?
PS 1921	"Underneath Hawaiian Skies"	Ernie Erdman	Fred Rose	WH, EH	?
PS 1921	"Weep No More My Mammy"	Lew Pollack	Sidney D. Mitchell, Sidney Clare	WH, EH	?
PS 1921	"She's the Mother of Broadway Rose"	Max C. Freedman, Nelson Ingham	Willie Howard, George B. McConnell	WH	?
PS 1921	"Carolina Rolling Stone"	Eleanor Young, Harry D. Squires	Mitchell Parish	WH, EH	?
PS 1921	"Kentucky Blues"	Clarence Gaskill	Clarence Gaskill	WH, EH	?
PS 1921	"Wonderful Kid"	Lew Pollack	Willie Howard, Sidney Clare	WH	?
PS 1921	"Becky from Babylon"	Abner Silver	Alex Gerber	WH	?
PS 1921	"Spanish Love"	Abner Silver	Howard Brothers, Alex Gerber	WH, EH	?

Table 3.1. (Continued)

Show	Song Title	Composer(s)	Lyricist(s)	Performer(s)	O/I
PS 1921	"My Wife"	J. Schwartz	H. Atteridge	WH, EH	O
PS 1921	"My Lady of the Lamp"	J. Schwartz	H. Atteridge	WH, EH	O
PS 1921	"Rigoletto Quartette"	G. Verdi		WH, EH, V. Englefield, I Hayward	O
PS 1921	"Sweetest Melody"	J. Schwartz	H. Atteridge	WH, EH	O
PS 1922	"Carolina in the Morning"	Walter Donaldson	Gus Kahn	WH, EH	I
PS 1922	"Wanita (Wanna Eat? Wanna Eat?)"	Sam Coslow, Al Sherman		WH, EH	I
PS 1922	"Do You, Don't You, Will You, Won't You"	George A. Little, Larry Schaetzlein, Howard Brothers		WH, EH	I
PS 1922	"Sonja" (Op. 98)	Eugen Partos	Beda/ Al Wilson, James Brennan	WH, EH	I
PS 1922	"My Coal Black Mammy"	Ivy St. Helier	Laddie Cliff	WH, EH	I
PS 1922	"Ten-Ten-Tennessee"	George Meyer	Joe Young, Sam Lewis	WH, EH	I
PS 1922	"I Love Me (I'm Wild About Myself)"	Edwin J. Weber	Jack Hoins, Will Mahoney	WH, EH	I
PS 1922	"In Italy" (Burlesque Aria)	Al Goodman	H. Atteridge	WH, EH	I
PS 1922 (t)	"Underneath the Palms"	I. Morris (pseudo. of I. M. Schlenoff)		WH, EH	I

Show: (r)—replacement; (t)—added during tour.

Performers: WH (Willie Howard); EH (Eugene Howard); C (Chorus).

O/I: O—Original song from the show; I—Interpolation

performing in front of the curtain alone With no sets and wearing tuxedos instead of costumes, the Howards could manipulate the moment as they saw fit. Changing songs helped to keep the show fresh and gave them something new to do during the revue. The third tendency is an interest in songs about the South. Even in 1912, a fascination with Dixie is apparent, and it continues into the later editions, with Mammies, cotton, and southern state names used as the subjects of song after song. This vestige of the minstrel show was an aspect of the *Follies* too, and also popular among other performers; Jolson certainly sang his share of these song types, but unlike him, neither Howard performed in blackface. And finally, the duo specialized in numbers inspired by Italian opera. Whether they performed as members of an ensemble or together, their voices had enough range and strength to effectively mimic (and parody) operatic singers. This remains evident in the Vitaphone short years later, solidifying the fact that this style of song was a favorite of the Howards.

One feature of the brothers' performances in later years is that they included a moment where the two would perform "selections," which was a place in the show where they had *carte blanche* to do anything they wished. The first time this device is used by the Howards was during the tour of *The Passing Show of 1918*, when it was written that near the end of the second act, the two would perform "selections and imitations." This was not something new to either the Shuberts or their shows; Al Jolson had an open-ended spot like this (often referred to as a "specialty") first in *Dancing Around* (1914, unlisted in the program) and then in *Robinson Crusoe, Jr.* (1916, credited). The flexibility of this moment must have proven inspirational to either the producers or the Howards, because the next Winter Garden revue (in the spring) was *The Show of Wonders* (1916), which included the same kind of opportunity for the duo. In Table 3.1, the reason for the question marks is that it is impossible to reconstruct a musical sequence of songs without some clear "set list" that would demonstrate a single night's performance. From an entertainment standpoint, this elasticity of structure must have been quite welcome to the singers, as they could make choices based on audiences, locations, and which songs got the greatest response. It is not hard to see why the practice continued into the new decade.[36]

The rise of the specialty number coincided with a change in musical and comic presentation of the revue—an unraveling of the overall dramatic narrative of the shows. By 1921, the reoccurring characters that had appeared during the earlier *Passing Shows* were entirely absent, with the exception of a song or dance interrupting a single scene. However, the thin plot that drove characters to some sort of conclusion had disappeared completely, and it may be that the choice to focus on stars as performers in their own right rather than as characters in a show was partially responsible for this dramatic disunity. But despite the change in the revue's structure, it gave audiences an opportunity to see and hear more of the stars they loved.

However strong they were as singers, the songs sung by the Howards did not display an unusual complexity of rhythm or the kind of vocal extremes one might hear in contemporary operetta. This does not mean the tunes did not present challenges, though. For example, "I Love Me (I'm Wild About Myself)" includes a bouncy chromatic passage in the final phrase of the chorus that can become even more active if it is gently swung, which it is in Jack Haley's 1923 recording of the song (Cameo 327). "Dreaming of a Sweet To-Morrow" is typical in that it has an octave range, with many of the other melodies using one or two notes beyond this in either direction. An earlier song, "The Bacchanal Rag," is more complicated, because this is an opera-inspired piece with multiple sections. The range is expanded (an eleventh) and the phrases are more challenging than in many of the other pieces too, alternating between active rhythmic patterns and long-held notes. "We Want a Mighty Navy," an interpolation in *The Passing Show of 1915*, follows the pattern of many of these songs, with a lower, more constricted patter-like verse followed by heightened range and scalar activity mixed with an ascension to the song's highest pitch in the chorus. While most of their numbers were fast-paced and upbeat, some, such as the waltz "Isle D'Amour," were ballads that necessitated powerful lungs for successful execution.[37]

While one might expect the songs sung by the Howards to be primarily comic, this was not the case, with a variety of types assigned to them (or chosen by them) over the course of the revue series. Many of their songs played to their comic sensibilities, with "The Metropolitan Squawk-tette" and "Wanita (Wanna Eat? Wanna Eat?)" employing both funny lyrics and catchy tunes to keep the audience interested. In the latter song, four full verses are included in the sheet music, which could extend the song significantly if one chose. However, none of the Southern-themed songs offer any of the silliness of something like "I Love Me." "My Coal Black Mammy," for example, is a song about someone down on his luck who wants to go back to his Southern mammy, who represents comfort and home (a common thread in songs of this type, with "Swanee" being the most famous example). In "Carolina Rolling Stone," the main character has seen a movie where a cabin door reminds him of home sweet home, where "the fields of snowy white" are "calling [him] tonight." It is highly unlikely that the Howards would have performed these numbers with intentional irony, instead injecting serious elements into their act. One title that suggests it might be a parody, "She's the Mother of Broadway Rose," is instead a story of the woman who must bear the shame of her daughter's reckless, carousing lifestyle (referencing the song "Broadway Rose," by West, Fried, and Spencer).

However, a short description of one song, "Sonja," challenges the notion that what is written on the page is equivalent to how a number was performed. "Sonja" was written by Eugen Partos (music) and Beda (words), and was published by Wiener Boheme Verlag in Vienna in 1920. Two years later, Marks Music Company announced that the song was the hit of Europe—which indeed was true—and that they had "won the race among publishers for securing this prize," purchasing copyrights in the United States, England, Mexico, and Central and South America.[38] Willie Howard, they announced, "had a special version for himself written on the lyric," and the sheet music included both the original words and the new text. The original words, concerning a man wasting away in a Siberian prison after killing the lover of his cheating wife, are described in the article as "a ballad lyric as sung abroad." The English version is about a Russian immigrant who sees a play that reminds him of the simple life he and his wife, Sonja, enjoyed before coming to America. He sings of how he misses "old Russland" and remembers meeting his wife at Ellis Island, where "they had you locked up in a big iron cage / the moment I saw you, it put me in a rage / everyone was pushing each other around / and so was I, until I found / my Sonja." Although nothing about this story or its accompanying music, in a haunting E–harmonic minor, seems anything other than heartfelt, these new words, by Al

Wilson and James Brennan, are described by Marks as an "American comedy version." It is hard to imagine these new words presented in a humorous way, but a still different set of words were used on a record by Mory Leaf (Columbia 951-D, 1927) that successfully parody the original. As any performer knows, the delivery can transform virtually any song to fit the singer's wishes. However the song was performed, this overall musical flexibility of the performers closely aligns with comments made about Eugene and Willie's versatility onstage even at the outset of their careers.

Part of the story of the Howards' relationship with songs does not have to do with the Shuberts, but rather, with publishers. The relationship between performers, publishers, producers, and the recording industry is incredibly complex and desperately needs greater attention from scholars to help untangle the related threads. In some instances, it seems that publishers sought out vaudeville performers who were doing well, while in other cases, those who were trying to make a name for themselves sought out the publishers. There were advantages to both sides for these arrangements, but without significant documentation, the details of these transactions are almost impossible to detect. The Howards, as mentioned earlier, were fortunate to forge a strong relationship with Witmark at the very start of their vaudeville days, and this led to their picture being used on the covers of a number of songs (including "That's Yiddisha Love," 1910, by James Brockman). The attention in the trade papers about their song hits was also good for both parties, and this certainly played a part in helping each side stay active on the performing scene. The Howards signed three separate contracts with the Shuberts—in 1912, 1914, and another in 1920—before they retired as a team, and it is significant that none of these contracts includes a clause concerning sheet music (although the last contract states that "you may make phonograph records at such times as do not interfere with your performances.")[39] And, although the Shuberts had an arrangement with Remick (discussed in depth in chapter 5), the Howards could work with whomever they wished when it came to show interpolations. The most concerted collaboration happened for *The Passing Show of 1921* when the brothers made an arrangement with Witmark to work with Abner Silver (music) and Alex Gerber (lyrics) for three songs, each published with the other "available" titles on their covers. [40] The songwriting team began working together in January of 1919, and their first assignment for the Shuberts was to write a song for Al Jolson in *Sinbad*. By September, their song, "Give Me the Sultan's Harem" was being used in three Shubert shows simultaneously.[41] Thus, it is not surprising that the Shuberts made arrangements with Silver and Gerber to produce some interpolated hits for *The Passing Show*. This did not signify an exclusive relationship, as the tunesmiths had also written for Ziegfeld in 1920 and would soon produce melodies for Earl Carroll, but the Shuberts (and their stars) worked with them when they could. [42]

As with any theatrical figures (including some of the chorus girls), the Howards appear in several "human interest" stories throughout their career, sometimes engineered by the Shuberts' press department, but they could also be events of real importance. The former type of story includes an instance where the Howards were arrested in front of the Winter Garden for "disorderly conduct," with no explanation given for their public disturbance.[43] Eugene's announcement that he had become a "captain of the Police Reserve"[44] received mention, while still another was a clambake "for the entire [Passing Show] company" hosted by the brothers at the Lakewood Restaurant in New York.[45] A slightly more serious story was the saga of Willie Howard's stolen car. While performing The Passing Show of 1921 in Chicago, Willie's $4,500 automobile went missing for a time and then turned up smashed and burned. The entire event was quite strange, with the possible framing of a hapless suspect and Willie Howard's wish that the matter would disappear after trying to bail out the person who was charged with the car's destruction.[46] Sadly, no conclusion to the story was ever printed. On a more positive note, Willie was secretly married to Emily Miles, a featured member of The Passing Show of 1921 and a veteran of five previous editions, and their disclosure of the nuptials made the list of Broadway gossip in a number of papers. The two wed while the show was on tour in Montreal in July, but they did not announce it until November.[47] They may have been waiting to see if the arrangement worked, but it must have been successful as it lasted until Willie's death in 1949.

The bulk of other stories about the Howards concern their continued relationship with the Jewish community. Throughout their careers, they frequently performed benefits and celebrations that positively and publicly reaffirmed their ties with their cultural roots. Sometimes events helped a group to accomplish a financial goal; when the Young Women's Hebrew Association wanted to "purchase and equip an ambulance to be sent overseas" for World War I troops, they enlisted the brothers to help them raise money.[48] Other occasions were simply entertainment. They performed alongside Cantor Josef Rosenblatt, Jack Pearl, and Ben Bernard (brother of Sam), for the anniversary dinner of the Hebrew Kindergarten and Infant's Home on WGL radio.[49] One of the more colorful benefits took place in 1918, when Harry Houdini organized a group called the "Rabbi's Sons Theatrical Benefit Association," bringing together many of the men in show business who fit the group's title. "Twenty charter members" were enrolled, including "Houdini (president), Al Jolson (vice president), Irving Berlin (secretary), Bert Cooper (financial secretary), Walter Hast (traveling representative), and the Howard Brothers (sergeants-at-arms)."[50] The new members each contributed as much as a week's salary, providing $8,000 with which, according to Houdini, they could "become a power for good."

Circumstances changed for the Howards in 1925. Requests began to appear for extended periods in vaudeville, which J. J. Shubert granted beginning in late 1924.[51] Changing their strategy, the brothers split up for the first time in March of the following year. The Shuberts agreed to build a show around Willie, and using his old "Sammy Meyers" character, he became the star of a musical called Sky High. Eugene was still involved, but this time it was as a coproducer instead of an entertainer. The show was a success and ran for six months, but it spelled the end of the relationship with the Shuberts for a time. With no plans for another Passing Show during that year, and a failed attempt at bringing one together in 1926, the Shuberts had decided instead to focus their efforts on operetta and smaller-scale revues.[52] With the end of their Shubert contract in 1926, the Howards took a position with George White, signaling the beginning of a multi-year run as a central feature of the Scandals revues. It was the eighth year of White's annual series, and the Howards continued with the shows until 1939. With the notable exception of Willie's solo performance as Gieber Goldfarb, the taxi driver-turned-sheriff in Gershwin's *Girl Crazy* (1930), the Howard Brothers worked together until Eugene retired to become Willie's business manager in 1940. This did not mean they never worked for the Shuberts—they appeared together in the Shuberts' version of the *Ziegfeld Follies of 1934* and *The Show Is On* (1937)—but they never again headlined a major theatrical franchise for their former employer. Willie, however, would have an important relationship with another *Passing Show*, but this would not come until many years later; Willie's story is discussed in more depth in the final chapter.

Before leaving the Howards, it is worth considering why their legacy did not survive the vaudeville era. The most frequent suggestion is that they simply missed the great media expansion of the 1920s; they were not regulars in recording or on the radio and made only a few film appearances. I agree with this assessment, but want to add to the story by noting that the great wave of nostalgia musicals, both on film and onstage, also omitted the brothers. One document, however, teases a tantalizing possibility that never came to be, reminding us of why some figures of the past get remembered while others fade away. An agreement was signed between Eugene Howard and Jule Styne (composer of *Gypsy* and many other important productions) on January 20, 1956, for the "irrevocable, exclusive option to purchase the exclusive world-wide motion picture rights in the life story and works of WILLIE & EUGENE HOWARD for the purchase price of $50,000."[53] However, Styne never completed the project, and thus the impact of a movie such as *Funny Girl*, which could have changed the reputation of the Howards and *The Passing Shows* for future audiences, sadly never materialized.

NOTES

1. Memo from J. J. Shubert to Lee Shubert, June 20, 1912, Shubert Archive, program files for *The Passing Show of 1912*.

2. See US Census Data, 1900 and 1910. Matilda was born in 1854, Leopold in 1858, and Sam in 1884.

3. "Who's Who in the Theatre," *New York Times*, March 15, 1925, X2.

4. "New York," *New York Dramatic Mirror*, December 8, 1900, 21. It may be that Willie resisted calling himself "Willie Howard" at first because there had been a famous dwarf by the same name who had been a celebrated figure in Congress in Washington (although he had died in 1887).

5. The contract is reproduced in Isidore Witmark and Isaac Goldberg's *From Ragtime to Swingtime: The Story of the House of Witmark* (New York: Lee Furman, Inc, 1939), 220.

6. "Telegram Newsboys at Wondrous Banquet," *New York Herald*, January 6, 1902, 4.

7. Witmark and Goldberg, *From Ragtime to Swingtime*, 219–22.

8. Robert Speare, "Nothing New in It," *New York Morning Telegraph*, February 27, 1904, 9.

9. "Music and Song," *New York Clipper*, May 6, 1905, 272.

10. For more on the black dialect, see Jennie Lightweis-Goff, " 'Long time I trabble on de way': Stephen Foster's Conversion Narrative," *Journal of Popular Music Studies* (20/2), 150–65. Irish and Dutch are described in more depth in Charles Hamm, *Irving*

Berlin: Songs from the Melting Pot—The Formative Years (1907–1914) (New York and Oxford: Oxford University Press, 1997). These stereotypes continued well into the 1960s in different media.

11. "Howard and Howard," *Variety*, May 9, 1908, 8.

12. Chicot, "Vaudeville," *Variety*, March 24, 1906, 9.

13. Rush, "Vaudeville," *Variety*, May 26, 1906, 9.

14. "Amphion," *Variety*, March 17, 1906, 11.

15. "Alhambra," *Billboard*, June 18, 1910, 9.

16. "Howard and Howard," *Variety*, May 9, 1908, 8.

17. Sime Silverman, "Hammerstein's," *Variety*, May 29, 1909, 15.

18. "Vaudeville," *New York Dramatic Mirror*, August 6, 1904, 15.

19. "Hammerstein's" *Variety*, May 21, 1910, 18. A modified version of this act was incorporated into *The Passing Show of 1921*.

20. The short is included on Warner Brothers' Archive Collection of six discs, entitled the *Vitaphone Cavalcade of Musical Comedy: Shorts Collection*, released on DVD in 2010. Dozens of performers, bands, and acts can be found on these (and other) Vitaphone discs that await greater attention by scholars.

21. "Sam Bernard Receives Offer of $4000 a Week," *Variety*, June 24, 1911, 4.

22. "'The Grass Widows' Are Passing Fair," *New York Morning Telegraph*, January 14, 1901, 9.

23. "Hebrew Comedians as Stars," *Variety*, February 8, 1911, 5.

24. "Colonial," *Variety*, May 20, 1911, 23.

25. "Winter Garden's Good Show," *Variety*, December 16, 1911, 4.

26. "United vs. Winter Garden," *Variety*, March 23, 1912, 6.

27. Ibid. The contract is at the Shubert Archive, Personal Name Series—Howard Brothers, box 7.

28. "Winter Garden Reopens," *New York Clipper*, August 3, 1912, 6; "Passing Show of 1912," *Variety*, July 26, 1912, 20.

29. "Passing Show of 1912," *Variety*, July 26, 1912, 20.

30. "Winter Garden," *New York Press*, October 20, 1912, 5.

31. "'Passing Show' Has Good Burlesque," *Brooklyn Daily Eagle*, December 9, 1913, 8.

32. The name of the song was actually "The Yiddisha Rag" by Joseph H. McKeon, Harry M. Piani, and W. Raymond Walker (1911).

33. Production file, *Passing Show of 1912*, Shubert Archive.

34. Memos and correspondence, E. R. Simmons Papers, *Passing Show of 1918* file, letter, March 10 1918, Shubert Archive.

35. He was to be dressed as the orphan from the play *Daddy Long Legs* (1915). The R. J. character was the "mysterious detective" of *Under Cover* (1914).

36. Other revues, by Ziegfeld, Cohan, and Dillingham followed suit, offering such performers as Van and Schenk the same kind of mid-show spotlight.

37. Jose Collins had performed the song during the *Follies of 1913*.

38. "Sonja a Hit for Marks," *New York Clipper*, November 1, 1922, 18.

39. All three contracts are held at the Shubert Archive, Personal Name Series—Howard Brothers, box 7.

40. Silver's career had just begun at this point, and he continued to write songs into the 1960s, writing hits for performers as diverse as Benny Goodman and Elvis Presley.

41. Advertisement, *New York Clipper*, September 24, 1919, 22. The song was used in the *Gaieties of 1919, Oh, What a Girl,* and *the Greenwich Village Follies*.

42. Like Jolson, the Howards are sometimes credited on song sheets as co-creators of a song. In 1921, Willie Howard worked together with Sydney Clare and composer Lew Pollack to write "Wonderful Kid," which was then interpolated into *The Passing Show of 1921*. The song was dedicated to child star Jackie Coogan, who played "The Kid" in Charlie Chaplin's film of the same name.

43. "About You! And You!! And You!!!," *New York Clipper*, September 25, 1918, 21.

44. "Notes from the Theatres," *New York Herald*, October 31, 1918, 8.

45. "Stars Give Clambake," *Billboard*, February 12, 1921, 28.

46. "More Trouble over Howard Car," *New York Clipper*, August 10, 1921, 6.

47. "Marriages—In the Profession," *Billboard*, November 19, 1921, 102.

48. "Notes from the Theatres," *New York Herald*, October 21, 1918, 7.

49. "Stage Stars in Benefit to be Heard on W.G.L.," *Brooklyn Daily Eagle*, January 29, 1928, 10.

50. "Sons of Rabbis Organize," *New York Clipper*, July 24, 1918, 14.

51. See Shubert Archive, Personal Name Series—Howard Brothers, box 7.

52. The Shuberts returned to the format in the 1930s, discussed more in depth in chapter 9.

53. The letter has been available on the American eBay site for many years, but, much like Styne not taking up the $50,000 option, no bidder has purchased the letter for the $2,000 asking price.

4

A DOWNPOUR OF TALENT,
A NIAGARA OF BEAUTY
• • •
CHORUS GIRLS AND CHORUS BOYS

Despite the star power of the Howard Brothers and the many principals for *The Passing Shows*, there was little doubt that the draw for many theater-goers was the "super-captivating divinities" of the chorus. And although the chorus employed men and women, the featured attraction was the girls. The numbers speak to this imbalance, with usually three or four women to one man. If there was any doubt that the Shuberts understood the vital role of the girls, a memo sent to J. J. Shubert in 1914 from the advertising department clarifies why so many female choristers were hired:

> There is no mistaking one fact,—"The Passing Show" is a leg show,—and so, I take it the thing to do, is to let everybody know that we have legs and plenty of them. This being the case, how do you like the use of the 'Sloping Path' picture used in an advance? . . . Hope you agree that we must advertise legs, and let 'em know it good and strong.[1]

"The Sloping Path" number involved placing rows of women on slanted runways that took up the whole of the stage, from the proscenium to the floor, allowing the bodies to become geometrically related so both the arms and legs could form mesmerizing visual patterns.[2] For the women in this bit and in all the Winter Garden shows, taking part in a revue meant placing one's body on display for "The Tired Businessman" in the audience, an issue that has been discussed in several recent monographs.[3] Young women subjected to the "male gaze" while wearing minimal costuming, all the while getting paid a pittance for their work has, I think rightly, become an area of great interest for many cultural critics and historians. But there is more to be said. For some authors, the excitement lies in "discovering" people who went from chorus member to star. Others, however, are more interested in reclaiming the life histories of these hard-working actresses who eventually faded into obscurity after quitting show business altogether. The majority of the writing, however, centers on the cultural practice of placing women in the position of being an object, used primarily for their physical attributes and, frequently, nothing else. The rampant sexism these young women faced on a daily basis, from being forced to deal with philandering, lecherous husbands and youthful, aggressive "stage door Johnnies," was a treacherous—and sometimes—sloping path that led to bad reputations and public humiliation. It is worth noting that by World War I, the French revue was far more risqué than its American cousin, often featuring topless women at the Casino de Paris or The Moulin Rouge, but even in the United States, the women had to face the stereotype of the promiscuous chorus girl. There were reasons so many women participated in these revues, however, and those opportunities, for many, must have justified the endeavor. The life of a chorus man offered its own complications and rewards. Examining this world through the lens of *The Passing Show* provides many clues as to how life unfolded for these largely forgotten entertainers.

The young women of Broadway came from all around the world to find fame on the Great White Way. But, mostly, they were from Manhattan. In a brief article in the *New York Sun* entitled "Chorus Girl Home Towns," the "125 young women of the chorus in 'The Passing Show of 1919'" were asked about their origins:

> Thirty-eight came from New York, eleven from Brooklyn, sixteen from Chicago, ten from England, nine from France, seven from San Francisco, four from Philadelphia, three from Boston, two from Baltimore, two from Canada, three from St. Louis, two from Switzerland, and one each from Bombay, India; Bucharest, Romania; Mizzoula [*sic*], MT; York, PA; Warren, PA; Vincennes, IN; Pittsburgh, PA; Middleton, CT; Cincinnati, OH; New Orleans, LA; Saginaw, MI; Louisville, KY; Hartford, CT; Huron, OH; Reading, PA; Indianapolis, IN; Norfolk, VA; and Scranton, PA.[4]

Although the number of girls advertised and those included in the survey do not match up, they do reveal something of a pattern. The first three cities and the first two countries listed were the primary locations in the world for musical productions, especially revues. By 1915, US audiences would have seen multiple editions of the *Follies* and *The Passing Shows*, the other Winter Garden revues, and the countless smaller revues that played in restaurants and as part of vaudeville. Revues had been equally popular for the British and French (mainly centered in London and Paris), and they had also made it to Australia.[5] The smaller cities listed in the survey read, in part, like a list of stops for the touring productions of Shubert shows (often played in a "Shubert Theater"), and these spectators would have been aware of the glamour and spectacle associated with these revues. As has been the case for countless generations of young people, traveling entertainers represented an escape from whatever world the teens felt trapped in, promising adventure, laudatory attention, and the romantic possibilities of the limitless unknown. Making their way to New York and joining a Broadway revue would have been enticing for many starry-eyed youth of both sexes.

Tales of modest beginnings and long-shot successes graced newspapers and magazines regularly. The small-town kid becoming a star through chorus work was one of the great Cinderella myths of the late nineteenth and early twentieth centuries, especially because there were so many examples of it actually happening (several instances in *Passing Shows* will be discussed later in the chapter). The urge to stand before the footlights was always intense, and probably even more common during the pre-television era, where performances in a theater, be it variety, vaudeville, or

Broadway-based were always live. In an informative interview with chorus girl Lois Josephine (from *The Passing Show of 1913*), she tells young women that the "best cure for [being] stagestruck is the stage, and lots of it."[6] When Lois first became interested in theater, she found "her mother violently discouraged her daughter from becoming an actress." However, she worked "for the dressmaker" during the day while "secretly" rehearsing with acting companies around her hometown of Boston. Lois was "so interested in the pictures and billboards" of the theater, the manager finally noticed her and she was invited to participate in the chorus of a small musical comedy. She did not tell her mother about her hidden passion until she was already upon the stage, and even though she had to struggle through the rain in outdoor performances, slipping and falling, she eventually gained her footing and found a home in the theater. "To show my approval of the stage, I will let you know I am encouraging my little sister to go on. Since going on the stage, I think I have succeeded fairly well, because I have not only gained experiences, but a husband. As he happens to be on the stage with me all the time, it works out very well," explains Lois. This part was true; Lois Josephine had married Wellington Cross and the two became active in vaudeville (as a ballroom specialty act) and on Broadway, at least through the mid-1920s. And, for Lois at least, her passion led to the leading role in *June Love* (1921), which had a brief run in New York and an extensive American tour. The article also points out that Lois's start "is identical to that of [international star] Mlle. [Irene] Bordoni, the French actress." This no doubt signaled to the hundreds of readers curious about their own chances for success as members of the chorus that they, too, might become stars.

The number of young women who were ready to try out for these chorus positions was often staggering, with thousands of hopefuls appearing at the doors of the Winter Garden whenever an open call was made. What is interesting is that the giant Shubert theatrical machine never needed a small number of women; instead of auditioning chorus members only for a *Passing Show*, the call was for multiple productions at once, including the touring versions of shows that would be starting their transnational engagements. Since the Shuberts offered five to six new shows a year, and then sent each of these on tour, dozens, perhaps even hundreds, of girls could find chorus work depending on the producers' need. The most vivid description of this process was published in the *New York Press*. On the morning of Monday, June 9, 1913, Ned Wayburn and a team of Shubert employees sorted through over 3,000 women who appeared at the door of the Winter Garden to find jobs as chorus girls.[7] Postcards had been sent out to the 5,000 women who had applied, and when the doors opened at 10 a.m., hopefuls came ready to dance, sing, or simply display themselves in front of the director. The scene was so impressive that two weeks later, a detailed description of the process was printed as a full-page feature in the same paper, offering Wayburn's criteria for choosing which girls would be a part of which production.[8] One main table was set up on the Winter Garden stage, and this is where Wayburn himself sat and would look at those auditioning. After making his choices, he sent them on to a series of five tables behind him. None of the young women knew what they represented, but it was the center table that was the most desirable; this was the station where the girls who would receive callbacks to be in *The Passing Show* were sent. The rest would have their information taken by staff and were not given any indication on a time when they might receive a notice to return. For those that were offered jobs, the pay was between eighteen and thirty dollars a week, depending on which show they were hired for. Of all the productions, *The Passing Show* paid the highest salary and was the most desirable placement for chorus members.

The task of choosing girls, according to the *Press*, was not an easy one. First, J. J. Shubert explained to Wayburn what kind of women he wanted to hire. The director used this information to match the "atmosphere of the piece" to the right chorus. When he had the hopefuls in front of him, he collected basic information, including age and experience, and then the girl might be asked to do something, such as dance or sing. "Three steps and I can tell whether or not the girl is a dancer," says Wayburn. "Experience and constant practice tell. Especially in their walk, they betray the sprightliness of their calling."[9] The central factor for hiring was not looks or skill, but proficiency. "New York theatrical managers haven't the time to 'break in' new material. They want a girl who can dance a bit, who has a good chorus voice, and who has attractive features of face and form." An article from the following year, 1914, spotlights Jack Mason, who was responsible for later revues. Mason reiterated Wayburn's sentiments about the importance of dancing in choosing girls, but he added that he should be able to do the steps himself too; as an active professional dancer, Mason performed many of the dances the girls were expected to learn, demonstrating what he wanted.[10]

The Wayburn article also mentions that chorus hopefuls are more diverse than one might think, especially in terms of age. The young made up the majority of the group, but "they keep on attending these 'round-ups' until paint and powder are no longer able to hide the tell-tale traces of maturity. Even grandmothers can be detected . . . and of mothers there are a-plenty. But youth and beauty predominate."[11] There was no place for women whose features did not suggest innocence, though, and the images of the chorus members from the first *Passing Show* until the last continually highlight the young woman. As the anecdote concerning Willie Howard as a vaudeville "water boy" demonstrates, starting young was the goal. Many performers from this era, such as Fred Astaire and Marilynn Miller, discuss the loopholes for being hired as a minor. In Miller's case, the fact that she was hired by the Shuberts in her mid-teens became the means of getting out of her exclusive contract. For most, though, misrepresenting age was a common avenue for getting a job despite strict laws against child labor.[12]

For those who were accepted into the ranks of the chorus, a variety of roles could be assigned. The chorus was not a homogenous unit; instead it was divided into groups based on the featured talent of the performer and/or their physical dimensions. The Mason article explains that the taller girls were only recently becoming known as "show girls" ("a term, by the way, they for some reason or other particularly relish"). Throughout *The Passing Show* series, women who were taller were placed either at the back of the stage or (unsurprisingly) along the side, sometimes even as stationary figures. If the second option was used, they would wear remarkable costumes that highlighted their figure and the costume simultaneously. An excellent example of this type of chorus girl can be seen in the number "The Language of the Fan," from *The Passing Show of 1917* (see Figure 4.1). The elaborate costumes were

Fig. 4.1. "The Language of the Fan," The Passing Show of 1917. *Shubert Archive.*

meant to represent the "Girls of All Nations," and the three women shown are China (with a dragon), Egypt (with a scarab), and Hawaii (with a grass skirt).

The next "special" category for female choristers was the "small girl." These were women who were short and particularly petite. Marilynn Miller fit this category; she was the smallest member of the cast for *The Passing Show of 1915*. These women would usually be given some sort of diminutive outfit that was meant to accentuate their size. In *The Passing Show of 1918*, the costume list prepared by E. R. Simmons mentions "16 little girls" to be made up to look like chicks for the song "Squab Farm," the first number where Fred Astaire was the featured performer.[13] The girls accompanied Astaire, who was called a "farmer," but wore a "light summer suit and a gray derby hat." The costume can be seen on the cover of a flyer for the show (see Figure 4.2), with the girls wearing yellow feathers and blue shoes and stockings. Astaire sang the verse, suggesting each farmer (meaning young man) should go to Broadway (the squab farm), where he can watch the little squabs parade around the town. The girls then sang the chorus, written by Atteridge:

On a squab farm in our town / squabs of every size
Some chickens, too—and quite a few / Have those eagle eyes.
You'll see the cutest chickadees / and some old crows—if you please
If you'll need 'em—you must feed 'em / or those little squabs will tease.
You'll see most every kind of bird / if you're down our way,

Fig. 4.2. A Squab Farm "chick," The Passing Show of 1918. *Shubert Archive.*

> You can buy some feathers too if you're a jay
> You'll need a lot of chicken feed / on the squab farm if you'll stay
> For the chickens raise the dickens / on the squab farm called Broadway.

The small size of the women was no doubt a way to match the nature of the little "squabs" mentioned in the song, but it was also a good fit for the nineteen-year-old Astaire, who was only 5'9" tall.

By the standards of the twenty-first century, the imagery of young women as chicks seems entirely patronizing toward the girls. No doubt there was some of that present, but, like so many elements of the revue, the number was more complex than it seems. First of all, it was a direct reference to a play of the same name, *The Squab Farm*, which played at the Bijou Theatre in March of 1918 with a plot centered on life in the movies. The story was about a director who "has a great weakness for ingénues and, in consequence, produces picture after picture in which attractive young girls are the principal features."[14] Even though it was a comedy, the story was a cautionary tale for women, but also for men, with the moral that chasing many women in one's life (instead of being faithful to only one) will lead to a path where they all reject you in the end. In *The Passing Show*, the number leads to a scene about a director who is bored with women, all of whom shower him with affection and kisses. This intertextual pattern also ties the Squab Farm in the show to the new fusion between a *chick* and a *squab*. The term squab had been in use to describe small people since the late eighteenth century, and "chick," as a reference to women, was relatively new (from a 1910 cartoon by T. A. "Tad" Dorgan, who was known for his many contributions to American slang).[15] No doubt the inclusion of the number in the revue helped to popularize the term on the national scene, but it would have engaged the audience on other levels too. Knowledge of the source material would have reminded viewers of the moral positioning of the play and would have led to a thorough enjoyment of the ridiculous topsy-turvy burlesque that followed the song in *The Passing Show*. At one level, *The Passing Show of 1918* was displaying the women onstage in a way the "director" character from the source material would have championed. But by referencing *The Squab Farm* in the first place, the criticism of *only* viewing women in this way would also become part of the moment (see chapter 7 for more on the way references were used in the revues). All semiotic complexities aside, the "Squab Farm" number was one of the only scenes where the smaller girls where featured during this particular show.

Groupings of women are impossible to ascertain from the programs themselves. Since the chorus girls were never identified by name, the audience would not know which girl was part of which section. The most illuminating source for this information comes from the notes and memos to and from the man responsible for "taking care" of the costumes for the series, E. Romaine "Ma" Simmons. Among the thousands of extant documents of the Shubert Archive, Simmons's papers demonstrate that he was another employee who J. J. Shubert, in particular, relied on heavily. Although he did not design each costume himself, he organized the costume process, from making detailed suggestions to getting quotes from costume makers for specific items and eventually working with the production team to ensure that the chosen outfit worked. It also seems he had an encyclopedic knowledge of items held in storage that could be reused or modified to become something new. Fred Allen includes a vivid description of Simmons in his memoirs of *The Passing Show of 1922*:

> The chorus boys had christened him "Ma," and this maternal sobriquet served him through the years. Ma's memory was uncanny. In August, when the new Shubert shows were in rehearsal and the older shows were being readied to go on the road, Ma might be supplying wardrobes for eight or ten different shows. This entailed supervising the making of new gowns for the women stars in the modern shows and period costumes for the principals in operettas; remodeling old costumes for the chorus girls and boys; and furnishing such items such as shirts, ties, and shoes for each show. Working around the clock during his hectic season, Ma knew the name of every chorus girl who had torn her farthingale at the *Passing Show* rehearsal in New York, the name of the *Blossom Time* principal whose peruke was too tight, how many buttons were off of the chorus boys'

trousers in the road company of *Bombo*, and how many moths were flying around at any given hour in the Shubert wardrobe building.[16]

Allen claims that "very few" of the costumes for this edition of *The Passing Show* were new, and Simmons's notes confirm that many were from "stock."[17] However, the records prove that Allen's memory was inaccurate; almost every item the chorus girls and boys wore (as well as most of the historical and foreign costumes) were made by Anne Spencer, Inc. specifically for this production.

Simmons's detailed written notes clarify who wore what in the chorus, providing the most exact information possible about how the chorus was organized.[18] The show had forty-eight girls total, but they were only used as a homogenous group once, during the "Camp's Daily Dozen" number, where a group of twelve exercises was performed by the chorus. The breakdown of girls for the "Pretty Hat Number" is more indicative of how chorus members were usually used. Simmons prepared different costumes for ten "show girls," eight "girls," and eight "poppies," meaning the smallest women. The "poppies" were also to be dancers, which is sometimes a category unto itself. During the Circus Scene, the breakdown included some of the men from the chorus as well as some of the second-tier stars; the scene called for nine male clowns (including the Three Mackweys), sixteen girl clowns (including Ethel Shutta), and four jockeys. All the clowns wore costumes of cerise and white sateen, while the jockeys wore coats and capes made of the same material, with each individual costume costing the firm fifteen dollars.

Creative groupings of the chorus were necessary to keep these large-scale revues moving and to differentiate one year's offerings from another. Costumes helped make the numbers unique, with some editions using outlandish finery to present the chorus in sometimes wonderfully ridiculous garb. One of the most striking of these costume-based arrangements was for the "Gold, Silver, and Green" scene of *The Passing Show of 1924*.[19] Eight girls wore gold coins, eight wore silver, and eight wore large-size greenbacks of various denominations. Multiple designs by Myra Butterworth remain, as well as one by William Weaver, all of which feature the tricolor scheme, but unfortunately no photograph has emerged to prove which design—or designs—were used (see Figure 4.3 for one of the Butterworth sketches). And, much like the "Language of the Fan" mentioned earlier, almost every revue would have an exotic scene, exploring some distant (from New York, at least) nation, from Spain to India to Argentina. This afforded the creative team numerous opportunities; costume designers explored traditional garb, dance instructors introduced new steps, and composers used music with "local color." All of this usually stayed well within the bounds of stereotype, but it also fulfilled one other role: it provided an excuse to put a young woman in the skimpiest of outfits.

Alternating arrangements of chorus parts for songs were another way of keeping audiences engaged with something new at every turn. The song "Baby" used a four-part breakdown because the number was for women alone (Soprano 1 and 2 and Alto 1 and 2), but the standard four-part harmony (soprano, alto, tenor, bass) was employed if the whole company was singing, which for opening act production numbers such as "We're Working in the Picture Game" (*The Passing Show of 1914*)

Fig. 4.3. "Gold, Silver, and Green" Chorus girl costume sketch, The Passing
Show of 1924. *Shubert Archive.*

was always the case. One extant choral arrangement, for the "Royal Wedding" from
The Passing Show of 1923, only used baritone and alto voices. [20] Changing the groups
aurally would have helped make numbers stand out, especially if, as in the example
with Fred Astaire earlier, the star's solo singing alternated with the chorus. It was
also essential to create a memorable relationship between the featured soloist and
the chorus through characterization to ensure the audience understood why the
combination made sense.

It is very clear, however, that women's physical attributes were of primary concern when arranging them onstage. A major trope in press releases about the girls
was an emphasis on their incomparable beauty as well as their "freshness," a term
meant to indicate they were mainly young, certainly innocent, and inexperienced
(and not far removed from the nineteenth-century definitions of "chick" or "squab"

for a child). An article about what types of women were chosen for the chorus was penned in 1923:

BATHING BEAUTY JOINS "THE PASSING SHOW"
In accordance with their policy of presenting the most beautiful girls in the world at the Winter Garden, the Messrs. Shubert yesterday engaged Sidney Nelson, artists' model and winner of the bathing beauty prize last summer at Atlantic City, for "The Passing Show of 1923." Miss Nelson, who is 19 and a native of New York, will appear in the "Living Chandelier" and "Animated Curtain" and other scenes which call for unusual feminine pulchritude.

With the addition of Miss Nelson, "The Passing Show" has the most beautiful group of girls that has ever been seen at the Winter Garden. In the large company are models for such artists as Howard Chandler Christy, Clarence Underwood, and Knowles Hare as well as winners of beauty contests held in all parts of the United States. There are 24 girls in the ensemble who have never before been on the stage.[21]

Most elements previously mentioned for the "ideal" girls are present here. Miss Nelson was young, successful, gorgeous, and new, much like the twenty-four girls who were recently plucked from obscurity and would be included in the body-spectacle-fantasy of the "Living Chandelier." Presenting the as-yet-unseen beauties of America was one of the revue's specialties, and each of the large-scale shows staged by Ziegfeld, Earl Carroll, or George White made use of this language to entice those with hungry eyes to attend.

A feature of the revue similar to the Living Chandelier could be found in every *Passing Show*, and although these numbers were presented in a variety of ways, the attraction combined vast numbers of girls with imaginative settings, fabulous costumes, and take-your-breath-away moments. On some occasions, the participants were static, carrying on the tradition of the "tableaux vivante." The "Living Cross" from *The Passing Show of 1926* (which did not make it to New York) is a perfect example of this. One woman stood roughly thirty feet in the air as the handle of a sword/cross amalgamation, and two women lying on their sides were placed next to her. Far below them, two lines of girls stretched out toward the audience, with a singular line of women holding place in front of the sword/cross. But unlike this scene, a lively dance accompanied the female chorus, providing them with a chance to show off their dancing and singing abilities.[22] These were referred to as production numbers, and were the most extensive sequences that happened during revues. In *The Passing Show of 1912*, the "Harem of Sewer-Man" falls into this category, while the "Sloping Path" from the 1914 show was one of the highlights of that edition. Each show had at least one production number per act, situated halfway through or later. Both "The Capitol Steps" and "Camp's Daily Dozen" are examples of this audience-pleasing theatrical device.

Part of the reason these numbers worked was that they made use of the famous runway that was a staple of the Winter Garden. It was referred to by some as the "Bridge of Thighs" because of the dancing girls on it.[23] The structure was taken from a Kabuki-styled runway in Max Reinhardt's pantomime *Sumurun* (1912), another Shubert production, in this case imported from Berlin. One writer described the original runway as a "softly-lighted path leading from the front of the theatre over two rows of orchestra seats to the curtain . . . Those who enter the scene from the street when the curtain lifts do so over the heads of the orchestra."[24] When the illuminated runway was installed in the Winter Garden, it was changed slightly, with the end reaching the center of the stage in the middle. One description, from a 1915 advertisement, proclaimed that the runway went far higher than one might expect: "Out over the heads of the audiences—up to the gallery—the Rose Tinted Runway brings you nearer the fun."[25] Although stars were placed on the stage extension, it was almost exclusively used for chorus girls to make their way out into and over the audience. This effect was a signature element for *The Passing Show* series, providing the spectators next to the runway a proximity to the chorus they never got at a Ziegfeld show and causing some to speculate that the price of tickets for the seats directly underneath went for a premium.[26] Reviewers were split over the use of the runway, its effectiveness at maintaining a true feeling of theater, and also the dangerous immediacy of the chorus to the audience. At least one reviewer felt that showing off the "ponies" in such a way was troublesome: "The performers being thus brought intimately to the audience . . . although nothing in particular is gained, for in the theater, above all other places, it is distance that lends enchantment, and to see the make-up—the paint and powder and the India ink—so near at hand is rather disillusioning."[27] For many in the audience, however, this unusual feature was delightful, and a runway was taken on each revue's tour throughout the country.

The relationship between the women of the chorus and their (mostly male) admirers was an issue that was trod as repeatedly as the runway. One of the more surprising perspectives was voiced by Marie B. Schrader, who had a regular column called "Madame Critic" in the *New York Dramatic Mirror*. Schrader's article concerning *The Passing Show of 1915* is partially a review, with the remainder an extended musing on what the life of the chorus girl from a revue must be like. One might expect a blistering reproach about "The Tired Businessman" from such a discerning theatergoer as Schrader, but to her they were merely falling prey to the dazzling allure of the girls, who use the "runways and fishing tackle" to attract attention.[28] "Quite a spirit of camaraderie is established in a very short time and bridges over that bare space between the first row of the orchestra and the former front row of the stage far more effectively than [lofty 'legitimate'] productions could ever do," wrote Schrader. Channing Pollock, author and playwright, wrote in the *Green Book Magazine* that the runway became a moral problem because the girls were barelegged; when causing "its girls [to] go to the heads of men, literally as well as figuratively," the runway "is of questionable propriety," most especially "when it serves to project real nakedness into the bosom of one's family."[29] Pollock admitted to having never liked any show at the Winter Garden in his review of the first *Passing Show*, but this was probably more because he was allied with Ziegfeld than because he did not like the show. His aversion for the runway is a central issue in criticism of the 1912 edition, and it is featured in a cartoon accompanying his writing (see Figure 4.4). Curiously, no families are depicted in the image, with the artist instead focusing on the elongated necks of the men, which while certainly a type of "rubbernecking," also suggests an audience formed entirely of erect human-phallus hybrids.

SCANTILY CLAD NYMPHS WALK THE PLANK RIGHT INTO THE BOSOM OF YOUR FAMILY, AT THE
WINTER GARDEN

Fig. 4.4. Cartoon by Herb Roth in Green Book Magazine, *1912.*

The fact that the Shuberts deployed a chorus of young women without stockings was a major issue when *The Passing Shows* went on tour, especially when the issue was morality. Posters for the 1913 revue caused such a stir in Buffalo, New York, that "strips of white paper" had to be placed over the girl's legs "to keep everybody happy."[30] Three years later in the same city, the 1916 edition encountered significant opposition when the United Preacher's Association issued a proclamation warning the Teck Theatre to reject the "outrageous disgrace" that was *The Passing Show.* The Reverend Robert J. McAlpine said that while he "enjoy[ed] a good play as well as the man next to him," he felt that this "piece of moral unfitness" was "a distinct menace to the common morals of Buffalo." As a response, the people of Buffalo saw the show in "record-breaking numbers."[31]

The truth was that discourse concerning reputation was in play whenever chorus girls were mentioned long before *The Passing Show of 1912* came to be. The chorus girl "problem" was already an issue when *The Black Crook* was performed in 1866, stemming partially from French productions in the 1840s in New York. The first *Passing Show* in 1894 also faced criticism for how some girls were displayed, what they displayed, and what was morally acceptable: "Regarded from one point of view, those four Phrynettes in the 'Passing Show' are more exhilarating than is the thorough nudity of living pictures. They also serve to illustrate the voluptuous tastes of modern society. A shrewd man, who understands his public, has attired these four young women in dresses that are rapturously shocking."[32] And audiences were shocked. Shocked enough that they paid to see the show in droves, no doubt influencing the young minds of the Shuberts and Ziegfeld as they began working in theater in earnest. Throughout the slow and steady disrobing of the American chorus girl, another chorus—of outraged moralists—continually threatened boycotts of theaters and the closing of doors, all in hopes of turning the inevitable tide away from what they felt was dangerous for society and also dangerous for the women in question.[33] It is certainly true that chorus members faced difficult choices as well as criminal behavior, both directed toward them and sometimes perpetrated by them. For example, during the summer of 1915, a major bust inside the King James Hotel revealed a pair of tango dancers who were supplying opium, heroin, and cocaine to chorus girls.[34] Producers and managers complained that "somebody was supplying ... drugs to chorus girls from a secret storehouse in the 'lobster belt,'" and when George Bennett and his wife, Mae Malloy, were arrested, they also found a young woman who had "been trying to break herself of the drug habit but had been unable to do so because of her knowledge of Bennett's supply." The unnamed chorus member told police, "if their stuff is taken, I can't get it so easily and maybe I can quit." In another story, chorus girls were told to watch out for S. Stanley Skop, who was selling them fake shares of ten dollars each for a show in the Progressive Circuit that was not real.[35] Drugs and scams, however, were not the only hazards for these women. Their access to men, combined with their own tragic beauty, might also lead to the dangers of sex.

One of the more personal documents I discovered in the Shubert Archive was directly about the awareness women had of how they were seen by the public. Found tucked inside the rehearsal piano music for *The Passing Show of 1918*, folded and within its original envelope, was a letter written by "one of your girls" to J. J. Shubert accompanied by a newspaper clipping. The young woman's note was an attempt to get another chorus member (who had been in the Ziegfeld *Midnight Frolic*) fired because of her bad reputation—and her public involvement with criminal activities:

> I am writing to protest to you against one of the girls who is rehearsing in the new Winter Garden show, Alice Wagner. She was arrested last January in Wanamakers in company with a notorious street walker for shoplifting. She was working in the Midnight Frolic at the time and Mr. Meers, the manager who was madly in love with her, succeeded by bringing a lot of influence to bear in getting the case settled out of court after obtaining two adjournments. He also got Mr. Ziegfeld to take her back. She hadn't been back a week when one of the girls at the Frolic, Eleanor Dell, told me she caught her red handed with a purse she stole from her in the dressing room ... The enclosed article which appeared in the [New York] Review verifies most of what I state. I don't think it fair to the other girls to have a notorious shop lifter and street walker in the company. We have a bad enough reputation as it is. I know anonymous letters are not very nice and shouldn't be paid any attention as a rule, but if you will take the trouble to investigate this, you will find that it is all true and I think you owe it to the nice girls in your company to do this, Mr. Shubert.[36]

Of course it is difficult to tell how much of the letter stems from honest concern for the group as opposed to personal distaste for Alice Wagner, but whatever the case, Wagner was not included in *The Passing Show* chorus, although the Shuberts must have thought enough of her skills to include her in the chorus for *Monte Cristo, Jr.* the following season. But whatever the arrangement with Wagner, the author of the letter clearly states that there was an established negative image that could further be threatened; the hope was that J. J. Shubert would do something to mitigate the problem. The article does support the chorister's accusation of Wagner's problems with theft, but Wagner herself is not called a prostitute (or streetwalker) in the clipping. The public's view of the women of the theater as "ladies of the night" was an attitude that stretched far into the past, but stories of notorious, lewd gold diggers and fallen angels were rife in the pulp magazines of the time. It may be that Wagner's association with someone who had a record of prostitution was combined with her own role as a chorus girl, setting off a powder keg of gossip against her.

Jack Mason addressed the issue of reputation in 1913, explaining that the public had an entirely fictional view of the chorus girl that, while fanciful, did not make sense when consideration was given to the details of the job itself.[37] "The idea that the chorus girl is necessarily immoral is a provincial idea," he told the reporter, "[and] the idea that [they] are or have to stand ready to be friendly with managers is even more provincial." Mason felt that equating beauty with stupidity and being sexually "available" was poor business sense both for the producers and for the women.

> I have known more thoroughly good girls in the chorus than I have in many other types of business in which girls engage. The chorus girl has to have . . . more brains and more cleverness than, say, a saleslady. Chorus girls are shrewd judges of human character and they haven't many silly illusions. They have common sense, which is the best ally of morality that I, for one, know of. Of course, they like a good time, but if they knew how hard they have to work, no one would wonder . . . They are self-reliant.

Mason's defense was one of dozens published in periodicals about how incorrect the general opinion toward these women really was. And, no doubt, the central reason for these repeated outcries from the industry was because it was such a widely held belief, repeated so frequently. One reason for the reputation was that, at least by the early 1920s, small booklets were published featuring chorus women in various states of undress. One of these, *Red Pepper*, a "Peppy Periodical for Peppy People," included eight photos in its pages, all of which were chorus women; girls in *The Passing Show*, Earl Carroll's *Vanities*, *Kid Boots*, *Artists and Models*, *The Dream Girl*, and *Keep Kool* (all shows playing in 1924) were featured (see Figure 4.5).

No doubt using these magazines fueled speculation that the women were willing to take risks and (presumably) open to promiscuity. Even Madame Critic cocked her eyebrow at the $700 floral arrangement that adorned the stage during *The Passing Show of 1915*, noting that "these beauties are so spoiled" that "automobiles, flowers, and the sons of millionaires waiting at the stage door make life one continual round of excitement."[38] But with even a theatrical professional like Schrader suggesting that women *did* take advantage of the wondrous and wealthy world outside their dressing rooms, how true to life was the myth?

Of all the components of Mason's argument for the high moral standards set by the chorus members, nothing rang more true than his comment concerning hard work and professionalism. The daily work lives of chorus members, both female and male, were not primarily the life of comfort, excitement, and splendor that Madame Critic so blithely suggested. Instead, the work was a real struggle, especially in terms of rehearsal hours and wages, and sometimes with the issues of reputation added to the mix. One response from the women can be found in an early, but brief, article about the chorus girls for *The Passing Show of 1912*. Louise Brunelle, who had taken over the part of the "Quaker Girl" from Anna Wheaton on the tour, organized eight

OH! FOR THE LIFE OF A CAMERA MAN

Photo De Mirjian Studio

ALYNE WHALEN
In the "Passing Show of 1924" at the Winter Garden.
No wonder Broadway is wild.

Fig. 4.5. Alyne Whalen in The Passing Show of 1924. Red Pepper *(December 1924).*
Author's Collection.

other women to become a sorority they called "Theta Delta," which for them was specifically an "Anti-Johnny" society.[39] Brunelle had been a part of the chorus of other shows, and felt that coming together as a group meant the members would offer important structure for the women who were bound together through their work. That following year, Loretta Healy (the tour replacement for Jobyna Howland) attempted to create an official union for chorus members, hoping to "fix a minimum wage for each class" that would ensure fair wages despite the price wars between producers.[40] Supported by outspoken suffragette Trixie Friganza, Healy's efforts did not result in an established protectorate—this would have to wait until 1919, when the Actor's Equity Association demanded a large-scale Broadway strike. Alfred Harding's account of the union indicates that the chorus bore the brunt of the high stakes involved in theatrical enterprises, receiving no pay until the show began and having to go without pay entirely if a production failed.[41] The chorus for *The Passing Show of 1919*, he indicated, went without any remuneration for the twenty-two weeks they rehearsed.[42] Monica Stufft's informative dissertation, entitled *Chorus Girl Collective*, explores the working conditions, collectivist efforts, and, when possible, personal experiences of chorus girls from this era and beyond, convincingly demonstrating that there was little time to become spoiled, and virtually no room in one's life for the ego that critic Schrader imagines.[43]

A positive element of Winter Garden revues, at least from the chorus perspective, was that the shows were guaranteed to run successfully and then were followed by tours. The relative stability of a Shubert production must have made it a far more enticing prospect than many musicals put on by competing producers. And beyond the assured trajectory of a single show, the Shuberts had multiple tours active simultaneously. Romberg's pseudo-autobiography describes a situation wherein most choristers were expected to perform one show while learning the next:

> At the theatre Sigmund found that things were a little different from the way he remembered them in Vienna. The speed and rush of New York, so different from the more leisurely Viennese way, was nowhere more evident than backstage. He found that the girls who were to appear in "The Whirl of the World" were the same girls who were appearing in the currently running Shubert revue, and that they too had to double—between the show in rehearsal and the show on the stage. The girls, among the most beautiful on the Broadway stage, were understandably short-tempered and exhausted under the grueling routine.[44]

As Atteridge stated, this probably represented the very start of the process after preliminary production plans left the office—teaching the chorus the music and the dancing. And even though Romberg only remembered the female members of the chorus, there were certainly several men who appeared alongside them. Table 4.1 lists the chorus members for the Broadway runs of *The Whirl of the World*, *The Passing Show of 1914*, and the touring production of *The Passing Show of 1914* when it appeared in Boston. The common entertainers in the first and second columns of the table have an asterisk (*) by their name, while the common performers between the second and third columns have a double asterisk by their name (**). Each of these chorus members is in bold and underlined for clear identification.

From Table 4.1, it is clear that there was a certain amount of crossover between chorus members in *The Whirl of the World* (the Spring revue at the Winter Garden) and *The Passing Show of 1914*, but not so much that the entire cast would have been involved in the rehearsals for one revue while preparing for the next. Of the forty-nine women and twelve men, only three (or possibly four) women and stayed on the Winter Garden stage: Rena Markey (called Rene Markey in *The Passing Show of 1914* programs), Helen Marche, Bobbie Roberts, and possibly Marion McDonald, who might be the "Miriam McDonald" of *The Passing Show of 1914*. The list of the chorus from the tour of *The Passing Show of 1914* is also included since it is far more likely that cast members would remain involved with the show once they had learned the part. Since youth was a requirement for these positions, it was probably not too difficult for them to depart New York City and join the touring cast—most of them had not established families yet and many either skipped or had finished school. The

Table 4.1 Chorus members in three Winter Garden revues.

The Whirl of the World	The Passing Show of 1914	The Passing Show of 1914 (Boston, touring production)
Women (49)	Women (53)	Women (37)
Muroff Allo	**Betty Berry** **	**Betty Berry** **
Dorothy Barnette	**Hazel Black** **	Mary Berry
Myrtle Bauer	Dorothy Cameron	**Hazel Black** **
Mabel Benelisha	Margarite Carmen	**Helen Carrington** **
Lena Betts	**Helen Carrington** **	**Cecil Carter** **
Pearl Betts	**Cecil Carter** **	Carolyn Clark
Jennie Callen	Adele Christy	Edna Coigne
Ruth Carbury	Estelle Christy	**Ethel DuBois** **
Lucille Cavnaugh	Barbara Clark	**Lottie Franklyn** **
Grace DuBois	Jeanne Dare	**Vivian Gordon** **
Vera Dunn	**Ethel DuBois** **	**Marie Gray** **
Alice Eldon	Gertrude Foy	Virginia Harvey
June Elvidge	**Lottie Franklyn** **	Sadie Howe
Follie Faulker	**Vivan Gardon** **	**Irene Hutchins** **
Grace Georgian	Lauretta Grant	Fannie Kidston
Mazie Gilmore	**Marie Gray** **	Ida Kramer
Helen Glenmore	Dolly Grey	**Nita Lamadrid** **
Evelyn Hall	Carrie Hahn	**Gertrude Mackey** **
Edna Hettler	Eunice Hamilton	Connie Magnet
Lillian Howell	Elfrida Hanswarth	**Rene Markey** *, **
Rosa Huber	**Irene Hutchins** **	**Blanche Marr** **
Florence Kern	Virginia June	Myrtle Marsh
Dorothy Landers	Ida Kramer	Rose Marye
Mazie Lawless	**Nita Lamadrid**	Anna Maywood
Vivan Lawrence	**Dorothy Landers***	**Emily Miles** **
Lena Lorelli	Fife Lissier	**Irene Mitchell** **
Helen Marche *	Daisy Lovell	**Georgie Moore** **
Rena Markey *, **	**Gertrude Mackey** **	Marjie Moore
Marion McDonald (?) *	**Helen Marche** *	Nemo Ormston
Dorothy Moran	**Rene Markey** *, **	Beatrice Percell
Dot Page	**Blanche Marr** **	Kitty Rahn
Lillian Parrish	Mae Marrell	**Grace Robinson** **
Claire Pearl	Lucy Maurelli	Alice Rogers

(*Continued*)

Table 4.1 (Continued)

The Whirl of the World	*The Passing Show of 1914*	*The Passing Show of 1914 (Boston, touring production)*
Rena Pelham	**Miriam McDonald (?)** *	**Raye Shirley** **
Nellie Pennington	Emma McGrath	**Mae Tarmey** **
Anna Perrine	**Emily Miles** **	Katherine Ward
Trixie Raymond	**Irene Mitchell** **	Dorothy Wilson
Bobbie Roberts *	Emily Monte	
Dot Rozell	Marion Mooney	
Emily Russ	**Georgie Moore** **	
Elinore Ryley	Anna Pauly	
Marie Salisbury	Carinne Picard	
Virginia Shelby	Alice Randolph	
Paulita Sherman	Josephine Raye	
Lois Stowe	**Bobbie Roberts** *	
Vera Tirrell	**Grace Robinson** **	
Elinor Wallace	Ida Scaife	
Ethel Wheeler	**Raye Shirley** **	
	Mae Tarmey **	
	Margarite Ward	
	Anna Waywood	
	Edna Wentworth	
Men (12)	Helen West	
Fred Bates		Men (8)
Allan Fagan	Men (12)	**Jas. Curran** **
Irving Finn	**Jas. Curran** **	**Frank Durand** **
Art Garvey	**Frank Durand** **	**Edward Gordon** **
Ray Goodrich	**Edward Gardon** **	Bob Hastings
Irving Jackson	Robert Gilbert	**Walter Smith** **
Arthur Kelly	**Bob Hastings** **	Stanley Vickers
Larry Mack	Fred Hudler	Herb Weir
Winnie Parker	Dave Marshall	**Arthur Whitman** **
Stanley Rayburn	**Walter Smith** **	
Charles Towns[h]end	Charles Turner	
William Wilder	**Arthur Whitman** **	
	Bob Wynne	
	William Young	

table demonstrates that the number of chorus members diminished when the show left Broadway, dropping from sixty-five to forty-five, but many of the choristers were retained as the revue began to tour the United States. Overall, twenty-four chorus members (eighteen women and six men) reprised their roles on the road.[45] Although several changes were made to the revue during the tour, there is not sufficient space here to examine this in the depth it deserves.[46] What is certain, though, is that the recollection of "overworked" and "exhausted" chorus girls was not very accurate, at least for this particular show. This does not mean they did not face challenging working conditions; a rare candid picture taken backstage at Chicago's Garrick Theater during the tour of the 1914 edition shows that many chorus members shared small spaces for dressing rooms (see Figure 4.6). But despite these difficulties, chorus members hired along the path were partially instructed by their fellow entertainers.

Fig. 4.6. Candid photo taken backstage at the Garrick Theater, Chicago, The Passing Show of 1914 tour. Author's Collection.

Once a part was learned, it was perfected by chorus members who would then have sufficient knowledge to teach newcomers the role.

Despite some of the challenging workplace conditions, there were several advantages to being a part of the chorus. Probably the most important was that it was possible to be noticed and then given a more important role—one with either a small bit of dialogue, a unique costume, and maybe even a featured moment in the show. Of course, the greatest difficulty in being a successful part of an ensemble is the ability to fit in, but if a chorus member blended in too much, they would never be noticed. Maintaining an identity as part of a mass while at the same time finding a means of asserting some individuality was a delicate balance, but luckily there were some ways a chorister could achieve this. The programs for *The Passing Shows* are filled with minor roles that were taken on by people who are not co-listed in the chorus, and the scripts demonstrate that most of these parts had only a few lines. The lucky performers who were given these parts were placed alongside the principals in the program, where their role was acknowledged and they could be more easily identified. One performer who achieved this kind of "lucky break" was June Elvidge (see ▶Figure 4.7), who is listed as a chorus girl in *The Whirl of the World* (see Table 4.1), and then received a speaking part in *The Passing Show of 1914*. Elvidge is listed as "Miss Leeds" in the program and, though it is not clearly marked in the script, this character was almost surely one of the five girls who appeared just before the entrance of Kitty MacKay (played by José Collins), each sporting Scottish-inspired monikers—Miss Glasgow, Miss Leeds, Miss Edinburgh, Miss Henrietta, and Miss Heather.[47] Three of these girls had lines, and whichever actress was "Girl Number 1" was given numerous speaking parts. It is likely Elvidge was one of these three fortunate women.

When *The Passing Show of 1914* went on tour, Elvidge was given a more important opportunity, taking over Collins's star role and becoming "Kitty MacKay" herself.[48] Thus, beginning in the chorus, Elvidge experienced the *42nd Street* dream of becoming a star, eventually finding her way onto the screen. Many of the other roles in the revue are similar to Elvidge's, and there is no doubt they were coveted by each chorus member who recognized the value of having even a minute of featured stage time.[49]

The reason that the Cinderella tale of the backstage musical—the chorus girl who finds fame and fortune—was used in so many pulp, novel, and film plots is that, quite simply, it actually happened. All it took were two people being in the right place at the right time for the moment to strike, and there is no doubt this was the secret hope of every young man and woman who trod the boards. As with Lois Josephine's tale of catching a manager's eye, the vast majority of rags-to-riches stories involve leaping from one stage role to the next, from taking the place of an ailing established star to being noticed for one's own skills. Marie Cahill and Eva Tanguay started out their careers in the chorus and so did Sallie Fisher, who starred in numerous operettas and musical comedies from 1900 to the 1920s, most notably in Berlin's *Watch Your Step* (1914). Fisher described her beginnings as a disaster: "I was probably the most awkward chorus girl in the world, and the worst."[50] In *The Passing Show*, many women found expanded stage time and featured roles for years after serving faithfully in the chorus. Helen Carrington, for example, was a chorus girl in the 1914 and 1915 editions, but after she sang "I'm Forever Blowing Bubbles" in the 1918 show, she was given more substantial parts, eventually becoming a successful character actress into the 1930s. She told one reporter "the life of a show girl is no pipe. I began my career at a salary of $25 per week. I wore out thirteen pairs of dancing pumps during my first season as a chorus girl, and at the end of the year found out that instead of saving money, I was $5 in debt to the management for those necessary articles."[51] Despite the difficulties, however, Carrington survived and became well-known. She even recreated her stage role for the movie version of *Queen High* (show, 1926; film, 1930).

For many, the chance to make the move to motion pictures would change their careers forever. Little did the chorus girls of the early 1920s know that sound films were just around the corner and that musical movies would be some of the first huge hits. But even in 1912, there was speculation that film was going to offer young women new opportunities. Bessie Shannon, a chorus member in *The Passing Show* of that year (and later), treated her fellow choristers—mostly women, but "with a chorus man seated here and there"—to a showing of one of her movies on a screen in the Winter Garden late one night.[52] Although "the management" was credited with offering the event as a "class," it is also noted that the moment was merely "a lark." With composer "Lou" Hirsch at the piano accompanying the movie, "the girls seemed astonished with the success achieved by their comrade and applauded her frequently. She was greeted with a hearty laugh when, in the picture, a dog in showing its great affection kissed her." The article about the event in the *New York Press* made it clear that movies were not for great stage presences, but only "for those who ability just falls short of a speaking part."

If film was seen as a benign competitor at this early stage, in only a few years the Shuberts knew that losing girls to the movie industry was a real possibility. In a letter to Gilman Haskell, the manager for *The Passing Show of 1915* tour, J. J. advised great care when reaching Los Angeles: "Out on the coast the moving picture people get crazy and make outlandish offers to our people and you must keep them in line and watch everything they do."[53] Shubert was right to be worried, and the chorus members probably tried to evade Haskell as much as possible. In fact, the emergence of the West Coast–based film industry coincided almost exactly with the Shuberts' revues at the Winter Garden, with the first movies in southern California appearing in 1910. Over the following three years, over seventeen film studios set up shop, and the location of Hollywood, California, quickly became synonymous with moviemaking, which, before that time, had taken place mostly in New York. However active the film representatives were in luring performers away from touring shows, they were even more aggressive in watching the Great White Way for new talent.

One of the classic examples of a chorus girl turned movie star was Nita Naldi, whose first large-scale revue was *The Passing Show of 1918*. Naldi was listed as a show girl in the program, probably because of her height, and she made a distinct impression. According to a 1941 interview given to the *New York Sun*, Naldi credited E. R. Simmons with encouraging and promoting her.[54] "He took a great fancy to me . . . He always wanted to dress me in black tights, and he did," she explained. Morris Gest saw her at the Winter Garden and hired her for the Century Midnight Show, where she was in turn spotted by John Barrymore and a director, John Robertson. The article continued: "Both Johns wrote her long, insistent letters urging her to quit the show and join the cast of a picture called 'Dr. Jekyll and Mr. Hyde' . . . Naldi thought they were kidding her, until, one evening, she received a visit in her dressing room from Josephine Lovett [the script writer for the movie] . . . She was tested for the part of the villainous dancer and engaged." Naldi's dark complexion and mysterious eyes made her one of the most infamous "vamps" of the 1920s, so it is not surprising that she would have been one of the Alluring Vampire Girls during the song "My Vampire Girl." And her memories of Simmons's efforts were accurate, even a quarter-century later; she was wearing a black velvet dress, a cerise fan and headdress, black stockings, and black shoes with red heels.[55] Additionally, she was cast as "Halloween" in the "Holiday Girl" sequence, with a costume designed by Cora MacGeachy (see Figure 4.8).

The most famous of all movie stars to rise from the ranks of the chorus was Joan Crawford, who made her stage debut as a chorus girl in *The Passing Show of 1924* as

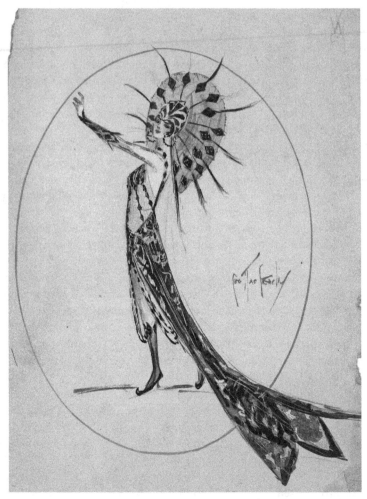

Fig. 4.8. Nita Naldi's "Halloween Girl" costume, The Passing Show of 1918. *Shubert Archive.*

"Lucille LeSeuer." After dancing in several shows throughout the Midwest, she was spotted by J. J. Shubert in Detroit. He offered her a spot in the chorus of *Innocent Eyes*, the Winter Garden revue for the spring. As was customary, some of the chorus (including LeSeuer) stayed in New York and continued with the summer production. Crawford's comments on chorus life suggest that the Stage Door Johnnies could, at times, be amusing; "Dancing was the main thing. And I dated. I'd learned . . . you couldn't take those dates seriously because the men were just out of college or married or engaged, and having a fling with a chorus girl was the 'in' thing. But those 'Johnnies' treated us to some damn good times."[56] In *The Passing Show,* she performed in the generic line of girls (neither "show girl" nor "little girl"), participating in "The Beaded Bag" number, where women danced around a giant purse (see Figure 4.9), and the "Gold, Silver, and Green" sequence, where, as mentioned earlier, she wore one of the oversized money costumes. It was on the Winter Garden stage that M-G-M producer Harry Rapf saw her perform and invited Le Seuer and some of her fellow chorus-mates to take a screen test. Crawford publicly recognized the role her chorus days had played in providing new opportunities for her career; in a syndicated article called "How I Broke into the Movies," she wrote, "Little did I suspect that I was to dance myself right out of this show and into the movies. But that's exactly what happened."[57] Nancy Carroll (who had been a chorus member in the 1923 edition and became a movie and stage star) was one of many other women who found a lesser, but not insubstantial, degree of fame through the same process. And finally, there was the rather unusual case of starlet Beatrice De Roe, a movie actress who sometimes welcomed the chance to appear in the chorus, this time in *The Passing Show of 1918*.[58]

As dramatically depicted in Stephen Sondheim's *Follies*, marriage was another possible outcome for some women. In most cases, both male and female chorus members were young and single, and this is the way producers wanted to keep things. In many of the letters from tour managers back to J. J. in New York, disparaging comments are made about stars and "hitched" choristers who try to bring their spouses on the trip, especially concerning the difficulties of trying to accommodate the couples on rail cars. For most chorus men and women, marriage signaled the end of one person's time onstage, and more than likely it was the woman who "retired" from theatrical life. This did not always happen; Fred Allen's marriage to

Fig. 4.9. Joan Crawford in the "Beaded Bag" number (seventh from right),
The Passing Show *of 1924. Photo courtesy of Grapefruit Moon Gallery.*

Downpour of Talent, Niagara of Beauty: Chorus Girls and Boys | 109

Portland Hoffa was not the end of either performer's careers. But, more than likely, a married chorus woman would not return to the Winter Garden. When asked "What becomes of the chorus girl?" actor and producer Lew Fields replied, "Well, the dear girls get married."[59] He continued, "Everybody wants one. And what will hardly be denied, they make good wives!" Fields felt that the work ethic of chorus women was of such high caliber that they were sought after by everyone and were appreciated by both their husbands and their children. Unfortunately, Fields also perpetuated the mythical notion that "nine times out of ten . . . she is the wife of some sickeningly rich old codger or the admired helpmeet of some silken son of dalliance." But, like so many scraps of showbiz lore, there were several examples of girls marrying well. For example, when nineteen-year-old Anne Dunning (from *The Passing Show of 1918* tour) was wed, the announcement of her ceremony to Dr. Joseph E. Wilson was celebrated in the society pages.[60] The difficulty of tracking chorus girls' lives after marriage is due to changing names; most women took their husband's surname, but even more difficult to track was the fact that many girls used stage names in the first place. In a now-lost booklet written in 1924 entitled *Little Feet Which Have Trod the Runway*, Harold Atteridge chronicled the life of every chorus girl who had been at the Winter Garden since it opened, demonstrating that "half of them married or retired and that the other half . . . remained on the stage to become principals or stars."[61] Although the percentages listed are exaggerated in regards to stardom, there was no denying that matrimony was the most likely life choice for most chorus women in *The Passing Shows*.

Other than appearing onstage, chorus girls were used by the Shuberts to create a sensation, drum up business for the shows they starred in, participate in benefits, or act as the subject of a theatrical "brief" involving an interesting event they attended. For example, when *The Passing Show of 1922* played in New York, the chorus girls made a Thanksgiving Day meal for the "twelve wardrobe women" of the show.[62] Another interesting snippet about their activities was the swimming contest held between the chorus girls of *The Passing Show of 1916* and Lew Fields's *Step This Way*; the Winter Garden's Peggy Smith won the competition, which was held at Coney Island.[63] When the Shuberts wanted to create some buzz concerning their revues, stories like these would be released by press agents and sent along to newspapers to keep the shows active in the media. When a fire broke out in the offices of the Shubert-Colonial Theater in Cleveland and firemen rushed in and up the stairs, a story about the chorus girls performing "I'm Forever Blowing Bubbles" to placate the "restless" audience was circulated.[64] One chorus girl story that was hyped repeatedly involved the number, "Camp's Daily Dozen," from *The Passing Show of 1922*. Walter Camp, an athletic authority and the "Father of American Football," devised a set of twelve exercises for the US military in 1918 and the drills proved so popular that they became a part of larger American culture.[65] For the revue, a scene in an athletic camp was created to show the girls (in swimsuits, naturally) going through these exercises to the accompaniment of Alfred Goodman's music. Several articles concerning the necessity for fitness among young women stemmed from the inclusion of the scene, including a report that J. C. Huffman declared that all Shubert choruses across the country would do the "Daily Dozen" four times a week for necessary health.[66] The Shuberts found many ways to use the number to their advantage, including sending the "sixty athletic beauties" downtown to Madison Square Garden to perform for the National Physical Culture Exhibition.[67]

During World War I, chorus girls were deployed numerous times to sell tickets for shows that benefitted various soldier-related organizations. One of the most spectacular of these events took place during the summer of 1916, before America's official entry into the war, when the United States was facing a possible altercation with a German-cajoled Mexico. Chorus girls from three different shows—*The Passing Show of 1916*, *Very Good Eddie*, and *Step This Way*—joined forces to sell tickets to an exhibition at the Sheepshead Bay Speedway that would benefit families of the National Guardsmen who were serving at the border.[68] Two hundred girls flooded Wall Street selling the tickets throughout the afternoon, despite rainy conditions. Organized by Grace Vanderbilt, wife of Cornelius Vanderbilt, the groups rode in "six motor busses and five touring cars," and the group collected thousands of dollars. "They were all young and pretty," reported the *Binghamton Press*, "and the tickets went like Steel Preferred on a rising market." (See ▶Figure 4.10).[69]

It is important to address the serious claims concerning the Shuberts—most especially J. J.—and their abuse of the girls. At least one source has made claims that J. J. Shubert physically beat women on a regular basis, with Lee Davis calling the producer's behavior "monstrous."[70] One story used to support this assertion is that of Peggy Forbes, who was beaten when she argued with Shubert over being fired from the chorus. Davis recounts "two roundhouse punches that left her with a black eye," finishing his tale with a note that the suit was settled out of court. Forbes, whose real name was Marie Barnet, did make this claim, but Shubert countered that the entire affair was backed by the *Evening Telegraph* as blackmail.[71] No trial ever occurred, and no follow-up story was ever printed. Of Helen White, the other woman mentioned by Davis as being attacked by J. J., the only record of her is as the chorus member from the touring production of *From Broadway to Paris* (1912) who organized a strike against a reduction in pay while in Boston.[72] No mention of an attack is reported. Whatever the truth of these events, it is unlikely that any of the production staff could have repeatedly abused the people they worked with and not been held accountable, especially by performers who wrote about them after they had died. Neither Fred Astaire nor Fred Allen, both of whom devote lengthy descriptions in their memoirs of their experiences with *The Passing Show* (see chapter 2), describe the type of hostile environment Davis depicts. Letters sent to the producers while performers were on tour are almost entirely about the working conditions that people were unhappy with. These complaints involved a high degree of detail, demonstrating that most performers, male *and* female, were extremely sensitive concerning their treatment and did not hesitate to voice those concerns.[73] Although one cannot say with certainty whether or not Forbes was beaten, there is no evidence to demonstrate that Shubert participated in this behavior on a regular basis, if at all. In fact, I believe the remarkable lack of evidence supporting any ongoing legal battles suggests that J. J. Shubert was neither violent nor abusive. As Mason stated in regard to the myth of the promiscuous chorus girl, it just would not have been "good business."[74]

With such a plethora of stories about chorus girls in the press, one has to choose a point to stop relating their tales or become overladen with anecdotes. The opposite is true for the men of the chorus. Chorus boys, it seems, were a necessary part of the revue if only to provide more complete vocal ranges during production numbers and to give the girls someone to dance with. No lengthy explanations of hiring male chorus members appear in the newspapers, and very few (if any) descriptions of their skills as entertainers are included in reviews. Remarkably, there are even few mentions of these young men in the personal correspondence between the Shuberts and their shows' managers. What made these gentlemen virtually invisible to the world in which they worked?

Part of the answer is simply a matter of numbers. The average number of men in *The Passing Shows* was twelve, with a reduction to eight for the tours. This meant that far fewer men were part of the revue and they were certainly overshadowed by the quantity of women. They were also used less frequently onstage, rarely appearing as a complete group. For example, during *The Passing Show of 1918*, there are sixteen numbers that feature eight or more chorus girls. Of those, only seven include chorus men, with just six male dancers used for the "Minuet" in act 2. The full complement of chorus boys is used only twice—once during the opening hotel scene and once during the finale, set in Spain and pairing twelve male and female choristers together as dancers. Even when the men did appear, they were almost always clad in tuxedos, which was the same choice of menswear for the male stars in most of the scenes. Atteridge's scripts regularly call for people to perform small roles, much like the bit parts that June Elvidge played, and these were doled out to the boys to keep the show moving. Often, these transitional comments prepare other actors or ensembles for their entrances. Thus, the small numbers of men were not made to stand out either in terms of performance or visual presentation. It is not surprising so few people noticed these entertainers—they were not *meant* to be noticed. In fact, one contemporary author referred to them as "prop[s]" and "costumed furniture with nimble feet and legs."[75]

It is rare that the media paid these actors any attention either. Despite numerous stories surrounding Wayburn's audition for women of *The Passing Show of 1913*, only one article indicates that men had also come to the doors of the Winter Garden for an audition.[76] The only significant attention for the boys came during World War I, when most of the chorus men were sent to Europe. At first, this was not to fight, but to replace the English chorus boys who were currently in the trenches. Madame Critic related information from the Shubert pressmen that "the American chorus 'boy' is the hero of the moment," and that the choristers from *The Passing Show of 1915* "will leave at once on an American Line Boat."[77] The gumption of these young men surprised Schrader, who "should never have suspected the modest chorus boy of stepping forward in such a dire emergency." She told chorus girls that they would have to get along without the boys who held their bouquets and knelt with footstools, wishing the men a "voyage safe from submarines and a visit free from unfriendly Zeppelins." Little did she or the travelers know that over the next year, the Preparedness movement would grow alongside American troop numbers, and by the following year, hundreds of thousands of men would also be making a transatlantic journey. As these numbers swelled, the number of eligible chorus men in the

United States dwindled, and after war was declared in April 1917, theater managers glumly told *Variety* that "most of the men now marching time to stage airs are unmarried and eligible for service."[78] Ziegfeld decreed that he would use no boys at all in the *Follies of 1917*, and—for those who still had men as a part of their casts— explanations were printed in programs as to why these men were not serving.[79] The usual reason was that the men in question were not accepted by the military or that they were simply too young.

Soon after the end of hostilities, revues began to find ways around using chorus boys altogether. Producer Charles Dillingham was among the first to replace the line of men with "a dozen of Amazonian beauties who will probably satisfy the audience as well as would an equal number of male help."[80] The following year, the Shuberts declared that they, too, would be removing the chorus boys from their planned (and dropped) 1920 edition, with the headline reading "Shuberts Shock B'way and Bar Chorus Boys: Say 'Passing Show of 1920' Will Be Pure."[81] The article claimed "the technical staff . . . are glad of the passing of the chorus man. This is probably because of the frequent kidding reference to the species on other stages. According to J. C. Huffman, 'the chorus man belongs to the dark day . . . before the 1,000 watt lamp.'" One can imagine the depressing state this trend would have created for men returning home from the war, especially following the long periods of convalescence necessary after suffering in the trenches. Huffman added, "While the stage loses its chorus men, it gains in dramatic expression."[82] Gordon Whyte, the main Broadway writer for *Billboard*, offered a rebuttal, pointing out that the chorus boy's function in musical productions was not insubstantial: "Goodness knows the chorus boy has had few defenders in his time," wrote Whyte, "but this is a little bit too thick." Offering works by Gilbert and Sullivan, Victor Herbert, and Reginald De Koven as examples, Whyte suggested "anyone who has heard these 'dark day' operas would smash a lamp to hear them . . . well sung." Whyte used Douglas Fairbanks as an example that serving as a chorus man was akin to an apprenticeship that paved the way for more substantial roles. Despite the thoughtful comments by Whyte, *The Passing Show of 1921* followed through with the threat, and for the remainder of the revue series, chorus boys were eliminated from the roster entirely.[83]

Whyte was not inaccurate in considering the operetta a key place for chorus men to shine. As the large-scale revue began to falter near the middle of the 1920s, both Romberg and Rudolf Friml had major hits with shows such as *The Student Prince* (1924), *Rose-Marie* (1924), and *The Desert Song* (1926). Once again, the chorus man was needed, but in this incarnation, a strong voice was more important than the ability to dance. In a remarkable article in the *New York Times* entitled "Concerning the Return of the Chorus Man," the emphasis for the return was that the artistic integrity of the drama was served by the men onstage, who had a *reason* to be there.[84] This return to operetta "ha[s] revived the days when chorus men, as well as women, did more than make faces and shake their underpinnings at audiences." The old style of man "was dispensed with entirely:"

The point was reached where the chorus man market slumped to zero. The type became almost extinct, so far as visual appearance was concerned. It wasn't even to be found in the storehouse—it wasn't worth preserving, even as a relic . . . The men now sought are not the mere bipeds which musical comedy audiences have been accustomed to see. They are super-chorus men. Not only must they have trained voices of power and lyric quality and know how to use them but they must have at least the foundation on which stage manners can be built. Here has been the chief difficulty—to find a combination of adequate vocal proficiency present-able figure, and easy, finished bearing.

The Shuberts, who had employed so many men over the years in their *Passing Shows*, turned to operetta and to female-exclusive choruses in smaller-scale revues such as *Artists and Models*. The dapper tails-wearing, cane-wielding male chorus member was not a staple of the 1920s stage, as he frequently is depicted in histori-cal fiction, but instead was a citizen of the teens who was out of job in the new decade.

One cannot help but wonder at the terminology deployed in each of these dis-cussions of the chorus boy of the early twentieth century. Folded in between lay-ers of text are the unspoken, hinted-at, and elusive meanings that characterize the discourse surrounding chorus boys. Why were there "kidding references" on other stages? Why were there "few defenders" for chorus men? Dancing was one cen-tral complaint about these performers, but so was the vocal style they used, which emphasized a melodic line that made use of an unremarkable range and was often syncopated or a ballad. The physical fragility of these boys, at least according to the *Times* author, matched the weak voices they possessed, placed in juxtaposition with the virtuosic male voices (which one might call "audible heterosexuality") and solid physiques of the super (read "straight") men who participated in operettas. The sad truth is that all of this discourse was clearly a complaint about the homosexuals who played the majority of the parts, using oblique language and artistic judgment to justify an overall dislike for the aesthetic and (as is often common in this era) for the people themselves. One of the few overt discussions of this issue can be found in composer Johnny Mercer's unpublished autobiography, which is quoted at length by his biographer, Gene Lees. Mercer's experience during the end of the teens provides some insight into the rhetoric:

> Almost all the small parts [in the drama he had been chosen for], which would have gone to chorus boys had it been a musical, were filled with homosexuals. They had, like all good fairies, their water wings on at all times and it was a foot-race to get back to the dressing room or pass them in the halls without being handled. But I had been to a boy's prep school, so I knew how to dodge, and how to take the advances in the manner they were presented—lightly and casually, that is—and not act as if I were insulted.[85]

Although there is a certain amount of disdain in Mercer's comments, there is noth-ing of the simmering hostility that was certainly present in the larger society. Of course, just because some chorus men were homosexual, not all of them were. Loy Vannatter, a young singer auditioning for the touring revival of *Blossom Time* in 1938, described a meeting with E. R. Simmons where the Shubert employee "rubbed his hand over [his] rear-end" after he sang.[86] Simmons must have expected that some young men would have been receptive to such advances. Nonetheless, this provides a historical backdrop for discussions on queer representation that authors focus on in later eras.[87] It also is a topic that deserves more attention, especially in relationship to the girls who were performing alongside the chorus boys. The later careers of these men also remain a mystery, with most of the members dropping out of show business as the jobs disappeared.

The remarkable experiences of the women and men who played their parts in the chorus would become legendary near the end of the twentieth century, in large part because of fictional representations of them. But rather than myths that provided foundations for characters in movies or television shows, these people were real and basked in the glow of the footlights, singing and dancing for audiences that continued to support this style of revue for over two decades. And what those audiences saw (and heard) kept them coming back for more.

NOTES

1. Letter from F. P. Wilstack, agent, to J. J. Shubert, October 21, 1914, Shubert Archive, correspondence, box 1168.

2. This highlight of *The Passing Show of 1914* was used for the advertisement shown in Figure 6.4. This dance is probably the model for the vertical dance sequence in the movie *The Show of Shows* (1929).

3. See Kellee Van Aken, "Race and Gender in the Broadway Chorus" (Ph. D. diss., University of Pittsburgh, 2006); also Linda Mizejewski, *Ziegfeld Girl: Image and Icon in Culture and Cinema* (Durham, NC: Duke University Press, 1999). The term "Tired Businessman" was widely used in magazines such as *Variety* during the 1910s and 1920s to describe men who attended the theatre specifically to see the young women on display.

4. "Home Towns of Chorus Girls," *New York Sun*, February 1, 1920, 9.

5. The countries less associated with the culture of musical theater, such as India, Canada, Switzerland, and Romania, were still places where American and British touring companies would take their shows. The history of international touring companies (especially in non-English speaking countries) awaits an ambitious and dedicated scholar to tell its tale.

6. "Best Cure for Stagestruck Is the Stage and Lots of It," *New York Press*, September 14, 1913, 6.

7. "Only 37 Girl Firsts in 3,000 at Winter Garden," *New York Press*, June 10, 1913, 12.

8. "Attention Girls! The Shubert "Dimple Department" Is Laying in Its Fall Stock of Beauty," *New York Press*, June 22, 1913, 3.

9. Ibid.

10. Harold E. Stearns, "Small Chorus Girls Most Popular, Declares Shubert Stage Director, Who Is an Expert in Selecting Them," *New York Press*, May 17, 1914, 2. The paper explains that Mason could be seen performing regularly at the Shubert-owned Folies Marigny, which was a cabaret in New York fashioned after the Parisian theater of the same name. The location did not open until 11 p.m., according to the February–May issue of *Munsey's Magazine*.

11. "Attention Girls!," 3.

12. Harris, *The Other Marilyn*, 32–34 (chap. 2, n. 30). Harris discusses issues that the Five Colombians had with child labor laws, including times when the family was fined for overworking children. Miller's contract issue is covered in chapter 8.

13. Memos and Correspondence, E. R. Simmons Papers, *Passing Show of 1918* file, costume list, July 7, 1918, Shubert Archive. There is a tremendous mound of materials produced for and by Simmons at the Shubert Archive, and only a small portion of the documents have been studied. Simmons's career and activities would make for a fascinating monograph.

14. "'Squab Farm' Amusing Play of the 'Movies,'" *New York Clipper*, March 20, 1918, 10.

15. For more on Dorgan, see Leonard Zwilling, *A TAD Lexicon: Etymology and Linguistic Principles*, vol. 3. (Rolla, MO: G. Cohen, 1993).

16. Allen, *Much Ado About Me*, 269 (see chap. 2, n. 42).

17. Ibid.

18. Notes written by Simmons are scattered throughout the Shubert Archive, and can be found in general correspondence papers, specific show files, and also in a group of papers filed under his name.

19. See J. J. Shubert's notes for the show from July 16, 1924, Shubert Archive, box 96, package 5.

20. The choral arrangement for "Baby," from *The Passing Show of 1921*, is written for just the women, whereas the published Schirmer score for *The Passing Show of 1915* frequently uses SATB. For the former document, see Shubert Archive, box 93, package 2. "Royal Wedding" can be found among the piano parts of *The Passing Show of 1923* materials, Shubert Archive, box 95, package 4.

21. "Bathing Beauty Joins 'The Passing Show,'" *Brooklyn Daily Eagle*, July 8, 1923, E7.

22. The opening shots of the "Loveland" sequence from Ziegfeld's movie, *Glorifying the American Girl* (1929), provide a glimpse as to how this type of event was experienced by an audience. The curtain would open with the entire company in place while music played (possibly accompanied by a singer or singers who are unseen); the audience would be able to view the static figures for a period of time, and then the music would end and the curtain would close. The purpose of the event is to be able to take in the full scene, especially noting the bodies of the chorus members as well as their elaborate costumes.

23. Chache et al., *The Shuberts Present*, Shubert Archive, 268. The runway was taken from a Kabuki-styled runway in Max Reinhardt's *Sumurun* (1912). The nickname is a reference to the "Bridge of Sighs" in Venice.

24. J. C. G., "'Sumurun at the Casino, Enchanting Pantomime," *New York Press*, January 17, 1912, 12.

25. Advertisement for *The Passing Show of 1915*, *Buffalo Courier*, April 2, 1916, 50.

26. The only exception to this proximity concerning Ziegfeld was that during the *Midnight Frolic*, which took place on the New Amsterdam Roof Garden, women would walk through the audience. However, being below a chorus girl was not the same as being next to her.

27. W. E. M., "'Passing Show' Is Among The Best." *Baltimore News*, April 29, 1913.

28. Marie B. Schrader, "Madame Critic," *New York Dramatic Mirror*, July 7, 1915, 4.

29. Channing Pollock, "When Lovely Women Stoop to Follies," *Green Book Magazine*, July 1914, 325.

30. E. P. Thayer, "In Buffalo," *Variety*, May 16, 1913, 30.

31. "Big Stars Missing in 'Passing Show' Spectacle," *Buffalo Evening News*, October 24, 1916, 17. "Censure Teck for Performing 'Passing Show'," *Buffalo Evening News*, October 30, 1916, 8. "'Passing Show' Menace to Morals of Buffalo," *Buffalo Evening News*, October 1916, 13.

32. "Masks and Faces: Unobscured Femininity Now All the Rage in Theatricals," *National Police Gazette*, July 14, 1894. The author continues with a well-written description of the event and its probable trajectory: "He clothes them from their waist to their feet in tights that are made so that the dancers appear to be wearing black silk stockings ending near the knee. Above these stockings you seem to behold the natural woman, shining luminously through brief, transparent skirts. The ladies dance vigorously, and as they whirl before the eye the inevitable impression is that they have all left an important garment in their dressing-rooms. I am rather curious to know just where this stage business is going to end. It shall be interesting to make the acquaintance of a manager who shall out-Hammerstein Hammerstein, and to see what the authorities will do when four Phyrnettes attempt to dance on the stage in black silk stockings and earrings. I am bound to say that we seem to be reaching rapidly towards a glittering climax."

33. An excellent source for the conditions of everyday life for the women in entertainment can be found in Sandra E. Adickes, *To Be Young Was Very Heaven: Women in New York before the First World War* (New York: Palgrave Macmillan, 2000).

34. "Big Drug Raid on Chorus Girl's Tip," New York Press, July 28, 1915, 12.

35. "Look Out for Skop," *Billboard*, April 18, 1914, 12.

36. Unsigned letter, May 17, 1918, Shubert Archive, *The Passing Show of 1918* show file. For the article the writer included in her letter, see "Midnight Frolic Girl Is Arrested for Shoplifting," *New York Review*, February 2, 1918, 1.

37. Harold E. Stearns, "Small Chorus Girls Most Popular," 2.

38. Marie B. Schrader, "Madame Critic," 4.

39. "Chorus Girls of 'Passing Show of 1912' Organize to Preserve Their Rights," *Buffalo Courier*, October 5, 1913, 49.

40. "Chorus Girl's Union," *New York Dramatic Mirror*, May 28, 19132, 13.

41. Alfred Harding, *The Revolt of the Actors* (New York: William Morrow & Company, 1929).

42. Ibid., 97.

43. Monica Eugenia Stufft, "Chorus Girl Collective: Twentieth Century American Performance Communities and Urban Networking" (Ph.D. diss., University of California, Berkeley, 2008).

44. Arnold, *Deep in My Heart*, 213–14 (see chap. 1, n. 36).

45. That is, of course, as long as some of the name changes are for some of the same people. The changes are slight, but the touring production probably got the names correct after they were misspelled on the Broadway program. The changed names are as follows: Vivian Gardon to Vivian Gordon, Edward Gardon to Edward Gordon, and Mae Tarmey to Mae Tormey.

46. The need for detailed descriptions of tours is evident from the research I have completed with this show. With only a brief perusal of the items at the Shubert Archive, it is clear that songs were changed, some of the dialogue was different, and even some of the roles were modified between the Broadway *Passing Show* and its touring production. The enormous number of towns that the show visited had a profound impact on audiences around the country, and so the numerous questions about what happened to a revue when

it became mobile are certainly important. One excellent model for this is bruce d. mcclung's *Lady in the Dark: Biography of a Musical* (New York: Oxford University Press, 2007). In chapt. 6, mcclung details the myriad changes that were made in the musical over time.

47. The character of Kitty MacKay is a reference to a play of the same name; the reference is discussed in more depth in chapt. 6.

48. See the Boston Program for Shubert Theater during the week of November 23, 1914, Shubert Archive.

49. It was also the case that some could be appointed as understudies and prepared to take one or several of the principal parts when changes were made. Emily Miles took on this position during *The Passing Show of 1917*, mainly as the understudy for Irene Franklin, and she was given better parts as a result in later editions.

50. Sallie Fisher, "Lessons You Learn in the Chorus," *Green Book Magazine*, April 1915, 747.

51. "At the Temple, Fairport," Herald-Mail, November 20, 1930, 5.

52. "Future for Chorus Girls in Front of the Camera," *New York Press*, August 10, 1912, 5. Bessie Shannon may have used another name for the movies, as I have been unable to find her listed in any film-related articles outside of this.

53. Letter from J. J. Shubert to Gilman Haskell, April 29, 1916, Shubert Archive, *The Passing Show of 1915* tour, general correspondence folder 1540.

54. Malcolm Johnson, "Nita Naldi, Now at the Diamond Horseshoe, Recalls Her Life as a Film Vamp," *New York Sun*, June 6, 1941, 25.

55. Memos and correspondence, E. R. Simmons Papers, Shubert Archive, *The Passing Show of 1918* file, costume list, July 7, 1918.

56. Quoted in Donald Spoto, *Possessed: The Life of Joan Crawford* (New York: Harper Collins, 2010), 29–30.

57. Joan Crawford, "How I Broke into the Movies," *Clyde Herald*, March 29, 1933, 3.

58. "Movie Star for Passing Show," *Billboard*, July 13, 1918, 5.

59. "What Becomes of the Chorus Girl?" *New York Sun*, July 2, 1916, 2.

60. "Actress Physician's Bride," *New York Sun and Herald*, April 14, 1920, 5. Her sister, Lillian, who is mentioned in the article, stayed with the production after Anne (listed as "Anna" in the program) left in Montreal.

61. "Shuberts Bring Back the Runway," *New York Sun*, August 28, 1924, 10.

62. Gordon Whyte, "Musical Comedy Notes," *Billboard*, December 9, 1922, 31.

63. "Mrs. Dillingham's Hat Wins," *New York Dramatic Mirror*, August 5, 1916, 11.

64. "Chorus Girls Prevent Panic," *Billboard*, December 13, 1919, 26.

65. The exercises are described in detail in "A Daily Dozen Set-Up," *Outing*, November 1918, 98.

66. "New Plays: Gossip of Stageland," *New York Evening Telegram*, October 13, 1922, 9.

67. "New Plays: Gossip of Stageland," *New York Evening Telegram*, October 16, 1922, 11.

68. "200 Chorus Girls Aid Militiamen's Benefit," *New York Sun*, July 27, 1916, 3.

69. "Show Girls Help Soldiers' Fund," *Binghamton Press*, July 28, 1916, 1.

70. Lee Davis, *Scandals and Follies*, 116 (chap. 1, n. 14). Foster Hirsch also recounts this tale in *The Boys from Syracuse*, 109 (chap. 1, n. 2).

71. See "Punched, She Says," *Syracuse Herald*, April 11, 1911, 9; and "Jacob J. Shubert Held on Girl's Charge," *Evening Telegram*, May 3, 1911, 8. Davis incorrectly gives the year as 1913.

72. "Chorus Girls Strike," *Billboard*, November 16, 1912, 6.

73. An excellent example is that of the dance team of Adelaide and Hughes. Adelaide is frequently mentioned in Henry Lehmann's letters, requesting special dressing rooms or specific clothing. Her letters to Shubert indicate the same degree of specificity regarding unusual treatment. See general correspondence, Shubert Archive, folder 1020.

74. I want to clarify, however, that anything is possible, but I believe it would require evidence to indicate that events such as these took place. The testimony of many of the interviewees in Foster Hirsch's *The Boys from Syracuse* indicate that J. J. Shubert was a bully, and there is even a statement from his son John about J. J. being a notoriously violent person. The lack of charges against the Shuberts after Equity is founded in 1919, and the lack of evidence in the Shubert Archive suggests that these assertions may have been more fiction than fact. The casual observer might suggest that it was not in the Shuberts' best interests to keep documents that portrayed them in a negative light, but that observer would be truly surprised at the vast number of items that remain, including a wealth of negative letters and memos. If frequent beatings, accompanied by complaints, had happened, there is a high probability they would still be among the documents.

75. "Concerning the Return of the Chorus Man," *New York Times*, May 10, 1925, 2.

76. "All in Short Skirts, Some Bathing Suits," *New York Press*, June 13, 1913, 8.

77. Marie B. Schrader, "Madame Critic," *New York Dramatic Mirror*, July 14, 1915, 4.

78. "Conscription Sure to Draw Stage Men in Army Service," *Variety*, May 4, 1917, 4.

79. "The Passing Show," *Syracuse Herald*, October 23, 1917, 8.

80. "Chorus Men a Minus Quantity in New Dillingham Show," *New York Dramatic Mirror*, August 24, 1918, 264.

81. "Shuberts Shock B'way and Bar Chorus Boys," *Variety*, December 17, 1920, 15.

82. Gordon Whyte, "The Chorus Man Should Be Given a Chance," *Billboard*, December 25, 1920, 26.

83. Although the *Follies* programs do not include full lists of chorus personnel—no full list of women or men is provided—it seems Ziegfeld upheld his earlier decision and cut these parts.

84. "Concerning the Return of the Chorus Man," 2.

85. Johnny Mercer, quoted in Gene Lees, *Portrait of Johnny: The Life of John Herndon Mercer* (Milwaukee, WI: Hal Leonard, 2004), 55.

86. Loy Vannatter, *And Then It Was Winter*, vol. 2 (Tucson, AZ: Wheatmark, 2010), 27–28.

87. See John M. Clum, *Something for the Boys: Musical Theater and Gay Culture* (New York: Palgrave, 1999) and David Haldane Lawrence, "Chorus Boys: Words, Music, and Queerness (c.1900–c.1936)" *Studies in Musical Theatre*, 3(2), 157–69 for well thought-out discussions of these topics. The statements I present here show that Clum's insightful remarks about chorus men in later decades had even earlier historical roots.

5

THE MASTODON OF MUSICAL EXTRAVAGANZA

• • •

SONG, DANCE, AND SCENIC EFFECTS

The creative team for *The Passing Shows* worked diligently to provide high-quality revue content for both the first-rate stars and the impressive chorus members. The sonic and visual components were among the many reasons the shows were so successful, and (despite claims to the contrary) the Shuberts filled their productions with good material, hiring composers, dancers, and designers that would generate the requisite theatrical thrills.[1] Each new edition required fresh acts that would bring people back to the show, sometimes following already established trends, but frequently introducing audiences to something entirely new. *The Passing Shows* were engineered to move through this content with remarkable speed, parading a dizzying array of entertainments before audiences.

As discussed earlier, Atteridge and his team only had a few short weeks to piece together each show, selecting the numbers and sketches that would eventually be assembled into a complete revue. This process of working and reworking material had to be precise if the enormous revue was to unfold smoothly, and in many cases, awareness of a performer's capabilities was a central part of the decision-making process. When choosing what worked best for a particular performer, everyone on the team had to be ready to tailor parts for that star. For example, when Bernard Granville was engaged for *The Passing Show of 1914*, his talents influenced choices made by the team; he had a powerful tenor voice, he was charismatic and funny, and he was also an excellent dancer, with a "specialty" eccentric dance that gave him the appearance of performing while inebriated. Sigmund Romberg wrote the "Grape Dance" for this last number, and Granville performed four other times during the revue, for the songs "Omar Khayyam," "You're Just a Little Bit Better (Than the One I Thought Was Best)," "Eagle Rock," and "Good Old Levee Days." Of these, only the first tune was written by Romberg (who penned most of the score), while the latter three were composed by Harry Carroll; Atteridge provided the lyrics for all the songs. "You're Just a Little Bit Better" was a duet with José Collins while the "Eagle Rock" was performed alongside Ethel Kelly, and both numbers included a dance that followed the song. "Levee Days" used a quartet of singers (Granville, Marilynn Miller, Ethel Kelly, and Lew Brice) and also had a large dance component. "Omar Khayyam" was engineered to be the hit of the show, and since Granville portrayed the character, it was probably his most important song to learn; the tune was also Granville's only solo number.[2] Additionally, of the whole cast, only George W. Monroe had more spoken lines. This ubiquitous placement in the revue required that Granville be the most versatile male performer in that year's edition. The shared compositional duties between Carroll and Romberg and the significant spoken material and lyrics by Atteridge demonstrate just how attuned the creative team was to Granville's abilities. In writing tunes for Granville, the team had to understand his capabilities while, at the same time, producing songs that the public would enjoy.

When approaching the music from any of *The Passing Shows*, it is essential to remember just how active every member of the team was in creating the final product. There is a strong tendency to see musical theater through the lens of classical music or film, assigning a single author (or *auteur*) the role of creator. But numerous studies reveal how untrue this is for many pieces of musical theater, showing that different people were responsible for building the musical framework. The contributions Richard Rodgers received from rehearsal pianist Trude Rittman, and Sondheim's close partnership with orchestrator Jonathan Tunick, are only two examples of this creative overlay. For *The Passing Shows*, the original materials reveal the remarkable number of people it took to create the music for a single show. What is even more interesting is that some jobs were performed by many different people, with multiple orchestrators, composers, lyricists, and others participating. Or music was simply borrowed from other sources; sometimes printed dance band arrangements were used, even if only for a few measures of music. Ballets were included in most editions, and music that fit the mood of the scene was cobbled together from a variety of sources. Interpolations were common, and not because the main composers were unable to write hits. The Shuberts were always looking for music that worked, and as the team swiftly (yet carefully) pieced each revue together, new solutions were always sought to improve the show.

Music

J. J. Shubert assigned one person to oversee the musical needs of each *Passing Show*, and it was this individual who would write most of the songs, work with the chorus and principals, and attend rehearsals with Atteridge to shape the final product. More often than not, that person was Sigmund Romberg, who (as previously stated) was the main contributor to six editions of the series.[3] Contracts and paperwork make it clear that these lead composers were paid for their scores upon receipt of the total show, and then they received royalties every week the show ran. Romberg signed a contract with Lee Shubert to this effect on May 27, 1924, where he acknowledged the payment of $1500 given to him for his work on *The Passing Show*.[4] As a result of this single sum, he "releas[ed] and relinquish[ed]" all rights to the "book, score, and lyrics of the said musical play," including publishing rights and payment for the use of the music in any other future production. The musical duties of the head composer included writing a variety of songs, several dance numbers, and smaller pieces of musical webbing (scene changes, underscoring, and other incidental music).

Preparing the overture and finale were not part of this job; they were pieced together by the orchestrator after the final structure for the show was determined. No entr'actes exist for any of the series. At the rehearsals during the workshop period, Romberg was on hand when changes were required. It is worth noting that Romberg was paid the same amount for the entire 1924 show as the Howard Brothers made for every week they performed under a contemporary Shubert contract.

Surprisingly, only one contract remains extant for an interpolation during the initial run of the series. W. Franke Harling was paid $50 for his song, "Venetian Hawaiian Love Song," which was purchased for *The Passing Show of 1924*. The payment assured that Harling transferred all rights over to the Shuberts for performance. However, if the Shuberts arranged to publish the song, they would pay 25 percent to Harling and would further grant him an additional 25 percent if the song was recorded. Although the song was ultimately not included in the show, Harling was an excellent choice for a contributor; over the next few years, he wrote operas, many more songs (such as "Beyond the Blue Horizon," 1930), and eventually a host of film scores.

For the most part, however, *The Passing Shows* were written by tunesmiths who, like Romberg, produced music full-time as part of the Shubert machine. From the moment Romberg was contracted by the producers until he began work on *Maytime* in mid-1917, he was a contributing (and usually primary) composer on an astonishing fifteen shows over a period of only twenty-two months. The effort included writing for all the Winter Garden revues as well as other Shubert productions. This pattern of "rapid-fire" work matched Atteridge's schedule; it was he who wrote lyrics for most of the musicians involved, and the composer would fashion the music around the words. With such a remarkable rate of production, Atteridge and Romberg must have worked together for hours on end, continually (and simultaneously) writing songs for multiple shows. And, as mentioned before, not all the finished products were included onstage. From documents in the Shubert Archive, it appears that roughly one-quarter of the songs were never used in either a *Passing Show* or any other production, relegating dozens of numbers over the years to a silent limbo. But even if the tunes were unheard by audiences, they were nevertheless prepared for performance by the Shuberts' orchestrators.

As discussed in chapter 1, the central orchestrator for the early *Passing Shows* was Frank Saddler. Working closely with the conductors and composers for the shows, most especially Oscar Radin, Saddler crafted the sound that the audience would actually hear. No matter the quality of the original tune, many felt that Saddler's touch could transform any material he was given into something worth hearing. In the words of one contemporary observer, "the Saddler orchestrations were subtle and beguiling, an intricate lace-work; he could embroider a commonplace theme into rare distinction."[5] Saddler worked on each revue in the series between 1912 and 1919. His instrumentation for 1912 (shown in Table 5.1) reveals that the orchestra for these shows was quite large and included some surprises.

The orchestra is similar to a chamber orchestra, with a smaller number of strings but several wind and brass instruments to provide a range of colors. The one instrument that was infrequently played in pit orchestras after this time was the harp, but it was used in the other Winter Garden revues until it was removed in 1916. Over the years, Saddler and his fellow orchestrators added and subtracted from the list.

Table 5.1. The Instrumentation for *The Passing Show of 1912.*

2 flutes (1 with piccolo)	1 drum / percussion
1 oboe	1 harp
2 clarinets (A and B♭)	3–4 1st violins
1 bassoon	2 2nd violins
2 horns in F	2 violas
2 cornets in A \ trumpets in B♭	2 cellos
1 trombone	1 string bass
Total orchestra members: 23–24	

A second flute was dropped in subsequent editions, for example, but the other pairings were left intact. One E-flat alto saxophone was added to some numbers of *The Passing Show of 1916*, and a second was added the following year, with the saxes being employed in more tunes. By 1923, a part was included for a tenor/baritone saxophone player. Some additions were very specific, sometimes only being used in one or two places; a banjo part is extant for "Lotus Flower," from *The Passing Show of 1923*, but it is not included throughout the production. The percussionist, not surprisingly, was the busiest member of the pit. Tympani, gongs, train whistles, wood blocks, bells, and drum set were standard for the run of the series. The only instrument that holds an unclear position in the fabric of the orchestration is the piano. Since no pictures or documents are extant that show the full ensemble, it is hard to know if the piano was used outside of rehearsals. The piano/vocal parts are well worn, but none of Saddler's partiturs include indications for the instrument. The careful approach Saddler and other orchestrators took concerning the sound of each number would have been doubled in many places, and therefore, it is unlikely the piano was a part of the performances.

As a point of interest, many of the orchestral parts also show heavy use, but beyond this, they also reveal some fascinating insights into the lives of the pit musicians. Given the number of months each show was performed, it is not surprising that the pieces, prepared by copyists at the direction of the orchestrator, are bent and often soiled at the point where the page is turned. Life on tour was just as grueling for the instrumentalists as it was for the other entertainers. In most cases, it appears a variety of conductors took charge of these traveling productions, leaving Radin to work at the Winter Garden. Unfortunately, it is not entirely clear how many people from the pit were included on tour, but from the parts, there is no indication that the orchestra was scaled-down on the road. In fact, some of the comments left on the parts themselves reveal a long association with the show, which is not the standard practice with most musical tours in the twenty-first century. The most entertaining pair of part-scribblers were the two clarinet players from *The Passing Show of 1919*, and it is their comments that suggest they traveled with the revue. On the back of a song, one writes to the other about where they will be

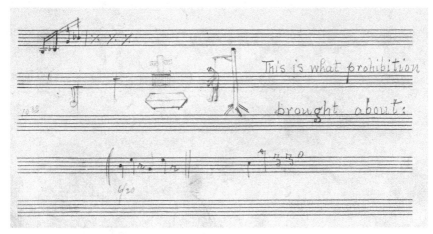

Fig. 5.1. Prohibition cartoon from Clarinet Part, The Passing Show of 1919.
Shubert Archive.

playing for Christmas. The stand partner then wrote "Merry XMAS" below it, adding "Saves [sending] A Card." And throughout their music, they included some remarkable drawings, including one of a man with a huge protruding nose and another of a woman singing. Many small dogs ("His Master's Voice") and creative figures are scattered across the pages, demonstrating the type of boredom that every pit musician knows well—the dullness of playing the same show night after night. One of the most interesting sketches shows a man being hung, with a particularly pointed comment alongside it (see Figure 5.1).

Prohibition of alcohol in the United States began during the tour of this revue, and there is no doubt that it made many, including these clarinet players, unhappy. Other comments are more about the day-to-day experiences. The piccolo part from *The Passing Show of 1921* was very challenging, and the player wrote "MORE COFFEE" in bold letters above the music. And one particularly astute violist from the 1914 edition kept track of every instrument that was left out of each piece of webbing, allowing for a more comprehensive recreation of the original score.[6] The orchestra parts for about eighty-five percent of each show remain extant. While most of it is in manuscript, the music in the Shubert Archive shows the players were quick to make use of published dance-band arrangements if an interpolation was to be changed during the show's run.

The relationship between the Shuberts and composers who were not under general contract—the writers of interpolations—was often not as simple as Harling's contract suggests. Instead, a major mediating factor in the musical choices for interpolations was the producer's highly charged and often volatile association with music publishers. The first three editions of the revue were published by Shapiro Music Publisher (later Shapiro, Bernstein, and Co.). Using a blue and red color scheme, the sheet music included a large inset of the singer associated with the number. The cover of "Carnegie" (sometimes called "Handy Andy" in the programs) even included Clarence Harvey in his Andrew Carnegie kilt-clad costume (see Figure 5.2).

Fig. 5.2. *"Carnegie" ("Handy Andy") sheet music cover,* The Passing Show of 1912. *Author's Collection.*

The only deviation from this pattern was Jean Schwartz's music from *The Passing Show of 1913*, which he published through his own company, Jerome and Schwartz. It was Al Brown's songs that Shapiro printed. In 1915, Schirmer published the full score, but this was the only *Passing Show* to receive this treatment. Schirmer also provided many individual songs from that year and continued to do the same for the following two shows. Remick was the principal publisher in 1918, and in 1919, 1921, and 1922. Finally, Harms printed the music for 1923 and 1924.

The most extensive correspondence between the Shuberts and a publishing house is with Remick.[7] The Archive houses dozens of exchanges between J. J. and Remick himself, with some letters from composers, lyricists, and Remick employees included. Their connection began on May 15, 1916, when Jerome Remick wrote a telegram to Shubert informing him that he had a new song called "Pretty Baby"

(Gus Kahn, lyrics; Egbert van Alstyne and Tony Jackson, music) that he was hoping to place in a show.[8] The song had not yet been published, and Remick promised that if J. J. would find a home for it, he would "hold" the song back from being released. Thirteen days later, J. J. wrote to Fred Belcher, Remick's New York agent, that he had discovered Melville Ellis and Irene Bordoni were using the song in their vaudeville act at the Colonial Theater:

> I had your assurance ... that you would keep the number for me but it seems I cannot do anything with publishers. Their promises do not go very far. If it continues, I will take the number out of Chicago and I won't use it in New York. I have always refrained from putting in interpolations for this very reason—that you would rather have a lot of vaudeville actors do your numbers than put them in a production.

Remick personally wrote J. J. and assured him that the two (former Shubert employees, no less) had been told to cease performing the song and had done so. Once the matter had been settled, Shubert ordered a twenty-eight–part orchestration from Grace Le Boy, a Remick composer and arranger who had published several songs with (and was married to) Gus Kahn. A few months later, Kahn himself inquired about the use of the song, and was assured that it was being used in both *The Passing Show of 1916* at the Winter Garden and *The Show of Wonders*, which was touring. Advertisements in *Variety* and *Billboard* proclaimed "Pretty Baby" the top Remick hit of the season and had the word "RESTRICTED!" prominently displayed to dissuade any vaudevillians from using the tune.

It makes sense that the issue of interpolations would have frustrated Shubert. From a songwriting standpoint, the publishing houses were the main competition for Broadway producers. Remick kept a staff of writers too, and for them, funneling songs into vaudeville was indeed more profitable. Not only could they simultaneously introduce the song through multiple venues, but they could do it nationally. This would result in more sales, allowing the sheet to be sold everywhere in a short period of time. Tales of vaudeville acts finding success with particular songs comprised a large space in trade papers. Such a relationship is exactly the kind the Howard Brothers had with Witmark in their early days, and it could be a fruitful connection for both parties. By placing a song with a Broadway production, however, the publisher would have to wait patiently as the show finished its New York run and then hope the tour was extensive. The trade-off was that the number would get a more grandiose treatment, often by a higher profile performer, and it could also have a longer lifespan onstage. J. J. remarked that he did not like to use interpolations, but he did so regularly, even in his pre–Winter Garden revues such as *The Mimic World* (1908). But the negotiations for using a song were not always easy, and many times Shubert required the publisher to go to great lengths to "put a song over." Remick was very excited to have "I'm Forever Blowing Bubbles" (Jaan Kenbrovin, lyrics; John Kellette, music) placed in *The Passing Show of 1918*, but Shubert asked the company to pay $2,185 for the backdrop, costumes, and bubble machines that were used to stage the piece.[9] When Remick agreed, the interpolation was included, and the Shuberts then paid $500 back to them as royalties for the first five weeks and another $25 a week as long as the show continued. "Bubbles" had replaced "Smiles" in the revue, but they were both among the most successful songs of the season; "Smiles" was the top-selling song in the nation for three months (October–December 1918), while "Bubbles" held the top position for four (June–September 1919) (see Figure 5.3, which references the past hit of "Pretty Baby," as well as the more recent "I'm Forever Blowing Bubbles").[10]

Belcher's frequent reports to Shubert also indicate how arrangements of songs were circulated. During this era, one of the surest ways to get audiences to hear a melody was to have the piece played across as many outlets as possible. In regard to the music for *The Passing Show of 1918*, Belcher wrote the following to J. J.:

> We have already distributed among the orchestra leaders in the various cafes and restaurants arrangements of "My Baby Talk Lady," "Galli-Curci Rag," "Trombone Jazz," "and "You're Over Here and I'm Over There." We got these out very quickly

Fig. 5.3. *Remick's advertising proof for "Pretty Baby" and "I'm Forever Blowing Bubbles."*
Shubert Archive.

in order to have them ready for the New York opening. I am having an excellent dance arrangement made of "Baby Talk Lady" and "Galli-Curci Rag" as I find these two numbers are the most likely for that purpose . . . We will also get out a Winter Garden Medley for orchestra, which will include [the above] and one or two of the other numbers.[11]

What is surprising about this letter is that Belcher—not Shubert—made the decisions about which songs would be suitable for various musical treatments. Additionally, it is fascinating to note that the versions of songs that went to local eating establishments were not necessarily the ones that were turned into dance band arrangements. Instead, the entire array of multi-musical marketing was handled by the publisher, who was making profits for the producer and the publisher through musical choices made at the administrative level.

This did not mean that the new versions of the tunes were completely different from the original orchestration, but rather that they were created for a new purpose. Frank Saddler was one of many orchestrators under contract for the Shuberts, and he was often responsible for producing the original arrangement. The next version, the one Belcher would have agreed upon, was built using the original parts as a model. For instance, an examination of the song "Kissable Lips" from The Passing Show of 1923 demonstrates just how close the products really were. The song (Harold Atteridge, lyrics; Jean Schwartz, music) was first written for the revue itself, with the rehearsal piano part arranged by J. Dell Lampe as an in-house product. [12] Curiously, the rehearsal part includes several new notes penciled in alongside the inked melody, suggesting Dell Lampe may have adjusted the music after it was received from Schwartz, probably in rehearsals. The piano/vocal part, along with the full orchestration (in this case, by an unidentified orchestrator), was then sent to Harms, who was under contract to publish the music. A new piano/vocal was made for publication, and for most of that part, the Dell Lampe arrangement was used. But by the third phrase in this new version, changes to the melody begin, and the printed music deviates from the handwritten part until the chorus begins. The new material in the third and fourth phrases is based on melodic material found in the original piano/vocal, but the line is shorter and more compact. After the piano/vocal sheet music was finalized, Harms then gave the song to one of their orchestrators, Robert Russell Bennett, and he produced a dance band "fox trot" arrangement. Bennett (who had learned much from Saddler) would later be known as one of the most illustrious Broadway orchestrators of his generation, providing a host of arrangements for Kern, Gershwin, Porter, and, most notably, Rodgers. Bennett was responsible for the sound of Lady Be Good (1925), Show Boat (1927), Anything Goes (1934), Oklahoma! (1943) and Camelot (1960), among many others. But at this point, Bennett had just begun his career, and creating arrangements for dance bands was part of his daily routine. A comparison of the original first violin part and the new one shows a remarkable similarity on the surface, but Bennett adds several subtle differences to "Kissable Lips," especially during instrumental "fill-ins" between vocal phrases. The main contribution from Bennett is an obbligato solo violin part that works as a countermelody to the main line, using rhythmic elements from the song to great effect (both the first violin line and the obbligato from this arrangement are shown in

Example 5.1).[13] Bennett's orchestration is smaller than the original one heard at the Winter Garden, with only eighteen to twenty instruments used (depending on the number of string players). The medleys mentioned by Belcher circulated as widely as the individual songs, with these "Selections" arriving across the country months ahead of the touring version of a show.

Sheet music sales were one of the ways to make a song a hit, but another was through phonograph records, referred to in contracts and letters as "mechanical reproduction." Some of the mysteries that elude modern-day scholars of musical theater are the relationships between shows, songs, performers, and record companies. Many important songs from the theaters were never recorded at the time of their success, and there are numerous performers who never made any records. In many cases, well-known stars were not the ones who made the first records of the songs they had made famous. The entire conundrum remains relatively opaque, but the negotiations between Remick and the Shuberts do make one thing clear—the choice to record a song was not in either of their hands but left to the discretion of the recording company. Joe Keit, an important employee at Remick, was the expert on the subject, according to Belcher, and it was to Keit that Shubert wrote in December 1919 about an idea he had for marketing songs at the shows themselves:

> I have a thought in mind about putting out records of the song hits of our shows in the lobby of the theaters. What do you think of taking the song hits of an attraction and instead of giving it to the Columbia, or to the Victor, or to others, and wait for months before they get the record out, to have it done immediately and sell them the same as you do song sheets?
>
> We can see a great many records because 9 cases out of 10 the show has exhausted its New York run before they get one hit number out of the show. There are thousands of people who cannot play the piano, yet every household in America has a Victrola, or one of those sorts of things, and which they use for that purpose.
>
> I think that a great deal of money can be made if the records can be manufactured as soon as the successes are gotten out, and sold simultaneously with them in the lobbies of the theaters where the attraction is playing.[14]

J. J. was obviously a man ahead of his time with his marketing strategies, and Keit tried for a time to make the arrangement work. After all, he agreed, records were released, but "it has always been weeks or months after the production has opened." Unfortunately, the two do not seem to have found any record company willing to consider the proposition, and they let the matter drop. Although this does not entirely clarify why so few Broadway recordings were made, it does show that the business arrangements between the various parties were problematic enough to prevent the "original cast album" from existing in the teens.[15] Relatively few documents from phonograph companies have been uncovered, but such a discovery would clarify a wide array of questions about the mysterious inner workings of the business.

The format of the songs and the manner in which they were performed is also worth noting, as some documents offer insight into how a performance happened. The songs themselves include three main elements, with a fourth present in other pieces: the introduction, the verse, the chorus, and, sometimes, a dance. In virtually every part throughout the series, a first and second ending is given to the chorus, allowing for a repeat of that section alone. However, Atteridge wrote second verses for songs too, but it is nearly impossible to tell when these were used. The markings "1-1," "1-2," "2-1," and so on, are used throughout the parts, and this seems to indicate the section that was repeated ("1" represented the verse and "2" indicated the chorus), and the order in which it was to occur. The reality is that *The Passing Shows* were massive endeavors, and to keep the revue moving swiftly, the songs were very brief onstage, avoiding too many repetitions and eliminating encores. Proof of this can be found in a timing sheet for *The Passing Show of 1914*, which shows exactly when each dialogue, song, and dance began and ended onstage.[16] The songs are surprisingly short. "The Moving Picture Glide" began at 8:49 p.m. and was off the stage by 8:51:30, while "A Modern Wedding Day" ran from 10:18:30 to 10:20. There was no time to repeat sections, which strongly suggests most songs omitted a second verse. The other means the Shuberts used to shorten the overall length was to ban encores. After attending the 1912 edition, a reviewer for the *New York Press* explained that he "had always been sore on encores, particularly in the bad shows, when the poor devils who were gambling their money on the result clutched at one or two saving numbers."[17] The Winter Garden ushers were quite firm about discouraging the practice during the opening night. "At first, when the 'New York Town' girls tripped up the runway," he related, "the Johnnie-boys went wild and it looked for a little while as if the no encore rule would crack right there. The number would have had a dozen recalls under the old order of things." But the applause did not stop the show, and the rest of the revue moved along with no interruption.

The topics of songs from *The Passing Show* series were as varied as the theatrical seasons they represented. One theme that is frequently invoked was the competing world of the moving picture, which during these years was just a burgeoning industry. Songs such as "The Maude Adams of the Screen," "We're Working in the Picture Game" and "The Moving Picture Glide" (all from 1914) and "There's Something Missing in the Movies" (from 1915) simultaneously celebrated and lampooned what film offered audiences, with silent pantomime considered less spectacular than what one could see in the theater. New inventions were sometimes subjects of songs; "My Telephone Girl" (from *The Passing Show of 1917*) was in the tradition of "Hello, Ma Baby!" (Joseph E. Howard and Ida Emerson, 1899) and "Hello, 'Frisco" (Louis Hirsch, 1915), connecting the importance of the telephone to romance. New types of music were referenced, including "Trombone Jazz" (1918), "American Jazz" (1922), "The Dancing Blues" (1921) and "Society Blues" (1924), even though, like early rock musicals, the music of the songs did not match the style in question. Recent sports events and figures were also mentioned. In 1923, "Golfing Blues" was singled out by reviewers as a possible hit, including the lines, "I curse the Heavens, Hagens, Barnes, and that Chick Evans," referencing some of the sport's top players. "A la Hockey" spoofed that activity in 1919, while baseball was the subject of 1915's "Summer Sports," which featured a chorus of girls dressed in uniforms, complete with balls and mitts.

But no matter what elements the revue included, the most common thing to sing about in any *Passing Show* was the beauty of women, or the beguiling nature of women, or new types of women. "Radiance" (from *The Passing Show of 1922*) starred the "Radium Girls."[18] The number used a type of luminescent paint called Undark on the costumes to create a dazzling effect for the audience; according to the lyrics, the light from the stars actually comes from the female object of the song (more about this number is discussed in chapter 8). This song was rarely performed in the later years, however, when the qualities of "purity" and "shyness" were less frequent in the lyrics than those of a salacious nature. The last three *Passing Shows* on Broadway (1922–1924) were more blatant about the sexuality of the female chorus. A cut song from 1921 was "Beautiful Girls Are Like Opium," where "kisses so exotic" would "get you so idiotic"; the verse concluded with the lines, "like the flames of the Yenshe / are her serpentine charms / all the glamour that men see / in her serpentine arms." "Beautiful and Damned," from the 1923 show, was a large production number that featured Bob Nelson and a handful of vamps. Atteridge's lyrics comment on the scandalous nature of "to-day's" blue literature, which focused on the fallen woman— a reference to F. Scott Fitzgerald's novel of the same name from the previous year.

Chorus:

> All the girls are beautiful / but they are all damned,
> And they think that vice is nice / so often it is shammed,
> All the ladies in the books these modern days,
> Oh, the Hades they raise,
> With their ways so very naughty,
> All the biggest sellers tell of vampires bold,
> All the greatest authors dwell on women so bold,
> Though by the critics they may be slammed,
> Oh, how we love them, if they are beautiful and damned.

The epitome of the overt sexualizing of women onstage was in *The Passing Show of 1924*, with the song, "(There's) Nothing Naughty in a Nighty." Opening the second act, this number took place on a large canopy bed, with twenty chorus girls together under the sheets. The color scheme of lavender, white, cream, and violet were used in the set and the costumes, with the latter being made so that "they [could] pull up" the dresses as they started the dance.[19] The brashness of the lyrics speak to an attitude toward women that would never have been articulated in 1912.

Verse:

> When a girl is naughty then she has no one to blame,
> No matter how she tries / She can't hide her disguise,
> She may dress old fashioned and be naughty just the same,
> And it matters not a bit in what gown or what outfit,
> Anything she wears makes a naughty thing of it.

Chorus:

> There is nothing naughty in a nighty,
> Without a naughty little girl inside.
> There is nothing shocking, nothing even flighty,
> In a little bit of lingerie with lots of colors gay,
> Simple dresses make a girl look bashful,
> But her glances she can never hide.
> There's lots of charms about a girl that men admire,
> But when she says "Good Night," and dresses to retire,
> There's nothing naughty in a nighty,
> Without a haughty naughty girl inside.

The song puts the onus of sexual manipulation on the women themselves, suggesting that their behavior and their "knowing" looks are more charged than any clothing could ever be. The corset of the past had disappeared from fashion by the 1920s, and women's clothing became more casual and more revealing, with knee-length skirts worn by many urban youth by the middle of the decade. But, as Atteridge suggests in his lyrics, even if a girl still wears old styles, she is probably inclined to accept the advances of a modern man.

Despite claims to the opposite, none of The Passing Shows included nudity, although this edition (and this song) was close to doing so.[20] Without chorus boys to block the view, the chorus girls became more objectified into the 1920s, a trend that coincided with the demise of The Passing Show and the rise of Artists and Models in 1923, a Shubert series that dared to finally remove the nighty—and everything else—entirely.[21]

Dance

Chorus girls in Passing Shows were not only required to have a good voice, but also to display the ability to dance. Good "movement" skills were stressed by Ned Wayburn when he discussed what he sought while choosing a woman for the chorus, and this was because dance was an essential component of these revues. Being able to glide while wearing glamorous yet unwieldy costumes was a skill that the young ladies needed in order to find a place in the show. Their ability to adapt to new dances was also important; as fad dances would be included to follow new trends, the chorus girls needed to be able to master the steps in a short time. And in many cases, these featured moves were attached to a performer hired specifically for their specialty. Just as they did with high-caliber performers who had other gifts, the Shuberts filled their revues with dance professionals who brought the newest styles to the Winter Garden.

If there was any question as to the importance of dance in The Passing Shows, it is worth noting that Wayburn, the first director in the series, was primarily a dance specialist. Jack Mason, one of the principal choreographers throughout the series, was adamant that dance was one of the reasons that revues worked; he pointed out that "without dancing, no musical show can 'get over.' A few years ago there was a chance for repose. In some of the numbers the principals or the chorus could assume one position and keep to it throughout the refrain. Now everything must be movement. Even in the case of sentimental songs there must be plenty of action. And there must be all sorts and kinds of dancing."[22] From the personal notes made by J. J. and Lee, it is clear they agreed with the need for a "snappy" show with lots of "pep," and nowhere was this desire to feature dance more apparent than in their presentation of *The Passing Show of 1912*.

The program for the first revue in the series actually offers two different productions, although they were conceived as part of a single evening's entertainment. The first work listed is *The Ballet of 1830*, a "mimo-dramatic ballet" written by Maurice Volny and staged by dancer Emile Agoust. The event was an import from the Alhambra Theatre in London (and Paris before that) and included the original sets, costumes, and principals. The story was about an art student who, because of his love for alcohol, nearly loses his sweetheart, who is wooed by a crafty baron. A vamp then tempts the student, but in the end the couple finds true love. The *New York Herald* pointed out that the piece was a pantomime, not unlike what one would see on film, and called it an "optic opera."[23] This opening work only lasted thirty minutes, but the critics agreed that it was in excellent taste, well performed, and according to the *New York Clipper*, "extremely well received."[24]

The inclusion of ballet as part of this production was not an accident or an afterthought; it was something the Shuberts had intended from their earliest conception of the show. Ballet had been used in Lew Fields' revues, Ziegfeld's *Follies*, and was also—surprisingly—popular in a number of nightclubs. During the planning stages of the 1912 *Passing Show*, Melville Ellis wrote from Paris to J. J. Shubert, suggesting the producer engage the Russian Ballet (the Ballet Russes).[25] Although he does not mention the specific piece, Ellis must have seen the group and its star, Nijinsky, perform Debussy's *Prélude à l'après-midi d'un faune*, and hoped to bring the company to the United States. Shubert felt that such a piece would be too unusual for New York, but he agreed that something shorter might work and had *The Ballet of 1830* adapted for the Winter Garden. The inclusion of this opening has been much maligned by modern authors, with some claiming it was "pretentious" and an addition that was "tacked on" to add a sense of grandeur to the event.[26] But in truth, ballet was a central feature of the revue, with most editions including it on the program. And even when other producers constructed their revues, they maintained the tradition; the *Scandals*, the *Music Box Revues*, and the *Greenwich Village Follies* (among others) found a place for ballet amidst the surrounding acts. Additionally, classical dancers could be seen on New York stages—even on Broadway—in numerous works of musical theater. For example, the British ballerina Adeline Genée was featured in Ziegfeld's *The Soul Kiss* (1908), while the Russian Anna Pavlova was included in the cast of *The Big Show* (1916), a revue produced by Dillingham.

In subsequent editions of *The Passing Show*, ballet was not separated from the main event but was a feature of its all-inclusive cavalcade of entertainment. Classical dance was usually given an exotic theme and set in a locale far-distant (either geographically, chronologically, or both) from New York. Much like the production number, the foreign setting allowed for experimentation with the design, music, and sets, while simultaneously suspending the audience's expectations of verisimilitude. This way, one could surreptitiously place a ballet sequence within the setting without disrupting the flow. In the 1915 edition, Hungary was the location of choice, while Paris (during the Second Empire) was the spot for 1923. Midway through the first act of *The Passing Show of 1914*, Marilynn Miller starred in the "Divertissement," a title borrowed from the French designation for a dance included in an opera. The setting used was orientalist, with huge ornate vases and flowers strewn across the stage. Although the audience would not have realized it yet, this would be the set for the upcoming "Omar Khayyam" sequence that would follow the dance. Exoticism was not a requirement for classical dance though, and neither was using the specialty within a larger framework.

In many cases, ballet was important enough that it was given structurally significant placement within the revue as a component of the opening or the finale. This was the case in *The Passing Show of 1918*, when both acts ended with ballets; the first was part of a burlesque of Oscar Wilde's *Salome*, while the second was a Spanish number. Both scenes starred Isabel Rodriguez, the Castilian "queen of the castanets," who did a signature dance at the end, while adhering to more traditional styles for the requisite "Dance of the Seven Veils" for the first finale. What made the Salome piece even more interesting was that Rodriguez finished by presenting the head of the Kaiser on a plate (in place of the head of John the Baptist). This would have been especially fitting for the dancer, since her own Parisian troupe had been disbanded when World War I broke out, "smashing all her plans."[27] Rodriguez was another of the transatlantic performers the Shuberts engaged to specifically make her Broadway debut at the Winter Garden, and like so many others, she took the opportunity to continue performing in vaudeville as a star.[28] Many of the other *Passing Show* editions placed ballets in opening spots, allowing the audience to experience dance while they were freshly in their seats. The result was that some dancers, such as Miller, became instant stars through the audience's enthusiastic embracing of their talents.

The prelude to *The Passing Show of 1912* may have been a ballet, but the inclusion of this dance style did not stop there. Although no documents remain extant to support a meeting, Ellis probably approached the Ballet Russes about building an American audience, and Diaghilev may even have introduced him to one of his dancers, Theodore Kosloff. Active with the troupe since 1910, Kosloff probably saw the chance to work for the Shuberts as a way to establish himself successfully in the United States after several successful years stunning audiences from London to St. Petersburg. Theodore (whose true name was Fijodor Mikailovitch Koslov) came from a family of prominent musicians in Moscow, and he graduated from the Imperial Theatrical School in the same city.[29] He also studied visual art and acting, and was already thoroughly established by the time he made his debut in Paris with the Ballet Russes in 1910. The Shuberts engaged him shortly after he came to the United States in 1912 in order to choreograph the first *Passing Show*, and soon afterwards, he was managing American tours for the Ballet Russes. He continued working with the Shuberts as Miller's dance partner and as coach in the 1915 edition and some of the other Winter Garden revues, but then he left New York to become a pioneer of dance on film in Hollywood's early days. There, he befriended and worked with Cecil B. de Mille, eventually finding enough support to open a ballet school. The studio flourished, and one of his most famous students was the director's niece, Agnes de Mille.

Alexis Kosloff, Theodore's younger sibling, followed his brother to America, and by 1915, he was also working with the Shuberts in *The Passing Show*. He chose to stay in New York, however, where he continued to work on Broadway into the later 1920s (also working with Marilynn Miller), eventually wrote a dance manual, and finally opened his own ballet school. Both of the Kosloff brothers were highly influential in the perpetuation of classical dance styles in the United States, but they were also especially progressive, encouraging their students to develop new styles and expand their skills to embrace more modern steps. The flexibility of the two dancers (and the addition of Maria Baldina, Theodore's wife) dramatically enhanced the ballet sections that they choreographed and performed. The trio, along with Miller, was so impressive during *The Passing Show of 1915* that the reviewer in the *New York Press* said that the show was good, but that "the dancers were the best of all."[30] Their "Spring Ballet" (see Figure 5.4) was the conclusion of the first act and Baldina's turn "won a storm of approval by her dainty dancing of a little conceit entitled 'The Nightingale,' which Rodion Mendelvitch feelingly played on the fiddle."[31] The enterprise received so much praise that Kosloff and Baldina took over a part of the Winter Garden that had previously been a restaurant (the Persian Garden) and, for a short time, opened their own ballet school.[32]

The engagement of Theodore Kosloff speaks to the Shuberts' vision for *The Passing Show* series—one that could be concurrently artistic and entertaining. Hiring a member of the most famous avant-garde dance company in the world in 1912 meant the producers were serious about appealing to a broad audience base. It would be a mistake to see the "Ragtime Overtures of Grand Operas" performed by the Howard Brothers and feel there was a dissonance with the "Spring Ballet" that followed. Not only would spectators accept the free-flowing movement from one style of performance to the next, but they would expect it. After all, two of the most important models for the revue—the variety show and later vaudeville— were based on an ever-changing stylistic dissonance. The difference for the revue, though, was that it abandoned vaudeville's hierarchical model, which featured the most important performers in the penultimate position. Instead, every moment of a revue needed to be of the highest possible caliber. The performance of numerous phenomenal acts was part of the appeal of the revue, and especially exciting was that a favorite act might return at any time. If ballet was to be used, then, it was essential that it be an equally exceptional feature, showcasing some of the best dancers available. Year after year, the Shuberts produced Winter Garden revues that offered acts that actively surpassed the appeal and the scale of even high-quality vaudeville fare.

The music for these ballet sequences was culled from a variety of sources, much of it French or Russian instrumentals slightly reworked for the forces in the pit. For example, in 1914, the accompaniment to Miller's "Divertissement" used Francis Tomé's "Sous la Feuillee," arranged by William Kretschmer. Tchaikovsky excerpts were used for the 1915 production, along with Cécil Chaminade's "Callirhoë" (Op. 37) during the second act "Polo Ballet." The music for the ballets came from previously printed sources and was (literally) cut and pasted into the musicians' parts. The only exception to this was when the sequence was more modern, such as in the Cubist ballet, "A Study in Black and White," which had music written by Alfred Goodman for

Fig. 5.4. Theodor Kosloff, Maria Baldina, and Alexis Kosloff, The Passing Show of 1915. *Author's Collection.*

the 1922 edition. The cut-and-paste music suggests that the dance, much like other elements of the show, used multiple transitions to keep the audience engaged.

A goal of *The Passing Shows*, it seems, was to find a place for ballet that could be built around one or another performer, much like with Isabel Rodriguez. Miller was hired, in part, for her classical abilities, and her replacement while she was in other revues was Countess Thamara Swirskaya (also called Swirsky), a Russian dancer and pianist. Like the Kosloffs, Swirskaya had performed throughout Europe before coming to the United States in 1909, after which she made a living performing in vaudeville, on Broadway, in film, and at the Metropolitan Opera.[33] The many stages she trod demonstrates how deeply enmeshed classical dancing was in American culture at this time. That she could move easily between such a wide range of entertainment media challenges the assumption that classical dance was only for those of the highest classes.[34] Swirskaya had studied in St. Petersburg, but because of her high social position, her parents did not wish her to become a dancer, so instead she went to Paris to become a concert pianist. However, her inclination toward dance held sway, and she began to specialize in numbers that made use of "Greek, Oriental, and Slav" forms.[35] Reviewers repeatedly pointed to her versatility, mentioning that she was comfortable making use of all her skills in her act. When the Shuberts hired her in the spring of 1916, she provided a letter that included items she felt were essential to finding success while working with a large production. She told J. J. that she "had so much difficulty with contracts in the past that I want this one to be absolutely carefree"; she insisted—quite justifiably—that she needed to know the exact start date of the revue, she would only attend the part of the rehearsal that she was needed for, she could give two weeks notice if she had to leave, and she requested that her name "have a place among the principals."[36]

In *The Passing Show of 1916*, Swirskaya danced with William Dunn and Ma-Belle in an "Olympian Ballet" that took place in the Grecian Baths. As the famous Helen, "a slave of enchantment," Swirskaya dazzled even the harshest critics of the production; one writer from Buffalo, New York, claimed she "made toes tingle and shoulders sway" and insisted that the ballet was one of the best parts of the revue.[37] The *New York Evening Telegram* critic went so far as to suggest that this dance alone was good enough to keep audiences coming to the theater, saying, "it is so excessively beautiful that the success of the new Passing Show is assured ... Superb in costumes, movement, and color, [it] is made even more thrilling by the presence and poses of Thamara Swirskaya, whose beautifully modeled physique was lavishly displayed."[38] The dance itself was lauded repeatedly, as was the setting and the other members of the scene, but the final comment made by this last reporter was also echoed through the papers—the paper-thin costume left nothing to the imagination. And with Swirskaya's performance, a trend began wherein dancers began to remove the traditional costumes of the past, such as the tutu, which had been worn by Miller during her appearances. The costumes of Swirskaya and Dunn (seen in Figure 5.5) are loose-fitting yet tailored, allowing for a full range of movement while simultaneously flattering the body. And, inevitably, with the visibility of a woman's body came outcries of vulgarity.

As the ballets continued into the 1920s, the costumes were made with less material and the performers sometimes had reputations mixed with scandal. One of these was Mlle. Olive Ann Alcorn, who was principal female danseuse for *The Passing Show of 1922*. Alcorn's main number was the "Ballet Les Conquerants," alongside Frances Renault. This dance is mentioned in more detail in chapter 2, and it was certainly one of the most notorious features of that year's edition, especially for its sensuality and risqué content. However, what some in the audience would have known was that Alcorn had a different life in California, both in the movies alongside Charlie Chaplin (*Sunnyside*, 1919) and also as a prominent nude model. The largest collection of nude photos of Alcorn was released earlier the same year in a collection by photographer Alexander Stark called "Alta Art Studios, Volume 1." Although the studio-created photos were published collectively and were ostensibly for artists, Alta was aware that the "nonprofessional" might also have an interest in the female form, and sold a number of photographs individually. Alcorn was not unprofessional—she had studied under Ruth St. Denis at her Denishawn School of Dancing and Related Arts—and

Fig. 5.5. Swirskaya and Dunn, The Passing Show of 1916.
Author's Collection.

she was lauded by many reviewers for her technical skills. However, the question of whether or not her performance in the "Ballet Les Conquerants" was in good "taste" became a heated discussion in the media. Even the *New York Clipper*, a trade publication, disparaged Alcorn's appearance, saying, "Alcorn [is] a very good dancer [and] is generous with her body display" but the dance overall "is in exceedingly bad taste. There's nothing artistic about it, and it only detracts from the merits of the entire show."[39] *Billboard* was no less unhappy with Alcorn's turn, stating "no one could wear less and not get arrested, and it is an open question—yes, very open—as to whether she is not crowding the censor a lot. In addition, Mlle. Alcorn chooses to dance the most pornographic dance that has ever come under my observation. It is lewd all the way thru and if the authorities stand for it, I will be much surprised."[40] It is perhaps not surprising that the harshest criticism of the dance was not leveled at Francis

Renault—Alcorn's partner in the endeavor—but was reserved for her alone. This is particularly unfortunate given that she did not choreograph the number (Allan Foster was responsible), nor did she choose her costume. But, as is often the case, Alcorn, as the lead (female) performer, received the brunt of the angry discourse during the show's run. The thin line between art and voyeurism became one of the most debated issues concerning Shubert shows into the 1920s (especially *Artists and Models*), and it was dance that was the target for much of the criticism.

Despite this negativity, modern numbers—as opposed to popular or classical ones—were included in many of the editions from the mid-1910s onward. One of the more vocal proponents of new styles was Dorsha [Hayes], who danced alongside Rodriguez in *The Passing Show of 1918*.[41] The twenty-one year old shared her thoughts on the future of dance and the power of different styles with the *New York Sun*:

> I want the dance to be something more free and more wholly imaginative. The crisp, neat difficult technique of the classical ballet has its vivacity and charm, but it is not the medium for emotion. The dances of the East have their primitive lure and feeling, but expression through them is naturally limited. The faithful revival of Greek dancing, beautiful and perfect as it is, cannot be the sincere expression of to-day's music or to-day's emotion. The skirt dancing of to-day has one enviable quality—a free joyousness—but it is lacking n beauty and refinement.
>
> I want the dance to be a new, free expression of all emotions that is not limited or dependent on the steps or poses of any type or period of dancing and is bounded only by the laws of beauty and sincere feeling.[42]

She continued, suggesting that all elements of a revue, from color to set design to blocking, were essential to transforming the experience of any kind of dance into something that would become immensely popular. Dorsha's hope was that by presenting dance within an artistic context that fused all the elements of stagecraft (a dance-centric *Gesamtkunstwerk*), all styles could speak to audiences more effectively. Given her time with the Shuberts and their theatrical machine, there is no doubt she felt that the enormous production numbers in *The Passing Shows* were a potentially effective means of providing high-quality dances that could fuse artistic vision under the right circumstances.

Of course, not every audience member was convinced of the power of dance, and reviews over the years show that some critics were thrilled with the inclusion of ballet, while others felt it was tiresome and pretentious. Usually, it was the latter breed that made a plea for dropping "artistic" movement to focus instead on popular dance. The Winter Garden revues were constructed to appeal to a wide audience. Huffman and his choreographers knew that dance was necessary to make the whole show work. As Mason states, the movement of bodies onstage was equated with the movement of the show itself, and stagnation—physical or otherwise—would kill a large revue.

In addition to ballet and modern styles, an array of other popular dances was woven into the show's framework. Dance partners were some of the first to be targeted and engaged by the Shuberts for the revue, and preproduction lists of possible headliners always included two or three significant dance duos. The pair's style was not necessarily important as long as they were exceptionally gifted and had a routine that fit effectively into a larger context. Often, dance duos were framed by a section of dialogue and a song, using the same set and theme, building a unified section of the revue. It was rare for two dancers to be featured without connecting it thematically to other portions of the production. For example, *The Passing Show of 1912* presented Adelaide and Hughes, a successful international pair, during the third scene. The scene built up to the "Harem of Sewer-Man," a burlesque on *Kismet* and *Sumurun*, but before the parody, two songs were sung and the dance team performed "The Spark of Life." The work was a "dancing fantasy" that was set in an imagined India, keeping it as "Oriental" as this time of stereotyped characterizations allowed. It even included a narrative printed in the program.[43] The number used "tricky toe-work" and waltz steps by Adelaide. For many reviewers, this was a high point of the show, with the *Clipper* describing the dance as one "where electricity plays a prominent role. The scene is of Oriental splendor. Adelaide is borne on the stage with all the pomp of a queen of Egypt of the old days, and she and Hughes did a dance that took the audience by a storm."[44] Folding the "Spark of Life" into the larger context helped to maintain some sense of cohesion to the overall scene, and even though the songs and dances may have made sense only to an audience for whom the Far East was more of an idea than a reality, the dance became more dramatic when placed within a larger milieu.

Other dancers who were hired for their specific talents were Ivan Bankoff and "Girlie" (Winifred Gilrain), both of who appeared in *The Passing Show of 1914*. Bankoff had been a vaudeville success for several years, working with a number of female dancers (thus naming his act—'Bankoff and Girlie'—so he could change partners when needed). His incorporation of Russian traditional steps into his style provided him with a distinctive niche. The pair performed a specialty dance in the first act, and were later augmented by Elsie Pilcer for the "Sari Dance," a number that referenced the music (and perhaps choreography) of the operetta, *Sari*, starring Mitzi Hajos. The notoriously difficult-to-please critic for *Green Book Magazine* (and a Ziegfeld employee), Channing Pollock, said of Bankoff that he "proves to be the most remarkable acrobatic dancer of this dancing epoch. His steps are Russian in character, but far more violent and amazing than anything heretofore brought out of the land of the Czar."[45] A more clear description of Bankoff's motions comes from an unusual source—Dewey Weinglass, an African American tap dancer who attended the performance at the Winter Garden. Weinglass explained that he "started experimenting with Russian steps" after seeing Bankoff's performance, specifically borrowing "moves like drops, squats, sweeps, splits, tumbles, and flips and added them to his dance routine."[46] There was no large-scale scene incorporating Russian plays or stories into the overall revue, but Bankoff and Gilrain's talents were still featured in a number that was of Eastern-European flavor. Here the team had an opportunity to demonstrate their own act and to work on new choreography that included other cast members. Zita and Naro Lockford, the "adagio" duo discussed in chapter 2, were featured in much the same way, and this trend continued for most of the other dancers and dance acts throughout the series.

One of the most elusive but popular of styles was called "eccentric" dancing. In many cases, it is nearly impossible to know what type of moves were comprised within a certain performer's routine, but the requirements for this dance were that it had to be highly unusual and it had to be associated with one individual performer. Although there are exceptions, most eccentric dances were done by solo artists, and were not choreographed for large groups or even pairs. Bernard Granville, mentioned earlier, offered a "Grape Dance" as a part of *The Passing Show of 1914*, where he pretended to be drunk and fell backwards with his knees bent, catching himself from falling just in time. Bessie Clayton's specialty the previous year was also an "eccentric" number, but it is described as "break-bone toe dancing," partially exciting because her movements up and down the Capitol Steps were dangerous, "where miscalculation of a hair's breadth might easily result in a temporary suspension of activities."[47] When Marilynn Miller danced, she would often include unusual steps; therefore she was seen not only as an exemplar of classical and popular types, but of her own individual style as well.

Another means of incorporating dance into the revue was to focus on new styles, or fad dances. In the teens there was an explosion of new dance types on the New York scene, and there is little doubt that integrating these trendy steps was important for nationwide dissemination of the craze. Among the styles highlighted in *The Passing Shows* were the turkey trot (1912), the tango (1913), the Brazilian maxixe and the foxtrot (1914), the hula and the fandango (1915), the apache (1916), the shimmy and "jazz dancing" (1918), and "blues dancing" (1921). On occasion, numbers in the show were performed by the dancer who had brought the new style onto the national scene, as with Rodriguez, although her Spanish moves did not spark as large a craze as some of the other styles. However, it was more likely that dancers were successful enough on their own (or with their own troupe) or too active in vaudeville to take time for a revue. For example, the woman credited with introducing America to the hula was Doraldina, a Spanish-Hawaiian dancer who was given the spotlight in Lew Fields's production of *Step This Way* (1916) after performing the dance on smaller stages. The young woman had lived in Hawaii for most of her childhood, and it was there that she studied hula. However, she returned to her native Spain in 1912 and concentrated on traditional Spanish styles. But when Doraldina came to New York in 1915, and it became known that she had learned the Hawaiian dance, she was asked to repeat it so frequently that it became her signature style (much to her chagrin). This coincided with a growing number of Hawaiian-themed songs, the expansion of Hawaiian orchestras from the West Coast onto the national circuits, and the birth of a new trend.[48]

In *The Passing Show of 1915*, the "hula-hula" became the basis for the revue's finale. Two songs were put into the scene, each with an emphasis on the exotic: "My Hula Maid" and "The Panama Pacific Drag" (both with music by Leo Edwards and lyrics by Atteridge). Frances Demarest, a veteran *Passing Show* performer, danced alongside Ernest Hare and the "Royal Hawaiians," a sextet of chorus girls.[49] A dozen other choristers joined in behind the dance, diving into a large pool that was placed on the stage; the critics liked the number, but thought the swimming portion was amusing in "supposedly being Hawaiian in character," as it was clearly just an excuse to show women in bathing suits.[50] Both songs were made available as sheet music, and they were also recorded and released as phonograph records by Victor.[51] "My Hula Maid" is a ballad that incorporates a ukulele part (performed on mandolin for the recording) that provides a slow, chordal basis for the flowing melody and the necessary slow rhythm that allows for swaying back and forth. The *New York Press* found this number "the best of the show" for two reasons. First, it featured "a group of Hawaiians with their native music and dancing (some dancing!)." And secondly, "There is a pool of real water, and in the pool there are a dozen or so real girls . . . Ned Wayburn showed one girl in a tub. Here are a dozen in a tank. Nuff ced."[52] The hula was a perfect choice for a dance that would work well in a revue. Not only could it include a novel song, but it could also use a number of chorus girls as solo dancers without male partners and also without much in the way of costumes. The exotic setting, mixed with this new style of dance and its accompanying music, was a perfect fit for *The Passing Show*, and it was at the forefront of a tidal wave of Hawaiian songs that would dominate the stage, the publishers, and the phonograph in the following year.

The *Passing Shows* were a showcase for dance in its myriad forms, and the Shuberts and their creative team always featured skilled, unique performers in any way possible. For the most part, critics praised the dances and the dancers, but not always. Dance, more than comedy and much more than song, was a display of physicality. Both the dancers and their costumes could became the target of the shocked religious leader or the scandalized theater critic. But despite the few instances where chorus girls without tights or "pornographic" choreography (as with Alcorn) attracted negative attention, dance remained a high point for most who attended the shows. The series was essential to bringing new dances to the fore, and it is probable that extensive national tours were a key means for popularizing new dance styles throughout the country.

Scenic Effects

The extended production number was also a way to put dance into the revue, and there were several of these gargantuan, multi-act showstoppers incorporated into *The Passing Shows*. While we do not know the details of the choreography for most of these numbers, some specific moves are mentioned by reviewers, while still others are suggested by the music that accompanied the dancers. The most complete discussion of an extended production number is discussed by Mary Simonson in her book *Body Knowledge*, where she provides an analysis and narrative of the Capitol Steps scene (as well as others) from *The Passing Show of 1913*.[53] Simonson convincingly integrates reviewer descriptions with melodic and rhythmic suggestions found in the music to piece together portions of this lost performance. Simonson follows the number as it flowed through dialogue, chorus dancing, solo dances, and even self-burlesque—Charlotte Greenwood's high-steps and costuming were in imitation of Bessie Clayton's dancing and image that had just happened on the same stage. In the midst of the scene, lighting and film effects were also employed to make the Capitol Steps a remarkable tour-de-force to finish the show.

Although it is impossible to discuss all of the extensive scenic effects that were highlighted within the shows, a few examples provide some insight into how the system worked. Technical innovations were woven together into the whole using stars and chorus, music, and dancing, usually in one brief but unforgettable moment. Although these components of theater are often dismissed as gimmicks today—the use of a helicopter in *Miss Saigon* springs to mind—they were an essential part of the theatrical world of the nineteenth century and remained staples of the theater at the turn of the century. Critical reactions both in New York and throughout the United States make it clear that audiences often waited breathlessly for these moments in the show, even if they knew they would only last a moment. Every *Passing Show* used technical elements in creative and unexpected ways. Sometimes Shubert staff engineered the scenes, but other agencies or innovators were often hired to formulate and construct a spectacle to dazzle the crowd. One of these individual contractors was Lincoln J. Carter, who had been devising mine collapses, fiery infernos, and train wrecks for decades before he was contacted by the Shuberts to create the Cavalry Charge for *The Passing Show of 1916*. The effect used live actors atop mechanical horses that reared up, back, and toward the audience amidst smoke, fire, and a furious musical accompaniment. It brought down the house when it finished the first act. Although this scene was onstage for only a few minutes, the critics lauded it as a thrilling portion of the revue which brought audiences back to their seats after the intermission. *The Passing Show of 1914* featured an airship making a nighttime trip across the ocean; chorus girls danced and waved on the plane from high above the stage while the orchestra provided a breezy, busy musical setting, and an offstage engine replicated the ship's whirring motors. To further enhance the realism, a film of the ocean was projected at the bottom of the stage while a movie of clouds passed above the ship.[54] The incorporation of filmic pieces to the effects began at the Winter Garden in 1913, and the driving force behind its use was Frank D. Thomas, the creator of the earliest *Passing Shows* effects.[55]

Thomas's contributions are almost always mentioned by critics, but it can be difficult to formulate what, exactly, audiences experienced. Photographs exist for a few of the effects, and the music remains extant at the Shubert Archive, but many of the other details are lost to time. But, by collecting reviews and placing them alongside documents in the Shubert Archive, one can begin to get a sense of the scene. Some of the most intriguing components are suggested in the correspondence between Thomas and J. J. Shubert. So what went into an *effect*?

Each scene was set against a painted backdrop that provided the color basis, but with limited imagery. Augmenting this was a combination of filmed footage and projected images. For the burning of San Francisco (used near the end of *The Passing Show of 1914*), Thomas reported that he had filmed two separate fires that could be projected onto different parts of the stage, using two operators simultaneously.[56] For *The Passing Show of 1915*, Thomas planned to use three projectors and add to this a popular attraction of the last century—a double stereopticon, or "magic lantern," which projected three-dimensional images.[57] However, he asked Shubert for $175 a week, and the producer felt the price was too high and only hired him again when the two came to a less expensive arrangement. Once the background imagery was established, the set pieces were placed on top of the whole. Thomas wrote Shubert more than once about fitting the airship to the correct measurements so that the proportions would make the illusion (as he called it) work. Additional sounds, such as sirens, bird calls, or machine grinding could be paired with scent-producing constructions (sulfur, fragrances, or powder was sometimes used) in order to fully enmesh the audience into the spectacle. The final additions were the chorus members (usually the women) who sang, danced, or did both. Each show contained at least one remarkable moment of visual splendor to enchant its audience in some way. In 1917, a football game between Yale and Harvard was simulated, with seventy-five thousand cheering spectators, while a year later, a full-fledged air raid on London was shown, complete with bombs and explosions. The important difference in the use of scenic effects after 1920 was that they seemed to incorporate fewer theatrical or purely visual devices; they focused more on depicting the chorus girls in the most imaginative ways possible, setting the stage for the imagination of Busby Berkeley in the next decade. A brief "futuristic study in black-and-white" was a feature of the 1922 edition, while *The Passing Show of 1923* had three spectacles—an "Animated Curtain," a "Jeweled Curtain," and a "Living Chandelier." The trend toward depicting people as objects through costuming (mentioned in chapter 4) was trumped by this elaborate staging; the dehumanization of women was immensely popular and would become a defining feature of film musicals in their first five years.

Similar to the choreography, most of the elements of the sets, including props and lighting, are lost. In some cases, however, there are a number of plots made for an array of technical specialists that remain extant at the Shubert Archive. The lighting plots for *The Passing Shows* of 1914, 1917, and 1919 provide some important clues as to the color requirements for the shows and the different ways the lighting technicians creatively developed scenes. The 1919 plot is especially detailed; it includes not only a complete inventory of required lights, but also specific instructions on where the lights should be placed in the theater and how they should be used during the performance.[58] Accompanying this list are the full requirements for the carpenters, scene and drop painters, and property managers. The prop lists, mostly devised as checklists for the touring productions, are the most common document relating to the sets; these remain for over half the revues, providing the colors, materials, and sometimes even the brand names used. The 1919 technical papers also include a list of how some of the scenes would function. For example, the drop made for the "Road to Destiny" needed to be painted carefully, making it nearly transparent. By turning on and off different 500-watt bulbs behind the curtain, different cities would come into view at the end of each road.

These features of *The Passing Show* series—songs, dances, and scenic effects— were important features of a production that was as light and effervescent as it was transitory. They were tailored in a very specific way to the moment itself, devised for an audience that would have been hungry for modern performances and topics. Songs had to be in the newest styles and about issues that the audiences cared about and understood. The dances were also "fresh" and new, sometimes adhering to classical forms presented in new ways, but at other times introducing audiences to a type of dance that they had never before witnessed. And, as any current movie or theater fan can attest, the latest visual techniques remain essential to entertainment today. Thus, these facets of *The Passing Show* were some of the most lauded elements of the revues and should be considered on their own terms as a part of their own culture and as a reflection of the people who conceived them. The context of each show was part of what made them so wonderful for audiences of the time, with a major part of the fun being the numerous references that filled each *Passing Show* to the brim.

1. Lee Davis in *Scandals and Follies* (chap. 1, n. 3) and Robert Baral in *Revue* (chap. 1, n. 3) both take this approach toward most revues, and they are especially negative when dealing with *The Passing Show* series. Davis uses the terms "inferior," "forgettable," and "atrocious" to describe the scores, while Baral is more neutral, simply calling the music as a whole "dull." It is interesting to note that most of the music from these shows was never recorded, and therefore it seems unlikely that either Davis or Baral ever heard a score performed with its original instrumentation. My experience conducting and performing some of this music has convinced me it has merit from a musical standpoint.

2. See Jonas Westover, "Shaping a Song for the Stage: How the Early Revue Cultivated Hits," *Studies in Musical Theatre* 6, no. 2 (2012), 153–71, for more on how the team tried to make the song memorable.

3. An excellent discussion of Romberg's music for both *The Passing Shows* and beyond can be found in William Everett, *Sigmund Romberg* (New Haven, CT: Yale University Press, 2007).

4. Contract between Lee Shubert and Sigmund Romberg, Shubert Archive, *The Passing Show of 1924* Show Series, box 58. The rehearsal attendance and the rest of the supervisory duties are not mentioned in this contract, but it would be surprising if the Shuberts paid extra for this additional work given the relatively few rights of "for hire" employees before the founding of the unions of the later 1910s (both musical and theatrical).

5. Newton A. Fuessle, "Broadway's King of Counterpoint," *The Outlook*, April 20, 1921, 635.

6. Unfortunately, there is not enough space here to go in depth concerning the webbing for the show. Many of the players' parts are filled with glued-in music that is both printed and in manuscript, sometimes only using a few measures of a tune for a transition.

7. Remick correspondence, Shubert Archive, general correspondence, folder 4229, box 468.

8. Tony Jackson was an African American jazz musician active in New Orleans and in Chicago, and his inclusion on the sheet music was the only acknowledgment he received. It is unclear how much of the tune was written by van Alstyne and Kahn, but they never hid their source of inspiration.

9. Letters between F. Belcher to J. J. Shubert, February–April 1919. Remick correspondence, Shubert Archive, general correspondence, folder 4229, box 468. J. J. was quite concerned that he needed to "have someone who could get the process they use for making the bubbles," because he wanted "to fill the entire stage and auditorium" with them, guaranteeing "the song will be a big hit."

10. Edward Foote Gardner, *Popular Songs of the Twentieth Century: Vol. I—Chart Detail and Encyclopedia (1900–1949)* (St. Paul, MN: Paragon House, 2000), 79–81.

11. Letter from F. Belcher to J. J. Shubert, July 26, 1918. Remick correspondence, Shubert Archive, general correspondence, folder 4229, box 468.

12. The Dell Lampe piano/vocal, Shubert Archive, package 95, box 3.

13. The dotted portion of the rhythm does not enter into the first violin part until the last four bars of the part. It is worth noting that the inclusion of an "obbligato" line was

not unique to Bennett. Edgar R. Carver was the orchestrator for Romberg's "Rose of the Morning" from the same show, and his arrangement also used this device, although the new voice does not match the rhythmic patterns of the original line.

14. Letter from J. J. Shubert to Joe Keit, December 17, 1919. Remick correspondence, Shubert Archive, general correspondence, folder 4229, box 468.

15. The most expansive collection of early recordings from Broadway is Jack Raymond's exceptional *Music from the New York Stage, 1890–1920* (GEMM CD 9050-2, 9053-5, 9056-8, and 9059-61). This collection is essential for anyone interested in theater music from the era.

16. Sequence of Time of Scenes, Dialogue, and Numbers, compiled by Caro Miller, August 5, 1914, Shubert Archive, general correspondence, folder 3594, box 425.

17. J. C. G., "New Winter Garden Piece a Joy to Stay-at-Homes," *New York Press*, July 23, 1912, 5.

18. The moniker was famously associated with the women who applied the substance to watch faces in the factories, many of whom, by the mid-1920s, sickened and died from radiation poisoning. The subsequent lawsuit was an important step in labor safety laws for employees working with dangerous substances.

19. J. J. Shubert's notes, June 29, 1924, Shubert Archive, *The Passing Show of 1924*, show series, box 58.

20. Baral claims explicit nudity first appeared in *The Passing Show of 1922*. See Baral, *Revue*, 114.

21. For more on the debate concerning nudity, Broadway, and the Shuberts, see Rachel Shtier, *Striptease: The Untold History of the Girlie Show* (New York: Oxford University Press, 2004), 71–78.

22. Stearns, "Small Chorus Girls Most Popular," 2 (chap. 4 n. 10).

23. "Winter Garden Has Gorgeous Reopening," *New York Herald*, July 23, 1912, 7.

24. "Winter Garden Reopens," *New York Clipper*, August 3, 1912, 8.

25. Letter from Melville Ellis to J. J. Shubert, June 3, 1912, Shubert Archive, *The Passing Show of 1912*, show file.

26. Lee Davis, *Scandals and Follies*, 104.

27. "Many Theatres Doing Fine Business during Summer," *Brooklyn Daily Eagle*, July 14, 1918, 7.

28. Unfortunately, Rodriguez married Dr. Carlos de Mandel, whom she divorced in 1921 after he used his "silken beard" to lure vamps and commit adultery. See "Spanish Dancer Sues Husband after Whiskers Vamp," *Chicago Tribune*, February 10, 1921, 6.

29. Carolyn Lowrey, *The First One Hundred Noted Men and Women of the Screen* (New York: Moffat, Yard, and Co., 1920), 96.

30. "Riot of Beauty in 'Passing Show,'" *New York Press*, May 30, 1915, 17.

31. "Bewitching Dancers, Gay Satires in 'Passing Show of 1915,'" *New York Herald*, May 30, 1915, 10.

32. "Take Over Persian Garden," *New York Sun*, July 1, 1915, 10.

33. A fascinating and extensive document comparing the skills and gifts of a variety of contemporary female dancers can be found in Shamus O'Sheel, "On with the Dance," *The Forum*, 45 (Jan–June 1911), 189.

34. The debate between low-brow and high-brow (and middle-brow) culture is a vast and ongoing debate among scholars.

35. More on Swirskaya's history can be found in the memoirs of her one-time manager, Rudolph Aronson, *Theatrical and Musical Memoirs* (New York: McBride, Nast, and Co., 1913), 212.

36. Letter from Thamara Swirskaya to J. J. Shubert, May 14, 1916, Shubert Archive, general correspondence, file 3, box 10. Shubert wrote to Simmons, "I do not care to grant any one of [Swirskaya's requests]. The contract she signed is the one I will hold her to."

37. "At the Lyric," *Buffalo Courier*, October 22, 1916, 46.

38. "'Olympian Ballet' Delightful at the Winter Garden," *New York Evening Telegram*, June 23, 1916, 10.

39. "New 'Passing Show' at Winter Garden Is Big Spectacle," *New York Clipper*, November 1, 1922, 30.

40. Gordon Whyte, "New Plays," *Billboard*, September 30, 1922, 34.

41. The life of Dorsha Hayes is a remarkable one that, like so many in this book, needs a voice to aid in its telling. She and her husband, Paul Hayes, ran a dance studio in Manhattan for many years, and she eventually turned to writing novels, poetry, and essays after suffering from rheumatic fever in 1936. She died in 1990 at age 93. Some of her work is held by the New York Public Library. "Dorsha Hayes, 93, Dancer and Writer," *New York Times*, November 30, 1990, http://www.nytimes.com/1990/11/30/obituaries/dorsha-hayes-93-dancer-and-writer.html.

42. "News and Gossip of the Theaters," *New York Sun*, September 15, 1918, 4.

43. The narrative is as follows: "Mahaba, a Hindoo [*sic*] sorcerer, is fascinated by the grade and beauty of a dancing girl, and carries her captive to his palace, where she is held under his magic spell. Nypah, in a trance, and dressed as a Buddha goddess, is brought into the presence of the sorcerer. Being constantly in this state of hypnosis, Nypah has become so weakened that she is a slave to the influence of Mahaba, and he causes her to be awakened and commands her to dance. During the dance she becomes weak and falls. Mahaba, after much effort, restores her and commands that she continue to dance. He then loses his head and embraces her. In vain she struggles, but finally, as she ascends the throne, she throws Mahaba from her, and the sorcerer falls backward on his neck, which is all but broken. He staggers to his feet, making a last attempt to overcome Nypah, when a mysterious power from heaven, showering its rays, protects her from malign influence. Mahaba drops dead. The spell is broken and Nypah falls on the throne lifeless."

44. "Winter Garden Reopens," *New York Clipper*, August 3, 1912, 8. The second dance performed by the couple was an "American Dance," which they had performed in other locations and as part of their European tour.

45. Channing Pollock, "When Lovely Women Stoop to Follies," *Green Book Magazine*, August 1914, 325–26.

46. Michael Holman, "Breaking: The History," in *That's the Joint: The Hip-Hop Studies Reader*, edited by Murray Forman and Mark Anthony Neal (New York: Routledge, 2004), 34. This statement proves that blacks could attend shows at the Winter Garden, but I am aware of no research that delves into the racial mix of audiences during this time. Given the important role (and subsequent disappearance) of "all-black" shows at the turn of the century, this would be a fascinating and challenging topic for further study.

47. "Much to Please in New 'Passing Show,'" *New York Times*, July 25, 1913, 7.

48. "New York's Newest Dance-Craze," *Green Book Magazine*, September 1916, 481–83. For more on the Hawaiian connection to popular songs of the era, see Charles Hiroshi

Garrett, *Struggling to Define a Nation: American Music and the Twentieth Century* (Berkeley and Los Angeles: University of California Press, 2008), chap. 5.

49. By August, Demarest had been replaced by Helen Eley.

50. "The Passing Show of 1915 Premiere," *Billboard*, June 12, 1915, 4.

51. "My Hula Maid" (Victor 17812-B) was recorded by James Reed and J. F. Harrison, and "The Panama Pacific Drag" (Victor 17978-B) was recorded by Joseph Moskowitz as a cembalo solo. The latter song was a reference to the Panama-Pacific International Exposition in San Francisco in 1915.

52. "Riot of Beauty in Passing Show," *New York Press*, May 30 1915, 17.

53. Mary Simonson, *Body Knowledge* (New York: Oxford University Press, 2013). One of the central concepts to Simonson's argument is the idea of "intermediality," where multiple media influence each other across previously perceived boundaries. This theoretical framework is both insightful and useful.

54. Procuring the necessary footage was not always easy, and Thomas wrote J. J. a memo earlier in the year that he was having trouble getting good images of the ocean because of high waves.

55. Memo from Gertrude Bock, secretary, July 18, 1913, Shubert Archive, general correspondence, file 3, box 7. The letter accompanied the money for the expense of taking the moving pictures, which amounted to $22.25.

56. Letter from Frank D. Thomas to J. J. Shubert, May 19, 1914, Shubert Archive, general correspondence, folder 2603.

57. Letter from Frank D. Thomas to J. J. Shubert, January 12, 1915, Shubert Archive, general correspondence, folder 2603. For a remarkable contemporary guide that details the use and expectations for these projects, see Oscar B. Depue and C. Francis Jenkins, *Handbook for Motion Picture and Stereopticon Operators* (Washington, DC: The Knega Company, 1908).

58. The plot is located in the Shubert Archive, box 92, package 1.

6

A SURE CURE FOR THE BLUES

• • •

CREATING *THE PASSING SHOW OF 1914*

After two successful editions of *The Passing Show* and five Fall and Spring Winter Garden shows, the Shuberts were confident they had a formula for their revues that worked. The next installment, *The Passing Show of 1914*, began production in March of the same year. By today's standards, the work was extremely fast, with the entire process taking just over three months. This chapter examines the genesis and structure of *The Passing Show of 1914* as a case study for how revues in the series were created. I will provide an example of how the creative team worked on this show from start to finish, with a close look at Atteridge's writing process. The remarkable collection held at the Shubert Archive allows for an in-depth inspection of script drafts and associated materials, revealing how this edition transformed over time.

A wide range of items pertaining to the creation of the script for *The Passing Show of 1914* remain extant, illustrating the process Harold Atteridge described, wherein the creation of the show begins with the collection and arrangement of a sprawling, "open" event with no real constraints.[1] Unfortunately, no drafts for the music remain, but the completed songs that were cut before the revue opened are still packed together with the scores for the show. As both Atteridge and J. C. Huffman explain in contemporary interviews, the goal of putting together the revue was first to arrange a long list of events that "might" work together and then to whittle the show down to its most effective numbers.[2]

CASTING AND DEVELOPMENT OF THE SCRIPT

The first step for building a *Passing Show* was to come up with ideas that might work in the production and then fitting those together in an order that made sense. First, Atteridge wrote several scenarios to determine where comedic scenes could unfold or where songs could be placed, often dependent on the actors portraying the roles. If someone was to play the gypsy princess Sari, for example, this person should be a skilled dancer and should be young.[3] Whichever performer became the Queen of the Movies needed to be loud, over-the-top, and a good comedian. So, the question that arises from this issue is very similar to the age-old "chicken and egg" problem: which came first—the role or the actor?

Several early lists were made of performers who might be available to participate in *The Passing Show of 1914*, but there are no specifics about which characters they were to play.[4] However, one version of the cast list that remains extant is not based on pay scales, but instead on roles. Table 6.1 pairs certain players with characters they might portray, complete with alternative roles or, in some cases, composite roles (where a performer would take on more than one role in the show—for example José Collins's portrayal of both Kitty MacKay and Lady Shireen).

Table 6.1 was an early list, but not the earliest. It originates sometime in early- to mid-April (at least before April 20, 1914). As evidenced here, many roles were already assigned to particular actors from the beginning of the writing process. José Collins was the female star, and would portray the two roles previously mentioned. Frances Demarest was going to be a secondary player with a variety of roles, from Panthea and Leonora (characters with dialogue) to a singing role, the Midnight Girl. The roles of Jerrold McGee and Omar Khayyam were meant to be paired the same way as Collins's roles, but in this case, two actors were being considered for the part. As Jerrold and Omar were both young male leading roles—the juvenile parts—it may have meant there was some flexibility in the creation of the character; since the part was fairly generic in its design, it could be played by a variety of actors. In this table, both Robert Emmet Keane and Franklin Ardell were considered for the role, though neither of them ended up with the part. Keane instead took on several roles mentioned in the lower right-hand area of the table, like Imam Allafake and Teddy Roosevelt. Since Harry Fox did not end up in the revue at all, the roles assigned to him were handed out to others (such as King Baggot being given to John Freeman), while others (Bertie the Lamb and the Crinoline Girl) were eliminated entirely. This suggests that these two roles might have been specifically written for Fox and removed because he was no longer part of the production. In the case of George W. Monroe, the character of the Queen of the Movies seems to have been connected to him from the beginning; the role incorporated his vaudeville and Broadway "schtick," bringing to the Winter Garden an entertainer whose act was part of what would unfold in the revue.

Table 6.1 also reveals that a number of roles were still unassigned. These positions required a variety of performer abilities. For example, the three "Vagabond Players" would all be expected to dance in order to play their role. A character actor like Monroe simply would not have been appropriate for such a position. And though Bankoff and Girlie had been engaged by the Shuberts by this time, no one knew that they would eventually fill two of those positions. The case of Jenny Dolly (one of the Dolly Sisters and a famous dancer and a singer) follows much the same story: she was to portray Sari (a fictitious gypsy) and Gaby (a real-life dancer and singer). However, Dolly was not retained for the production, and the role of Gaby was eliminated. Elsie Pilcer, a relatively unknown actress, was given the part of Sari, but as the revue developed, the role was scaled down.

Another issue raised by Table 6.1 is the chronology of the script. As a few of the roles were already conceived and assigned, it meant that Atteridge had begun at an earlier date. So when did the development of *The Passing Show of 1914* begin? It was

Table 6.1 Early Cast List with Roles (Undated).[1]

ACTOR	ROLE
Harry Fox	Bertie the Lamb, and the Crinoline Girl. King Baggot
Robert Emmet Kean [sic]	McGee & Omar Khayyam or Franklin Ardell
Bankoff and Girlie Specialty.	
George Monroe	Queen of the Movies
Frances Demarest	Midnight Girl, Panthea, & Leonora
Jenny Dolly	Gaby and Sari
Laura Hamilton	Adele, Billie Burke, Mary Pickford
George Whiting	Moving Picture Operator
Sadie Burt	Mary Pickford? Or Girl in love with Moving Picture Actors
Mack & Walker?	
Artic Mellinger?	
Jennie Lucas?	
Jose Collins	Kitty McKay & Shireen
	Roosevelt
	Huerta
	Napoleon or the Nut
	Baron (combination of the Baron from *Panthea* and *The Yellow Ticket*)
	Imam Allafake
	Vagabond Players. Maxixe, Tango, and Turkey Trot

[1]Undated cast list, Shubert Archive, box 87, package 5. Some names differ in spelling from later versions or actual names.

probably around March 15, 1914, when the first cast list was prepared. Luckily, several documents exist that, although undated, provide clues to the development of the show. Four scenarios—two of which are signed by Atteridge—sketch the basic structure of the show in its early form. This coincides exactly with Atteridge's description of creating a show in his featured article from 1914: "Seven or eight weeks ahead I have a private conference with J. J. Shubert, who engages the cast and chorus, plans the scenery and lighting effects, and superintends the production, and together we map out a skeleton idea of the forthcoming revue."[5] These "skeletons" are fascinating windows into the creation process.

The first of these scenarios is the shortest, and it is written in a way that merely suggests topics, imagery, and some of the shows that will be burlesqued by the upcoming Winter Garden revue. Many of the plays Atteridge wanted to burlesque are discussed more thoroughly in chapter 7.

[**SCENARIO 1**]
SCENARIO FOR PASSING SHOW OF 1914.
The curtain to rise on an elaborate Persian Garden with the embellishments and environments of "A Thousand Years Ago" and "Omar the Tentmaker."
At the rise of the curtain, the stage to be absolutely empty, with the accompaniment of the oboe and the harp, until the appearance of the leading female character.
Then the appearance of "Omar," the vagabond musician, embodying the parts of "Omar the Tentmaker" and [Henry] Dixey's part in "A Thousand Years Ago."
There should be a pretty love scene, and then the Waltz Song, which shall be the theme all through the entire play.
After that, the various characters in both plays aforementioned are introduced, until the scene becomes a Persian Cabaret, which shall be a very good number with all the color of the Orient, balloons, confetti, lanterns, and make it a sort of a carnival.
After this big carnival scene, Omar is arrested as a heretic for professing that there shall be a Broadway a thousand years from now; also that the man shall see the women's faces, and that there shall be Tango dancing, turkey-trotting, Zepplin [sic] airships, and all the funny sayings of the present period. He is taken and put into the stocks. He is told that he will be given his freedom if he answers correctly three riddles that a la "Thousand Years Ago." He fails in the last riddle, which must be made very funny, and he is again put in the stocks the same as in "Omar the Tentmaker." As they are about to beat him, LIGHTS OUT.
The next time you see him, he is floating over the heads of the audience on a crane, and there he tells what will happen in the future. This scene to be about 3 or 4 minutes long, until the scene can be set on the stage for the Napoleonic Period, the directoire, in which the character of the crazy man from "The Misleading Lady" playing the part of Napoleon. This scene to run for about 15 minutes.
Then a scene in "one" where we are brought to the Gambling Palace at Monte Carlo. This is where we want to show semi-modern dances, the kan-kan [sic]. This is to be entirely French.
From there we take the Zepplin [sic] airship and sail across the Atlantic with the [Frank] Thomas Effect.
The opening of the second act to be some big scene in New York City, either an idealized restaurant, dance palace, or a locale which will lend itself to dress and color.

From there we want a scene in "1," which shall be the railroad station where they get on the train—the New York Central, showing three cars instead of one car as they do at the Princess Theatre. They are going to the Exposition in San Francisco. After that scene, a scene in "1," a semi-oriental scene, like the modern Chinatown of San Francisco, or some scene which will lend itself to environments and atmosphere, and then to the Presidio overlooking the Panama Exposition in San Francisco and the Golden Gate.[6]

This single-page, typewritten scenario is an extraordinary document, demonstrating a wide range of interests and expectations that Atteridge (and probably J. J. Shubert too) had for the revue as a whole. Some of these ideas survived to become part of the actual production, while most of the concepts were dropped or altered significantly by the time the revue premiered. Beyond the basic structural ideas, however, is the surprisingly detailed information concerning dances, places for song numbers, the visual makeup of the scene, and even the duration of some events. Atteridge wanted to create a show with good entertainment possibilities in the visual language of the production—a "Persian Cabaret" and a ride in a "Zeppelin airship"—but he also wanted to make sure there were opportunities for other items within the larger framework. Atteridge explains what he wants not just by means of a location, but also in terms of what that site can do for the show—for example, a "scene which will lend itself to environments and atmosphere." Atteridge even conceived of specific theatrical moments where characters were placed in carefully devised situations, such as on an empty stage or in three railroad cars. Without having written lyrics or dialogue (presumably), Atteridge was already deciding which scenes could be several minutes long and which should be shorter. He even prepared for places where jokes would be a necessity, specifically in the "failure" of Omar to answer the final riddle and be sentenced to death. Atteridge seemed to be striving for a balance of both past and present (a thousand years ago and the modern age) and the exotic and familiar (France or Persia and New York). The revue, then, was meant to embrace a wide variety of elements, but in a balanced, thoughtful way, a feat that would remain important throughout the development of the show.

A key element of this scenario is the desire by Atteridge for what musicologists call *thematic unity*, wherein a single musical motive or theme can provide a thread of consistency throughout a complete work. The idea is a common topic for scholars writing about the music of Beethoven and other classical music, but some musicals (post-1940) use this idea for very specific purposes—*Lady in the Dark* and its use of "My Ship" comes to mind.[7] It is very surprising, however, to find the idea embedded in this scenario, so far removed (chronologically) from the musicals of the so-called "Golden Age." This tells us many things: Atteridge wanted there to be a central song in the show—a "manufactured" hit; there was the expectation that the score could provide unity instead of a script; that the motive could come from a song within the show that was based on a waltz; and, perhaps most importantly, that the revue itself was to have a feeling of wholeness through an important theatrical device. Atteridge's consideration of a waltz to perform this function may have been a mistake in 1914, although waltzes were still popular and one was even included later on in this particular revue. The dance sensation of this year though was actually the tango, and as the production grew, this dance was used more extensively, making for a better, more modern musical thread.[8] The notion of a unified musical is the most important feature of the preceding outline, showing that Atteridge wanted something that felt whole rather than piecemeal—not just a loose collection of vaudeville acts.

Another interesting element of this scenario—one might even venture to say that it was the central concept of the show in the beginning—is the idea to use Omar Khayyam as a leading character. The harem scene is one of many mentioned in the original sketch that manage to remain intact through all the show's transformations, making it an excellent focal point to explore while considering the three remaining scenarios. After the first one was written, Atteridge expanded each consecutive scenario, adding more details. Considering the significant size of scenarios 2 through 4 (see appendix 2), I focus only on the scenes involving Omar Khayyam, examining the transformation of this scene without trying to cover every aspect of the revue. The other components, however, will be included in the discussion of large-scale structure.

In Scenario 1, the unnamed female lead from "Omar the Tentmaker" appears onstage first, bringing an end to the sparse entrance music. Though no transition is mentioned, Omar is then ushered onto the stage as a "vagabond musician"—an idea that survives through to the final version of the show. Scenario 2, however, offers a wider variety of trajectories for the narrative, labeled "A," "B," and "C." Table 6.2 delineates the various scenarios, showing where different ideas migrate in the separate scenarios. At first glance, this would seem to be the first sketch for ideas, but a single sentence in scenario "B" clarifies the matter, placing this document in at least the second position: "First scene and prologue . . . introducing Omar and combining the best things of 'A Thousand Years Ago' and 'Omar Khayyam,' a Broadway prophecy, etc., etc., as in original scenario." Scenario 2 greatly simplifies the kind of ideas Atteridge suggested in Scenario 1, cutting each of the three narratives down to half-page mini-paragraphs. Omar is omitted from scenario 2A, where the action revolves around a movie studio and its boss, the Queen of the Movies, but Omar is retained for scenarios 2B and 2C. In 2B, the revue begins with Omar and the Persian Garden, but moves away from the past in the second scene, where the movie studio idea returns. However, an interesting turn happens in scene 3, where "the re-incarnated 'Omar,' now the modern novelist (a la 'Seven Keys to Baldpate'), applies for a position. [The Queen] makes desperate love to him, tempts him with wine, etc., etc., a la '1999' and reversing the second act situation of 'The Yellow Ticket.'" What Atteridge wanted was a way to have part of the show take place in the past and part in the present. In the modern age, Omar is reincarnated to achieve the effect of using the same character to tie these sections together.[9]

Scenario 2C is another attempt at trying to use Omar as the unifying character, again bridging old and new worlds. Atteridge writes that the "first scene [is] a Persian Cabaret, where Omar is in love with Kitty Mackay, who is being hounded by the Russian Secret Police (the Okrana), at the instigation of the Queen of the Movies, who is in love with Omar. The entire story [is] to be modern with all characters of the plays used." This brief scenario allows for the colorful "Oriental" charm while at the same time creating the possibility of modern events happening in a place dedicated to the old-fashioned. This theme, too, re-emerges in the final edition of the

Table 6.2 Scenarios for *The Passing Show of 1914*, with Topics for Each Act.

Scenario 1	Scenario 2A	2B	2C	Scenario 3	Scenario 4
Act 1	*Act 1*	*Act 1*	*Act 1*	*Act 1*	*Act 1*
Persian Garden	Moving Picture Office	Persian Garden	Persian Cabaret	Moving Picture Studio	Persian Garden
Persian Cabaret					Moving Picture Office
Prophecy	Novelist Adventures	Moving Picture Office	Kitty MacKay In Trouble	Novelist Adventures	Napoleon Scene
Napoleon Scene	Kitty MacKay Rescue	Novelist Adventures		Kitty MacKay In Trouble	Moving Picture Studio
Monte Carlo		Napoleon Scene		Moving Picture Office	Novelist Adventures
Airship Effect		Kitty MacKay Rescue		Persian Garden	Kitty MacKay In Trouble
Act 2				New York Scene	Crinoline Girl Bit
New York Scene				Airship Effect	Moving Picture Action
Railroad Scene					Airship Effect
Chinatown Scene					
Panama Exposition					

show. And, importantly, this is the first indication of a love interest between Kitty and Omar, an idea that, in its own way, is eventually transferred to the final version. Although it is not explicitly stated, the Russian secret police come from "The Yellow Ticket," one of the many plays parodied by *The Passing Show*. There is some question about just *how* the Queen of the Movies would make "desperate love" (desperate wooing) to Omar onstage, but since the idea did not expand, it remains a mystery.

Scenarios 3 and 4 are somewhat more difficult to place in order, and therefore I have chosen to label the shorter of the two, which includes some ideas from scenario 2, as scenario 3. Here, the opening scene is labeled, "discovered—stenographers," which transfers to the final version, in a movie studio where "a new film to be made called 'From a Thousand Years Ago to Today'" is being made. King Baggot and Mary Pickford appear prominently, as do three actors who have been hired to be in the movie, including the Midnight Girl, the Crinoline Girl, and Sari. Atteridge even mentions some possible songs, including a "number between Adele and McGee," a song that is performed by "Kitty MacKay and Scotch girls," and the "Sari Number." This scenario gets closer to some events that later actually *happen* onstage, but the insistence that there be a Persian scene seems less urgent. Kitty MacKay, McGee the novelist, a Baron, and the Queen of the Movies are all present, and for the first time, Omar is relegated to a small part of the show: the movie within the revue, which takes place in scene 3. Some of the same themes are maintained—the jump to the past, the exploration of the present, the parody of many other theatrical productions—while at the same time making the whole story somewhat more plausible. This does not mean that the inclusion of the Russian Secret Police and Roosevelt (who is to be "lost in Brazil") are more likely to happen, but it means that opportunities for song numbers and dances become possible in the same way that music can happen during a backstage musical: when McGee holds a "rehearsal" for the movie, the scene can "end with the Moving Picture Glide," and the end of scene four depicts an escape where "the Baron and the Russian secret police . . . take [Kitty] away in an airship." These two moments are still theatrical spectacle, but they are created for specific reasons. They are not "empty" plot moments that have no connection to each other, even if the plot does seem thin. Instead, these two examples show how Atteridge conceived of the show, much as in the same way as scenarios 1 and 2: he thought of it as a whole, with a framework that would provide a multitude of moments for specialty acts or events.

This revue is not aligned with what is now called an "integrated" musical (one where every aspect, including dance, is part of the narrative thrust), but it does exhibit a sense of forward motion. This may simply be an idea that did not continue to grow into the revues of 1919 and beyond, but current research does not yet support that. It is important, however, that even if the revue did not make use of a plotted trajectory—a teleological, dramatic narrative—this did not mean that there was no feeling of change over time. Susanne K. Langer's seminal book, *Feeling and Form*, provides some fascinating ideas on the ways in which comedy intersects with dramatic forms. Tragedy, she asserts, is a narrative that is fundamentally linear, but comedy can take a more circular shape. Both narratives produce a link to real life while at the same time invoking the "virtual" world, but both forms manage to create a strong connection to an audience. On comedy, she continued with the following:

Because comedy is abstract, and reincarnates for our perception the motion and rhythm of living, it enhances our vital feeling, much as the presentation of space in painting enhances our awareness of visual space. The virtual life on the stage is not diffuse and only half felt, as actually life usually is: virtual life, always moving visibly into the future, is intensified, speeded up, exaggerated; the exhibition of vitality rises to a breaking point, to mirth and laughter. We laugh in the theater at small incidents and drolleries which would hardly rate a chuckle off-stage. It is not for such psychological reasons as that we go there to be amused, nor that we are bound by rules of politeness to hide our hilarity, but these trifles at which we laugh are really funnier *where they occur* than they would be elsewhere; they are *employed* in the play, not merely brought in casually. They occur where the tension of dialogue or other action reaches to a high point. As thought breaks into speech—as the wave breaks into foam—vitality breaks into humor.[10]

Atteridge's careful structuring of the revue seems based on the ideas Langer suggests will most likely create an empathic bond between audience and the characters onstage. In scenario 3, by developing a more plausible flow of events for the revue, especially in dramatic reasoning (the cause-and-effect of events), the writer comes closer to forging a reality that could elicit a stronger reaction from his audience. The careful line one must maintain in these terms is that it is not the closer one gets to real life that will work best in drama, but that some connection between the two should exist, at least on a structural level (and perhaps on an emotional level also?) to most effectively work with one's audience. Again, where this line begins and ends for the revue deserves significantly more attention.

Scenario 4 is by far the most extensive of the four documents. Here, we begin to see Atteridge working out not only a list of songs that could fit each scene, but also a much more thorough version of the revue across the entire first act through five scenes. The progression is quite complex, with a detailed list of what might happen next. The Persian Garden scene is listed first again, with the motion picture office scene placed in the second position. Omar is still a vagabond player, but in this scenario, he comes "in quest of the hand of Shireen," which eventually happens in the revue. The prophecy section is intact, though the group of three songs in this section is not yet in its final form. In truth, the Omar scene eventually uses only two main songs, "Omar Khayyam" and "Dreams from Out of the Past," but Atteridge's original ideas were for "A Persian Night," "A Thousand Years Ago," and "Oh, Oh, Omar!" The general outline of songs (one for setting, one for the past, and one about the main character) is nearly kept, but apparently the number that "set the stage" did not make the final edit. However, throughout the rest of scenario 4, Omar remains a character in modern day (again reincarnated), and he deals with Mrs. Shireen, who is now the Queen of the Movies. Her daughter—just called "Shireen"—is going to play the part of "Kitty MacKay" in a movie. The relationship between Shireen and Omar is still used in this case, and it becomes the backbone for the rest of the action. First, the two are separated by a gang of White Slavers while Shireen is "forced to work as Kitty MacKay in the new film being made," and the following scenes continue to expand this narrative. The story—about Napoleon and the Mona Lisa—is appropriately nonsensical, but in the midst of this scenario, something very important happens: Atteridge labels one section with "The Picture as Played."

Although it was suggested in the previous scenarios, there is in scenario 4 a clearly delineated section where the revue actually becomes *a film within a play*. Of course, humor is added because Omar does not realize that Shireen is playing the role of Kitty, and therefore he thinks that everything that is happening to her is real rather than part of a story (and, as one would expect in this type of screwball moment, he is the only one who thinks this). The enactment of a movie is strange because it is done through the use of songs and dances as well as a plot and, therefore, lampooning cinema while at the same time retaining the qualities only possible (at the time) in theater; it is easy today to forget that the movies in 1914 were still silent and would be until 1927, but in this scenario, the Midnight Girls, the Sari Dancers, and the Crinoline girl (a female impersonator) each get a song, belying the true medium of *The Passing Show*. This mimesis of a motion picture continues in the following scenes, which Atteridge labeled as "The Second Reel," wherein Omar becomes one of three characters dressed as Napoleon and general chaos ensues until the airship effect. In an interesting addendum, Atteridge writes a note about the scene and its possible actors: "(This ... would be an ideal scene of [George] Whiting and [Sadie] Burt, as Whiting could easily do the Magee, Novelist)."

There are a few items in scenario 4 that give question to their chronological position, but the results are not conclusive. First of all, the reincarnation idea (for Omar) from scenario 2 is still made use of here, and this does not happen in scenario 3. However, Shireen is entirely absent from the previous treatments, and since she becomes such an important part of the relationship between the lead actors in the final script, it is surprising that she would somehow be left out after being introduced here. The scene in which there is tension between the Queen of the Movies and her daughter in the studio is retained, as is the idea of the Queen and her White Slaves (meaning her regular employees). The second half of this scene, wherein the Queen tries to seduce a man in her office, also makes the final cut for the show. This strange mix of events, though, especially in the beginning of scenario 3—with the stenographers dancing with the movie executives—is far closer to the final shape of the show than scenario 4 is. In all probability, Atteridge took ideas and moved them around many times before he decided on an order that made sense to him and also satisfied the other members of the creative staff, especially Huffman, who would have contributed his thoughts on where a scene was placed.

Whatever the chronology of the scenarios, the four different sketches of how this particular revue should unfold presents a fascinating glimpse into the creative process of Harold Atteridge (and probably unmentioned others as well). It is surprising just how much of scenario 1 was transferred into the final version of the show onstage, including the huge airship effect, the Persian scene, and the idea to connect the show with the movies. Even the move to New York, the spotlight on different dances, and the eventual relocation to San Francisco stay in the show throughout its creation. It must also be mentioned that with the exception of the first draft of ideas, none of the other scenarios include any information *at all* about act 2, unless those pages have simply been lost, as improbable as that might be. Even in the final script, the first act is where most of the action happens and where the most complicated shifts of location take place. Atteridge's efforts to develop the show depended, at least for him, on the first act, always building to a climax with the final "effect."

In addition to the scenarios, two other types of lists also exist demonstrating further development of the revue. One is the cast list for roles, with no suggestions made about the people who will play the parts, but merely a catalog of which parts will be used in each situation. The remaining four documents are collections of song numbers for each scene, and they are also included in appendix 2. Two of the four have no performers assigned to songs, while two indicate specific entertainers for the various numbers. The list of songs (song list 1) was created to explicate the numbers for scenario 3. In a single instance, the title would remain unchanged even in the final version of the show; "The Moving Picture Glide" is the only song that retains its title from song list 1. A few of the songs are assigned to characters, but many of them are still awaiting further details. For example, no. 2 is listed as "Midnight Girl Number," but it is followed by no. 3, which is called a "Boy and Girl Number." There is no song title, but instead only an idea of what *type* of song would contrast with those around it rather than the *content* of the actual piece. As is the case with the scenarios, the conceptual framework devised by Atteridge took precedence over the details, allowing songs to migrate to different positions depending on the flow of the production at any time. Additionally, songs could not only switch places, but they could also be removed if they did not seem to work. Both Huffman and Atteridge explain that the show begins rehearsals as a much longer, five-hour show that is honed to a perfect two-and-a-half- to three-hour revue.[11] By writing conceptually, no single number is given a position that cannot be changed or reconsidered when the whole takes shape.

The most extensive of the documents is the pairing of the cast list with song list 2. Both of these coincide with the creation of scenario 4, and they are quite detailed, with many song titles written in specific locations. There are indications that some songs are fairly well set in Atteridge's mind, while others are still being formulated. Song no. 4 is called the "Big Scotch Number" and the title, "Kitty MacKay," is written next to the idea; but song no. 9 is labeled as the "Big Hungarian Rag Song, 'That Haunting Hungarian Tune' or etc., built on the 'Hazaazaa [sic] Number' from *Sari*." In one instance, Atteridge even identifies the song he will be parodying in the show. He calls song no. 13 "Any Night," which he wants to be "built on the type of 'In The Night' from *The Queen of the Movies*." The general type of song is still listed first, in several cases, but this catalog has a wide variety of titles that suggest where Atteridge may have been heading with this draft of songs for the show. In the cast list that accompanies the song list, Atteridge simply mentions which characters will be needed to complete the different scenes. There are many, many names overall, but Atteridge succinctly states "many of these characters double, and other incidental characters introduced."

The striking thing about the first two song lists is that they deal almost entirely with the first act, very much like the scenarios before them. The final two song lists, however, are only about the second act, and these differ from the previous versions in that they not only include which character will star in the number, but in most cases, the actors are also specified. Because of the different performers who are included on the lists, it would seem they were written much later than the previous two documents. Song list 3 deals with cast members and their songs, but in some cases, no song title is included. For example, scene 2 is a "railroad drop in 'one,'" and the number that follows the action is listed as "Freeman-Dunham's Specialty." Scene 5 is the "Sloping Path," while scene 6 is José Collins's "Bohemian Rag." Scene 7, though, lists each event in its entirety, with dialogue and transitions included to show how one song moves to the next. Finally, song list 4 most closely relates to the revue on opening day, with song titles, actors, and choruses listed after the scene location is specified. The only significant difference between the two lists is the inclusion of Marilynn Miller on song list 4, where she is referred to as "Baby Miller," suggesting that this list came after the previous one, where Miller is not present.

Atteridge clearly had some difficulty deciding what to do with the famous dance duo of Adelaide and Hughes. At the bottom of song list 3, "Adelaide and Hughes, 'Fountain Dance'" is written followed by an underlined question mark. Also, a song called "Silence and Fun," performed by Hughes, is written in between a dialogue and a burlesque (followed by "Eagle Rock") in scene 7. This song is dropped in song list 4, but it is replaced with a song called "On the Levee," also to be performed by Hughes. Since the dancers did not appear in the show when it opened, Atteridge had to quickly decide what to do with the "Levee" number, which he renamed "Good Old Levee Days" and reassigned to four other dancers. Even though the word "yes" is circled at the bottom of song list 4, suggesting that this was the combination the producers were going to keep for the opening of the show, there were still changes to be made at the very last moment. A closer look at the various scripts for *The Passing Show of 1914* suggests just how major (or, in some cases, minor) the transformations for the final version really were.

THE SCRIPTS

There are five versions of *The Passing Show of 1914* in the Shubert Archive; most of these scripts are dated on the cover, providing a clear chronology of when the different versions of the script came to be.[12] Table 6.3 displays the various versions of the scripts alongside the number that will be used here to discuss them.

Script 1, though undated, is very different from other versions of the show. The cover, first of all, is made of brown paper, while the others are all bound together in blue paper. But it is what lies on the inside cover of the undated act 2 that is the most surprising and, at the same time, suggests that it is part of the very early stages of the writing process. There is a cartoon of several women sitting "In the Gymnasium of a Women's Club," (see Figure 6.1). This cartoon was an inspiration for Atteridge, who used it to write a scene that takes place inside a gymnasium. The men in the gym, Atteridge's own addition, were part of the Nat Nazarro, Jr. Troupe, all acrobats and contortionists, and according to at least one of the early scripts, some members were little more than (or possibly only) boys.[13] The joke in the cartoon is that although there may be several women at the gym, the most strenuous thing they would do is play cards. In an interesting turn, this does not become part of the humor of the scene.

Table 6.3 Scripts for *The Passing Show of 1914*.

Number	Date	Acts
1	Undated	I, II
2	April 18, 1914	I
3	May 8 and 9, 1914	I, II
4	May 23, 1914	I, II
5	June 13 (17), 1914[1]	I, II

Note: Each script is typed and on letter-sized paper.

[1]Both dates are included on the front of the script, which probably suggests the show remained the same for at least a week. The script was changed quite soon after opening, however.

Fig. 6.1. *Undated cartoon of women's club (gym). Unknown magazine source. Shubert Archive.*

The physical stasis required for the source joke would not have worked onstage, so Atteridge instead used exercises popular in 1914, including passing a medicine ball back and forth, jumping through hoops, and tossing around footballs. The footballs were a special touch, with the women of the chorus carrying them on the runway and throwing them to people in the audience. The costume designs from the show were more closely modeled on the cartoon. ⓅFigure 6.2 shows the costumes for the scene, with chorus girls in their uniforms, complete with a large black belt.

Although the costumes are not identical, they share a few important elements. One of these is the short skirt, ideal for displaying the girls' legs, while another shared trait is the low "V" neckline, though *The Passing Show's* necklines are substantially lower than those in the cartoon. Even the collar for the actresses is reminiscent of the ones in the picture, although the "sailor" motif is dropped for the revue, as are the bows on the front of the blouse.

A second cartoon is also included in this undated script on page 8 of the second act. This cartoon, seen in Figure 6.3, depicts more closely an event that happens in the revue, "A Eugenic Wedding," which is the title used in the final program for the Winter Garden show.

The joke of the cartoon is that the physical perfection brought on by exercise—a new idea in the 1910s—should become the most important part of choosing a spouse (perhaps trumping love?). In the cartoon, the bride wears a veil, but her gown is unusually short to show off her shapely legs. The groom is in a full body exercise suit,

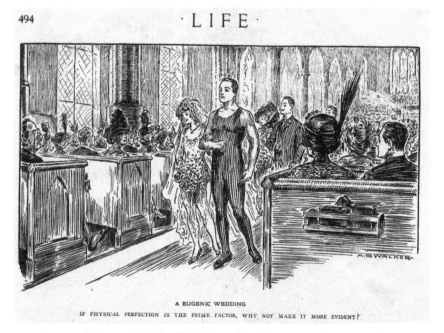

Fig. 6.3. *"A Eugenic Wedding" by A. B. Walker (fl. 1900–1930)*, Life Magazine, *date unknown. Shubert Archive.*

similar to those worn by college gym teams, such as the one at Vanderbilt University in 1909–1910. Such a costume would clearly show off the physical prowess of any young man in his prime. Although no photograph from the Eugenics Wedding scene in the musical is extant, there is little doubt that Bernard Granville, who was a young and lithe dancer, would probably have worn a similar outfit to most clearly explain to the audience what was happening onstage.

This wedding is only one of many such scenes that took place early in the writing of the revue (from April until May) that managed to remain until the opening of the show. Even among the changes that take place over each scenario, each cast list, and each pay list, one topic remains salient: the love of Omar and Shireen is the basis for the plot of the play. In the earliest scripts, Omar and Shireen have significantly more prominent roles, with Atteridge going so far as to reincarnate the characters from "A Thousand Years Ago" into the modern age, to allow for up-to-date dances, music, and comedy. Eventually, Omar and Shireen are relegated to just one place in the revue—the Persian Garden—which becomes a movie, and where the characters are roles played by Jerrold McGee and Kitty MacKay, respectively. The love of these two protagonists remains the seed from which the rest of the script grows. Jerrold and Kitty become the primary couple, but the love they share (even when donning the roles of Omar and Shireen) is still the crux of the plot, and remains so throughout every draft of the script.

Kitty and Jerrold's love is endangered by a jealous Baron, and a number of secondary characters either help or hinder their union from taking place. As the rest of the chapter demonstrates, the wedding scene ends the tension of the plot (such as it is) in the very first scene of the second act, allowing the rest of the revue to move from one location to another, loosening up the story to allow for a variety of specialties. A plot did exist in the first act—probably to lure audience members back into their seats after the intermission—but, once patrons were seated again, the director could let go of the narrative and simply employ spectacle. As is true with the plot elements, each version of the script suggests the lack of structure in the second act to be the norm.

As Table 6.3 demonstrates, the earliest copy of the script (script 1) is indicated both by the different-colored brown binding as well as by the "inspirational" cartoons pasted into the second act. Each act is bound separately, as is the case for each version of the script. Instead of doing a line-by-line analysis of the script, I will focus mainly on the placement of scenes, as well as the differences between the scene as it appears in script 1 and the transformations that take place over the creation of the other scripts.

Script 1 begins with the scene set in the Persian Garden. A substantial amount of this dialogue is retained throughout the different scripts, and most of it is used in script 5 (dated June 13, 1914), which was completed the week the show opened. It is not a surprise to find that the pattern of act 1 follows scenario 4 exactly, down to the same listing of songs and characters that are to be used from moment to moment; it is likely, therefore, that scenario 4 was completed just before Atteridge sat down to write the dialogue. Though no handwritten material is included in script 1, there are a large number of "pieces" of scenes both typed and handwritten that possibly were created somewhere between the scenario and the process of compiling the full script.[14] One of the only significant changes from scenario 1 comes in Omar's answer to the last riddle; instead of making a mistake and paying for it with his life, he passes the test, only to be dragged away and beaten when he preaches of a mysterious place in the future called Broadway. This change would remain intact to the day of the performance.

The second scene is extensive, and takes place in the Office of the Queen of the Movies at a moving picture studio. This scene retains many of the same features between script 1 and script 5, especially in terms of placement and tone. The most important difference, however, is that in this early version, the scene is very long, stretching over ten pages and encompassing at least six different collections of characters. This scene introduces the Queen of the Movies; here, she is also known as Mrs. Shireen, Shireen's mother. In the opening, the Queen sits with Leonora, her lawyer, and with Billie Burke, an office girl. Equating Burke, who was Ziegfeld's wife at the time, to an "office girl," was incredibly demeaning, and the scene would only get worse for her as it was altered over time.[15] Many of the actual lines, however, are still included in script 5. The scene then changes to include Bertie the Lamb and Gaby Deslys, two characters who are not included in the June version. A song, "You're Just a Little Bit Better Than the One I Thought Was Best," is even assigned to these two. Following this, the scene moves back to the Queen, Billie, and Bertie, eventually introducing Mr. Omar as a nervous wreck of a writer trying to get a job with the Queen of the Movies. Only the second part of this section is kept in the final show, but Mr. Omar is removed (as he is in scripts 2–5), replaced by Mr. Verenka, a Russian inspired by the play, *The Yellow Ticket*. Following the introduction and attempted seduction (by the Queen) of Mr. Omar, Shireen appears, as if out of the ether, and announces that this man is the one she was destined to love for all eternity. Atteridge suggests that an as-yet-unnamed song be written to finish off the scene. Script 1 includes some of the songs, but the final decisions about what number goes where (or even if one should happen) is not made until later, suggesting that Atteridge was fully aware that this script was only in an early stage of development.

The third scene in script 1 is also quite extensive, and filled with dialogue that, for the most part, is cut before script 3. The section opens with Mary Pickhard, who becomes Mary Packard by script 4. This character, meant to parody Mary Pickford, includes William Hallowell Magee, who is "the hero from [George M. Cohan's play] 'Seven Keys from Baldpate'" and an unnamed cameraman. This scene eventually becomes scene 1 on opening night. The Cameraman (William Dunham) is eventually given a more substantial role, including several interactions with characters who dance and sing; this role represents the glue that ties the whole scene together. The revue becomes vastly more complicated when the Queen insists that her daughter should not run off, but instead portray the character Kitty MacKay in a movie. The flood of secondary characters, from Huerta (the Mexican President), one crazy "Nut" who thinks he is Napoleon, and a cross-dressing detective, "The Crinoline Girl" (played by Harry Fox), all transform this scene into a nightmare of continuity and relationships. To make matters more complicated, multiple characters are usually introduced just before a song and/or dance *about* that person. For example, when the Baron Stefan Andrey is introduced (and announces himself "a combination of the Barons from 'The Yellow Ticket' and 'Panthea'"), the script indicates a "Big Russian

Number" to be inserted. By script 2, this song is eliminated entirely, and by script 3, this part of the scene is also gone. Over time, it appears that Atteridge streamlined the characters, the lines, and the songs, eliminating sections when the scene either felt too long or did not hold together. At this point in the show, there is very little information about the love connection between Mr. Omar and Shireen other than the complications leading to—of all things—Omar donning a Napoleon costume to save Shireen, who he thinks is "in mortal danger" because he does not know the difference between the movie and reality. As one might expect, when Magee becomes a third Napoleon, there is "a Big French Number."

Script 1 only indicates some basic ideas for scene 4, though Atteridge wants to keep the location as the movie studio. He suggests specifically that there should be a number for "whatever specialty is used," opening up a place in the script for whichever specialty act is hired. At this point, he was probably considering a large dance number with Adelaide and Hughes. Finally, he ends the scene with the airship effect, something that began in the scenarios and remained until the night of the first performance.

Act 2, as mentioned, is much less specific than the earlier sections. The scene begins in a Eugenics gym, with an opening number entitled "Calisthenics and Eugenics," which would become the act 2 opening chorus by script 4. A choice Atteridge makes in script 1 is to include many new characters at the opening, including Frances Starlight, the women's gym teacher, and Buldoon, a coach. After a fair bit of dialogue about how hard exercise is, Buldoon and Bertie the Lamb have a conversation that is interrupted by the Queen of the Movies. Some of this dialogue is used in the final script, even though the scene takes place between only the Queen and the Baron. One particularly fantastic joke that is added by hand in script 4 is used on opening night:

"BARON: Why don't you try to exercise on the bars?
QUEEN: That's where my first husband took all of his exercises—at the bars. That's why I haven't any first husband."

Eventually Shireen and Magee join in with the rest of the group, ready for a wedding. Shireen, as Kitty, says that she must be ready for a modern wedding, and they sing the only song missing from the edition of the script compiled for this edition: "The Girl of 1914, or The Girl of Today." Thus Shireen as Kitty, and Magee as her betrothed, get married as part of the film. The wedding itself remains mostly intact in script 5; two major differences, however, are that the Baron is the minister here, while the Misleading Nut becomes the minister for the show, and several of the jokes are shortened and changed. Even the ordering of the gags seems to have been important. On page 12 of script 4, three sections of dialogue are circled and assigned numbers one through three, to be reorganized for script 5. The song, "A Eugenics Wedding," is eventually changed to "A Modern Wedding Day" for the finale of the scene.

The next scene takes place in a railroad car. Atteridge includes in his very brief opening description that the song, "Manhattan Mad," could easily "fit here," though by script 3, the song is cut from the revue entirely. An extensive interplay between Mr. and Mrs. Bertie Lamb (Gaby) occurs when the two of them split up into different groups, each trying humorously to seduce Mr. and Mrs. Harlem, respectively. There is no apparent reason for the Harlems to appear, except to act as foils for the couple, and there is absolutely no indication of why the name is chosen. The new plot involves Frances Starlight trying to steal Magee's money on the train, which leads into scene 3. Scenario 1 suggests that three train cars be seen at once, but in this script, the number is down to two ("a la the Prince's [Princess Theater] play *It Can Be Done*"), which is also used in the final version of the show. Again, there are some new characters (including a conductor, a passenger, and a dummy passenger), but the action is mostly between two of the new couples (Mr. Harlem and Mrs. Bertie Lamb) and Frances Starlight and Magee. The scene is remarkably complex and lends itself more to confusion than it does to comedy. And, as seems to be the case with each draft of the second act, this is where script 1 ends, with no ending written.

Instead of examining scripts 2 through 4 in great detail, it is more useful to consider them works-in-progress. They are full of scratched-out lines with new dialogue written in the margins or on the back of the previous page. These drafts depict the sharpening of the show, especially in terms of characters and length. It is not until script 5 that Bertie the Lamb and Gaby are gone, but many of Bertie's lines are given to the Misleading Nut during the handwritten revisions in script 4. Frances Starlight is almost entirely eliminated by script 4. The fundamental difference between the first and last script is the transformation from a revue that focused on Omar and Shireen into one about Kitty MacKay and Jerrold McGee. The first time this relationship is abundantly clear is in script 3, although it is not yet well developed. McGee is his own character by this time, and not split between different actors, as he is in script 1. Script 4 shows that, though a great deal of the new plot is in place, some characters could still be added—like Lady Windermere as a foil for The Nut, and Mr. Dullplot and Miss High Jinks in the second act. In many cases, whole sections are crossed out, never seen by a Winter Garden audience. Atteridge is clearly thinking about ways to place new jokes into the show, with the musical reference to another song included in the midst of the number. The result was the "slimming down" of the show—exactly what Atteridge claimed happened in his interview in the *New York Times*.[16]

One important alteration is the departure of Adelaide and Hughes at the last moment. In script 4, they are the dancers who portray Pierrot and Prunella in scene 5, but their names are crossed out and "Kelly and Pemberton" are written in next to theirs. Since Stafford Pemberton does not appear even on the final pay list dated May 16, 1914, it would seem that he was the dancer specifically chosen to replace Hughes, with Ethel Kelly stepping in for Adelaide at the last moment. It is not known when the handwritten revisions were added to this script, but it was only days before the curtain went up.

The majority of the songs, however, are not jettisoned in script 4. For the most part, both the titles and the order of the songs are quite similar to script 5. One of the most glaring modifications comes from dropping a Freeman and Dunham specialty in scene 2 (to balance out their song in act 1), "Ragtime in London," which was to take place right after the first scene in the train cars. In addition to this, another number from the second act, Adelaide and Hughes's "Dance of the Fountain" was also crossed out in this script. The two pieces of music surrounding the Fountain number—Lady Windermere's waltz and Marilynn Miller's "Imitation" song—were both retained for the final version of the show. Even though changes were made, it seems that much of the material in script 4, at least in its corrected form, is quite close to the final form of the revue.

Overall, the various versions of the scripts (1–5) coincide with Atteridge's claim that the show begins as a behemoth that must be slowly cut down over time, perfecting the flow of the musical over a period of several weeks. There are some musical changes, but many of the songs do not seem to have been written even by the time of script 4—that is, early- to mid-May. The most severe changes come in the length of the dialogue and in the interactions between different characters. By script 5, the plot lines that tie characters and scenes together are significantly cut down. Frances Starlight's gold-digger mischief and the "swingers on a train" narratives are totally removed. The revue was, in part, reliant on humor, but it seems that music—both song and dance—was more important than the sketches were, at least from Atteridge and Huffman's point of view. Since it is not clear who made the changes in the scripts, we will never be certain whose decisions are represented throughout the process, but the long, drawn-out comic scenes are drastically reduced. The revue appears to be about music and to flow in a way that a "book" musical-comedy would not, as it was based on material that could be reworked on a large scale, free from narrative constraints, and this flexibility probably led to the revue becoming the plotless, musical-driven show that it became by the end of the twentieth century.

THE STRUCTURE OF *THE PASSING SHOW OF 1914*

Once the script was finalized, just days or perhaps even hours before the show began, the audience got to see a version of *The Passing Show* that would only last for a short time. Luckily, the scripts for most of the shows give the date it was performed, and even though the revue would go through more changes, this at least allows for a glimpse of what one night's entertainment included. An analysis of how this edition of the show functioned reveals the relationship between dialogue and music, but it also gives a sense of what points were structurally the most important. Certainly the two large "effects" were vital to the show, but were they really the highlight of the production? Only a step-by-step assessment can reveal the flow of the show.

In Table 6.4, the large-scale structure of *The Passing Show of 1914* is provided, demonstrating key elements of the revue. The music is diagrammed to indicate where dances were included, what the songs were, and how many soloists appeared in each song. In almost every case, songs seem to have unfolded as *verse/chorus/chorus*. There are many indications in the parts, however, that a second verse is sometimes used; in each case, one was written, but it seems they were only used when a song was especially popular. The addition of male or female chorus is also clearly marked next to the solo character. As a final remark, there are moments where the dancers do not seem to portray specific characters, and they are referred to only by their names in the program. The descriptions of dialogue can be understood as follows:

Very short dialogue = seven lines of dialogue or less
Short dialogue = one to two pages of dialogue
Medium dialogue = two to three pages of dialogue
Long dialogue = three to four pages of dialogue
Very long dialogue = four pages or more of dialogue

This dialogue key shows how much talking happens in between songs, but not necessarily the duration of a scene. In several cases there are stage directions, referred to in the script as *business*, that could significantly alter the timing of a section. Since most of this stage business is not described, there is no way to know exactly what happened. As any comedian will attest, timing is everything, and we can only speculate about what entertainers performed in these sections.

Table 6.4 shows that pacing, an issue mentioned specifically by Huffman in his article, was an essential part of determining how the show would function.[17] There are long stretches of music and long sections of dialogue, but they rarely follow one another; even if an especially extensive section of comedy takes place, there is always some type of musical number inserted to keep the moment fresh and full of life. The largest sections of dialogue are always placed after the beginning or just before the end of an act, with musical sections providing bookends. The end of act 1—the scene that leads to Omar's death and the delivery of the prophecy—is offset by the huge airship effect that follows it, assuring that the most visually stimulating image of the act was the audience's last memory.

Surprisingly, several sections of songs appear to be layered on top of one another. For example, in the beginning of act 1 and at the end of act 2, there is almost no talking whatsoever. Brief portions of dialogue take place in the Moving Picture Studio merely to introduce a character, whisking them off into their *introduction song* as quickly as possible. Most numbers are solos backed by the chorus, an interesting way to construct a show in that it provided a much larger range of featured singers than a book musical would, at least according to Huffman.[18] Moments for the full chorus alone are rare, and they are saved for the opening of acts. ("We're Working in the Picture Game" and "Eugenics Girls" are the only two examples in this revue.) The two duets—"You're Just a Little Bit Better Than the One I Thought Was Best" and "Eagle Rock"—are placed squarely in the center of the two respective acts in order to provide some variety. There is only a single solo song, and this is sung by José Collins near the end of the first act, as would be appropriate for her leading role. To balance her solo number, Bernard Granville has a solo eccentric dance near the end of act 2. This allowed the stars to shine on their own for a brief moment.

Uses of the chorus seem to be carefully measured out too. For the most part, a mixed chorus is used to support the solo performers in their songs, chiming in during the refrain rather than during the verse. The larger chorus featured the women in every scene, but the men onstage added a wider musical range and would have given the women someone to dance with. Only a single number, "The Bohemian Rag," uses the men of the chorus as background singers. For "Don't' Hesitate with Me," the

Table 6.4. The Structure of *The Passing Show of 1914*—from Script 5, Dated June 13 (17), 1914.

Act	Cast involved
Overture	None (Instrumental)
Act 1	
Scene 1	
"We're Working in the Picture Game"	Chorus (M, F)
Very Short Dialogue	2 Stenographers, Camera Man, Mary Packard
"The Maude Adams of the Screen"	Packard and Chorus (M, F)
Very Short Dialogue	Midnight Girl, Camera Man, Baggot
"The Midnight Girl at the Midnight Cabaret"	Midnight Girl and Chorus (F)
Medium Dialogue	Camera Man, Roosevelt, Huerta, Queen
"Sari Dance"	Sari and Chorus (M, F)
Very Long Dialogue	2 Camera Men, Windermere, 2 Attendants, Nut
Medium Dialogue	Baggot, Camera Man, Panthea, McGee
Very Short Dialogue	2 Camera Men, 3 Girls, MacKay
"Kitty MacKay"	MacKay and Chorus (F)
Long Dialogue	MacKay, Baron, McGee
"You're Just A Little Bit . . . "	MacKay, McGee
Very Short Dialogue	2 Camera Men, Baggot, Gaby, Camera Man
"The Moving Picture Glide"	Baggot, Gaby, Camera Man, Chorus (M, F)
Scene 2	
Long Dialogue	Queen, Burke, Leonora, Stenographer
Medium Dialogue	Queen, Verenka, Burke
Scene 3	
"Miss Kelly's Dance"	Kelly

(Continued)

Table 6.4. (Continued)

Scene 4	
"Ballet"	Miller, Pemberton, Kelly, Bankoff, Pilcer, Gilrain
Scene 5	
Short Dialogue	Omar
"Silence and Fun"	Pierrot and Prunella
Very Short Dialogue	Omar
"Omar Khayyam"	Omar and Chorus (M, F)
Medium Dialogue	Zarah, Shireen, Omar, Imam, Priest
"Dreams from Out of the Past"	Shireen
Very Long Dialogue	Omar, Shireen, Imam, Priest
Short Dialogue (Prophecy)	Omar, Shireen
Very Long Dialogue	Baron, Queen, McGee, MacKay, Dullplot, Aviator, Mechanic High Jinks
AIRSHIP EFFECT	Instrumental
Act 2	
Scene 1	
"Eugenics Girls"	Chorus (M, F)
Medium Dialogue	Buldoon, Baron, Queen
"Girl of 1914"	MacKay and Chorus (F)
Medium Dialogue	MacKay, Nut, McGee
"Modern Wedding Day"	Packard, Buldoon, Chorus (M, F)
Medium Dialogue	Baron, Queen, Gateman, MacKay, 2 Men
"Bohemian Rag"	MacKay and Chorus (M)
"Sloping Path"	High Jinks and Chorus (F)
Scene 3	
"Don't Hesitate With Me"	Windermere and Chorus (M)
Very Short Dialogue	High Jinks, McGee
"Good Old Levee Days"	Miller, Granville, Brice, Kelly and Chorus (M, F)
Scene 4	
Very Short Dialogue	Midnight Girl

Table 6.4. (Continued)

"In 'Frisco Town"	Midnight Girl and Chorus
"Specialty"	Bankoff and Girlie
Short Dialogue	Baron, Queen, McGee, Jerry
"Imitations"	Jerry
Long Dialogue	Baron, Queen, Nut, MacKay
Very Short Dialogue	McGee
"Eagle Rock"	McGee, High Jinks, Chorus (M,F)
Waiter Scene	McGee and Brice
"Grape Dance"	McGee
"You Can Count On Me"	Salvation Nell and Chorus (M, F)
Very Short Dialogue	Baggot, Camera Man, Native Son
TRANSFORMATION EFFECT (Fire)	
"California"	MacKay and Chorus (M,F)
Very Short Dialogue	Baron, Queen, Nut, MacKay, McGee, Midnight Girl
Finale	None (Instrumental)

performers dance with Lady Windermere instead of adding their voices to hers, since the number is instrumental.

The all-female chorus is featured in several numbers. These particular songs are interspersed throughout the musical, with the first of them being the third song, "The Midnight Girl at the Midnight Cabaret." The audience did not have to wait too long for the next appearance of this "mammoth" mass of women; they appear again behind Kitty MacKay during her self-titled song. The second act balanced the first, with two numbers featuring the female chorus. The first song is the only one that is no longer extant, entitled "The 1914 Girl" or "The Girl of 1914." This was another moment for Kitty to act as soloist, while the women cavorted around in the gymnasium outfits seen in Figure 6.3. The major showcase for the female chorus in act 2 was the "Sloping Path" production number, complete with song and intermezzo. This scene was a huge success with critics; the entire female chorus danced and sang on ascending platforms that gave the song its title. Figure 6.4 shows how this was accomplished, and exhibits how high the ramps were in relation to the cast. The soloist was Miss High Jinks, played by Ethel Kelly, but there is no doubt that the chorus girls were the stars.

The "effects" occur in two different sections, once during act 1 and once near the completion of act 2. Thomas's effects of the ride in the airship and the burning of San Francisco (complete with earthquake) were central to presenting an over-the-top musical, and it is this element of the genre that is most closely linked to the

Fig. 6.4. "The Sloping Path," The Passing Show of 1914. Shubert Archive.

nineteenth century spectacle and extravaganza. The placement of these two events is interesting, also. There is no doubt that the finale of act 1 needed to be powerful enough to lure the audience back for more of the show, which, if it wore on to two-and-a-half hours, was a long production. The placement of the second featured spectacle, however, is a bit of a surprise. One might expect that it would conclude the second act, which it nearly does, but since it is labeled a "transformation" scene, it probably depicted the fire and then the *restoration* of the city; the song that follows the scene is all about the beauty of California, and not about its destruction, a wise choice on the part of the creative team. The song allows for a celebration just before the finale, a perfect farewell before the show ends.

There seems to be a certain balance to the four lead characters (Jerrold McGee, Kitty MacKay, the Queen of the Movies, and the Baron von Criquet). Jerrold and Kitty take the stage as the "romantic" couple, usually singing and speaking about each other, although they are given several humorous lines as well. The tension between the couple and the possibility that they might not get married is resolved quickly in the beginning of act 2 (in the wedding scene), and thus the rest of the act does not resolve around this plot issue. Kitty and Jerrold share a duet, but they also have a large number of solos and appear in different situations with the entire chorus. The other two characters, the Queen and the Baron, are comic relief throughout the show, and it could even be said that they represent the comic couple for this revue. They are not a romantic couple, to be sure, but as they frequently share scenes, most of the extended scenes use these two as fixtures. The Queen and the Baron do not sing or dance (which is unusual for the comedic couple), but their amusing interplay would have been enough to keep the audience entertained. These four characters are each given a brief line to close the show in the final dialogue, representing a farewell from each performer.

Of the secondary characters, the most prominent is the Misleading Nut (played by T. Roy Barnes), who explains his insanity in the final line ("I wrote *The Passing Show of 1914!*") and he is also given plenty of dialogue instead of taking the lead in a musical number. His wife, Bessie Crawford (Lady Windermere), had a fair amount of dialogue, but other secondary characters are mainly used to sing and dance wherever appropriate. This is most certainly Marilynn Miller's role in the show. Many reviewers were surprised by just how little she appeared as "Miss Jerry," and they wanted more of her in the revue. Others performers who danced or sang their way into the show were Frances Demarest, Muriel Window, Stafford Pemberton, and Ethel Kelly. Freeman and Dunham were responsible for a single song, but they also had some dialogue—probably connected to the type of vaudeville routine they performed outside of this revue.

The development of the script for *The Passing Show of 1914* was just as rapid-fire as Atteridge made it sound, with changes incorporated into the script almost as fast as new material was being produced. However, one of the most surprising aspects of the show is that some of the basic ideas suggested in the very first scenario were maintained throughout the production. Even though the Persian Garden scene went through frequent alterations in placement, meaning, and function, Atteridge found a way to make the scene still fit into the whole. The idea of putting a "movie within a play" first appears in scenario 4 and becomes the solution for this scene. The device worked on many levels: it allowed Collins and Granville to perform more than one role in the same show, provided the audience with some variation, and included a bevy of beautiful, scantily clad chorus girls. Not only does the idea for the scene remain fixed throughout the five versions of the script, but this scene even retains most of the dialogue written for it in the earliest extant script. In some cases, dialogue goes through a great deal of transformation, especially in terms of jokes and gags. The last sections to be changed were the musical numbers, which were subtracted most extensively near the opening of the show. As some performers dropped out (such as Adelaide and Hughes), Atteridge and Huffman worked carefully to make sure that the new version of the script could accommodate the flow they were hoping to achieve. The progression of the script toward the stage was an extensive process involving a complicated interaction of writers, composers, performers, and other members of the creative team. The key term to describe the revue on opening night was *balance*; from the first scenario to the final working script, Atteridge and his colleagues forged a show that maintained an equilibrium of entertainments, from large sections of dialogue to the duets and dances. No doubt overseeing all of this was J. J. Shubert himself, who probably gave his blessing before the show finally opened at the Winter Garden. One can only imagine him sitting in one of the front rows of the house, silently judging every joke and every transition, every duet and every dance number, expecting excellence from a team that was given only eight-to-ten weeks to create a "perfect" revue for his flagship theater.

OPENING OF THE REVUE AND RECEPTION

The first mention of rehearsals for the show was in April of 1914. A notice in the *New York Times* read, "The management of the Winter Garden announces that rehearsals will begin on Monday morning [April 20] for the new Summer show, called 'The Passing Show of 1914,' which will be produced at the Winter Garden in June."[19] The planned date for opening night was June 6, 1914. Newspapers included several briefs about the show in the weeks before the curtain went up, a result of Claude P. Greneker's work in the publicity department. One of the attractions mentioned was the inclusion of the special ramp brought to New York from England: "One of the several spectacular novelties will be 'The Sloping Path,' the American rights for which were secured by Lee Shubert from the Alhambra Theater in London."[20] The excitement generated by these announcements culminated in the official notice, released only days before the musical was to open. Due to a heat wave that happened that week, however, the Shuberts postponed the show until June 10, taking the time to fix the air conditioning in the Winter Garden. When the doors opened, audiences flocked to see the new revue. The show played daily at eight in the evening and also gave matinees at two, but not every day of the week.[21] Tickets were $1 and $1.50 for the "best orchestra seats," but the prices for other tickets— the "cheap" seats—are not mentioned.[22] There was a large culture of ticket scalping (run by "ticket brokers"), with prices much higher than those that were advertised ($4 to $4.50 was common), and several notices indicate that the best seats were usually only available from third parties who waited outside the theater to attract buyers. Both the *Follies* and *The Passing Show* were incredibly popular with brokers, with one notice proclaiming, "It will be a fortunate person who can purchase a front seat ticket at either the [New] Amsterdam or the [Winter] Garden box office during the summer months."[23]

The reviews were generally very positive, with the emphasis mostly placed on the spectacle that was to be seen. *Theatre Magazine* said, "To those who have the good fortune, or the misfortune, to be in New York during the warm weather, 'The Passing Show of 1914,' with its breezy atmosphere will bring new life to the overheated. It seems that the managers have gone the limit in gathering the headliners who during the evening appear to enjoy their parts as much as the public."[24] The grandeur of the revue is mentioned repeatedly as one of the reasons to see the production, but it also seemed to puzzle some as to "where to begin" in talking about it, as seen with the following *New York Times* commentator:

"The Passing Show of 1914" . . . simply out-summers and out-shows anything in its line seen in a New York theatre, and sets considerable of a mark for Winter entertainments as well.

Local theatergoers are accustomed to seeing things done on a big scale, but even the massive productions at the Hippodrome must take a back seat when compared to the entertainment which began at 8 o'clock last night and ran along merrily until after midnight. Of course, some of it will have to be cut out. Four hours of almost continual laughter is too much for the tired business man, but just what to cut is something which will prove puzzling to the Shuberts. Perhaps they will chop off an hour and a half and use that part in another theatre. . . .

"The Passing Show of 1914" is really so big that it is hard to find out just where to start in telling about it. Most of the plays which scored here last Winter are burlesqued during the course of the evening, and each burlesque is exceedingly clever. The lines are funny, something unusual for a Summer show, and the music is catchy and bright.[25]

While the *Dramatic Mirror* exclaimed, " 'The Passing Show of 1914' Sets a High-Water Mark in Musical Extravaganza,"[26] the *Herald* reported, "Girls by the scores to look at, costumes of brilliant colors and original ideas by the hundreds to marvel at, and scenes by the dozen to wonder at—all this, but little to laugh at—and then came the intermission after the first part of the new musical revue."[27] Though at first it would seem that the lack of humor was a problem, the anonymous reviewer remarked in the next paragraph that "the audience, sweltering in the June heat, was more than awakened. 'The Passing Show' won easily after a slow start, and everyone went home satisfied after three and a half hours of kaleidoscopic amusement. That the laughs were not forthcoming in the first part was not due entirely to the librettist, Mr. Harold Atteridge, for the book is the best he has written, but rather to the late arrival of a large portion of the audience."[28] For the most part, critics found the show to be fun and "breezy," full of light entertainment perfect for the audiences of the hot New York summers. The only major detractor to this litany of praise was the review written in *Green Book Magazine*, where Channing Pollock (who worked for Ziegfeld) found problems both with Atteridge's script and with the "bare-leggedness" of the chorus girls: " 'The Passing Show of 1914' without its book, would be a lively and unbroken entertainment. In spite of its book, it is a particularly and unusually attractive specimen of the kind of thing that New York seems to crave in summer."[29] Even from the harshest critic, *The Passing Show of 1914* still passed inspection, offering an entertainment that easily fulfilled its audience's expectations.

The illustrious "Madame Critic" from the *Dramatic Mirror* had her own view of the show, and her commentary about the first night is particularly helpful for understanding the effect the show had on its audience. She also had some insightful comments on costuming and chorus girls:

When "Pinafore" was produced, I thought that the Shuberts had surpassed themselves for the last time, but the opening performance of "The Passing Show of 1914" at the Winter Garden proved that, evidently, there is no such word as *last* in the Shubert vocabulary.

The new attraction was presented on a hot night. We do have hot nights, occasionally, in New York, although the majority of visitors from the Southern United States will tell you we complain without reason, while those from the South American States are warm in their declarations that the lands near the Equator are portions of the temperate zone when compared with tropical Manhattan.

At any rate, when I stepped within the doors of the Winter Garden and beheld the display of perspiring male humanity lined up six rows deep in the rear of the house at the rise of the curtain—fancy anybody being on time on a stifling Summer evening when nothing can induce them to attend earlier than eight-thirty on a Winter night, no matter how great the play—I sincerely hoped that their every word would not be wasted. The curtain rose on time—a fact which A. Toxen Worm [the publicist for the show] was wordfully exultant. Really, a prompt curtain has been as rare as a snowstorm in July. I looked around and observed that all the World was present. Pretty soon along came the Flesh—never before was so much of it seen in a musical production. The Devil must have been hiding about somewhere, but we were not permitted a glimpse of his majesty. After all, something was left to the imagination.

Speaking of the Flesh, I fear the results of such a wholesale exposition of founded knees and shapely calves, for the first thing we know the tight makers will form a union for the restoration of their wares. If other musical productions follow the example of the Winter Garden, the younger generation will look back upon tights as a curious fashion once inspired by our Puritanical notions. Several seasons ago there was a short-lived musical comedy in which the broilers—I will use the antiquated term in order to keep strictly within the period—appeared in rompers, bare legs, and socks. This novel costume was considered intensely shocking, although its wearers look not a day older than twelve years. They acted like children, too. Then we have had the Greek dancers of various ages and weights. They, too, were shocking until we became accustomed to the innovation.

But never before has there been such quantity of undisguised female bare attractions in full bloom on a stage in this country. These charms were not confined to the stage, either. They tripped gaily out on the runways into the audience. One could see legs *in the real* by the dozen. I fancy their owners' faces were lost sight of in the contemplation. It must have been a unique sensation for Diamond Jim Brady[30] suddenly to behold a pair of dimpled knees right in front of his nose. But that is what happened at the Winter Garden. Diamond Jim couldn't have seen the stage if he had wanted to. And when a coquettish girl in fluffy chiffon skirts of the crinoline period, unconsciously brushed his hair with her ruffles, I felt sure that Mr. Brady must have realized that a new epoch in musical comedy had arrived. . . .

There were so many notables present at the opening that to name them would be to call the roll of nearly all the prominent professionals, and tired businessmen left in town. It was a great event—and the women present seemed to enjoy it as much as the men. They discussed the good and bad points of the various female anatomies as impartially as though they were mere pictures, or cold, cold marble.

The New York woman is a thoroughbred. I couldn't help wondering, however, what the wives of the sight-seeing Hirams and Ezekials will do if by chance they should accompany their husbands to "The Passing Show."

The tossing of the footballs [during the gymnasium scene] was another feature which established a thought transference between the players and played-to. It was really quite exciting, especially when a man could feel a certain pretty pitcher was deliberately making him the catcher. . . .

The performance lasted until past twelve, but few in the audience cared to leave before the final curtain. Even then many lingered, until the players who had been working hard must have feared that they would never be permitted to rest. Jose Collins was the particular star among the women. New York has always liked her, but now I am sure it has taken her to its heart for good and all. The audience finally left the theater with the satisfaction that it had had its money's worth, and then some. There were no ifs, ands, or buts.[31]

Madame Critic's commentary is more concerned with what the revue represented rather than what it contained, and it echoes what several of the other reviewers said—especially the critic from the *New York Times*, who suggested that the theater *sans* tights would bring grumbling from a community that expected girls to be wearing these garments while onstage. Her column brings to life the opening night of a Winter Garden revue, which was clearly an important theatrical event during the hot summer season. The revue went on to perform at the Winter Garden until September 3, 1914, with a run of at least 133 performances.[32] The production immediately set its sights elsewhere, and would travel across the country until returning to New York late in the spring, just in time to prepare for the next *Passing Show*.

NOTES

1. "Harold Atteridge, A Rapid-Fire Librettist," X8 (chap. 1, n. 23).

2. Ibid. See also J. C. Huffman, "Revue Proves Hardest Test of Craftsmanship on Stage," M–5 (chap. 1, n. 27).

3. Numerous references to other plays and other people are indicated in this chapter, but the details for each of the references are not explained until Chapter 7, which is specifically about how reference and parody functions in this musical.

4. These cast lists are considered in more depth in Jonas Westover, "A Study and Reconstruction of the *Passing Show of 1914*," (Ph.D diss., Graduate Center of the City University of New York, 2010), chap. 2.

5. "Harold Atteridge, A Rapid-Fire Librettist," X8.

6. Harold Atteridge, undated scenarios, Shubert Archive, package 87, box 5. Each scenario (1–4) is located here.

7. See bruce d. mcclung, *Lady in the Dark* (chap. 4, n. 46).

8. The role and use of the tango in this period is discussed in more depth in Jonas Westover, "A Study and Reconstruction of the *Passing Show of 1914*" (Ph.D. diss., Graduate Center of the City University of New York, 2010), chap. 4.

9. Many revues from the 1910s and 1920s include a of harem scene, no doubt as an opportunity to show off the figures of the women and men of the show. An extensive study of their content would provide the basis for a fascinating study.

10. Susanne K. Langer, *Feeling and Form: A Theory of Art* (New York: Charles Scribner's Sons, 1953), 344–45.

11. "Harold Atteridge, A Rapid-Fire Librettist," X8; and J. C. Huffman, "Revue Proves Hardest Test of Craftsmanship on Stage," M–5.

12. Harold Atteridge, dated and undated scripts, Shubert Archive, package 87, box 3. Each of the scripts (1–5) is located here.

13. Nazarro (or Nazzaro, as his name is sometimes spelled) was an acrobat and "acrobatic dancer" active on Broadway and vaudeville from at least *The Two Orphans* (1874). Nazarro was a regular performer for the Shuberts, appearing at the earliest in a revival of *Twelfth Night* and *Up and Down Broadway*, both in 1910. Apparently, Nazarro and his wife had adopted a young man in 1911 whom they made a part of their act, but may have also mistreated. See "S. Miller Kent Sent to Jail," *New York Times*, March 25,

1911, 1. For an example of Nazarro's vaudeville performance, see "Vaudeville," *New York Times*, November 30, 1913, X5.

14. There is a large amount of material extant at the Shubert Archive, but it is very difficult to understand where in the process these fragments belong. Some of the handwritten documents include shorthand, and were probably written by a secretary (maybe taking dictation from Atteridge?). The typewritten materials are also occasionally in pieces, though there are a few scenes that seem to be whole. Among these whole scenes are two versions of the Bequeath scene and the Eugenics Gymnasium scene; two versions of the Palace Hotel scene; two versions of the railroad scene; and an unrelated script for a scene called "1999." These documents are in the Shubert Archive, box 87, package 4.

15. The use of Burke in the scene made Ziegfeld furious, and he threatened to sue if it was not taken out. It was removed by the second week of the show. See "Ziegfeld Appeased," *New York Dramatic Mirror*, June 24, 1914, 8.

16. "Harold Atteridge A Rapid-Fire Librettist," X8.

17. J. C. Huffman, "Revue Proves Hardest Test of Craftsmanship on Stage," M–5.

18. Ibid.

19. "Theatrical Notes," *New York Times*, April 18, 1914, 11. The same announcement was printed eleven days later in the *Dramatic Mirror*. See "The Passing Show," *New York Dramatic Mirror*, April 29, 1914, 8.

20. "Theatrical Notes," *New York Times*, May 31, 1914, 11.

21. The advertisements for matinees vary, suggesting there was no exact schedule for which days would have a second performance.

22. "Advertisements," *New York Herald*, June 11, 1914, 15.

23. "'Follies' Prices Soar High Immediately after Opening," *Variety*, June 6, 1914, 11.

24. "At the Theatres," *Theatre Magazine*, 20, no. 161, July 1914, 37.

25. "Fun and Glitter in 'Passing Show,'" *New York Times*, June 11, 1914, 11.

26. "At the Winter Garden," *New York Dramatic Mirror*, June 17, 1914, 8.

27. "Third 'Passing Show' in Winter Garden," *New York Herald*, June 11, 1914, 15.

28. Ibid.

29. Channing Pollock, "When Lovely Women Stoop to Follies," *Green Book Magazine*, August 1914, 325–26.

30. Brady was a wealthy philanthropist and businessman who was a colorful figure on New York's social scene during his lifetime (1856–1917).

31. Marie B. Schrader,"Madame Critic" *New York Dramatic Mirror*, June 17, 1914, 5.

32. See <http://www.ibdb.com>. Accessed July 21, 2009. This number of performances seems suspect, however, in that the number of matinees may not be included. Also, the Sunday evening concerts were not included in the total, and deserve more prominence given how much material from the show was used.

7

A CARNIVAL OF TRAVESTY

* * *

TEXTUAL AND MUSICAL REFERENCES IN
THE PASSING SHOWS

In the first scene of *The Passing Show of 1914*, the revue's main comedic character is introduced to the audience through a combination of dialogue and entrance music, a common practice in musical theater. The setting is a movie studio, and a cameraman announces, "Here comes the Queen of the Movies. She's been playing in that Pinafore film." Before the actor enters, the orchestra plays a short instrumental piece to usher the character onstage. The music relies on the audience's theater-going experience to inform them about the person they are going to meet. The dialogue also sets up references that tell the audience the identity of the Queen. The second comment, about Pinafore, is reinforced musically; the statement is the cue for the orchestra to play music from Gilbert and Sullivan's *H. M. S. Pinafore*, namely the song "I'm Called Little Buttercup." The character one anticipates is a rotund young woman, but the other reference tempers this expectation. The first remark, about the Queen of the Movies, would not necessarily be recognized today, but contemporary audiences would have immediately understood this reference as both the title and the main character from another play, *The Queen of the Movies*, an earlier hit of the 1913–1914 Broadway season.[1] The woman referenced here was thin, petite, and beautiful. When the orchestra accompanies the Queen's entrance, the audience would have been thrilled and surprised to see a very fat George W. Monroe in a huge "exaggerated" frilly dress, boisterously bellowing, "I'm fresh little Buttercake . . . I'm what you call Little Buttercup on the Hippodrome scale." The audience had no trouble getting the joke; it was an exaggeration of Buttercup, a sendup of The Queen of the Movies character, and a reversal of the ingénue role, a tactic similar to what is used in modern theater satires such as *Forbidden Broadway*. Even if some in the crowd had not seen older productions of *Pinafore*, it had been revived earlier that spring at—where?—the Hippodrome, in a production that was called "colossal."[2] Audiences loved Monroe's over-the-top Queen, so it was no surprise that he was one of the featured members of the stellar cast.

The context for revues from this period is surprisingly rich and requires perseverance to extricate. Not only must one thoroughly know the theatrical season that preceded the revue, but one must also understand the history of almost every person associated with the musical. Throughout the writing on revues, the word *topical* is pressed into service, easily dismissing the way names, productions, events, and characters are used by the creators to refer to the world surrounding the shows. For example, Lee Davis proclaims that for *The Passing Show of 1916*, "topicality ruled; there were parodies of Charlie Chaplin, Woodrow Wilson, Charles Evans Hughes, Teddy Roosevelt, and yes, Pancho Villa."[3] However, Davis never explains the ways in which these characters interacted, what they wore, what was sung, and what it all meant. The problem with the word topicality is that it obscures the remarkable kaleidoscope of techniques used to connect the annual show with the complicated context that surrounded it. The word can still apply to these shows, but its application is not as simple as Davis suggests. A *Passing Show* took the efforts of composers, lyricists, scriptwriters, costume designers, choreographers, and performers to place layer upon layer of meaning throughout the show. Scholars usually use the term *intertextuality* to describe this intertwining of meaning, suggesting that it links one type of event with another. To best examine how the topical machine worked, it is necessary to focus on a single example—one revue—to understand the multifaceted references within the production. To this end, I examine *The Passing Show of 1914* in depth while considering the referential links between it and the larger theatrical (and cultural) context, providing a case study that could be applied to any of the Winter Garden revues.

When *The Passing Show* opened, the wide variety of acts, the quality of the dancing, the many genres of music, and the extravagant costumes and sets brought people into the theater in droves. But an important reason why audiences came to see the show was that they expected a certain type of entertainment—one that relied on the whole of the previous theater season for material. For *The Passing Show of 1914*, an article from May 29, 1914, promised that "some of the successes of the season to be travestied will be 'Kitty MacKay,' 'Help Wanted,' 'The Things That Count,' 'The Midnight Girl,' 'The Yellow Ticket,' 'Omar the Tentmaker,' 'Panthea,' 'Too Many Cooks,' and 'A Thousand Years Ago.'"[4] This list includes many types of theatrical productions. *The Midnight Girl* was a German operetta revamped for the American stage, while *Kitty MacKay* was a play about a young Scottish girl looking for love—a play that used incidental music to inject local color into the drama. *Omar the Tentmaker* was a straight play based on the novel by Nathan Haskell Dole about Omar Khayyam. Each of the shows listed was one that had been on the Broadway stage during the 1913–1914 season. But, as is clear from Little Buttercup's introduction, only a few theatrical references were included in the preliminary advertisements for *The Passing Show of 1914*. So in what ways, exactly, did these references appear, and what does that tell us about the audience for this revue?

Allusions surface in a wide variety of ways in this revue. As mentioned earlier, revues have been characterized as a genre where parody is quite straightforward: the source is satirized or made fun of from a negative point of view, especially when it comes to competing plays and/or musicals. Modern authors use many terms to explain the relationship between various *Passing Shows* and their sources, including "spoofed," "satirized," "roundhouse sendups," "lampooned," and "mugged."[5] In truth, though, the revues followed the grand nineteenth-century tradition of burlesque, in which a single work was used as the basis for another, mocking the source merci-lessly. For example, one of the most popular comic operas (*opéra bouffe*) of the 1860s and 1870s was Jacques Offenbach's *The Grand Duchess of Gerolstein* (1867). When minstrels Kelly and Leon put together a burlesque of the piece the following year, they called it *Leon's Own Grand Dutch "S,"* and it was so popular it ran at their theater for ten months.[6] However, in *The Passing Shows*, the use of burlesque and parody is not limited by a single approach. The creators used a plethora of methods to make connections to virtually any object or situation they wished. Throughout the revue, Atteridge used source materials as *models* rather than repeatedly using them as the butt of jokes. This does not mean spoofing did not happen—it most certainly did, and it was a key element of the show—but it was only part of the fabric of the overall revue.

There are two primary areas where reference is used: first, in the narrative (and its characters); and second, in the music. Additional elements of the show allude to almost anything that can be put onstage, such as physical motions, costumes, dances, lighting techniques, and props, but these are generally woven into one of the two aforementioned categories. Narrative references can appear in several ways. In some cases, a character is borrowed from another play, whereas in others, the object of parody is the actor or actress portraying the character. Atteridge often took characters and turned them into foolish and silly caricatures, but, just as regularly, he would use them more or less in their original forms, making use of the origi-nal production for his own purposes. Additionally, parody was used musically, most commonly in the webbing, but also in the songs themselves. Sigmund Romberg's musical borrowing for his score takes different shapes, too, sometimes "sending up" another song, while at other times, merely using its form or melody to refer to the source material.

Other entertainments were primarily referenced by the inclusion of characters taken in whole or part from the casts of other shows, both in terms of title and in function. For example, the main hero in *The Passing Show of 1914* is Jerrold McGee, an amalgam of Gerard Mordaunt, the well-to-do hero from Monckton Hoffe's play, *Panthea*, and the novelist/hero William Hallowell Magee, from George M. Cohan's *Seven Keys to Baldpate*. In both instances, the man in question is youthful and romantic, and this is what the newly created Jerrold McGee is meant to reflect. His function is to romance the heroine, although Gerard is significantly more connected to melodrama than his equal, Magee. The main plot in *Panthea* revolves around a young woman who fights for her love against the will of an angry aristocrat, the Baron de Duisitort.[7] The climactic scene from the play pits her confused lover, Gerard, against both herself and the Baron, who has tricked the poor hero. In an act of bravery, Panthea kills the Baron in order to be with her love, though she is sent away to Siberia with Gerard in tow. It is Gerard's relationship with Panthea that is lampooned in *The Passing Show*; instead of Panthea acting as the brave character, Jerrold (in the *Passing Show*) is the hero—it is he who has to find a way to overcome the Baron to win the heart of his lover, Kitty MacKay. The function of the new char-acter is almost as complicated as the plot of *Panthea*; not only must Jerrold McGee represent more than one plot from another show, but he also takes on attributes from these diverse characters.

In a few instances, only the idea of a character stems from another play. An example of this is the Misleading Nut, who is extracted not as a whole character, but simply as a moment from Charles W. Goddard and Paul Dickey's *The Misleading Lady* (1913).[8] The play was a success on Broadway, and ran from November of 1913 until May of 1914, so it would have been very familiar to audiences of *The Passing Show*. The Misleading Nut first appears in scene 1, dressed as Napoleon and followed by two attendants (meant to be workers from a sanatorium). So the audience would not miss the reference, the French anthem, "The Marseillaise" was played to usher the character on and off stage. The real Napoleon does not appear in *The Misleading Lady*, but there is a scene in act three where the character "Boney" dresses up as Napoleon, pretending to be someone from an insane asylum. In truth, the story is a melodrama about a man (Jack Craigen) who tries to kidnap another man's (Henry Tracey) wife, Helen. In this case, the *idea* for a character is derived from a humorous instance in another play, rather than using a specific role. The Nut's time as Napoleon is brief in *The Passing Show*, however, and he eventually takes on other guises, such as a minister in act 2 for the Eugenics Wedding; the overall purpose of the character is to destabilize the plot, adding a quality of randomness into the revue, and representing the unpredictable—all functions that are humorously accomplished by the Misleading Nut.

Several additional characters also emanate from other shows. Near the end of the second act of *The Passing Show*, the character of Salvation Nell sings a song called "You Can't Go Wrong with Me." At first, there no clear reason for her appearance—she does not stem from any play that was performed during the 1913–1914 season. Rather, the show she appears in is Edward Sheldon's *Salvation Nell*, which dates from 1908. The character could very well have been forgotten by 1914, at least as something *new*, but the fact is that there *was* a recent version of the character—from sheet music. The cover of "Salvation Nell" in Figure 7.1 (1913; lyrics by Grant Clarke and Edgar Leslie, music by Theodore Morse) shows a proud Salvation Army missionary, calling to men—presumably sinners—by playing her tambourine and singing about Jesus. The lyrics of the song describe the character.[9] In "You Can't Go Wrong with Me," the song from *The Passing Show*, the lyrics are not about Salvation Nell as a character, but instead about the deliverance she represents, as sung in the first person: Verse 1

> Oh, you sinners, come with me
> And join the army right away.
> And salvation you will see,
> Come follow right in line today—
> There is a place in Heaven, they say,
> Where you can tango all of the day,
> Don't wait another day but just decide,
> And try that real salvation glide.

When Muriel Window performed as Salvation Nell, she was acting out a combination of the play and the popular song.[10]

In this case, Nell does not become an object of ridicule but simply a borrowed character. As an element of the narrative, she merely fulfills the role of her

Fig. 7.1. *"Salvation Nell" sheet music cover. Author's Collection.*

character from the source play and song, alluding to the function, the features, and the style of the original Nell. No photographs survive of Window's "Salvation Nell" costume, but it is likely she was dressed in a similar manner to the cover of the sheet music, perhaps even holding a tambourine. The relationship between Nell and her song is not a sendup at all—there is nothing funny about her in the lyrics, in the music, or in the script (notably, there is no dialogue that precedes or follows the number that has anything to do with Nell). She merely *is* Salvation Nell, who appears as part of *The Passing Show* using the amalgam of media for the audience's entertainment.

A number of other characters also find their way into *The Passing Show of 1914*, but unlike Salvation Nell, many are lampooned in a humorous way. For example, a secondary character at the movie studio during act 1 is named "Deuce Baggot," a director. In reality, the Baggot in question was the real-life King Baggot

(1879–1948), who was an actor and director during the early years of film. The joke on the character's name comes from a deck of cards, wherein the deuce (2) is at the other end of the spectrum from the King. There does not seem to be any particular reason for using Baggot other than referring to his eminence in film at the time, and Freeman and Dunham, the comedy team who portrayed Baggot and the Camera Man, do not appear to have used any lines that were specific to any real-life depictions of people.

Another film figure to appear in the show was Mary Packard, a clear nod to movie superstar Mary Pickford (1892–1979). Pickford was known for playing immature girls long after she was an adult. She was usually seen in curls and wearing frilly dresses to invoke purity, even if it did not work with the narrative. The habit of portraying a much more youthful version of herself marked Pickford as ripe for spoofing in *The Passing Show*. Mary is introduced through a short bit of dialogue in the very opening of act 1:

CAMERA MAN: Well, here comes Mary Packard.
(ENTER MARY PACKARD (MARY PICKFORD) A DEMURE GIRL, CARRYING A DOLL.)
Hello, Mary. How is the "Maude Adams of the Movies?"
MARY: I'm all right, but I'm tired of playing these child parts. My husband doesn't like it.
CAMERA MAN: You're going to act in a great picture today. You shoot your uncle and stab your father with a bread-knife.
MARY: Must I always play those girl parts? This moving picture game is just one reel after another.

Already, Pickford's career is the object of ridicule, both from Mary and from the Camera Man. It is the Camera Man's comment about Maude Adams, however, that prepares the scene for the upcoming song entitled "The Real Maude Adams of the Screen." By connecting Mary Pickford to Maude Adams, Atteridge ties together two women from different media who perform the same kind of roles. Maude Adams (1872–1953) was a stage actress who also frequently played young women, though one of her most well-known performances was as a boy, when she portrayed the title character in J. M. Barrie's *Peter Pan* (1904). Atteridge and Romberg's song, then, is a satire of two different actresses at once; the lyrics of the verse and chorus reinforce the joke:

Verse 1

I'm little Mary who poses,
I'm little sunshine and roses.
On the film my face you've seen,
I always play the daughter,
Who's very milk and water.
I'm really one of the fixtures
I am the star of the pictures
Mary, the child-like fairy.
Mary, the Queen of the Screen.

Chorus

> I'm the girlie who is always on the screen.
> In the pictures, any place you go, I'm seen.
> I am playing, always so demurely.
> And you're saying: -"She's a nice girl, surely."
> I'm the "sweet thing" playing all the childish parts.
> In Hoboken, I win all the native's hearts.
> I play every clinging scene,
> Simple child, so young and green,
> I'm the real Maude Adams of the screen.

The song lampoons what Pickford does in the movies as well as the response she gets from people who may not really understand drama (i.e., the residents of Hoboken). Packard is Pickford as a caricature in no uncertain terms, and she is ridiculed through the deployment of many elements—including lyrics, dialogue, and (though no photograph is extant) probably through costuming.

Moving pictures get their share of parody in this show, and it is not coincidental that they—still silent at this time—are referred to as *pantomimes* in the song, "We're Working in the Picture Game." The movies were still a growing industry, and they were only beginning to evidence a commercial appeal that was a threat to both vaudeville and the stage. Specific movies are mentioned in the dialogue of this revue by their titles, and in most cases, the Queen of the Movies delivers the lines; she was the ideal candidate to send up the films that were mentioned in the show. Scene 2 of act 1 takes place inside the Queen's office, and many of the movies she comments on (made in *her* studio) are actually scrambled or reworked versions of films that had been on the screen in or around 1914. For example, when she says they're making a picture of *The Nights in a Bar Room in Ten Reels*, the Queen is alluding to *Ten Nights in a Bar Room*, which was made into a motion picture three times, in 1910, 1911, and 1913. *Why Girls Leave Home in Two Parts* directly recalls *Why Girls Leave Home* (1913), a movie that was lampooned again in 1929 by another picture, *Why Gorillas Leave Home*. Many references in the script are made about white slaves, deriving from the movies that appeared during the previous season, including *The Inside of the White Slave Traffic* (1913), *The White Slave; or The Octoroon* (1913), and *The White Slave Catchers* (1914). Other characters mention different pictures and each suggestion for a treatment is a reference to a movie that had already been made.

In some cases, plays are referenced in *The Passing Show* by dissecting their plots into smaller pieces and rearranging them. This is how the play *Panthea*, mentioned earlier, is used. The *Panthea* scene in the revue happens midway through act 1, scene 1. The references in this situation are small pieces of the source play that become fodder for Atteridge's parody. For example, in the revue, we see Panthea—the character—brought ashore after a shipwreck, and she is shivering because she is cold. The joke here is that the acting of Olga Petrova, who played the role at the Booth Theater in the spring, was overdone and over-the-top; the actress in *The Passing Show*, Frances Demarest, would have had to play Panthea in way that lampooned the other actress and her character simultaneously.[11] ⏵Figure 7.2 is a portrait of Petrova. Without reading the original play, one would not realize that *The Passing Show* actually refers directly to the opening scene of *Panthea*, where the Mordaunt family is gathered in their home and is suddenly aware of a boat that has had a terrible accident. One of the women pulled ashore is Panthea, and this is the description of her first appearance in the original play:

> A group appears at the doorway surrounding the strange lady. SHE is slight and dark, her face is very pale, her hair is done (a la Hoffe), she has a strange mixture of odd garments on. She looks straight over to the fire, nods to it, then goes deliberately over to it. She sits on the footstool, shivers slightly and still stares straight into the fire.[12]

This scene is directly parodied in *The Passing Show*, but in several different ways. First of all, mention is made that the woman, Panthea, "fell overboard." McGee then says, "The poor woman's cold. I can tell she's an emotional actress the way her shoulders tremble. That denotes acting. (SHE LOOKS AT HIM AND GASPS SEVERAL TIMES A LA PETROVA) I beg your pardon. Have you asthma or are you hissing?" Some chorus men in *The Passing Show* actually exit the stage and bring on a moveable fireplace for Panthea to warm herself, but this scene is really all about sending up the opening of act 1 in *Panthea*. As the scene in the revue progresses, additional jokes are made about Petrova (and her hair), but there are several comments that point to other scenes in the source play too. McGee mentions Russians, spies, and Siberia. All of these moments can be found in *Panthea*, when, after a deadly battle wherein the heroine is forced to kill the Baron, she is followed by Russian agents in the next act. Eventually, Panthea is taken to Siberia, with Gerard Mordaunt professing his love and marrying her so that he, too, can be taken to Siberia. Even though these events are merely mentioned in *The Passing Show of 1914*, they were markers of the source play for the patrons of the revue; the scene requires the audience to have familiarization with the whole play, not just a single dramatic moment, in order to understand the events taking place onstage.

A similar situation is true for Percy MacKaye's version of *Turandot*, which he entitled *A Thousand Years Ago* (1914).[13] The complete play was not used to form a single part of a scene, but instead became the framework for a larger scene in *The Passing Show*. Specifically, *A Thousand Years Ago* becomes the template for scene 6, which is an extended Omar Khayyam sequence; the difference is that the structural outline of the scene is derived from the narrative of the source, rather than from a few pieced-together moments.

One instance of this is in the introduction of Omar Khayyam. When he appears in *The Passing Show*, he almost immediately mentions two characters from Italian commedia dell'arte, Pierrot the clown and his love, who dance together in "Silence and Fun." [14] There is no clear reason for the appearance of these characters in this scene, but two elements connect them to the theater world of the time. First of all, the play *Prunella* (Lawrence Housman and Harley Granville-Barker, 1913) had been playing at the Little Theater since October. In addition, commedia dell'arte characters had played a significant role in *A Thousand Years Ago*, where they were "Strolling Players." In *The Passing Show*, the commedia dell'arte theme is split between the ballet dancers and a group called the Vagabond Players, made up of Omar Khayyam and his dancing pals, Turkey Trot, Tango, and Maxixe (all dances that were popular fads of the day).

In *A Thousand Years Ago*, the character Caliph ends up wearing a false beard, which becomes a joke in scene 6 of *The Passing Show*. When Imam Allafake and his priests enter, they are all wearing long, fake blue beards and Omar says, "Ah, so they're wearing colored beards, now."

A Thousand Years Ago also provides the structure for the dramatic thrust of the scene. In the source play, Omar desires to marry a princess, Lady Shireen. To do this, he must first prove that he is a prince and must also pass a test involving three riddles. When successful, this will ensure that he has shown wisdom and can marry her. *The Passing Show* ties Omar Khayyam with the hero of *A Thousand Years Ago*, maintaining the riddle sequence and also calling Omar a "beggar prince," the same term used in the second act of the source play. The riddle scene is extensive in both productions, and, also in each drama, it is the means by which the hero connects with the heroine. Most of scene 6 in *The Passing Show* is modeled after this very play, and when Omar wins the hand of Shireen, he begins to announce his belief about a future place called Broadway. He eventually gets himself killed because of these "heretical ideas" and this leads to the dramatic delivery of his prophecy, which involves another "false" Omar hoisted into the rafters as a ghost.

The piecemeal approach taken with *Panthea* did not stop Atteridge from borrowing a whole scene intact. The Queen of the Movies is introduced to Mr. Verenka, who is trying to find a job, in a lengthy section of scene 2 of *The Passing Show*. He does not want to work as a "white slave" (a laborer who works for small wages at long hours), and hopes that the Queen will give him a job in the movies. However, he soon learns that she wishes to seduce him, which he protests vigorously. Verenka cannot explain why his honor will be ruined, but he says that if she comes closer, he will scream. Almost all of the narrative stems from the ending of the source play, Michael Morton's *The Yellow Ticket* (1914).[15]

Near the finale of *The Yellow Ticket*, the twenty-year-old Marya Varenka professes her love to Julian Rolfe, an American reporter. The play takes place in Russia, where Varenka, who has been working for some time with an English family, tries to tell Rolfe about the *real* conditions in the country. Of course, the Russian secret police (the Okrana) do not want the story told, and so they (and their agent, the Baron Stephan Andrey) keep a close watch on Varenka. They eventually expose her real name, Anna Mirrel, and that she carries a Yellow Ticket, which is a prostitute's license. This revelation disgraces her, and Rolfe rejects her. But, just before she is taken away, it is revealed that she is Jewish, and she had to use the passport to move around the country rather than be stuck in a ghetto her whole life—she announces that she has never lived as a "lady of the evening." All ends well, and Rolfe and Anna live happily together.

The scene with the Queen of the Movies and Mr. Varenka in *The Passing Show of 1914* is a topsy-turvy version of the original, borrowing an extended portion of source material for effect. Atteridge first changes the gender of the character in question, making him an older man begging help from an even older woman; nothing in the scene deals with young, sweet love, but rather with a strange, unusual, and silly love between a cross-dressing man and his (truly?) mutton-chop-sporting love interest (see ⏵Figure 7.3).

Not only is the situation itself reversed—wherein the woman is begging the man to love her, despite her situation—but even the prop itself becomes an object of mirth. Here, the Yellow Ticket is nothing scandalous, but is instead a huge yellow pawn ticket, which apparently connects Varenka to the Russians who get "six percent" of everything he makes each month. Any audience member who had seen *The Yellow Ticket* would have immediately recognized the ridiculousness of the situation.

In some cases, *The Passing Show* merely took basic principles and general situations from other Broadway offerings and placed them in a new context. An example occurs with "The Midnight Girl," who sings a song, "The Midnight Girl at the Midnight Cabaret." This reference is to the musical, *The Midnight Girl*, which premiered on February 23, 1914; the show featured music and lyrics by Adolf Philipp, who also premiered his *Adele* in New York earlier in the 1913–1914 theater season. The plot revolves around a young woman who is a nurse by day and a fabulous cabaret singer late at night. More will be said about the song and its musical aspects later in the chapter, but here, Atteridge merely makes use of the character in his revue, importing her attributes and her peculiar nocturnal habits wholesale and without humor.

Kitty MacKay (pronounced "*Kit*-tee Mack-*Eye*") was another borrowed character. Kitty's one special attribute is that, at her first appearance, she wears a costume that is also referential in nature—it comes almost entirely from the source play.[16] This was the starring female role in *The Passing Show*, and Kitty was played by José Collins. ▶Figure 7.4 shows Collins dressed as the Scottish damsel. Her costume was directly modeled after Molly MacIntyre's outfit from the source play *Kitty MacKay* (1914), by Catherine Chisolm Cushing, seen in ▶Figure 7.5. Harry Carroll, the secondary composer for *The Passing Show of 1914*, provided the character with an opening song complete with a chorus that sings and dances a Scottish can-can in the tune, "Kitty MacKay." The music, however, was entirely new—not referential—and provided Collins a feature role amidst a bevy of beautiful chorus girls.

Additional characters, costumes, and props are culled directly from other shows, but the degree to which the music itself was a referent to other musicals could vary greatly. In some cases, it was simply a lyrical or titular connection to the source, whereas in others, a sonic reference was used.

Some of the most complicated references to identify are song lyrics, and it takes a specialist in the music of the period to know which lines in the show are actually connected to popular music of the day.[17] In scene 1, the Misleading Nut is asked to explain more about who he is, and he replies, "I'm the guy who put the salt in the ocean." Though this may not seem like a humorous reply, it actually references the song by Gaskill and Shisler (1912), 'I'm the Guy,' about a man who can do just about anything.
Chorus

> I'm the guy that put the fish in the ocean.
> I'm the guy that causes all the commotion
> I'm a one-two-three-four wonderful man,

I can change your mind by shaking your hand.
I'm the guy that put the dough in the doughnut,
and the "cus" in the custard pie
Did you ever stop and wonder
Where did they get the noise for thunder?
I'm the guy, I'm the guy.

Several other tunes are also mentioned in the dialogue. When Omar Khayyam implores the priests in scene 6 with "Yes, don't blame it all on Broadway," he references the title of the song, "Don't Blame It All on Broadway," (1913) by lyricist Harry Williams and composers Joe Young and Bert Grant. Later, in scene 7, Jerrold McGee cries from offstage, "Kitty, Kitty, somebody has lost his cat." This is probably an oblique reference to the song, "What Do You Mean You Lost Your Dog?" (Henry Weil, 1914). Even if these comments flew by in an instant, audiences of the time would catch them without difficulty.

There are also moments where Atteridge uses songs from other shows as the basis for his own lyrics, even when the music for that particular song has no correlation with the original material. The best example of this approach is in "Kitty MacKay," which has already been mentioned. Although the play was not a musical, it appears to have music included—perhaps a holdover from the nineteenth-century tradition of using orchestras to play music for straight plays. A song from the show was published by the Edgar Selden Music Co., which is the only evidence of what kind of music could be heard, and, remarkably, the music was written by a member of the cast, Bernard Thornton, with lyrics by Edgar Selden. The cover warns buyers to "Beware of Imitations!" and there is little doubt they are referring to the song from *The Passing Show of 1914* by Atteridge and Carroll. The tune is in three-quarter time, and it has no connection to Carroll's melody. Selden's lyrics, however, were mimicked by Atteridge.

SELDEN LYRICS	ATTERIDGE LYRICS
Verse	Verse
There's a lassie who lives in old Scotland	Oh Sandy, wise Sandy, loved Kitty MacKay,
The pick o' the basket is she.	A dandy, real dandy, she looked to his eye.
But whenever I tell her I love her,	He quickly made most all the Highlands, the sigh-lands,
She'll laugh and nae listen to me;	Without knowing if he had a showing.
She's as bright as the bluebells about her,	So pretty, so pretty was Kitty MacKay,
In the highlands, the heather and glen;	That Kitty, fair Kitty, you never could tie.
I'll confess that I can't live without her,	Oh, every time that Sandy'd meet her, he'd greet her,

And I've said this again and again:

Chorus	Chorus
Sweet Kitty MacKay, say, won't you try	Kitty MacKay, my Highland maid,
And give me just one chance?	There's mischief in your eye.
Each day I wait from dawn 'til late	With all my heart-strings you have played,
For one wee loving glance;	You surely made me sigh, and try that Romeo-ing
Sweet Kitty my own, for you alone,	Kitty MacKay, what sweet charms lie
I'd build with love a golden throne;	There in your manner shy!
The piper will tune	Pretty Kitty!
For our June honeymoon,	Pity my heart, Kitty MacKay!
In the heatherland, you and I,	
My bonnie Sweet Kitty MacKay.	

Selden's lyrics are unsurprisingly sweet and appropriate for the melodramatic tone of the play itself, where poor Kitty must find a sweetheart who truly loves her. The song is from the point of view of a lover who continuously tries to woo Kitty, but to no avail. The number is also full of stereotypical items associated with Scotland, such as the heather (though not on the hill), the pipers, and the glen, with just a touch of Scottish dialect. Also, note that the lyricist nicely sets up the chorus by ending the verse with a lead-in to the title of the song.

Atteridge used this as the model for his own lyrics. Unlike the "mugging" that took place in "The Maude Adams of the Screen," Atteridge's text for "Kitty MacKay" is an example of strict parody rather than a satire or lampoon; the sentiments of the source song are maintained, as is the use of local color, the point of view (at times), and even the preparation for the chorus. In Atteridge's version, many indicators of the source song are present, including the use of the word "sweet," the coquettishness of the woman in question, and the hopes of the protagonist. There is no humor here, just homage to the lyrics of the original song used in *Kitty MacKay*. The tune introduces Kitty as a character in *The Passing Show*, and it does so without providing insight as to how she will be portrayed.

In many cases, music comments on a situation outside of the production numbers in order to create a joke. One of the characters that interacts with the Queen of the Movies is Teddy Roosevelt, who has just awakened from a long nap and is searching for his "big stick." As he enters, the intro music is one of Al Jolson's hits from *The Honeymoon Express* (1913), "Who Paid the Rent for Mrs. Rip Van Winkle When Rip Van Winkle Went Away?" with lyrics by Alfred Bryan and music by Fred Fischer. The song was then interpolated into *The Belle of Bond Street* in March of 1914, so it would have been fresh when *The Passing Show* opened in June.[18] This type of topical reference is perhaps more familiar to modern audiences. The song comments on Roosevelt's political career and the many years that passed between his first elected presidential term in 1904 and his campaign for re-election in 1912. After the music concludes, Roosevelt asks, "Where am I? Have I been asleep? Didn't the great Theodore Roosevelt say he wanted to retire from public life?" The scene-change music—only labeled as a "Melos" in the instrument parts—provided an aural joke that relied on a text that wasn't sung but was absolutely implied.

Another commentary in the musical webbing deals with the Panthea scene, and it is heard just after the audience learns that the woman playing Panthea (Petrova) has fallen out of a boat. Only a few measures of music are used, but it still manages to make a connection that would have probably tickled the funny bone of some in the audience. The fictional Panthea is involved in a shipwreck, but here, the scene-change music is for the song "Sit Down, You're Rocking the Boat" (1913) by William Jerome and Grant Clarke (lyrics) and Jean Schwartz (music). Since Schwartz had been the composer for *The Passing Show of 1913* and had worked with the Shuberts for years, there was probably no issue with using his music to aid in the joke; he wrote tunes for many of the later editions, so clearly no feelings were hurt on his end. Both *The Honeymoon Express* and *The Belle of Bond Street* were Shubert productions too, so the brothers were probably more than happy to advertise music from their other shows.

Many of the referential pieces of music were featured in the production numbers themselves, though at times Romberg made oblique nods to other songs. In one case, he merely used the form of the source tune and neglected the melody entirely. Early in the first act, a band of gypsies rushes onstage and begins to perform in the same movie studio set that acts as a backdrop for Mary Packard and the Midnight Girl. These players perform a number that (in the narrative) will be used in an upcoming movie, *The Sari Dance*, featuring three principals and several accompanying members. These gypsies are stragglers from Emmerich Kálmán's operetta, *Der Zigeunerprimas*, which opened in New York in January 1914 under the title *Sari*. One of the highlights of *Sari* is the "Ha-za-zaa," a whirling dance wherein the chorus is heard over and over, with each repetition increasing in tempo. The chorus for this song—the part that continues to speed up—can be seen in Example 7.1.

Example 7.1 Chorus from "Hazazaa," Sari. Emmerich Kálmán.

Quasi marcia moderato

Ha - za - zaa!_____ you start and a - way you go,_____

If it should make you diz - zy, Don't no - tice that, keep bus - y,

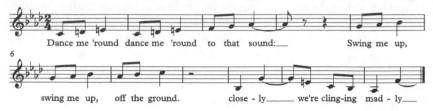

Example 7.2 *Chorus from "Sari Dance," The Passing Show of 1914. Sigmund Romberg.*

Example 7.3 *Chorus from "The Midnight Girl," The Midnight Girl. Adolf Philipp.*

While Atteridge's lyrics to *The Sari Dance* mention Mitzi Hajos (the star of the show) as well as the "Ha-za-zaa" dance itself, Romberg resists the urge to copy Kálmán's music directly. Instead, he merely borrows the music's dance-inspired function with only a small suggestion of its melodic content in the descent and leap in mm. 35-6.[19] The vocal line for Romberg's chorus can be seen in Example 7.2; it is this section that gets progressively faster.

The patrons of the Winter Garden would have had no trouble making the connection between the number and *Sari* itself and, again, the allusion was more celebratory than parody.

Some of the composer's melodies, however, are taken directly from other sources. Romberg's musical introduction for the title character from *The Midnight Girl*, as mentioned earlier, is called "The Midnight Girl at the Midnight Cabaret." Again, a character is referred to through costume, play, and plot, but Romberg takes the connection further by borrowing directly from Adolf Philipp's score.[20] Example 7.3 shows the opening chorus of Philipp's song entitled "The Midnight Girl." The up-and-down motion in the vocal line ultimately leads the melody upwards to a rousing "triple hammer blow" that was no doubt matched by a physical motion on the stage.

Romberg uses the exact musical figure to open *his* chorus, as shown in Examples 7.4a and 7.4b, even though he slightly changes the line by m. 5, when the new consequent of the phrase is introduced.

The connection between the songs would have been apparent, and no doubt the audience enjoyed seeing the character take the stage again. The character and the song retain many of their features from the source play, and they are not satirized in melody or in function. In *The Passing Show*, the Midnight Girl becomes a movie starlet, but she remains a nurse-turned-entertainer who likes nothing better than to show off her singing skills. She never is degraded as a mere laughing stock, turning the character on her head from the original context. Instead, she retains the verve and charm she possessed in the source play.

One common way of creating musical reference is to use a famous song for only a few measures as part of a newly composed work, and this happens in a few instances in *The Passing Show*. During the chorus of "Levee Days," there is a moment where Carroll quotes the opening of "The Old Folks at Home" (1851) by Stephen Foster. The reference would have been expected, because "Levee Days" is a song that recalls the antebellum South as a place of beauty now "lost in mem'ry's haze." "You Can't Go Wrong with Me" uses this type of musical borrowing as well. In the midst of the song's chorus, Romberg invokes part of "The Battle Hymn of the Republic" (1862), with music by William Steffe and lyrics by Julia Ward Howe. The moment is clearly identified by the use of the brass and by the text that it underscores. These types of musical reference are not too frequent in *The Passing Show of 1914*, but when they happen, they are always indicated by a significant change in texture so that the audience does not miss the gesture.

The *tour-de-force* of reference-based performance came in act 2 of the revue, which was the second time that Marilynn Miller performed alone onstage. In her first number, she danced in the *divertissement*, but in her second appearance, "Imitations," she used her acting, dancing, and singing skills together. Her abilities were so highly lauded that she received tremendous attention in the press. "Imitations" is an extended musical sequence that incorporates four popular songs within a separate musical framework, providing transitions between the different sections. Each of the four songs were associated with a different star from Broadway, vaudeville, or ballet. Miller imitated each of these in turn, trying to match the performer's voice, movements, and style—exactly what would be expected from any impersonator. Interestingly, this is the only section that changed substantially during the Broadway run and throughout the tour, where different programs and different versions of the script identify some of the changes that were made. The changes have caused confusion in identifying the targets of Miller's satire.[21] The parts and the copyist's score still exist in manuscript, however, supplying us with one accurate collection of the imitated stars, complete with one replacement. The music Romberg provides to frame these imitations is light and transparent, and it comes equipped with a clear cadence that allows for the insertion of whichever song she wished. This structure made exchanging the inner songs easy, as did the format of the specialty number itself. The framing music was more than simply a way to move from one imitation to the next though, because it also included lyrics that explained more about the parodies themselves:

Examples 7.4a and 7.4b Chorus from "The Midnight Girl," The Passing Show of 1914.
Sigmund Romberg.

I've seen the shows around the town,
And seen each shining star.
Petrova, Hitchcock and the rest,
I've worshipped from afar.
Sweet Ethel Levy [sic] I've admired,
And Eltinge as a girl,
And Gaby, very Frenchified,
All in a merry whirl.

(GABY IMITATION)

When Julian Eltinge first I saw,
All dressed in crinoline,
I thought he was the sweetest maid,
That I had ever seen

(ELTINGE IMITATION)

And Ethel Levy [sic] was divine,
Though simply-like arrayed,
My heart went quickly out to her,
When she sang the "Tango Maid."

(LEVY [sic] IMITATION)

And when Petrova I first saw,
I pictured don't you know,
How she would sing a song you've heard,
Here in the *Passing Show*.

(PETROVA IMITATION)

The first song was originally "The Tango Dip," performed by Gaby Deslys in the 1914 production of the *Belle from Bond Street*. It was replaced by an as-yet-unidentified piece (probably by Jerome Kern) performed by Hattie Williams in *The Doll Girl*, from the fall of 1913. The third song was "My Tango Girl," also heard in the *Belle from Bond Street*, but originally from the 1913 British revue, *Hullo, Tango!*[22] This was performed by the popular transcontinental actress Ethel Levey, who made several recordings in her career. The song also may have held a particular interest for the creative team since Louis Hirsch, the composer, had written the score for *The Passing Show of 1912* (and would contribute to later editions too); the interpolation may have been in part a means of plugging Hirsch's tune in America. The fourth song, "Omar Khayyam," was by Romberg and was from *The Passing Show* itself. Instead of lampooning a singer, Miller provided a version of Olga Petrova as a singer—something Petrova certainly was not—but gave a performance not unlike Robin Williams's impersonation of Marlon Brando performing Shakespeare in the movie, *Dead Poet's*

Society (1989), where the quality of the voice and the style of acting becomes the basis for the joke.

It was the second song, however, that caused the most discussion. Miller performed the song "When Martha Was a Girl," from *The Crinoline Girl*, which opened in March 1914.[23] She imitated the star (as well as contributing lyricist) of the musical, Julian Eltinge, seen in ▶Figure 7.6. Eltinge was quite a beguiling actress and was highly respected, not in the least because "she" was actually a "he," and one of the most famous female impersonators of the teens and twenties. Eltinge's style of impersonation was not like Monroe's hysterical *grande dame*; instead it was lauded for his veracity—he looked and acted like a woman, even though his picture was frequently published while he was dressed as a man. As with Francis Renault, it appears from contemporary reviews and articles that there were no suggestive or homosexual overtones in his act. He was seen as a first-class performer who was incredibly good at what he did.[24] Thus, when Miller sang this song as Eltinge, she was a woman performing as a man performing as a woman, and audiences loved it. In this single number, the references were what created the humor, both musically and physically, but it was the skill of a single performer that brought them to life.

This chapter details only *some* of the many references in the script. Other people are mentioned, such as Lew Docksteader, the blackface minstrel performer still popular in New York City in 1914. Many other shows are also included, using the different strategies discussed here. For example, a "Help Wanted" sign hangs in the office of the Queen of the Movies, briefly referencing the play of the same name by Jack Lait (1914). "Miss High Jinks," a character played by Frances Demarest throughout the revue, is from the musical *High Jinks* (1913, lyrics by Otto Harbach, music by Rudolf Friml). Locations from the surrounding area of New York are mentioned, like Hempstead, New York (Long Island), which is where the airship scene takes place. Frances Starlight, a character that is used in earlier drafts of the script, but dropped before opening night, is based on the famous actress Frances Starr. A full catalog of the references for the show is probably impossible from a twenty-first century perspective, but, as this chapter demonstrates, a contemporary reading of the show involves far more than just a mention of the other plays satirized in *The Passing Show*; it requires a nuanced approach that takes the full revue into account.

So what does this intricate web of references tell us? First of all, it suggests a methodology for an approach to the revue in its earliest years. Only by delving into the world surrounding the show in question can one begin to understand its structure, its characters, and its music and dances. Rather than simply calling revues topical, a more thorough study reveals that the pattern of references works on multiple levels, some of which are specifically based on recent events and prominent people, while others stem from the entertainment milieu of the day. This methodology points to the extraordinary flexibility of the genre and explains, in part, why the popularity of the revue lasted as long as it did, though much more research needs to be done to show how the genre changed over the years. And lastly, this approach not only helps to delve into the work (or the text) inductively, but also to look outward, toward the audiences who attended. The many types of references (physical, musical, verbal, visual, and so on) are entirely dependent on an audience's knowledge of the source material. An analysis of the revue suggests an audience that was more than just a passing crowd who saw a passing show. The audience was representative of a culture of theatergoers who saw everything that crossed the boards, from musicals to operettas to straight plays. Beyond that, these patrons had to know movies, tunes from the past, and lyrics from unrelated songs. The creative team for each *Passing Show* was open to a variety of media, and they rearranged and reworked the sources through equally diverse processes. The expectation was that most of the jokes were tailored to New York audiences, but the extensive touring circuits brought most shows through much of the United States, and it is probable these audiences understood a fair portion of the humor. The Broadway of *The Passing Show* series was very different from the Broadway of today—in that focused on a specific culture of New York that would become the basis for musicals in the late teens and especially in the 1920s and 1930s. By unpacking the references of these early shows, one gains a unique perspective into the theatrical culture of the past—one that reveals the revue to be at once familiar and distant simultaneously to twenty-first-century audiences. And it is within this remarkably rich format that the creative teams for the Shuberts—as well as Ziegfeld, White, Berlin, Cohan, and Carroll—all worked, hoping to find the right mixture of reference to keep audiences buying tickets year after year.

NOTES

1. For a contemporary review, "Review" *Theatre Magazine*, February 1914, 96.

2. Bordman, *American Musical Theatre*, 294 (chap. 1, n. 3). For a contemporary review of the show, see "The First Nighter" *New York Dramatic Mirror*, April 15, 1914, 12.

3. Lee Davis, *Scandals and Follies*, 134 (chap. 1, n. 3).

4. "Theatrical Notes" *New York Times*, May 29, 1914, 11.

5. Lee Davis, *Scandals and Follies*, chap. 5.

6. For a contemporary review, see "City Summary," *New York Clipper*, May 2, 1868, 30.

7. For a contemporary review of the show, see "The First Nighter," *New York Dramatic Mirror*, April 1, 1914, 12. For more commentary, see Marie B. Schrader, "Madame Critic" *New York Dramatic Mirror*, April 8, 1914, 5.

8. See Charles W. Goddard and Paul Dickey, *The Misleading Lady* (New York: Samuel French, 1914), Shubert Archive. The play inspired at least three movies of the same name in 1916, 1920, and 1932.

9. The first verse to the original song reads:

There's a girl of sweet seventeen,
Always has a cute tambourine,
Heavenly grace, heavenly face,
'Neath a bonnet with "Salvation" written on it.
Ev'ry fellow living in town,
Thinks she's mighty swell.
Ev'ry night they gather 'round
Sweet Salvation Nell.

10. The play was popular enough to spawn two film versions—the first in 1921 and the second in 1931.

11. See "The First Nighter," *New York Dramatic Mirror*, April 1, 1914, 12.

12. Monckton Hoffe, *Panthea*, unpublished script dated December 21, 1914, Shubert Archive.

13. Percy MacKaye, *A Thousand Years Ago*, unpublished, undated script, Shubert Archive. For a contemporary review, see "Review" *Theatre Magazine*, February 1914, 63.

14. For more information on Pierrot, see Martin Green and John Swan, *The Triumph of Pierrot: The Commedia dell'arte and the Modern Imagination* (University Park: Pennsylvania State University Press, 1993). The ballet was performed in *The Passing Show of 1914* by Stafford Pemberton and Ethel Kelly.

15. The play originally comes from the Victoria Morton's novel, *The Yellow Ticket* (New York: Grosset and Dunlap, 1914).

16. For a contemporary review, see "Review," *Theatre Magazine*, February 1914, 59.

17. One of these experts is Paul Charosh, whom I thank for suggesting these and other important references from the script.

18. For a contemporary review of the show, see "The First Nighter," *New York Dramatic Mirror*, April 1, 1914, 13.

19. The melodic leap in m. 34 of the "new" version is probably the closest melodic connection between the two pieces. The source dance is sometimes given the alternate spelling, "Hazaza."

20. Both Jean Briquet and Paul Hervé were pseudonyms of Philipp. See John Koegel, *Music in German Immigrant Theater: New York, 1840–1940* (Rochester, NY: Boydell and Brewer, Ltd., 2009) for a thorough discussion of Philipp and his music. For a contemporary review of the operetta, see "Review" *Theatre Magazine*, April 1914, 212.

21. Authors offer many different lists of the parodied stars. For example, Lee Davis suggests that Miller first "impersonated Mme. Adelaide Genée, then warbling in different octaves as she did takeoffs on Bessie McCoy, Fritzi Scheff, and Sophie Tucker"; Davis, *Scandals and Follies*, 119. This list, however, from Miller's biography, describes her act *before* she was cast in *The Passing Show of 1914*; see Harris, *The Other Marilyn*, 36 (chap. 2, n. 30).

22. Miller knew about *Hullo, Tango!* because she was performing in London during its run at the Hippodrome, and very possibly she saw the revue itself. She probably knew some of the cast, since they shared the same hotel. Harris, *The Other Marilyn*, 34.

23. For a contemporary review, see "Review" *Theatre Magazine*, May 1914, 227.

24. Both performers were targets of gossip, and it is probable both Eltinge and Renault were homosexuals, but theater reviewers do not make such suggestions in their columns.

8

AMERICA'S FOREMOST MUSICAL
INSTITUTION
• • •
THE SHUBERTS, ZIEGFELD, AND THEIR BATTLE
FOR SUPREMACY

In an advertisement for *The Passing Show of 1924*, the phrase, "America's Foremost Musical Institution" appeared in florid letters alongside the usual hoopla about the chorus girls, the enormity of the show, and the excitement of the "original New York cast."[1] It would be difficult to find a theater historian or aficionado in the early twenty-first century who would agree that the annual Winter Garden show could receive this title. Most people would identify the right answer as Ziegfeld's *Follies* without hesitation. But as difficult as it may be for modern-day enthusiasts to understand, an audience member or critic in 1924 could have identified either revue— *The Passing Show* or the *Follies*—as the finest series they had witnessed. Over the decades, the former production became overshadowed by the latter, and alongside the aggrandizement of the *Follies* came a mythology surrounding Florenz Ziegfeld as a person. The power of this fantasy has thrust all other revues (and their producers) into a dark and dusky haze in which they still remain. By exploring the development of the *Follies* legend, one begins to see that the Broadway of the teens and twenties was just as dazzling and as teeming with competitive splendor as it was in the years that followed. The illumination of the past brings with it not only stories of fierce competition and bitter rivalry but also of speedy business decisions and wise investments. And, like any good legend, the story now told about the past is built on a series of choices and omissions that began long ago and continued for years after the original participants had died.

The decision to launch *The Passing Show* as an annual revue series was, for the Shuberts, both effective and profitable. Although today many authors claim it was merely a way to compete with Ziegfeld and his *Follies*, the truth is that for Lee and J. J., *The Passing Show* was only a single cog in their ever-growing theatrical machine. It was not their first revue, nor was it the first show in their newly built Winter Garden Theatre. This does not mean that it was unimportant to the brothers, but the series was not the single-minded (and simplistic) means of competing with the *Follies* that many suggest it was. Bordman says the Shuberts were "Broadway's most

notorious copycats" and claims the Winter Garden revues "were not seriously rival-
ing Ziegfeld," either financially or artistically.[2] Baral claims "the Winter Garden girls
were plentiful and decorative but not always in the Ziegfeld class."[3] Davis calls the
Winter Garden shows "expensive vaudeville" and asserts that the Shuberts took
advantage of Ziegfeld's late opening for the *Follies of 1912* as a means of competing
with him.[4] What these authors miss, however, is that by 1910, the Shuberts were
working on a much larger scale than Ziegfeld. They owned or leased dozens of theaters by this time, and the brothers also had produced more shows than any of their
competitors during the teens. In the 1911–1912 season alone, the Shuberts had nine
shows on Broadway, and they also had over five touring productions. Their closest
competitor was the company of (George M.) Cohan and (Sam) Harris, who only put
on three shows that season. Furthermore, of the shows the Shuberts mounted, four
were revues. The suggestion that *The Passing Show* was an act of flat mimicry on
the part of the Shuberts simply does not consider the context in which the show
took form, and as documents demonstrate, the Shuberts themselves did not believe
Ziegfeld's approach to being a producer was one that they either could—or wanted
to—appropriate. Instead, the Shuberts rightly considered themselves as being on
a very different scale than Ziegfeld or, for that matter, Charles Frohman, Oliver
Morosco, Charles Dillingham, or the dozens of other producers who worked on a
single show at a time. The Shuberts' main concern was Marc Klaw and Abe Erlanger,
producers who rivaled them more vigorously on the national level and who were
controlling members of the Syndicate, the monopoly that the Shuberts had fought
against and bested in order to run their own theaters. So what was it that brought
Ziegfeld to the attention of the Shuberts? The heart of the matter had to do with the
one commodity that all the producers were eager to get—the best stars, the top of
the talent pool. Not only would this be the first issue that caused friction between
the producers, but it would become the defining problem between the Shuberts and
Ziegfeld until the latter's death in 1932.

In a wisely titled article in the *Green Book Magazine* from 1914, Ziegfeld was hailed
by Rennold Wolf as "The P. T. Barnum of the Theatre."[5] In part, the author explores
the many ways that the producer developed his career, especially noting that his time
connected the Trocadero Club of Chicago was the first real sign of his genius. Nearly
contemporaneously with Sam Shubert and his work with Mansfield in New York,
Ziegfeld became the promoter for another important star, Eugene Sandow (imagi-
natively called the "perfect man"), in the Midwest. Ziegfeld was impressed by this
bodybuilder and initiated a series of publicity stunts that would bring both the producer and the man great fame. These tricks of showmanship included an invitation
for women to come on stage to caress Sandow's muscles and a (fixed) fight between
the strongman and a lion. As Ziegfeld progressed in his career, other stars became
a part of his galaxy, and he found numerous ways to make major attractions of
W. C. Fields, Fanny Brice, Lillian Lorraine, and Sophie Tucker.

It may not have been revolutionary to recognize the possibilities inherent in
hiring a star performer, but for both the Shuberts and Ziegfeld—and thus for the
revue as a whole—it was a central feature for success. For both parties, the relationship between entertainers and producers was a complicated proposition. In the
twenty-first century, the Shuberts (specifically Lee and J. J.) still have a reputation as

angry, money-hungry tyrants, while Ziegfeld is often depicted as a man of class and dignity who treated all with respect.[6] This element of the Ziegfeld legend partially comes from his inclusion of Bert Williams in the *Follies*. An oft-told tale, repeated in numerous print sources, has Ziegfeld forcing his all-white cast to accept the black man, telling them, "I can replace any of you in a heartbeat, but Williams is one star you can't replace." This story puts Ziegfeld in the role of benevolent benefactor—a master showman with a big heart.[7] In point of fact, however, both Ziegfeld and the Shuberts were equally aggressive with stars when they felt they had to be. Rennold relates a tale of Ziegfeld's struggle with Nora Bayes during the *Follies of 1909*:

> Frequently, [his employees] have misunderstandings with him which are entirely justified, for sometimes he has a most exasperating way of ignoring the ethics of business or friendly relationship. Yet, so gentle, so suave and so ingratiating is he, that sooner or later a companionship and even a professional association is resumed . . .
>
> Miss Bayes, the principal luminary of [the 1909 *Follies*] withdrew abruptly. She said she was "ill." Whatever the real complaint, Mr. Ziegfeld's summer entertainment was dangerously close to the rocks, and he saved the day only by engaging Eva Tanguay at a staggering salary. His next step was to obtain an injunction restraining Miss Bayes from appearing elsewhere during the term of her contract. The action for an injunction was fought bitterly. Ziegfeld was ruthless, and time and again he halted Miss Bayes at the outset of a lucrative engagement. In court and out, and through the columns of the press, both parties indulged in vituperation and recrimination.[8]

This type of tumultuous relationship was common in theatrical circles, and the result of such combinations of strong personalities, flaring tempers, significant amounts of money, and artistic rights led to a flurry of interchange between performers and both the Shuberts and Ziegfeld. After all, the entertainers knew that one of the best ways to position themselves was to pit producers against each other to get the best possible contract. It was within this context that the ire between Ziegfeld and the Shuberts began.

One of the earliest documents in the Shubert Archive from Ziegfeld is a letter sent in 1908 not to the Shuberts, but instead to Ned Wayburn:

> "My dear Mr. Wayburn,
> If it is your intention to attempt to try and have members of my organization break their contracts and leave me to play in the Messrs. Shubert production, I would like to know it, because two can play at the same game,
>
> Yours very truly,
> Ziegfeld[9]

At the time, Wayburn was preparing the Eddie Foy vehicle, *Mr. Hamlet of Broadway*, and was going to open in the Lyric Theater on December 23. Ziegfeld was busy maintaining *Miss Innocence*, an extravaganza that had opened on November 30. In both cases, the productions had loose narratives and were more akin to a revue than a musical comedy. This meant that cast members who were not principals could probably be convinced to leave Ziegfeld's production if they received a better offer. None of the opening night cast from *Miss Innocence* seems to have been utilized in Wayburn's Hamlet comedy, so the details of the argument are obscured. But, whatever the truth was, the securing of talent contracts was an important exchange between the two camps.

And the truth of the matter was that Ziegfeld's associates put him in an adversarial relationship with the Shuberts before he had even met the brothers. As previously mentioned, the Syndicate and its allies had been at odds with the Shuberts since the earliest stages of the brothers' time in show business. Ziegfeld, too, had a connection with the Syndicate early on; he had been under Erlanger's protection since 1896, and he continued to work alongside the man and his monopoly for years. Ziegfeld was still a minor producer when Sam Shubert was killed in 1905 and thus was able to avoid being seen as part of the opposite camp. But, when Lee Shubert offered Ziegfeld and his star (and wife) Anna Held a chance to appear in *The Motor Girl* in 1906, Ziegfeld made a move that may have become the basis for years of bad blood. Ziegfeld and Held accepted the money Lee Shubert wired to them to sail back from Europe on the understanding that it was an advance for the show, but when they arrived in New York, Ziegfeld kept the money and then placed Held in a new Erlanger show.[10] The Shuberts were furious and sued, but Ziegfeld returned the money saying he "forgot" to pay it back.[11] By siding with the Syndicate in his early years and then turning a positive business arrangement into a personal affront, Ziegfeld went from being a nonthreatening small-time manager to one of the Shuberts' most disliked competitors.

When *The Passing Show* series was in development, the in-house memos, letters, and even overseas telegrams do not show a preoccupation with Ziegfeld, but instead show a desire to put on a production bigger than anything else summer audiences could see. For the Shuberts—or more accurately for J. J., who was the driving force behind the shows—the very function of the Winter Garden was as a home for revues or revue-like shows, and therefore, in many of the memos, the term *Winter Garden show* is used far more frequently than *Passing Show*. And, perhaps more importantly, Ziegfeld was not the only producer staging revues at the time—George Lederer, Joe Weber, Henry Harris, and Jessie Lasky had all put on revues during the 1910–1911 season. As mentioned in chapter 1, the original plan for the Winter Garden might have been as a showcase for Lew Fields, but J. J. took over supervision of the new theater when Fields fell ill in 1910.[12] By the time the first *Passing Show* was in production, J. J. was using Fields's model to manufacture his own contribution to his family's theatrical enterprise.

The key difference between Weber and Fields's shows and *The Passing Shows* was that the formula for creating the two were *not* identical, even though the former was a powerful influence for the latter. The Winter Garden revues, and *The Passing Show* series in particular, each followed unique paths in their organization. For *La Belle Paree* and *The Revue of Revues*, the Shuberts sectioned off the night into different "pieces," which separated the main event from extended ballets and "exotic" Chinese or Japanese one-acts. Fields's model, as the producer's descendants relate, was that the "class" section came first—usually a pantomime or ballet—with the "sass" portion to follow, built primarily on burlesques of other shows.[13] By the time Harold Atteridge and George Bronson-Howard began shaping the overall structure for *The*

Passing Show of 1912, they refined this general formula by developing a script that bound together numerous burlesques of other productions into a single, yet loose, narrative. Although the *Follies* made use of some burlesque, it more frequently featured medleys and skits that had no relation to one another.[14] The programs for the *Follies* between 1907 and 1911 show a structure that is quite unlike the 1912 *Passing Show*, and this difference was clear to audiences at the time. J. J. was focused beyond the *Follies*, but he was aware that Flo's shows would be important competition. Shubert acknowledged more than once in memos that the major summer production in New York was the Ziegfeld revue, which he felt would be "the show to beat," but they were not overly concerned about the *Follies*.[15] Contemporary theatergoers did not think *The Passing Shows* existed merely to challenge the rooftop entertainment, and that is most apparent in the reviews of the Winter Garden's first summer production. Not a single critic, from Channing Pollock to Sime Silverman, from the *New York Herald* to *Variety*, mentions Ziegfeld's series even once in their estimation of the Shuberts' entertainment. Instead, writers discuss the factors that made *The Passing Show of 1912* something new and different, with most of the discourse surrounding the extensive burlesque. Taking these facts into consideration, the suggestion that the Shuberts set out to copy the *Follies* is unsubstantiated. *The Passing Show* was a summer show, but it was a revue crafted out of new elements.

It would be a mistake to forget that part of what made each of the revues what they were was their location, and it further supports the notion that the Shubert revues were devised in their own right. An interesting set of memos contains comments on this issue and also provides some personal insight into Lee and J. J.'s thoughts about Ziegfeld. As mentioned, *The Passing Show* was specifically devised as a feature at the Winter Garden, running there from its first performance on Broadway to its last. As one reviewer mentioned while summing up the 1912 edition, "It is a paradox, but the Winter Garden has a fine summer entertainment."[16] This may seem like a trifling comment, but it is more significant than it seems on the surface. The very idea of summer shows was that they were light and simple, and as several reviews of *The Passing Show of 1912* point out, there was more content in that first edition than other summer shows could provide. *Variety* went as far as to say, "'The Passing Show' isn't a summer show—it is a regular show."[17] Part of what may have inspired the comparison to summer fare was that the *Follies* were originally in a small, open space. When it began in 1907, the *Follies* took place at the Jardin de Paris on the New York Theatre Roof, a small pavilion-like theater with folding seats and a small refreshment stand on the side.[18] The location could hold only a limited set and a small number of musicians and, despite changing the name to The Moulin Rouge in 1912 for *The Winsome Widow* (also produced by Ziegfeld), the venue was no match for the large-scale revues that had taken place in the Winter Garden. Figure 8.1 is the stage of the Jardin de Paris shortly before the time it was used by Ziegfeld, while Figure 8.2 shows the inside of the Winter Garden; no amount of theatrical smoke and mirrors could hide the fact that the larger space allowed for a completely different kind of revue on a much grander scale.

The move to the New Amsterdam for Ziegfeld, then, was not an arbitrary decision but a reaction to the enormous success of the Winter Garden shows, especially *The Passing Show*. Although the popular story has been that the Shuberts were

Fig. 8.1. *Jardin de Paris stage (ca. 1906, as the Olympia Roof Garden). Shubert Archive.*

Fig. 8.2. *Winter Garden interior, stage left. Shubert Archive.*

competing with Ziegfeld, the truth is that Ziegfeld and his backers were competing with the Shuberts. Many authors, including Ziegfeld's own descendants, say that the *Follies* had "arrived" when it moved to a new space, but none suggest why this might be.[19] Klaw and Erlanger made the decision to move Ziegfeld and his *Follies* to the New Amsterdam Theatre for the 1913 edition, and this is where the revue would stay until 1927, when Ziegfeld's own titular theater was built. Although the New Amsterdam was an older theater, it was beautiful and spacious, holding only one hundred fewer patrons than the Winter Garden at seventeen hundred patrons. The New Amsterdam was remodeled for the *Follies*, and parts of it, especially the Roof Garden, were continually reworked during the 1920s, allowing the revue to expand in scale and grandeur.[20] The change in venues was essential to keep Ziegfeld's production alive, and everyone involved with the welfare of the *Follies* knew it had to upgrade to stay competitive. When Ziegfeld announced he would be offering a smaller show on the roof in 1914 (the *Midnight Frolic*), the Shuberts were justifiably nervous, in part because Ziegfeld had approached them about using one of *their* theaters for the roof show during the previous season.

A series of inter-office memos passed between J. J. and Lee on January 17, 1914, illuminating their feelings on what a roof garden show could mean for them. The memos also show how they saw Ziegfeld as a producer. Although both their offices were located in the Shubert Theatre, J. J. and Lee were on different floors, and throughout the day, they sent several notes to one another, hundreds of which survive. Lee first wrote to J. J., saying, "With reference to Ziegfeld and the roof garden— he would make capitol out of this in every possible way. He wouldn't play his show with us on the road either as he is tied up body and soul with the other people [Klaw and Erlanger]. He is also a bad egg and we could never trust him."[21] Past events had convinced Lee that Ziegfeld was—correctly—someone they would never be able to work with. On the surface, this memo seems to be about the New Amsterdam's roof, but in fact, it is actually a reference to an unnamed roof garden in one of the Shuberts' theaters. When J. J. responded, he suggested that Ziegfeld had approached them with the possibility of using this space, probably long before he had considered doing the remodeling of the New Amsterdam:

> Regarding Ziegfeld, I think you are wrong. He would have made the Roof Garden a big paying proposition, and it is only a question of time when the other fellow would kick him out for some reason or other, and you would have a valuable asset even if he didn't make a dollar for you as he would not be against you. "The Follies" is the only big musical proposition today against the Winter Garden shows, and we would have it all our own way. I think I would have tied him up and let your personal feelings go. It is too much work to be bothered with the roof garden and the theater downstairs and producing all the time and he is just the kind of man for the place. He would have a certain following in that direction, and I certainly would have been in favor of having him take it. . . . You have to have somebody on the job all the time, and if he were interested, he would be there all the time, and he has a following of a class of New Yorkers who are the spenders.

In the end, Lee decided that Ziegfeld was too much of a risk, and the two moved on to other business. This fascinating document offers a unique window into their thoughts about the theater business in the first place, and also about how to work with others. The Archive is filled with letters of complaints over the years from every imaginable source, from actors to seat manufacturers. In many cases, however, no matter how badly a single situation might be at the time, the Shuberts (especially J. J.) were willing to rehire someone if they felt the individual's skills justified a separation from personal emotions. It is remarkable that, after losing a substantial sum on Ziegfeld only a few years before, J. J. was willing to suggest to Lee that they consider giving their competitor a chance. This is especially interesting given (as J. J. states) that the *Follies* was the only other revue in New York at the time that could challenge the Winter Garden's shows. For J. J. to put aside his own ego demonstrates his impressive gifts as a canny businessman, including the ability to look beyond his emotional reactions to the bottom line. This memo also shows that J. J. realized that Ziegfeld was someone who could focus on one theater at a time and be a success. In other words, Ziegfeld was relatively small-time, but had a knack for making one location prosperous. And every prediction J. J. made was true, probably much to his own chagrin.

Even though the Winter Garden shows were formulated differently than the *Follies*, there could be no mistaking the fact that they both required the same basic substance to build a larger production: talent. And when it came to composers, stars, set designers, makers of effects, and the many other jobs necessary to piecing a revue together, the Shuberts and Ziegfeld were at odds on every front. Surprisingly, there are a number of members of the creative team that worked for both producers, sometimes even in the same theatrical season. For example, Cora MacGeachy, one of the most versatile and gifted costume designers on Broadway, lent her services to both Ziegfeld and the Shuberts, and moved back and forth between these producers and others with ease. This was also the case with several composers, including Louis A. Hirsch, Walter Donaldson, and Leo Edwards. Hirsch provided the score for *The Passing Show of 1912* and followed that with music for the *Follies of 1915*. By the 1920s, however, he was writing the *Greenwich Village Follies* for the Shuberts and, only months later, writing for Ziegfeld's annual *Follies* (a cycle he made more than once). From the standpoint of a creative talent, finding ways to satisfy both the Klaw and Erlanger camp and the Shubert camp would have been an excellent business move, keeping one's options open while still working in high-profile positions.[22]

For the most part, though, once Ziegfeld and the *Follies* were housed at the New Amsterdam, each year would become a heated race between the two sides to hire fresh talent, feature the best effects, and generally outdo the other for every summer show. There were positive and negative facets for each side because of the way they ran their business, and this made the competition even more fierce between the two. Ziegfeld was concentrated in one place and working with only one show at a time. This focus—something J. J. had recognized in the preceding memo—allowed Ziegfeld to more carefully craft everything in his production, resulting in what has become known as the "Ziegfeld touch." He was notorious for spending huge amounts of money on single scenes, and if the reports of his spending are true, he saw extravagance for its own sake as part of his *modus operandi*. Thus, if he could get a visual effect or new device into his production, it was probably going to be quite grand. When it came to showing audiences new things on a national scale, though, the Shuberts had the advantage. If they could place music by a new composer or a new type of visual effect in a *Passing Show*, they could simultaneously insert it into whatever Winter Garden revue was touring the country, thus robbing Ziegfeld of wowing the country with the "newest thing." Additionally, since the Shuberts had so many more revues happening throughout the year, they could more easily offer lucrative (and long-term) contracts than Ziegfeld. This unique situation meant that both camps were hungry for whatever quality content they could get, and they were constantly trying to beat each other to the punch.

The many letters that passed between the Shuberts and their partners demonstrate that, after 1913, competition was on everyone's mind. One of the first instances to indicate the need to be aware of Ziegfeld's content was a letter from J. V. Foley, a Shubert employee who wrote for their in-house paper, the *New York Review*. Much like many Shubert shows, Ziegfeld offered previews of his annual revue in Atlantic City, and it was there, in the summer of 1914, that Foley attended a performance on May 26. Foley mentions that he and Harold Atteridge were both in the audience, and he encloses his written critique of the show with a note saying, "If you think it is O.K., I will send it to [the Review]."[23] In this case, Foley's review is not very favorable, suggesting that it was much too long and that the material was not very good. In his private letter to J. J., however, Foley says, "On the whole, the songs and music are rather poor, but for Beauty, Costumes, and scenic effect, the piece is wonderful. Without a doubt it will be a big success when the bad stuff is eliminated . . . It will be a hard one to beat." One piece of the critique, though, probably spoke to the Shubert brothers' mindset about the production, and to the relationship between the two camps. "Ziegfeld has spent money with a lavish, reckless hand in mounting and costuming the new offering," Foley wrote, "The 'K & E' [Klaw and Erlanger] treasury will have a pretty bill to foot when all is reckoned, but why should Flo worry since it isn't his money?"

One of the many employees whose position required him to be cognizant of Ziegfeld's shows was E. R. Simmons, whose watch over the Shuberts' costume collection and needs made it imperative that he be aware of the latest trends. As mentioned in chapter 4, several chorus girls in *The Passing Show of 1922* wore costumes that incorporated radium and were thus "glow-in-the-dark" novelties. Designer Homer Conant contacted Simmons in April, and the two began trying to find a way to beat Ziegfeld, getting the radium outfits on stage before the *Follies* producer could do so.[24] Simmons wrote to J. J. in London that the effect would be expensive—at least $1,000 for the materials. However, upon further examination, Simmons discovered that the exclusive American rights to the substance—called at this point "Radiana"—belonged to George Choos, a producer living in Paris who had worked along transatlantic theater circuits since about 1912. Choos and Ziegfeld had signed a contract, so there was no way for the new *Passing Show* to contain a similar effect unless the "mineral" could be purchased elsewhere or the contract expired, which it did on August 1. By May 4, Simmons knew how the New Amsterdam was going to use the material and wrote in a telegram, "Ziegfeld Uses Lace Curtain Lace Dresses [,] [Watson] Barratt Intends Making Willowtree Scene Entirely Different[,] Cost Scene 12 Costumes Approximately 2500 Dollars." By June 2, Simmons had managed to find some Radiana and had even incorporated it into a show before the opening of the *Follies*, which happened three days later:

> Today I just want to tell you that we had the radium dress last night in the number and that it worked beautifully. I finally got two pounds of the material from Denver and Conant and I painted it ourselves Thursday night. I had Adler make a dress of eight big lace curtains and a big headdress, also made of the same curtain lace, and it was really a very effective dress and in the darkness is looked like a great big butterfly. We had two bamboo sticks about six feet long to hold out the sides of the dress and Miss Campbell, who wore it, looked stunning indeed. . . .
>
> I am quite sure, of course, that Ziegfeld is going to have a tremendous effect as he is going to have fifty dresses on the stage, and I understand a lace curtain besides; but if we went on tour with the [Eddie] Cantor show first, I think we could in this way take the wind out of his sails. The principal thing is it works beautifully.

The show Simmons mentions was Eddie Cantor's *Make It Snappy*, which played at the Winter Garden during that spring, and it was Evelyn Campbell who wore the dress. But apparently Simmons was not the only designer to try and place the effect in a show; the revue entitled *Sun-kist*, mounted by the authors, Fanchon and Marco Wolff, was playing at the Globe Theatre and had included the luminescent paint a day earlier. Choos was furious and took out a large advertisement in *Variety* warning people that this was a violation of his arrangement, and thereby demanded that the Globe cease using the material immediately.[25] The *Follies* opened on June 5, and Simmons attended, offering Shubert a full critique of every scene. The "Laceland" spectacle was "quite beautiful and the effect was great," making it "the special feature of the show." The only hope of minimizing Ziegfeld's efforts was "to put this effect in all the shows that go on tour before the 'Follies' [to outdo him] in other the other towns." But, for all Simmons' plotting, the Laceland moment was indeed entrancing. The *New York Evening Telegram* describes it as, "the apotheosis of stage loveliness. Under the flood of beautiful lights, the lacemaker's skill is shown. Then, gradually, the lights go out, one by one. Then a faint luminous glow is dimly outlined in the blackness. It begins to grow. The gorgeous lace creations take on a varicolored luminosity. The lace stockings, the parasols, handkerchiefs, fans, gowns, and the veils assume the beauty of a rainbow."[26] By the time *The Passing Show* used the same effect, as beautiful as it was, most of New York had already seen it in the *Follies*.

Associates who did not work for the Shuberts also knew that mentioning Ziegfeld's name would be enough to catch their interest. When Remick Music Publishing's representative, Fred Belcher, was thinking about hiring two songwriters on a more permanent basis, he contacted J. J. about the matter. In a letter written on May 16, 1919, Belcher says, "We are contemplating bringing these boys on to New York and signing them up for a year. This, however, would mean an investment of about $10,000, and I am wondering, if . . . you would be inclined to give them some of your work to do." Astutely, Belcher included a clipping that reads "L. A. Boys to Write 3 Songs for Ziegfeld." Shubert agreed and the two wrote several hits for him, and for Remick. The boys in question: Richard "Dick" Coburn (lyricist) and Vincent Rose (composer), the writers of "Whispering" and "Tell Me Why," the latter of which was one of the *Follies* songs mentioned in the article that was a huge hit.[27]

When it came to people on stage, the rules were different; they were the face of a show, and whichever producer signed them was important for both parties. Over time, a reflexive relationship developed that partially defined both the employer and employee. Al Jolson, for example, was a Shubert star, and Will Rogers a Ziegfeld star. As mentioned earlier, disagreements between the Shuberts and Ziegfeld were almost entirely over stars, and tracing this issue across the years and through a number of cases, a picture emerges that paints Ziegfeld's business practices in an unfavorable light. Before I begin this discussion, however, it is important to point out that in pouring over the hundreds of documents in the Shubert Archive, I got a sense of the Shubert brothers' business ethics too. There were several occasions where J. J., especially, tried to manipulate actors into working, even when there was a dispute that had not been resolved. This happened many times during *The Passing Show* tours, where an actor would ask for a pay raise or for compensation for something that was not specified in their contract. On multiple occasions, J. J. would finesse paying some people while not paying others, with the stars usually getting paid while the second-tier and lower entertainers did not. For example, he did this by telling the tour manager to withhold information until the performers went on stage, and then claiming that the earnings from that night's show were not enough to cover the costs. J. J. instructed the manager to pay George Monroe, though, and tell him to keep quiet about it.[28] The most common form of maneuvering evident from the archives was suppressing information, although there are instances where J. J. simply refused to pay for things (such as new shoes) requested by the actors. However, in the many missives I examined, there does not appear to be a single effort to "steal" an actor from another production, nor do either of the brothers suggest working outside the bounds of contracts that they arranged. In fact, there are many cases when Lee and J. J. send messages to their attorney, William Klein, asking if one move or another would violate their arrangements. Since many of the extant documents are personal messages between the brothers that no one else would see, it is unlikely that they would try so carefully to adhere to these contracts if they planned on violating them on a regular basis. That said, it is certainly possible that they tried to make things work in their favor, especially when it came to reviews and the media. But the Shubert theatrical machine was far too big to be run on rampant deceit and misrepresentation, and the enormous paper trail that remains does not support a culture of bad business practices and the exploitation of employees.

An early issue involving actors took place in March of 1914, when Ziegfeld wrote to Morris Gest, a Russian producer who at the time worked for the Shuberts. Ziegfeld was angry with a vaudevillian, Walter S. "Rube" Dickinson, a specialist in the "hick" act, who had written him with an unusual request. "He wants me to send him a phoney [sic] offer of $400," wrote Ziegfeld, "evidently to carry out one of [Max] Hart's schemes to hold up the Shuberts, which game he has been playing to the fullest extent."[29] Ziegfeld included the telegram he received from Dickinson, and also the reply he sent to him in Cincinnati, trying to convince Gest he was sincere. Hart had recently spoken to Gene Buck on the telephone, said Ziegfeld, telling him "he would double cross a manager [producer] any time he could, and he was for the actor first, last, and all the time." The problem in dealing with entertainers was primarily the difficulty of dealing with their agents, in Ziegfeld's estimation:

> Any time the Shuberts are negotiating for anyone, and they hear I am, if they are first in the field, all they have to do is notify me and I will quit. It is about time we stopped cutting each other's throats to give all the money to the actors, and I know that I have been quoted a million times oftener than has been the case, when people have been offered to the Shuberts, as the agents and actors always considered that I would do everything possible against the Shuberts and they against me, when I have never had that feeling at all.[30]

When he wrote this letter, Ziegfeld had only recently become prominent, and he was sincere in his wish to maintain positive ties to Lee and J. J. This was the personality of the Ziegfeld that J. J. mentioned in the earlier inter-office memo, one who was willing to reveal the machinations of agents, who, after all, were trying to manipulate the producers for their own gains.

As the *Follies* grew in size and splendor, the competition between the New Amsterdam and the Winter Garden producers became more intense, and as his show garnered more attention, Ziegfeld became more confident and, as a result, aggressive. Ziegfeld hired Joseph Urban to transform the theater, especially the Roof Garden, late in 1914, and the following year, the master designer had begun working on the *Follies*. As more space became available to Ziegfeld, he started needing more talent to fill his (now two) stages, and the first large pool of applicants he drew from contained numerous chorus girls. Naturally, with more opportunities for the choristers came the chance to work for more than one producer at a time, both on tour and on Broadway. In May of 1916, J. J. wrote to Flo, asking him to refrain from hiring girls who he knew worked for the brothers. Ziegfeld replied, "In looking over my girls at rehearsal, I find five or six which I know are Winter Garden girls, at present playing in your company . . . but if you will take the trouble to send me a list of the girls engaged for your coming production, I will eliminate them from my chorus."[31] The language is more terse than what was used in previous notes, but it seems, on the surface, to be a relatively benign exchange.

It would be interesting to know just how many women worked for both parties, but unfortunately the truth will never be known. One of the greatest Ziegfeld myths is that he was the one who hired the most beautiful women, but this cannot be ascertained, and for the same reason. The fact is that in all his programs for the New Amsterdam (for both the *Frolic* and the *Follies*), Ziegfeld refrained from listing a complete list of chorus members. The only time the showman included a chorus member's credit was when they were featured in a small group or in some unusual act. This differs from the policy of the Shuberts, who published the name of every chorus man or woman in the program. And, as the shows went through changes in different cities, the Winter Garden programs reflected the members who came and went throughout the tour. Ziegfeld's choice to withhold a list of his "Ziegfeld Girls" has made research in this area difficult, thus contributing substantially to the legend suggesting his unerring eye for beauty as unparalleled.[32]

The first public sign of trouble between the two camps came in 1917 as *The Passing Show* was in preparation. Two comedians, Savoy and Brennan, had read through their sides, and were unhappy that their roles were rapidly decreasing in size. Savoy was a cross-dresser, who wore a bright red wig and affected the mannerisms of a ditzy, catty woman who commented on her adventures with her friend Margie. Brennan, on the other hand, was the winking straight man, always feeding lines to Savoy, who would deliver the punch line with a raucous laugh. The two had been enormously successful in vaudeville, and probably when they realized their Winter Garden debut was not going to unfold as they hoped, they quit. As *Variety* reported, "The Shuberts did not appear particularly concerned over the desertion … until they learned Flo Ziegfeld had tendered them an alluring contract … with the new 'Follies.'"[33] The Shuberts made several "futile friendly overtures," but when the team would not return, they threatened legal action. Savoy and Brennan went back to the Shuberts, but did not open with the show. They were kept "in reserve" until a new place was found for them. Eventually, the two accepted a Ziegfeld contract, but only stayed with him for two seasons before joining the *Greenwich Village Follies* in 1920.

If tensions had been inflamed with Savoy and Brennan, that was only a spark compared to the firestorm surrounding the most important young star in the Shubert firmament, Marilynn Miller. As discussed in chapter 2, Lee had recruited Miller while performing in England, and he spared no expense to bring her back to the United States to star in *The Passing Show of 1914* amid a flurry of publicity. She became a superstar, and the Shuberts paid for her to have (popular) dance lessons at the Ned Wayburn School, a facility the former director had run for many years. Miller's skills improved, and the Shuberts gave her starring roles in the 1915 edition, *The Show of Wonders,* and in *Fancy Free.* By 1918, Miller was a nationally recognized figure, due largely to the opportunities the Shuberts had provided for her. What they could not have known was that Wayburn had been in communication with Ziegfeld while Miller was studying with him, and when the young woman returned from the Chicago tryout of *Fancy Free,* she was approached by a representative from Ziegfeld, who told her she could be making much more money if she signed with his employer.[34] This would lead to a major battle, but although rival producers did not know it, there had been significant tension between Marilynn and the brothers years before—as early as the fall of 1915. The problem was not the young star. The problem was her mother, Ada Miller.

Marilynn had grown up as a vaudevillian, and her mother had married fellow entertainer Caro Miller while the girl was only a toddler. He never officially adopted any of the three girls that Ada brought to the marriage, but together they formed a group called The Five Columbians. When Lee Shubert approached the family in 1914, they were thrilled to be out of vaudeville and into more steady positions. The stipulation of the contract was that Marilynn and Caro would be jointly hired by the Shuberts for five years, with the girl performing and her stepfather acting as a stage manager. When Caro signed the contract, he did so on behalf of the girl, who was still sixteen and thus a minor. In the early part of their time with the Shuberts, this arrangement worked splendidly, with stepfather, mother, and daughter staying together during the run of the tour for *The Passing Show of 1914.* When the next *Passing Show* left New York in October of 1915, though, Ada had begun to cause trouble. Gilman Haskell, the tour manager, wrote J. J. about an event in May of 1916. The cast had performed an extra show while in Los Angeles, and the chorus members asked to be compensated for the day, since they were paid in small increments. When the principals found out that the chorus had been paid, a "kick" (complaint) was begun. Haskell wrote the following:

> I don't know who started the trouble, but I do know that Mrs. [Ada] Miller was running around to all the principals rooms before they sent for me to come into Miss Miller's room. When I got in there . . . it was Marilynn Miller who did the talking for the crowd . . . Mrs. Miller seemed to be under the influence of [a] spirit of some kind, as is often the case with her, and that may have had a good deal to do with her activity in the matter. She is a busy body when in that condition. Mr. Miller did no talking about it, so far as I know. In fact I am sure that he argued against the attitude that they assumed . . . I am glad you stretched a point to them as with all the movies out here. They are all getting offers from studios to do feature work and I know that Miss Miller in particular had a big offer, though as a matter of fact I know you must have her tied in such a way that she could not jump you.[35]

Haskell paid the principals for the extra show and managed to keep his cast together for the final stops of the production, but clearly, by this time, Ada Miller was already trying to maneuver Marilynn into a better position.

It should have come as no surprise that when Ziegfeld made an offer two years later, Ada Miller worked with the impresario's lawyers to find a way out of the Shuberts' employ. The loopholes they found were twofold. First of all, the lawyers stated that since Caro Miller had never legally adopted her, he could not actually sign on Marilynn's behalf. Secondly, the contract contained "joker" clauses, which meant that the Shuberts could place the young woman in any performance situation they wished, including "leasing" her out to movie studios.[36] The truth was that the original contract had been written for only one year, but it had given the Shuberts the right to "take up the option" for five years, something they had done each time. And, though the reports said that Miller was making $450 a week by 1918, what they did not realize is that the Shuberts had originally started her at $150 weekly and gave her raises annually.[37] Both J. J. and Lee were astonished by Miller's defection, but they were powerless against the decision. Ziegfeld paid her $600 a week, with an option for another year. Not only did she become one of the brightest stars of the *Follies* and *Midnight Frolic*, but she also starred in the Cinderella story, *Sally*, and other Ziegfeld shows. After this, the Shuberts became heavily guarded against any move Ziegfeld would make toward their employees, but it was they who would have the last laugh. The New Amsterdam producer fired Miller in 1923 in an antagonistic battle that became a war of words in the press, with both parties making scathing comments about the other for years.[38] At least one reporter called the break "poetic justice," saying that "now, after having made quantities of money and being independent, she turns about and practically plays the same trick on Ziegfeld that formerly she played on the Messrs. Shubert. Which goes to prove that a contract between friends just isn't."[39]

After the fracas with Miller, it should be no surprise that the contracts written by Klein for the Shuberts were very carefully prepared so that no such event could happen again. But, as all producers knew, agents were always trying to get their clients higher pay, and this meant that every arrangement became a balancing act for both sides. This had been true in the past, but, as the *Follies* blossomed during the late

1910s, the competition became increasingly virulent. By 1916, reviews were starting to compare *The Passing Show* and the *Follies* publicly; many critics both in New York and across America found it difficult to choose which production was more spectacular. The popularity of both series can be exemplified by looking at the titles of entertainments mounted in schools, churches, and community organizations everywhere. For example, the University of Kansas at Lawrence held numerous benefit concerts during World War I, and they called the February show the "K. U. Follies of 1916" and the April show the "K. U. Passing Show of 1916."[40] *Variety* reported that both New York shows had excellent receipts in 1917, with the New Amsterdam and the Winter Garden reportedly making around $19,000 weekly at their opening.[41] Two years later, each of the annual revues was maintaining their status, financially and artistically. "Of the bunch of musical comedies within the last three weeks, there are two really in the hit class—'The Passing Show of 1919,' regarded an equal to the 'Follies,' and 'Buddies,'" *Variety* said, adding, "'The Passing Show' and the 'Follies' are leading [the box office] on about even terms."[42] With such a close race, neither the Shuberts nor Ziegfeld could afford to lose any of the entertainers they had engaged without fear of selling fewer tickets. And, to make matters more challenging from the management's point of view, a major strike took place in the summer of 1919, causing mass closings and forcing the renegotiation of chorus and technical staff contracts. The Actor's Equity Association prompted action against the recently formed Producing Manager's Association (PMA), putting both the Shuberts and Ziegfeld (members of the PMA) on the defensive.[43] So much was on the line that when the next performers broke their contract and tried to move to Ziegfeld, the Shuberts spared no expense in bringing a lawsuit against both parties.

Preparations for *The Passing Show of 1919* began under excellent circumstances. The previous edition had been a colossal winner, and the tour was lasting well into the next season; the Howard Brothers, Helen Carrington, and the Astaires were still performing in Chicago at the end of June. The other Winter Garden shows had done equally well, with the semi-revue *Monte Cristo, Jr.* held over from the spring. Jolson's *Sinbad* (which contained his ever-popular, Gershwin-penned "Swanee") received enough attention that it reopened in the fall after its initial run. All three shows were touring, then, when *The Passing Show of 1919* opened in October. By the time the Shuberts assembled the cast, many of their performers were currently in shows, and thus, the 1919 show featured several stars that had never before been part of the annual revue. This included Blanche Ring, Charles Winninger, the Avon Comedy Four, Olga Cook, and James Barton. As was customary for a Winter Garden show, many prominent vaudevillians were also engaged. Two of the most unusual of this latter group were brothers, Dick and George Rath, a gymnastics-based adagio act that could also sing (see Figure 8.3). Called "America's popular athletes," the *Chicago Tribune* described the act with "one wafting the other about as languidly as a lady does her fan."[44] Their costumes sported a large "D" and "G," and they were considered both colorful and artistic. Morris Gest described one of their motions:

> One of the brothers takes his partner in his two hands, raises him from the floor, throws him over the heads of the audience, stretched out, his entire body, and raises him slowly over his head again ... It is so unusual that you have to use adjectives to express it.[45]

Fig. 8.3. *The Rath Brothers on the cover of "My Isle of Golden Dreams."*
Author's Collection.

Both in New York and during the tour, audiences greeted the Raths and their fellow entertainers eagerly, with box office receipts and critical reaction equally generous. Despite heavy competition with Ziegfeld, whose *Follies of 1919* was very strong and had an excellent score by Irving Berlin, the new Winter Garden revue managed to overtake it within the first few weeks of its run. " '*The Passing Show*' is now leading all Broadway," declared *Variety*, "Last week it went to about $40,000, that gross being aided by the Sunday night concert, which itself drew $3700. [It] is the only musical attraction playing nine performances weekly."[46] The revue had come at an unusual time in the season, and it stayed at the Winter Garden until the following summer, at which point the company began an extended tour.

Several months into the road production—on August 7, 1920—the Rath Brothers abandoned the revue. The crucial moment came when the Shuberts decided to "take up their option," and keep them engaged for another year. A letter was sent while the tour was playing the Detroit Opera House, notifying them in June that their contract, which was due to be renewed in October, was going to be extended.[47] Under normal circumstances, this would have been great news, and the two men could have rested with assurance that they had regular work somewhere in the Shubert system for the following year. Not only were they assured employment, but they also received a raise; the brothers had earned $275 a week beforehand, and would now make $325 a week. Instead of celebrating, however, the acrobats did not acknowledge the Shubert letter and began negotiations with Ziegfeld, who promised them they would receive $500 a week if they abandoned their former contract. The Raths signed with Ziegfeld on August 2, claiming the Shuberts had never contacted them. By mid-August, they were performing on the Roof as part of the *Midnight Frolic*, much to the anger of the Shuberts, who requested that Actor's Equity look into the matter and, in the meantime, file an injunction against the Rath Brothers performing while there was a dispute. Letters were sent to Max Hart, their manager, and to Ziegfeld, informing them that George and Dick were not available. J. J. wrote Flo on August 9, 1920, saying, "It seems that you do nothing but harp upon the people that we have under contract. I have not molested any of your people in any way. There are other managers in New York that have acts,—why not try some of them? Why do you persist in continually making offers to our people and making them dissatisfied?"[48]

Ziegfeld replied that he did not know that the brothers were working for the Shuberts, and said, "I have no intention whatsoever of taking anybody under contract with you, but when an artist proves to me they have no contract with you and would go elsewhere . . . I don't see why you should expect me to turn them down under such conditions."[49] When, after more letters, Ziegfeld said he had seen no solid proof of a Rath contract with the Shuberts, he was sent a letter by William Klein, the Shuberts' attorney, and specifically asked to stop using the acrobats on stage. When Ziegfeld refused, the issue became more serious and the Shuberts moved forward with a lawsuit.

By September 15, the newspapers carried the details of the trial, and *Billboard* eventually published the entire court document, noting that the "decision . . . contains important matter for the theatrical profession at large," and it "recommends a careful reading of it by all managers, agents, and particularly all artists."[50] The case was tried in the US District Court of the Southern District of New York, with Judge Martin T. Manton presiding.[51] The complete court document, including all the sworn statements and the final judgment, is quite thorough, and it demonstrates just how sneaky—for lack of a better term—the agents, actors, and managers could be if they wanted to break a contract. The main point the Rath Brothers tried to make was that the contract was unfair at the outset, and they should be able to leave whenever they chose. Klein countered with the fact that, as long as they were in the Shubert employ, the duo had been paid well for their services, with the producers going so far as to also give money to their wives so that all four could go on tour together. Klein says in his statement, "in addition to monetary consideration, the defendants enjoyed the prestige which came from identification with one of the great Broadway productions by the foremost theatrical producers; and they reaped the advantage of the Shuberts' great advertising campaigns and of publicity and appearance in all the great cities. The plaintiff had [even] built a special scene for them." Arthur Hammerstein, Morris Gest, Oliver Morosco (who had been an acrobat himself), and others testified that the performance itself was unique in the business in terms of quality and in content; they could not, in the eyes of theatrical managers, be replaced. Klein's legal argument pulled precedents from lawsuits throughout the entertainment industry, citing cases as far afield as circuses and baseball. In the end, the judge decided to grant the injunction, saying, "I am satisfied from . . . actually seeing the performance that it is incumbent upon me to hold that the services are of such a character as to require a court of equity to intervene by injunction and restrain the defendants from breaching the contract which they made with the plaintiff." The *New York Clipper* called the trial "one of the most hotly contested law actions in the history of American show business," and went into great detail in its reporting of the event.[52] Although the case was "hard fought," they concluded, it was fair. The Raths stopped performing for Ziegfeld, and—remarkably—continued to perform with the Shuberts for the remainder of the decade, making it clear that business was business and, for the Shuberts, at least, not personal.

During the trial, at least two similar events happened between the Shuberts and Ziegfeld. One involved Gilda Gray and another involved George LeMaire, both performers who were offered more money by Ziegfeld to abandon their previous engagements and join him. These two cases only added to the friction already inflamed by the Rath Brothers, and on September 25, the Shuberts decided to try to hold Ziegfeld to an even higher authority than the US Court—the Producing Manager's Association. They wrote an extraordinary letter to the Association, and included details not only of the Rath situation, but also of many events from the past. In light of the strike that had happened less than a year before, the Shuberts were livid that Ziegfeld would undermine the balance of the whole entertainment field for his "own personal gain," and had "chosen to utterly disregard the very principles which are the embodiment of this organization."[53] One of the methods Ziegfeld used, the Shuberts claimed, was to pay any legal expenses that might be sustained by the breaking of a contract, and therefore, many artists who might otherwise be fearful of making such a brash move would be convinced that they were making the best possible choice. The Shubert Brothers wrote the following:

> [Ziegfeld's] procedure has always been . . . to generally make inducements to those who have achieved some fame and who have been well advertised by one concern and who have been made and who have reached and attained the position and popularity they enjoy solely through the efforts and backing of the concert that originally discovered them and spent thousands of dollars in making them successful performers. The method pursued is indeed simply [*sic*] and consists of offering a performer a very substantial increase in salary, which has the inevitable effect of making them dissatisfied with the employment in which they are then engaged and which also tends to demoralize and have a very serious effect upon the companies with which they are appearing . . .
>
> Mr. Ziegfeld took Bert Williams from Comstock and Gest, Nora Bayes from Lew Fields, the Pony Ballet, Vivian Siegel, Jessie Reed, Magores Brothers, and Savoy and Brennan from the Shuberts. . . .

Mr. Ziegfeld did not accord to a brother member of the association that spirit of belief to which he was entitled, not only by reason of the fraternal relationship existing but by reason of the position obtained in the profession which in and of itself would lend toward more credibility than that of some persons practically unknown to him . . .

This institution cannot continue if the just and equitable principles of trade between producers and others are permitted to be so openly and flagrantly violated. At no time should we allow the personal gain and desires to override that which is right, just and fair and it is respectfully submitted that such action be taken which will be proper and in harmony with the principles of this organization.

This eleven-page letter asks for a censuring of Ziegfeld, and it was presented to the PMA and discussed at a meeting on October 2 at the Hotel Astor. Unfortunately, the result of their vote does not survive and was never made public. However, in the same month, Ziegfeld filed an injunction against the Shuberts for "stealing a scene" from the 1919 *Follies* and placing it in their *Broadway Brevities of 1920*, which was a Winter Garden Revue that starred Eddie Cantor, who had very publicly quit Ziegfeld earlier in the year.[54] To make matters worse, Ziegfeld ended up in a bitter lawsuit only two months later, when Mark Klaw demanded that he be paid according to the stock he owned in the *Follies*—which was 75 percent of the shares.[55] Ziegfeld refused, and said he did not want his books rummaged through by the courts. A public fight with his once-close ally would have been a horrible blow. Clearly, Ziegfeld must have been glad to see 1920 come to a close.

Although one must question the language of morality used by the Shuberts in their letter to the PMA, they were addressing an issue that had existed for some time and had grown steadily more problematic with the rise of Ziegfeld as a prominent producer. The trend, so the documents suggest, was that Ziegfeld took a markedly different track than the Shuberts when it came to mounting shows. While the Shuberts were generally cautious of overspending, Ziegfeld was a solid proponent of spending to extravagance. Not only was he willing to take risks in his shows, with single scenes being reported in the papers as costing $30,000 or more, but Ziegfeld was also willing to pay stars whatever he thought might entice them. This did not mean that his schemes always worked. As in the case of Marilynn Miller, her desire for more was fueled by Ziegfeld's own enticements, and she eventually lost her position due to following the path that Ziegfeld himself set out for her.

The volatile relationships between stars, agents, and producers were made far worse when one was pitted against another, and it seems that such a balancing act was constantly at play. The protections that Actor's Equity and the Producing Managers' Association tried to uphold were also frequently questioned, and although these organizations managed to secure some rights for both sides, all it took was a lawsuit to change the rules. The years from 1919–1921 were ones of great change, with new rules for chorus girls, the complete dismissal of chorus boys (as discussed in chapter 4), and a growing rivalry between producers. It is clear that the PMA must have been exhausted with both the Shuberts and Ziegfeld by the end of 1920, but it is hard to tell from the reports whether there was a feeling that these disagreements were petty or not. In the following years, Ziegfeld would challenge the PMA several times, eventually calling for a disbanding of the organization in 1923.[56] Whatever his relationship to the group became though, there is no question that having been beaten in court and then embarrassed in front of his peers must have fueled a fiery hatred in Ziegfeld for the Shuberts, and thus, the 1920s became a period of intense and unrelenting competition for both camps.

The mounting pressure Ziegfeld probably felt also came on two other important fronts. The first concern was shared with the Shuberts; in the 1919–1920 season, a host of new challengers came forward with important and successful revues. There had been popular revues staged during the teens, most notably the Cohan Revues (1916 and 1918) and *Hitchy-Koo* (four editions, begun in 1917), but they were not consistent enough or large enough to threaten either the *Follies* or *The Passing Shows*. However, when George White's *Scandals of 1919* opened in the spring, before either of the larger annual shows, it was only the beginning of serious rivalry from other fronts. White had worked for both Ziegfeld and the Shuberts, and, with this new series, he danced alongside Ann Pennington, who was also a veteran of both camps. The critics liked the show,[57] and the following year, White hired George Gershwin to write much of the score, impressing audiences even more. After the *Follies of 1919* had opened, it was immediately followed by the *Greenwich Village Follies*, a series spearheaded by another revue alum, John Murray Anderson. The term "Follies" had been borrowed by Ziegfeld—both from a small show in New York in 1906 and from an idea from Harry B. Smith—and so he could make no claims against the name. And, surrounded on all sides by new shows, the flood began. Small shows that went nowhere popped up (the *Frivolities of 1920*), and others were built around stars (*The Ed Wynn Carnival*). The following year, Irving Berlin introduced his first *Music Box Revue*, the first *Chauve Souris* was mounted in 1922, and Earl Carroll began his *Vanities* in 1923. This explosion required a response from the Shuberts and Ziegfeld.

The second problem for Ziegfeld was that he was starting to spend an extraordinary amount of money on his *Follies* and, as a result, was beginning to falter. His overindulgence was legendary, and the comparison between what he was willing to spend and what the Shuberts were open to doing was significant. The costs for a complete *Passing Show* are not indicated in the records, but my estimation from the documents suggest that mounting the early productions had cost between $100,000 to $150,000.[58] In a memo to a tour manager for *The Passing Show of 1923*, J. J. wrote that it cost him $15,000 a week to operate the show, and that included his addition of Ted Lewis and his band.[59] Lewis was very well known at the time and expensive to hire (even though he had been employed several times by the Shuberts), but this paled in comparison to the costs Ziegfeld was incurring. In a press statement issued in June of 1923, Ziegfeld claimed that it had cost him $20,000 to run the first *Follies* in 1907.[60] By 1923, the cost had risen to $237,000 to mount the show, with his most expensive actor (unnamed) receiving $2,000 a week for his services. The gross receipts were an amazing $1,820,000 from the show, which, remarkably, ran for a whole year at the New Amsterdam. But this figure is deceiving, claimed the producer. After the costs and taxes, Ziegfeld explained, his net profit from the entire engagement after an entire year was a mere $15,421, "less than half the amount paid the 'clearers' who move the furniture on the stage." The reason for this press release was that there were "close students of the higher drama" who did not feel these figures were accurate, meaning that some of Ziegfeld's critics were disputing the ledgers from the New Amsterdam in order to be paid their fair share of the profits—the same problem that had plagued his relations with Klaw in 1920. As Ziegfeld began to feel pressure from these outside onlookers (presumably financial backers), he continued to fight a bevy of lawsuits involving everything from art collections to royalties.

As tension grew for Ziegfeld, the Shuberts took a different path. They continued to produce *Passing Shows*, but when new revues began edging their way onto the scene in 1919, J. J. and Lee made a wise financial decision. First, they recognized the popularity of the *Greenwich Village Follies*, which had originally played in its titular neighborhood, and they made a deal with the production team to buy the rights to the show in 1920. They kept Anderson at the helm and placed the revue in the Shubert Theater. Next, they began to experiment with revue titles that included a year, suggesting they might become annual events; the *Shubert Gaieties of 1919*, the *Midnight Rounders of 1920*, *Spice of 1922*, and finally *Artists and Models of 1923*—all became possible names for a Shubert revue.[61] This diversification of possible titles would eventually become a key component to their strategy for keeping revues working. Most writers claim the last *Passing Show* that played on Broadway was in 1924, but few realize that there were several more shows that carried the title, even into the 1930s. For example, *The Passing Show of 1926* opened on September 12, 1926 in Chicago, but it had been called *The Merry World* when it played at the Winter Garden earlier that summer, and had been branded *Passions of 1926* while in previews.[62] This did not mean that the productions were poor and needed a new title to confuse audiences; a *Washington Post* critic proclaimed that *The Passing Show of 1926*, which featured a young Ray Bolger, was full of "pleasing melodies and talented singers to sing them [and] alluring dances and more alluring girls to dance them."[63] This model of changing names for different purposes became standard and was a brilliant way of simultaneously using a multitude of revue titles, which was especially important for making every venture seem brand new, even if it was only a slightly altered production. *The Passing Show of 1932* began its previews in Detroit, but lost its star, Ted Healy, and significant revisions had to be made quickly.[64] The new version, which then became the touring name, was the *Greenwich Village Follies*. *Passing Shows* were attempted again in 1933, 1934, and 1935, but none of them made it to Broadway, and none of them had significant runs, even under different monikers. This type of title switching was possible for the Shuberts because they owned enough properties—successful properties—that they were able to morph easily from one designation to the next without fear. The sheer size of the Shubert theatrical machine, grown even larger by the 1930s, allowed them a flexibility that Ziegfeld did not possess.

This was a problem for Ziegfeld, because he began to turn his attention away from the *Follies* in the following years, and instead became infatuated with book shows. The focus he had exercised with his revues became fractured, and once the first crack appeared, it spelled the end of Ziegfeld's career and, unfortunately, his life. The trend began when he produced the smash hit, *Sally*, which starred Marilyn Miller (who had dropped the second "n" at Ziegfeld's suggestion). *Sally* opened in 1920, and it was an immediate sensation. It ran for a year and a half, and it was during this run that Miller became such a big star that she and Ziegfeld argued often, leading to her dismissal. The "dissatisfaction" referenced by the Shuberts in their letter to the PMA was exactly what drove a wedge between Ziegfeld and his new star. The production was the beginning of a transition for the producer, and though he continued to do multiple editions of the *Follies*, he became more interested in narrative-driven musicals. He had one major success—*Kid Boots* (1923), starring Eddie Cantor—but he also had a string of failures until *Rio Rita* opened in 1927. The same year also saw the debut of *Show Boat*. Despite the confusion, Ziegfeld was also looking for new financial backers, befriending William Randolph Hearst, who set about building an exclusive new theater for the manager. To make matters more complicated, 1927 was also the year of *The Jazz Singer*, which inspired Ziegfeld (and so many others) to want to make Hollywood musicals. Over the next two years, Ziegfeld oversaw Mary Eaton (a chorus girl in *The Passing Show of 1919*) in *Glorifying the American Girl*, filmed at Kaufman-Astoria Studios in Queens. The end result was disappointing, but it did not stop Ziegfeld from pursuing other film undertakings.[65] By end of the 1920s, Ziegfeld had drastically changed his mode of operation, splintering his concentration and working up a fever pitch of projects and spending. By the time he produced the revue *Smiles* (1930), he could not even pay two of its stars—Fred and Adele Astaire, and they sued him, only to have the matter end in a settlement.[66] During the next two years, nothing Ziegfeld touched produced a profit, and he became as deep in debt as he had been wealthy. He died in July of 1932, exhausted and penniless. His wife, Billie Burke, and his daughter, Patricia, were left a sea of debt and the regret that Florenz had died under such terrible pressure and with so many burdens.

By the time of Ziegfeld's death, critics were no longer comparing the *Follies* to *The Passing Show*, or, for that matter, any of the Shuberts' revues. Instead, there were so many different revues being produced that it was difficult to pinpoint any one producer as a leader. The genre was beginning to suffer under the strain of its age, and the World War I–era show was desperately in need of a change. This did not surprise J. J. Shubert. Even in the first month of the 1920s, J. J. had a sense of what was to come, and, in a short note to Jerome Remick from January of that year, he made it clear he was setting his sights on a different theatrical genre. The letter from J. J. contains a vivid insight into his mindset at the time, and speaks volumes as to what the Shuberts would be doing for much of the next decade:

> Now, while I am on the subject, I am on my way to Europe on the 14th of February. I may buy a great many things over there in the way of publishing. Are you interested to any extent? If so, let me know what you want to do. The entire tendency now is towards operetta. You will find that within the next year or two everything will be operetta and the revue proposition will be confined only to one or two producers. It is almost prohibitive at present time to put on these big shows and the little shows will have to be the thing of the future.

This note shows that J. J. was beginning to turn his attention toward the operetta, and he and one of his most trusted employees, Sigmund Romberg, would flourish in this field over the next several years. The style of revue that had been so important to both men was quickly becoming a thing of the past, and J. J. knew, even in 1920, that the future was going to look quite different.

The Shuberts and Ziegfeld last exchanged correspondence in 1922, and a cold silence followed. With new parties mounting revues, the battle lines were not so clearly drawn between the old rivals. The Rath Brothers debacle was the last time Ziegfeld tried so openly to secure artists who were under contract with the Shuberts and, as he changed his focus, the Shuberts did too. The two camps could afford to despise each other from a distance, and that is exactly what they did. But what nobody could have known was that when Ziegfeld died, an opportunity would present itself that the Shuberts could not turn down. This event would have killed Ziegfeld again had he been alive, but even he could not have foreseen the long-term results. The broken shell that was Ziegfeld's reputation (and bank account) was about to become transformed, and it would be the Shuberts—two of his most virulent adversaries— who were going to help transfigure the Chicago impresario from a man into a legend.

NOTES

1. Advertisement for *The Passing Show of 1924*, *Buffalo Courier*, March 15, 1925, 72.

2. Bordman, *American Musical Revue*, 53–54 (chap. 1, n. 3).

3. Baral, *Revue*, 106 (chap. 1, n. 3).

4. Davis, *Scandals and Follies*, 97, 104 (chap. 1, n. 3).

5. Rennold Wolf, "The P. T. Barnum of the Theatre," *Green Book Magazine*, May 1914, 933–46.

6. As mentioned earlier, the Shubert reputation is primarily due to Foster Hirsch's book, *The Boys from Syracuse*. I discuss the reason for Ziegfeld's reputation in chap. 9. The tales told of Ziegfeld by those who worked with him vary from glowing (Fred Astaire in his autobiography, *Steps in Time*) to deeply critical (Richard Rodgers in his autobiography, *Musical Stages*).

7. The story, in a slightly different form, is repeated in Richard and Paulette Ziegfeld, *The Ziegfeld Touch*, 49.

8. Wolf, "The P. T. Barnum of the Theatre," 943–44.

9. Autograph file, Ziegfeld, December 16, 1908, Shubert Archive.

10. See Ethan Mordden, *Ziegfeld: The Man Who Invented Show Business* (New York: St. Martin's Press, 2008) for more on this event.

11. "Shubert Sues Ziegfeld," *New York Dramatic Mirror*, December 22, 1906, 50.

12. Hirsch, *The Boys from Syracuse*, 82.

13. Fields and Fields, *From the Bowery to Broadway*, 315.

14. The first *Follies* used two characters—Pocahontas and Captain John Smith—as "guides" through the show, but it did not include the type of plot-like features the early *Passing Show* scripts did, with a goal for the characters to reach.

15. *Passing Show of 1912* show file, Shubert Archive.

16. "Winter Garden Has Gorgeous Reopening," *New York Herald*, July 23, 1912, 7.

17. Sime Silverman, "Passing Show of 1912," *Variety*, July 26, 1912, 20.

18. Richard Ziegfeld and Paulette Ziegfeld, *The Ziegfeld Touch*, 41–42. The place was a multiplex of theaters, including the Jardin de Paris and at least two other stages.

19. See Mary C. Henderson, *The New Amsterdam: The Biography of a Broadway Theatre* (New York: Hyperion, 1997), alongside the many Ziegfeld biographies cited here.

20. For more details on the changes to the theater at this time, see Henderson, *The New Amsterdam*, especially chap. 3.

21. The series of memos is located in the Shubert Archive, general correspondence files (1910–1926), box 8, file 3.

22. It is worth noting that several employees stayed loyal to one side or another for most of their careers. Harold Atteridge, for example, remained a Shubert staff member for most of his theatrical life, while Joseph Urban, the designer, stuck by Ziegfeld's side for years. Additionally, there are several people who begin in one camp and end up moving to the other side for the duration. Victor Herbert, for example, worked with the Shuberts until after his show, *The Duchess*, was a disaster, after which he worked only for others, including Ziegfeld. John H. Young, the scenic designer, frequently worked both sides of the theatrical fence until 1915, after which time he worked only for the Shuberts.

23. Shubert Archive, general correspondence, file 157, box 177.

24. The Simmons/Shubert telegrams and letters are located in the Shubert Archive, general correspondence, box 260, folder 464.

25. Advertisement, *Variety*, June 9, 1922, 10.

26. "The Lace Ballet in the New Follies," *New York Evening Telegraph*, June 15, 1922, 8. The article relates that Ziegfeld had heard about the Norwegian mineral about a year before, when "he sent it to chemists to make an investigation and to see if the mineral could be adapted for stage ballet purposes." The effect, he claimed, had cost $30,000.

27. Remick file, Shubert Archive, general correspondence, box 468, folder 4229. Rose's career was extensive and prolonged. One of his last big hits was "Blueberry Hill" (1940), made famous by Fats Domino in 1956.

28. Examples can be found in the materials for *The Passing Show of 1914* tour. See letters between D. C. Curry and J. J. Shubert, Shubert Archive, general correspondence, folder 2791.

29. Letter dated March 24, 1914, Shubert Archive, general correspondence, box 233, folder 1056.

30. Ibid., n.p.

31. Letter dated May 2, 1916, Shubert Archive, general correspondence, box 381, folder 1523.

32. John Kenrick includes a note on Ziegfeld research on his Musicals101 website, stating, "There is no easy way to verify the full cast list for most editions of the *Follies*." Accessed November 5, 2015. http://www.Musicals101.com.

33. "Back to the Garden," *Variety*, June 2, 1916, 7.

34. Harris, *The Other Marilyn*, 53.

35. Letter from Gilman Haskell to J. J. Shubert, May 12, 1916, Shubert Archive, general correspondence, folder 1540.

36. "Shuberts Have Contract Row, But Star Goes to Ziegfeld," *Variety*, May 3, 1918, 12.

37. Memos between J. J. and Lee, April 15 and April, 18, 1916, Shubert Archive, general correspondence, file 3, box 10.

38. One of J. J.'s employees sent him a copy of a biting interview done with Ziegfeld in December of 1923. See "Monsieur Ziegfeld Reviews His Army of Beauties Here," *Pittsburgh Gazette-Times*, December 28, 1923, n.p.

39. "Marilyn Miller's Troubles," *Rochester Democrat and Chronicle*, December 30, 1923, 6.

40. Programs remain extant for these shows, and dozens of others like them held throughout the country even into the 1940s.

41. "Shows at the Box Office in New York and Chicago," *Variety*, August 31, 1917, 11.

42. "More Musical Shows Than Ever Supported By Rialto," *Variety*, 31 October 1919, 14.

43. This strike was mentioned in chap. 4 and is covered in-depth in Alfred Harding, *The Revolt of the Actors* (New York: William Morrow & Company, 1929).

44. Percy Hammond, "The Passing Show," *Chicago Tribune*, June 15, 1920, 17.

45. Second Circuit Court Document, Shubert Archive, general correspondence, box 3594.

46. "Broadway in a Slump Last Week," *Variety*, November 7, 1919, n.p.

47. Letter from J. J. Shubert to Rath Brothers, June 7, 1920, Shubert Archive, general correspondence, box 464, folder 4100.

48. Letter from J. J. Shubert to Florenz Ziegfeld, August 9, 1920, Shubert Archive, general correspondence, box 464, folder 4100.

49. Letter from Florenz Ziegfeld to J. J. Shubert, August 11, 1920, Shubert Archive, general correspondence, box 464, folder 4100.

50. "Rath Brothers Must Play Out Contract with Shuberts," *Billboard*, October 2, 1920, 1.

51. The complete document can be found in the Shubert Archive, general correspondence, box 3594.

52. "Rath Case Hard Fought," *New York Clipper*, September 22, 1920, 23.

53. Letter from J. J. Shubert to the Producing Mangers' Association, September 25, 1920, Shubert Archive, general correspondence, box 4100.

54. "Ziegfeld to Begin Action Against 'Brevities' Producers," *New York Clipper*, October 6, 1920, 1.

55. "Ziegfeld Answers Klaw," *New York Clipper*, December 15, 1920, 30.

56. "Will Still Act Together," *New York Morning Telegraph*, July 26, 1923, 2.

57. "First Nighters Show Approval of 'Scandals of 1919,'" *New York Clipper*, June 4, 1919, 28.

58. The Shubert Archive contains ledgers for the Winter Garden, but these are written in a form of accounting shorthand that is no longer legible.

59. Letter from J. J. Shubert to Lawrence Solomon, September 19, 1923, Shubert Archive, general correspondence, box 180.

60. "This and That," *New York Times*, June 3, 1923, sec. 7, x.

61. The term *Gaieties*, like so many aspects of the revue, was borrowed from French antecedents.

62. "Shuberts to Book All of Cohan Plays," *New York Times*, September 1, 1926, 27.

63. "1926 Edition of 'Passing Show' Here," *Washington Post*, November 28, 1926, F1.

64. "Ted Healy Leaves 'The Passing Show,'" *New York Times*, August 20, 1932, 7.

65. For more on the history and reception of this film, see Richard Barrios, *A Song in the Dark: The Birth of the Musical Film* (New York and Oxford: Oxford University Press, 1995), 194–98.

66. Mordden, *Ziegfeld*, 282.

9

AS NEW, BRIGHT, AND WELCOME AS THE MORNING SUN

• • •

THE BIRTH OF A LEGEND AND THE DEMISE OF A GENRE

In the 1951 Warner Brothers movie *I'll See You in My Dreams*, Danny Thomas portrays lyricist Gus Kahn, while Doris Day plays his songwriter wife, Grace Le Boy. The movie was part of a string of biopics that had audiences wallowing in nostalgia, remembering a pre–World War II America with its innocent entertainers and good old-time melodies. As mentioned in chapter 5, Kahn was the lyricist for "Pretty Baby," a major hit from *The Passing Show of 1916*. He also wrote the lyrics for "Carolina in the Morning," which the Howard Brothers introduced in *The Passing Show of 1922*. Both songs were important for Kahn and became draws for the Winter Garden revues in which they appeared. The movie, though, never mentions the Shubert brothers or *The Passing Shows*, despite their pivotal role in Kahn's career. Instead, the first time audiences see Kahn on a stage talking with a producer, it is Florenz Ziegfeld he talks to, and it is the *Follies* for which "Carolina in the Morning" is being considered as an interpolation. In the smoke-filled haze of the rehearsal, Ziegfeld (played by a very noble-looking William Forrest) thinks the song is good, but wants something more sophisticated for his leading lady, Gloria Knight (Patrice Wymore), a fictionalized version of Ruth Etting. The movie quickly jettisons most of the 1920s and transitions to Kahn watching a performance of *Whoopee* (1928) with Etting performing "Love Me or Leave Me." All traces of his early years have been erased and, like most of the biopics of this era, the real story lies somewhere outside the fictional frame of the camera.

The fact is that by 1951, the legend of Ziegfeld and his *Follies* had grown to a point where it was the only revue from the past worth mentioning and Ziegfeld himself was regal, tender, and powerful: a demigod of the theater. How is it that, in the intervening twenty years between the Ziegfeld's death and the release of the film, *The Passing Shows* had been erased as part of Broadway history? Many authors are quick to ascribe value to the quality of revues they never witnessed, and arrive at the answer that *The Passing Shows* were just not very good.[1] The truth is, in the two decades between the end of Ziegfeld's life and the heyday of the nostalgic biopic, a transformation had been engineered that turned the *Follies* into glittery dreamstuff and simultaneously raised Flo to new heights, effectively burying all other revues under heavy doses of mythology. And just who was responsible for this theatrical transformation? In the movies, it was mostly MGM, but on the stage, it was the Shuberts themselves. The very producers responsible for presenting *The Passing Shows*, J. J. and Lee, obscured their own past contributions in order to cash in on a brand that, by the mid-1930s, was worth every penny.

Not long after Ziegfeld passed away, Billie Burke, his widow, realized that she needed to quickly generate a significant amount of money to pay off the tremendous debt her husband had accrued in the final years of his life. The number of creditors who made claims on the estate was substantial, and the total they asked for in 1932 was between $500,000 and $750,000.[2] The case was sent to Surrogate Court in White Plains, New York, where the County Treasurer, William S. Coffey, tried to make sense of the claims and provide disbursements over time. The case was sent to White Plains because the family household, Burkeley Crest, had been located in Hastings-on-Hudson, New York, where Burke had lived since 1911. Burke and her daughter left New York shortly after Ziegfeld's death, quietly mourning in their Santa Monica home, and thus they avoided the scramble in the courts, allowing Burke to continue making films and focus on rebuilding her capitol.[3] She appeared in a number of advertisements too, including many for Enna Jetticks shoes. One asset she recognized, though, was that the use of the name "Ziegfeld *Follies*" could be worth money, and she took two important actions. First, with her lawyer, A. C. Blumenthal, she did what Grant Hayter-Menzies accurately labels as the "unthinkable": she leased the rights for a stage version of the *Follies* to the Shubert Brothers.[4] Secondly, she entered into talks with Universal Pictures to make a movie about Ziegfeld's life. Although she probably did not realize it at the time, these two actions became the basis for the Ziegfeld *Follies* myth and still affect the way both the man and the show are remembered in the twenty-first century.

The contract for theatrical productions was signed on May 16, 1933, between Producing Associates, Inc. (the Shuberts) and both Billie Burke Ziegfeld and the estate of Abe Erlanger, which still owned a stake in the revue. The agreement included a number of stipulations, including the first and most important: "The production is to be of the same character and quality as were the Follies produced by the late Florenz Ziegfeld."[5] Originally, this was just a licensing agreement, allowing the Shuberts to put on a single revue and to pay an initial $1,000, followed by 3 percent of the gross receipts. Additionally, any songs could be played over the radio in order to encourage business. Burke was to be named as a coproducer in all the materials related to the show, especially the advertising. This last move was quite astute for both parties. Not only did it allow the Shuberts to connect the theatrical production to a woman who, at the time, was a major star on screen, but it also anointed the revue in the public sphere with "a" Ziegfeld touch, even though it wasn't Flo's. The first of the stipulations is also informative, and more than anything else, it speaks to the fact that the Shuberts and their *Passing Shows* were considered equivalents to the *Follies*. If, as most modern authors suggest, the Shuberts were only capable of "cheap imitation," Burke would not have gone to them with the expectation that they could continue her husband's tradition.

The result of this venture was the *Ziegfeld Follies of 1934*. The producers had planned to open the revue in September of 1933, but last minute changes delayed it for several months. As preparations began, Lee announced he was visiting Burke in California in July to confer about the show, and the telegrams between the parties show that she was indeed included in the process of formulating the revue.[6] The production opened on January 4, 1934 at, of all places, the Winter Garden Theater. One can only imagine the inner glee that J. J. and Lee felt at acquiring the name and turning the *Follies*—and *Ziegfeld's Follies* at that—into one of its Winter Garden revues. But it would be wrong to suggest that they did not take the project seriously. Instead, the Shuberts made another wise choice in casting: they hired three principal stars for the revue, Fanny Brice and the Howard Brothers. If there were two acts that represented the amalgamation of the Shubert and Ziegfeld revues, these were the ones. Brice had last appeared in the *Follies of 1923*, after which she moved to Berlin's *Music Box Revue of 1924*, but she had remained on good terms with the Ziegfeld family and gladly returned. It was in this show that Brice introduced "Baby Snooks" to audiences, a character she portrayed for years afterwards. The Howard Brothers, as usual, both sang and performed skits, with Willie taking on the role of both the incoming and the outgoing presidents of Cuba. The critics declared the show a smash success, and Art Arthur, the critic for the *Brooklyn Daily Eagle*, provided some commentary on the opening night:

> The Shuberts threw the newest edition of the Ziegfeld Follies to the lions (social and otherwise) at the Winter Garden . . . and the lions liked it. That made it one of the few openings this season to justify the attending pomp and glory. The show itself is a hit and there's no doubt about it . . . The whole thing has been given a production worthy of Ziegfeld himself . . . Opening night brought out Earl Carroll, who applauded a show bearing the name Ziegfeld for the first time since his quarrel with the late Flo years ago. George O'Brien, the movie man, was there with his wife Marguerite Churchill . . . Max Gordon and Arch Selwyn gave the show a "thumbs up" verdict.[7]

The music and the script had numerous contributors; among them were E. L. "Yip" Harburg and Vernon Duke, Fred Allen, and Harold Atteridge. The vocal talents of Everett Marshall and Jane Froman were singled out as among the best, while the dancing of Buddy Ebsen and his sister Vilma was praised. The Shuberts were very pleased with the resulting revue, and Lee sent clippings of the critics' reaction to Billie in Beverly Hills. She responded in a telegram from January 12:

SO GRATEFUL TO YOU
FOR MAKING THE FOLLIES
SUCH A GRAND SHOW[.]
AM DOUBLY GRATEFUL IN FLO'S NAME[.][8]

As all the Winter Garden revues had done in the past, the *Ziegfeld Follies of 1934* went on tour nationally, ending in April of the following year.

An interesting postscript about this revue was that Lee issued a press release concerning the type of women he had chosen for the show, wanting to demonstrate that this was the dawn of a "new" chorus girl. The headline read, "Curves 'Out' for 1934

Beauties, Experts Say; Willowy Types Rule."[9] In the article, Lee Shubert, illustrator McClelland Barclay, and fashion designer Louis Brenner commented on the ways in which the woman of the thirties would be defined. First of all, this was a decisive "end to the flapper era," they said, and "she will be more her 'real self' than she has been in years." A more "natural" figure, as opposed to the full-figured or unusually thin bodies, was *en vogue*. Lee Shubert explained that "[Ziegfeld's] ideal was the cold, ultra-sophisticated young lady, not the 1890 type as represented by Mae West at one extreme and Katherine Hepburn in 'Little Women' on the other." Females were going to be smart, too, and would demonstrate a wealth of experience growing up under "Prohibition's jazz age and the four years of Depression." Cold, wise, and self-sufficient, the woman of the new era will be so stylish she won't have to pose, and she'll be less curvy than the women of the past. The "hotcha, peppery beauty type" is out, they stated, and boyish, clever women like Kay Francis, one of the most popular movie stars of the early 1930s, were in. This type of woman was, according the Lee, what future revues would feature.

Neither Burke nor the Shuberts could have imagined, though, how the term *Follies* would grow once Ziegfeld was dead; the word was now fair game for any company that wanted to use it. There was an explosion of Follies in 1934, both onstage (professionally and in amateur circles) and in the movies. Among the small-time groups, one could find the name everywhere: Saratoga Springs, New York, had a *Gay Follies of 1934* in the Hudson Music Hall;[10] a local Niagara Falls YWCA hosted the *Water Follies of 1934* in the pool;[11] and the town youth offered members of the Buffalo, New York, community the *Ubessa Follies of 1934*.[12] On the radio, Jimmy Durante had an "Inka Dinka Doo Follies of 1934" on New York's WEAF-NBC.[13] And, on the screen, William Powell starred in the *Fashion Follies of 1934*. The recognition that the term Follies was now available for use in the public without any fear of legal retribution made it ubiquitous, and there is no question that both the New York run and the tour of the "official" *Ziegfeld Follies* helped to legitimize every show that wanted to use the title. The other large-scale revues were either still active or their producers still held the rights to the specific names, but in the case of the Follies, Ziegfeld himself had made legal claims so complicated by his questionable maneuverings that there was nothing to stop anyone, great or small, who wished to employ the title, at least without his name attached.

For Ziegfeld's creditors though, there was still hope that by stopping the Shuberts from using "Ziegfeld's *Follies*" as a brand, they could recoup some of the funds that had evaded them upon the impresario's death. By March, only three months after the new *Follies* opened, both Burke and the Shuberts were called to testify in White Plains, where Coffey felt he could take them to task for using the name and therefore get some money back for Ziegfeld's many creditors.[14] Coffey's argument was that the estate, which was in arrears, actually owned the name. Therefore, any profit the Shuberts and Burke had made from the arrangement should go elsewhere. J. J. Shubert and Burke's personal secretary, Catherine Dix, both testified. Dix said that Ziegfeld had created a document that transferred all rights he had to his wife, but unfortunately the "paper" that he signed with the statement was lost.[15] When J. J. came to the stand, he brought the contract that had been mentioned with him, and Coffey had to concede that it was, indeed, legitimate.[16] In the end, Coffey and his lawyer failed to convince a judge that Burke had no right to use the name, but they continued trying to procure whatever funds they could from any "Ziegfeld" endeavor for years. In 1936, they again filed suit against Burke, but this time the co-conspirator in their eyes was MGM, who had released a film of the late producer's life called *The Great Ziegfeld*.[17] The second suit also failed to pay Ziegfeld's debts, and even though Coffey had been discharged as administrator of the estate by this point, he still felt an obligation to fight for cash. Finally, four years after Flo's death, Coffey and the creditors realized the debts would never be paid.[18]

The Great Ziegfeld was produced by MGM and directed by Robert Z. Leonard, neither of who were originally involved in the project. Hayter-Menzies explains that the screenwriter William Anthony McGuire (who had himself worked for Ziegfeld) demanded such a high salary that Universal sold the rights to MGM, a studio that had strong ties to Billie Burke. This would be the second component to creating and solidifying the mythos. After this movie was released, a host of other films followed in its wake, each adding another piece to the fictional Ziegfeld persona that remained strong into the twenty-first century. The slew of what I call "bio-fic-pics" (an appropriate genre category for the fanciful quasi-historical movies of the era) worked in tandem with the stage productions, both unknowingly constructing a past that never was. Although many of the overarching historical events of the pictures are correct—a Sandow here, an Anna Held there, and a Billie Burke to top it off—the scenes themselves are the stuff of pure imagination. The moody lighting and the shadowy private moments became delightful and gorgeous through the eye of the camera and, for once, the man who spent so many years directing the gaze of others became the object of the gaze himself. And, with an excellent cast and a generous helping of nostalgia, *The Great Ziegfeld* was a tremendous success, winning three Oscars the following year, and starting a trend that aided in the reinvention of Florenz Ziegfeld.

The film unfolds slowly, with an exploration of Ziegfeld's career. William Powell depicted the showman as a vibrant yet gentle carnival barker who, as much as he disdains it, cannot help but be a slave to the beauty of all the women of the world. Unfortunately, this image was in stark contrast to the true Ziegfeld; his biographers, Cynthia and Sara Brideson, point out that "by leaving out his personal follies, the picture neglected major parts of his character."[19] Burke agreed, telling Barbara Rush that he was "nothing, absolutely nothing like Flo."[20] In the movie, none of Ziegfeld's multiple sexual liaisons remain. At one point, when a woman he knew as a girl throws herself at him, Powell seems afraid of her sexual power, embarrassed to have his secretary see him embraced by a woman who is not his wife. His affair with Lillian Lorraine (who is shown as the fictional Audrey Dane) is entirely omitted and instead replaced with the impresario prudishly demanding she sober up and act professional. Powell's portrayal of Ziegfeld's professional reputation is also polished, omitting anger and bitterness and supplying a healthy dose of reserved maneuvering in place of grand gestures. Frank Morgan plays "Jack Billings," a fictional producer meant to be Ziegfeld's foil in the movie (as many suggest, probably based on Charles Dillingham). Perhaps the most honest element of their relationship is that Ziegfeld steals everything he can from Billings, including Anna Held, Billie Burke, and even his butler. Ziegfeld is a total cad, willing to lie, cheat, and manipulate to get whatever he wants, but he does everything with a smile. Morgan is easily flustered but, even as he visits a dying Ziegfeld, he cannot help but admit he cares deeply for him. When Ziegfeld/Powell dies, dreaming of "more stairs" (presumably leading to heaven), he goes gently into death, and there is a feeling of having lost the most important man entertainment ever knew. So many details of Ziegfeld himself and specific factual events were changed that it is hard to find anything in the movie that does not feel like it is manufacturing reality for its own terms.

The section featuring Fanny Brice's performance in burlesque is one of the highlights of the movie, but even this is dreadfully confused. Brice sings "Yiddle on Your Fiddle, Play Some Ragtime" (Irving Berlin, 1909) while she is "discovered," presumably in 1910.[21] The orchestra conductor plays the violin, as many theater directors did, and the audience is fairly small. Strangely, though, her inclusion in the *Follies* takes place in 1920, just before *Sally* opens. Unfortunately, the other performances that represent the *Follies* (both the main show and the *Midnight Frolic*) are overblown, with little connecting them to any actual performances. And then, there is the "official" *Follies* production number, which is really a remarkable piece of work, compressing twenty-four years of productions into one massive attempt to out-*Follies* the *Follies*.

The barrage of *Follies*-related elements is so confusing in *The Great Ziegfeld* that MGM was able to essentially reinvent the show into something it had never actually been. By juxtaposing songs from a variety of years into a short burst of the show-within-a-show, it would seem to the viewer that the *Follies* produced nothing but memorable numbers. The glamour of the *Follies* is exaggerated, too, with the central production number costing the studio $220,000 alone, which Cynthia and Sara Brideson note was more expensive to mount than any of Ziegfeld's entire shows.[22] The sequence begins with the *Follies* opening at the New Amsterdam Theatre, ignoring the modest cabaret-like performances at the Jardin de Paris. The audience in the movie first sees Eddie Cantor singing "If You Knew Susie" (by Buddy DeSylva and Joseph Meyer) from 1923. Although the song was first used in *Kid Boots*, which was a Ziegfeld production, it was never included in the *Follies*. As chorus girls are ushered onstage, the song underneath the action is "Shine On Harvest Moon," from the revival of the *Follies of 1908*.[23] As Ziegfeld converses with the costumer, the in-film audience listens to' "Hello, 'Frisco," (lyrics by Gene Buck; music by Louis Hirsch), which had been in the *Follies of 1915*. The next song, Berlin's "A Pretty Girl Is Like a Melody," is sung by John Steel (Buddy Clark); the song had been one of the hits of the *Follies of 1919*.[24] All of this is just a prelude to the extended two-shot extravaganza that follows. As the camera pulls back, an enormous curtain opens, revealing the edge of the enormous cake that slowly displays its sumptuous "Art" pieces. But again, there is a dissonance between the music and the image, with Dvorak's "Humoresque" (1894) accompanying an eighteenth-century scene inspired by the art of Fragonard. More could be said about this number (especially as the camera spirals upwards along the cake), but in terms of reinventing *Follies* material, it is a tantalizing fantasy.

Although it could be mistaken for a "best of" medley, the sequence uses mostly complete *Follies* songs rather than brief strains woven together through transitions. And, with the exception of the Cantor and Steel numbers, the others are so deep within the mix of sound that they are challenging to identify. Nothing lines up with factual events, and the strange vacillation between conscious and subconscious sound allows the viewer to slip into an oneiric state, where anything is possible. The "Pretty Girl" production number inspires awe, and it should. By manipulating the past and present, the film reassembles pieces of memory to create the basis for something new, which the entire extended "cake" embodies. This is mythmaking at its best, reforming the past through a clever deployment of historical and ahistorical fragments. For both the production number and for *The Great Ziegfeld* as a whole, the film represents not the Ziegfeld of the past—rooted in an objective historical framework—but the Ziegfeld of the future, with dreams of sumptuousness and splendor manufactured, in this case, for the medium of film. And, garnering several Oscars, including Best Picture of 1936, the movie sparked the national imagination by glorifying (and reinventing) Ziegfeld and his *Follies*.

The same year that MGM released the picture, the Shuberts put on the *Ziegfeld's Follies of 1936*. Fanny Brice, certainly busy that year, took on a starring role again, and was joined by Bob Hope, who had been active on Broadway since the late 1920s. It was an excellent show that received high praise from critics, due in part to the stunning art direction by Vincente Minnelli. Cynthia and Sara Brideson cover the show in their Ziegfeld book, with special mentions of Brice and ballerina Harriet Hoctor (who had appeared in *The Great Ziegfeld*). One comment they make, though, is telling: "Both editions [1934 and 1936] mirrored Ziegfeld's in nearly every way, except that their costs did not exceed their profits."[25] This could not have been more true, and it was one of the key differences between the Shuberts and Ziegfeld: the former were better businessmen, and they put on dozens of beautiful, lavish productions that could still make money. Both *Follies* revues were well-received on Broadway and throughout the country, and, playing simultaneously with *The Great Ziegfeld*, the ghost of the deceased producer began to haunt all corners of the United States.

The Ziegfeld legend continued to grow, both onstage and on the screen. *Ziegfeld Girl* (1941), featuring Judy Garland, Hedy Lamar, and Lana Turner, traced the lives of three different women who became Ziegfeld stars. This was an important step toward keeping both Ziegfeld and his shows in the public consciousness, but it was also a means of perpetuating the mystery and glamour surrounding the women themselves. The chance to become a member of a Broadway chorus still existed at this time, but it was rapidly diminishing, with choruses becoming smaller and fewer shows using the chorus line as *The Passing Show* and the *Follies* had done. Nightclub and dinner theater choruses were still active, but such a position could hardly compare to what revues had offered young women in the past. Still, the movie aided in building the myth.

In 1946, MGM released the *Ziegfeld Follies* movie. Although it did not purport to be a bio-fic-pic, it was packed with revamped nostalgia. It also featured skits from previous revues and costumes suggesting the shows of the 1920s. J. J. Shubert knew the project was in the pipeline as early as 1939, when he wrote to Billie Burke concerning an edition of the *Follies* he was trying to put together in Los Angeles. "Owing to the fact that M.G.M. are going to make a picture shortly, giving it the same title," J. J. said, "we might as well get as much as we possibly can before the picture is released."[26] The show was planned, but never opened, mainly due to the fact that nobody wanted to leave California ("I never knew it was as attractive as all that!" said J. J.).[27] Despite an attempt to put on a stage production ahead of the movie, there was no way they could have anticipated the film's content. The picture was hosted by Ziegfeld himself, now an angel in heaven, and of all the people who could have been cast as the producer, it was again William Powell, who the titles indicate was "recreating his role as 'The Great Ziegfeld.'" It was not that he was performing a role from another movie—even though this was true—the wording is important because the previous movie and its immense impact had transformed "Ziegfeld" into "The Great Ziegfeld." The casting was a brilliant means by which to build upon the invented story from the last decade, and no doubt it provided an imagined continuity that cemented the "New Ziegfeld" in the minds of thousands of viewers. As the film opens, we see the showman placed above the clouds of Shakespeare and P. T. Barnum, and when we meet him in his red smoking jacket, we cannot help but smile at the wonderful afterlife Ziegfeld enjoys.

The movie was directed by Vincente Minnelli, who continued to lend his artistic voice to that of Ziegfeld, this time from the screen. The colors were exciting, many of the scenes are gorgeous (especially the opening "Bring on the Beautiful Girls" number), and it was closer in structure to an actual revue than any previous film associated with Ziegfeld. As a film, it is beautiful and entertaining. But again, the references to history are fanciful—especially the opening stop-motion animation sequence— turning the past into little more than imagination. The Jardin de Paris is depicted as a large theater with a full orchestra pit (suggesting it probably is the New Amsterdam), and all of New York society has come to the opening night of the 1907 *Follies*, neither of which was accurate. The script also includes an insult to the recent theatrical productions: "Just because I have moved up here, did the Follies have to die, too?" Ziegfeld asks, "No, no I suppose not. After all, how could there be a Ziegfeld Follies without Ziegfeld?"[28] Remarkable performances fill the picture, with Gene Kelly, Keenan Wynn, Lucille Ball, and so many others taking their place as Ziegfeld entertainers, even though they never knew the man himself.

Other Ziegfeld movie appearances followed, reinforcing the characterization of the producer originating in MGM's films. *The Story of Will Rogers* (1952), *The Eddie Cantor Story* (1953), *Deep in My Heart* (1954), *The Helen Morgan Story* (1957), *Funny Girl* (1968), *Funny Lady* (1975), and *W. C. Fields and Me* (1976) all included the producer as a character, with performances ranging from brief appearances to extended scenes. There was a sense in most cases that Ziegfeld's presence was the signal that the star in question had arrived at the highest professional level. Cynthia and Sara Brideson offer excellent critiques of these portrayals, mentioning that Walter Pidgeon's turn in *Funny Girl* was probably the most nuanced, showing Ziegfeld as "as a man (not an untouchable god) who could be both teasing and argumentative with his stars."[29] They also point that on several occasions, Ziegfeld is an invisible presence, represented by a voice or an object rather than by an actual person, like in *Easter Parade* (1948).[30] With such an onslaught of movies reinforcing the mythical Ziegfeld persona over three decades, it is easy to see how the legend gained a foothold in the general consciousness of the entertainment world.

And as Ziegfeld's legend burgeoned, the Shuberts (for the most part) kept their presence out of the bio-fic-pics that celebrated the past. No doubt the fact that Lee and J. J. lived through this period kept them out of these fanciful representations; while many songwriters, entertainers, and other celebrities were becoming screen personalities, the Shuberts were still actively participating in the modern theatrical business. Their reputations as fairly unlikable people (at least according to Foster Hirsch) probably did not help matters. Several films that might have included their characters used a fictional stand-in to take their place. Marilynn Miller's character in *The Great Ziegfeld* is under contract with an unnamed man who has a single line, complaining that she is being stolen. But nobody ever mentions that the contract was held by the Shuberts, and, almost two decades after the "theft" occurred, few in the film's audience would have remembered the details of the event. The movie that should have prominently featured the Shuberts and *The Passing Show* was the bio-fic-pic of Sigmund Romberg, called *Deep in My Heart*. Walter Pidgeon portrays J. J. as a level-headed, handsome, and kind man. There is an interesting moment when Romberg and his love interest, Dorothy Donnelly (Merle Oberon), trick J. J. into putting on the operetta *Maytime* by pitting Shubert against Ziegfeld successfully. The reason for this invention is to show Romberg getting the chance to finally write operettas, as if the genre was his only love. But, as with the other films, neither producer was depicted on screen as he really was. And further, as William Everett points out, many connections with the Shuberts were replaced by Romberg's "manager" figure, Bert Townsend (played by Paul Stewart).[31] In another strange move, the early Romberg shows depicted in the movie—*The Midnight Girl, The Whirl of the World,* and *Dancing Around*—were long-forgotten by 1954 and only contained Romberg interpolations. Just as he was about to write his first full-length show, *The Passing Show of 1914,* the movie jumps years ahead, omitting the revue entirely. Unfortunately, the long-term effect that the lack of celluloid presence had was not only to make the Shuberts invisible, but to diminish the legacy of their own properties, including *Greenwich Village Follies* and, most of all, *The Passing Shows*.

Without representation in movies to remind audiences of the entertainment world before sound film, the Shuberts and their *Passing Shows* faded from the public's memory as an important part of the theatrical past. This was diminished even more by the aggrandizement of Ziegfeld and his fabled *Follies*. Billie Burke's deal with the movie studios worked the kind of enchantment one would expect from Glinda the Good Witch; it helped support her remaining family and, at the same time, provided a lasting legacy for her departed husband, rich in lore, slightly beyond the boundaries of reality, and full of lasting, inspiring theatrical magic.

* * *

In order to understand the effect of the Shuberts' choices more directly, one must return to the Broadway stage and also turn back to the moments just before Ziegfeld's demise. Even by the early-1930s, the Shuberts were tiring of revues. J. J. announced in 1931 after he was "cornered in Shubert Alley" that he "would produce no more revues . . . because the obstacles presented by temperamental players were too much for even the most willing spirits to cope with."[32] The unnamed author (most likely Brooks Atkinson) thought that Shubert might change his mind in the future. The following year, when the producer publicized another *Passing Show*, the author said, "the announcement of another 'Passing Show' is reassuring. It sort of helps to keep things in balance."[33]

The last group of *Passing Shows*, as mentioned in chapter 8, was frequently re-branded with other titles from Shubert revues, constantly shuffling names as the show moved from previews to Broadway and then touring runs. The 1930s had numerous Shubert revues, but they were decidedly less frequent and usually ran much longer than shows had in the past. The Winter Garden, for example, abandoned the rotating system by the mid-twenties, with the last Jolson production being *Big Boy* (1925). The following year, the revue *Gay Paree* exceeded expectations, running from November until April of 1927—almost an entire season. Other revues followed in the same venue, including two editions of *Artists and Models* (1925 and 1927), the short-lived *A Night in Spain* (1927), and another *Greenwich Village Follies* (1928). The revue that significantly changed the Winter Garden's calendar, however, was *Life Begins at 8:40*, which ran from August of 1934 until March of 1935. When this show ended, more revues continued to grace the stage until one of the most successful of all time, Olsen and Johnson's *Hellzapoppin*, moved there from the 46th Street Theatre in November of 1938. It would stay at the Winter Garden for three years, the type of engagement that would have been unheard of in the past.

By this time, several major changes had affected American life, and these had a profound effect on the large-scale revue. First of all, America entered World War II in 1941, diverting much of the young talent from the theatrical stage to the battlefields of Europe and the South Pacific. This loss of talent was a crisis for the entertainment industry, given that the previous decade had seen the slow crumbling of an institution fundamental to the revue: vaudeville. As the circuits began to shut down, with many live theaters revamped into movie houses, the primary proving ground for new talent became less and less useful for producers at the Shuberts' level.[34] A prophetic comment in *Vaudeville News* from 1926 asked the question, "What would the producing manager do were it not for the vaudeville theatres and their army of clever artists from which to draw?"[35] The answer by 1938 was threefold and would very soon be fourfold. Where to go? One could go to the movies, certainly, but one could also go to radio to find new talent. As radio coverage expanded throughout the 1920s and into the next decade, the Shuberts tasked some of the their talent scouts to listen carefully to amateur hours, looking for high-quality acts that could be inexpensively signed. The third venue for new talent is almost completely ignored by historians, partially because it is hard to track: the nightclub and dinner theater world. Small revues flourished in these locations by the late 1910s, and over the next four decades, they remained active and always in need of new performers. A glance at the club page of most New York papers gives a sense of the wide variety of show types during the mid-1920s.[36] And shortly after World War II ended, television became another medium for finding and recruiting stage personalities. The expansion of mediums radically shifted the possible starting places for young performers, and in the end, it spelled the end for the large-scale revue.

With Ziegfeld gone in 1932, the Shuberts still had quite a range of competition for their shows. But over the next two decades, this would also change. George White's *Scandals* ended in the late 1930s, and eventually the producer/director moved to film, with his last effort in 1945. Earl Carroll began to look beyond New York for his shows. It is worth noting that one of the many revues hosted by the Winter Garden was in fact the producer's newest launch, *Earl Carroll's Sketchbook of 1935*. It would be his penultimate Broadway gesture, with the last of the *Vanities* taking place in 1940. He found more success in Hollywood, though, setting up another self-named theater in 1938 that featured floor shows (which he called revues) until his death in 1948. The diffusion of the revue, beginning in the 1920s, into cabarets, nightclubs, and dinner theaters, has not been given the in-depth study it deserves, but it certainly had an effect on the Shuberts' choice of productions. The power of movies to depict the revue also meant that to compete, the stage show needed to offer something equally impressive as the filmic presentations, and this was simply not possible.[37] The cake scene from *The Great Ziegfeld* and the quasi-revue numbers from Busby Berkeley's influential films used the medium to present images that were theatrically impossible. The main attraction for attending a stage show was getting to see stars live, and even this was not a strong enough draw to keep audiences coming. As shows stayed in theaters for longer runs, as radio, movies, and television syphoned off more audience members, and along with the demise of vaudeville, the large-scale revue was beginning to falter.

As the 1940s began, these changes did not completely end attempts to offer audiences versions of revues they knew from the past. When *Hellzapoppin* finally left the Winter Garden, Olsen and Johnson put on *Sons o' Fun*, which had another two-year run. Following that, the *Ziegfeld Follies of 1943* opened, starring Milton Berle, Arthur Treacher, and Sue Ryan. The souvenir program put the show directly in line with tradition, calling it, "A National Institution Glorifying the American Girl." Burke was again involved, but the driving force behind the show was a revue veteran, John Murray Anderson, whose earliest connection with the Winter Garden Revues was a song for *The Passing Show of 1913*. Anderson's thirty years of experience put together a successful show, but, like the other revues that dominated film and footlights, this show was not about cutting-edge material, but offered audiences something more akin to their past experience. Like the bio-fic-pics, this was a mode of nostalgia, but this time it was dressed in modern-day costumes. Berle and his costars had all grown up in vaudeville, and the program included this pedigree wherever possible. For example, they advertised Sue Ryan as "clowning in vaudeville since she was old enough to lace her own shoes." But, unlike past stars, these players were known from all the other entertainment venues, with Berle singled out as having done just about every medium of showbiz available. A small line of chorus girls were present, but most of the entertainment was focused on skits; one was about two monkeys looking at a human in a cage, while another involved questionable customer service at a soda fountain. An extensive tour followed the Broadway run.

But even in New York, there was ambivalence about the show. Yes, it had the requisite chorus girls and comedians. But what did it have that was new? An insightful column written by Arthur Pollock in the *Brooklyn Eagle* compared two major attractions that had opened the previous week. It could not have been more apparent which production he thought the more important. On March 31, *Oklahoma!* opened at the St. James Theatre, while the *Follies of 1943* opened April 1 at the Winter Garden. Pollock sums up the difference thus: "The frenetic new revue of today is as old, and the old one is as fresh and new as a sunny tomorrow morning."[38] Pollock meant that the "old" show was about the past, whereas the revue was supposed to be entirely modern, with the *Follies* boasting "a right-up-to-the-minute revue with jive and zoot suits in it [and] glamorous girls in the newest type of skimpy but colorful colorings." Despite the revue's entertaining qualities, what it lacked was anything that was *really* new, by which he probably could have said "innovative." Pollock called *Oklahoma!* "historic," and he was absolutely correct and expounded on what, exactly, made the musical so new. His criticism of the new *Follies* captured the central problem with the genre. The revue made use of a structure that was entirely malleable, meaning that it could be presented in almost any way. During the later part of the 1920s and 1930s, however, a coalescence of form happened. Although the order of theatrical events could be shuffled endlessly, the *components* of the revue became fixed. The elements inside the revue—the comedians, popular dancers, ballet dancers, chorus girls, and the like—acquired a stale taste that no rearranging could mask. It is no surprise, then, that something like *Oklahoma!* would stand in stark contrast to the formulaic, standardized revue. After thirty-five years, audiences knew that a new costume or a tune in a popular style was just a gussied up act by an old performer. And that was not what they wanted.

And thus, with the end of World War II, the last of *The Passing Show* series took place. There were high hopes for the show, and in order to assure audiences that it was an authentic revue, much like those of the past, the star was—remarkably—Willie Howard. Howard had been busy during the 1930s and, as explained in chapter 3, Eugene finally retired in 1940 to become Willie's business manager. It is remarkable to look at a list of Willie's theatrical engagements, though, and even after he and his brother "broke up," Willie was always working. He opened the revue *Crazy with the Heat* in January of 1941 and was onstage continuously until October of 1943, in *Priorities of 1942* (a long-lived revue) and *My Dear Public* (a very short-lived revue). During 1944, Howard played in Chicago in Michael Todd's *Star and Garter*. And the following year, he was approached by the Shuberts to be in the newest *Passing Show*.

The last edition held two names, *The Passing Show of 1945* and *The Passing Show of 1946*, but the content was virtually the same in both. The reason for this was that the production began previews in several different locations, including Washington, DC, and Chicago, and as it was revamped, the Shuberts changed the title, hoping to open on Broadway. The process of constructing the show began in August of 1945, when Will "Mac" Morrissey filled the position that Harold Atteridge had held in the past. Atteridge had contributed to many Shubert shows until his retirement in 1934, and he had known Morrissey since the latter contributed songs to *The Passing Show of 1915*. Morrissey made brave attempts to produce, write, direct, stage, and perform his own revues throughout the 1920s and 1930s (including *Buzzin' Around* [1920] and *Polly of Hollywood* [1927]), but none of his own shows lasted more than a month on the Great White Way. However, he worked off and on for the Shuberts over the years, and by 1945, he was a showbiz veteran. Morrissey wrote to J. J. on August 27 concerning performers he felt would work well in the show:

> "Three pieces of talent you have to see right away. I know you don't favor colored talent in a revue, but this Bailey girl at the Zanzibar is something else. She has what Bert Williams had on the ball and [I] think she will top Ethel Waters. Bill Acorn at the Diamond Horseshoe new show. This is the dancer I spoke to you about last winter . . . He's young and already has more than Ray Bolger. Carl

Ravazzo—a piece of box office for the women. I saw him at the Martinique some-time ago and later at the Roxy . . . This is a young Latin-American personality that has to end up as the Chevalier type of star . . .

Although the war is over—do [you] think we should have either in travesty or pictures—something of the new G.I. Joe artist type [like Bill] "MAUDLIN."

[I] think we can cut the nostalgia of the "PASSING SHOW" and just make it present and future, as Billy Rose has enough nostalgia to make you walk into the Diamond Horseshoe feeling 30 and coming out feeling 90 years old . . .

[I] think we should have Russian Singing Choir similar to the Cossacks if we use sequence of "PASSING SHOW" in Russia. In fact, each of our allies should be represented—either in comedy or specialty act in the production.[39]

This interesting document offers a taste of what *The Passing Show of 1945* could have been. Many of Morrissey's ideas were interesting (and there are others that are somewhat questionable, such as using a dream sequence involving "the little crip-pled girl" from *The Glass Menagerie*), and they suggest a cosmopolitan show that was deeply rooted in the present. The "Bailey" girl he mentions was Pearl Bailey, who was appearing alongside Cab Calloway's Orchestra at the Café Zanzibar on Forty-Ninth Street. If Shubert would have been more open-minded, he could have given Bailey her Broadway debut a year before she appeared in Edward Gross's *St. Louis Woman*. It is difficult to tell what opinion J. J. had of African American talent beyond this com-ment. He had featured Josephine Baker in the *Ziegfeld Follies of 1936*, and there is no suggestion in the documents for the show that he had racial concerns. But even if Morrissey understood J. J.'s racism, he still felt he should promote the young singer. Bill Acorn was a dancer, singer, and comedian who was active in numerous New York night clubs around 1945–1946, but he seems to have disappeared afterwards. His voice was described by one reviewer as "oaky" like "Sinatra."[40] And as for Carl Ravazzo, his name was actually Ravazza, and he was a popular band leader, singer, and violinist who had been active since forming his own group in San Francisco in the mid-1930s. By the time Morrissey had seen him, Ravazza was headlining the Roxy alongside Phil Silvers, and reviewers agreed that the suave, handsome crooner could be a hit if only people could see his face.[41] He specialized in Italian, Spanish, and Cuban songs, a pan-Latin mash-up that mimicked performers like Desi Arnaz and Xavier Cugat. Morrissey's suggestions would have made the talent for *The Passing Show* far more representative of modern trends in entertainment and may have transformed the show into something far more successful. Even his overarching suggestions, tapping into the war through art and representation of the Allies, would have been wise. But alas, Shubert chose to use performers he already knew, maintaining the nostalgia Morrissey had attributed to Billy Rose.

Vaudeville was again the primary talent pool Shubert used to fill his roster. Beyond Howard, the principal female lead was Sue Ryan, a talent he had hired in the last *Follies*. The featured dancer, Bobby Morris, had been active in burlesque for many years, and was seen by Willie Howard while the two were playing theaters in Australia before the war. The cast list continues in much the same way, with mar-ried dancers John Masters and Rowena Rollins, and singers Ruth Davis and Ruth Clayton, all originating from the two-a-day halls. One of the younger cast members,

Gil Johnson, got his start in Hollywood as a child and was active in Broadway during the early 1940s, including as understudy to Ray Bolger in *By Jupiter* (1942). Another, Alice "Mimi" Kellerman, was the niece of Annette Kellerman, and had been on Broadway since a young age, beginning with *The Gang's All Here* (1931). Perhaps the only nod to something new was the inclusion of Bob Russell, a singer who was also the Master of Ceremonies from the "Miss America" pageant. Russell was well known on the radio for his excellent voice (singing both operatic and popular music), but he also penned the music and words for a number of songs. His most famous song was "Brazil" (1939), for which he wrote the words to Ary Barroso's samba melody. The chorus included nineteen women (eight showgirls and eleven dancing girls) and eight "dancing boys." While the cast was made up of solid performers, none of them were unique enough to carry the revue and offer something new to audiences.

The music for *The Passing Show of 1945* was more standard for its era, both in its composition and in its orchestration. The show used an orchestra similar in size to past productions, the most important addition being a larger string section. However, the biggest change from older shows was that by the 1940s, it was now common to assign multiple instruments to wind players.[42] An unsigned memo lists twenty-six members of the pit, with ten violins, two cellos, one string bass, piano, harp, five woodwinds doubling parts (flute/alto sax, oboe/tenor sax, clarinet/alto sax, clarinet/tenor sax, baritone sax/bass clarinet/clarinet), three trumpets, two trombones, and drums.[43] This sound was common in dance bands of the era, but it significantly altered the sonority of the Saddler orchestrations; not only is there no viola to add middle textures to the strings, but the midrange of sound in the brass was also removed with no French horns.[44] This was a melody-heavy group that spotlighted upper-register sounds and offered very little in the way of mid- to low-range support. One wonders if this was for a particular type of vocal need, but even during Irving Actman's "Dream Ballet" (listed as the "White Rhapsody" in the program), the same orchestration was maintained; the violins are written as three-part *divisi* with the "A" part sometimes reaching very high, supported by the cello, also very high in its register.[45] The balance must have been quite unusual.

Another attempt to make some of the songs more relevant to contemporary times was also tried. One of the first dance sequences was a "Bobby Socks Convention" that used swing music to show off the "Rug Cutter" (Gil Johnson) and the "2nd Hep" (Diana Marsh). Dance was more important than strong vocals for most of the show, and when the full company was performing (such as in "The Avenue of the Americas" and "Living in a Brand New Day"), or when it was only a couple singing (for "Then There's Romance" and "How Long Will It Be?"), dances between large groups and small ensembles were employed. The choreographers, Natalie Kamarova and Carl Randall, had to work with a number of different composers, including Will Morrissey, Eugene Burton, Ross Thomas, and Irving Actman, to make the music work.[46] One of the songs that was not centered on dance was "The Girl from Oklahoma Meets the Boy from Carousel" (by Morrissey), which was not musically connected to the Rodgers and Hammerstein shows that inspired it. This number was probably the most similar to *The Passing Shows* of the past, burlesquing the characteristics of each show through some of their main characters.

It was a complicated process to piece together the numerous numbers, however, because many of the men who were contributors were still in the military while the show was in production. For example, Bill Bunt, who wrote "You're My Kind of Ugly," was a sergeant stationed in San Antonio while negotiations were taking place. Shubert bought the song for a paltry $100, and shared the publishing royalties 50/50.[47] The number (a love song) was performed by John Masters and Rowena Rollins, but it was never published. Bunt was an active composer, lyricist, and conductor during the 1940s, but this did not help his career. The days of having a "lucky" interpolation in a revue were, like so many other pieces of the shows, coming to a close.

Willie Howard and Sue Ryan were responsible for most of the comedy, and they each had scenes that were their own, mimicking the specialty acts that Jolson had begun performing four decades before. One of Ryan's bits was called "Back to the Kitchen" and another was "Doughnuts," where she had to work behind the counter to satisfy several angry customers. Howard, on the other hand, played "The Psychoanalyst," named "Dr. Zoopf." Howard's shining moment, though, came near the end of the second act, where he came out and entertained audiences with his characteristic patter and Yiddish accent, honed from years of being onstage. Robert J. Casey, the critic for the *Chicago Daily News*, seemed to think most of the show was good, but he singled out Howard as the reason for attending: "Wars get themselves fought, glaciers melt, mountains erode and deserts blossom like a seed catalogue, but no matter when you hoist the curtain on the 'Passing Show,' there's Willie Howard, unchanged and unchangeable. Even in a revue as good as this, you're somehow glad he's there."[48] But despite that positive statement, audiences and most other critics did not agree, and most of what was said was that the show was terrible, with shoddy looking sets and unpolished dances. The show reopened in November in Washington, DC, and made some small changes in format, but nothing could save the production. The show closed in Chicago on February 17, 1946, with no chance of being revived for Broadway.

Part of the issue was undoubtedly that the effort to coordinate the revue was not as neatly arranged as in the past. The Shubert theatrical machine, constructed and run by J. J., no longer existed as it had during the heyday of the large-scale revue. Huffmann and Atteridge had stated that arranging the patchwork of a revue was the hardest part of the show, and it seems the right balance could not be found. One look in the Shubert Archive provides a key as to why the show did not work: there was an enormous amount of material written that was never used. Some of the pieces were in very poor taste, with the most glaring being a sketch for Willie Howard called "The Atomic Bomb," where the comic was to be "Professor Einswi" and play alongside "Professor Drifeer." The two eventually cause an enormous explosion that resulted in women appearing in test tubes. It would have been a bad choice to include in the show, and it was wise to cut it. On the opposite side, a song called "It Takes Both White Keys and Black Keys to Play the Star Spangled Banner," with words by John W. Bratton and music by Geoffrey O'Hara, would have been a progressive touch concerning racial issues and American identity.[49] The song tells of a child who takes piano lessons and learns from his "old Mammy" that "the greatest songs today take all the keys to play." Bratton (born in 1867) and O'Hara (born in 1882) had been actively writing music hits since the nineteenth century, and the antiquated title suggests an early Tin Pan Alley song.[50] The music had some gentle syncopation that seemed more ragtime than swing time, but perhaps in the hands of a good orchestrator, the song could have come alive. Whatever the reason that this song, and many of the skits, were cut, the sheer amount of material discarded is impressive. This suggests the director, Russell Mack, had great difficulty in finding the right combination and flow for the performance. Although he had been a part of revues during the 1920s as a performer, he did not have Atteridge or Huffman's skill at arranging a successful show.[51]

Among the documents for *The Passing Show of 1946* is an item that was one of the most personal and moving letters I discovered anywhere in the Archive. It also is the clearest indication of why *The Passing Show* ended during previews. And, sadly, it marked the end of the revue career for the man who, in many ways, was responsible for the great success of the original series. The undated letter is written on stationary from Washington, DC, and it was one of the last letters Mack wrote to Willie Howard.[52] As was usually the case, such a letter would be given to a stenographer, typed, and sent; in many cases, the originals were kept and have been preserved in the Archive. The letter must have been both difficult to write, and particularly difficult to get:

> My dear Mr. Howard,
>
> As our show is running too long it will be necessary for you to make proper cuts in all the scenes you appear in. You wait too long before you speak[;] in that way, you are taking up the time and it delays the speed of the shows. I have watched all the performances so far and you ad lib and never play the scene the same way[.] Besides, our stage manager never gets the same cue so he does not know when the scene is over ... We need to fix our show and I am cutting every scene possible and I must have your cooperation[.] Your material has been seen by almost everybody with the exception of the introduction and the Pscho[analyst][.] You said [illegible] four times last night and the Shyster line was not very nice. As the leading performer of the show you must remember you are not in a vaudeville picture house and audiences are not made up of a Jewish clientele. And most of the audience doesn't know what you are saying and besides a great part of our Jewish clientele resent it[.] Likewise, all Jewish comedians with a few exceptions resort to that sort of comedy which is in bad taste.
>
> I don't like to write letters, but you leave me no other recourse that my orders must be adhered to. You are well paid and my instructions are permanent.

This letter (or more pointedly, its consequences) marked the end of *The Passing Show* as a theatrical venture for the Shuberts and for Willie Howard since the series began in 1912. The memo was meant to be a warning to Howard about his stage presence and his comedic delivery, but the comedian did not change his habits, and the show did not continue. The letter speaks volumes not only concerning Howard as a performer, but also about the audiences he was playing for. The comment about vaudeville suggests that Howard was trying to do the same act he had done for most of his life. But with the end of World War II, a new place had to be found for Jewish identity in theater, and the Yiddish accent and jokes were simply outdated and, as Mack points out, considered offensive. The remarkable comic timing

Howard had been praised for in 1910—that he was quick and did not wallow in the moment—had slowed, and as he slowed, so did the show as a whole. The comment made by Casey about the "unchanged and unchangeable" comedian was true. But it was also true for the rest of *The Passing Show of 1946*—it was a show built on a nostalgic formula featuring a representative of one of the biggest stars from almost two generations before. It held very little relation to the postwar mentality, and although the documents show it could have looked forward, the cast, music, dances, and content did not add up to the kind of Broadway-quality production the Shuberts had hoped for. *The Passing Show's* time had come to an end.

During the following decades, the trajectory set by the Shuberts' choices remained intact. Ziegfeld's legend continued to grow, through film and theatrical shows, while *The Passing Shows* receded further and further into the past. An attempt was made by the brothers to put together a television series on NBC with *The Passing Show* title during the early 1950s, but the program never materialized. And as the Ziegfeld-themed productions continued, the brothers passed away. Lee died in 1953 and J. J. a decade later. During those years, the movies (discussed previously) continued to feed into the Ziegfeld mythology. Some attempts at staging another *Ziegfeld Follies* were made on Broadway, but only one had much success. The *Ziegfeld Follies of 1957* was staged in the Winter Garden Theater, but it was produced by Mark Kroll and Charles Conaway. It starred Beatrice Lillie and Billy DeWolf, and ran for a respectable three months (123 performances). Cynthia and Sara Brideson suggest that the next installments in the Ziegfeld lore were Stephen Sondheim's *Follies* (1971), followed by Joe Layton's British musical *Ziegfeld* (1988). However, in the 1950s and throughout the following decades, the Ziegfeld name moved from Broadway to a new location that the producer (himself an incorrigible gambler) would have loved: Las Vegas.

The first of the Nevada-based shows took place in 1953, and it happened because Billie Burke was given the opportunity to perform in a show called *A Ziegfeld Album*. She was booked at the Sands Hotel and Casino, and it was only the first of many productions that opened at this venue. Among several other versions of the revue, the Sands also hosted a *Ziegfeld Follies* in 1967, produced by Lou Walters, followed by another produced by Peter Gayle in 1970.[53] The long-legged Vegas showgirl with giant feather boas was not a phenomenon without a past, but instead an offshoot of the 1920s Broadway chorus girl mixed with the risqué French dancers featured in Parisian nightclubs.

Even after many *Follies*-style shows had successfully found homes in Las Vegas hotels, there could be problems if the elements for a production did not align properly. Mitzi Briggs, who became the owner of the Tropicana Hotel and Casino in 1975, presided over one of the last efforts to use the Ziegfeld name in the city. As part of her reworking of the establishment, she poured money into a new show that was to open along with the renovated hotel. The story of Briggs's struggle to put on the show is a classic showbiz tale. She wrote Fredric Gershon, one of the lawyers for the Shubert Organization, that she had arranged and completed almost every aspect of the show, including choreography, songwriting, and costumes,. Unfortunately, the financial backers, Rigler and Deutsch, "were three months into production when they consulted their astrologer and were told that there would be

[an] economic depression in [the] United States. They promptly abandoned [the] show."⁵⁴ However, Briggs continued to arrange the program, including a cast of thirty-eight that would perform many interesting numbers, such as a "salute to the cultures of the Native Americans and Alaskan Indians," a "San Francisco production number containing Chinatown and a Dragon Parade," and a "Polynesian Paradise with a waterfall and Laserium light show." Briggs was clearly determined to make the production a success, despite facing steep odds. "I have been threatened by nearly everyone involved, and have been laughed at and discouraged from every direction," she wrote. "I can assure you of two things: I continue to believe in the show and I know now how to make it happen." The performance took place at a smaller theater, and it became a part of Ziegfeld's legacy in the West. Other remnants connected to the producer also existed in Las Vegas, with the most well known being the MGM/Grand Hotel's "Ziegfeld Theater," designed by Donn Arden for huge musical extravaganzas.

Some of the most widely traveled versions of *The Passing Show* were not Shubert-related events but were revues organized by small-time producers trying to make a quiet profit from the title. The first of these toured the Midwest and East Coast as "Scibilia's Broadway Passing Show," playing small theaters during the 1939–1940 season. The producer, Anton Scibilia, had been a presence in vaudeville and even occasionally on Broadway since the 1910s, mostly as a manager, but also as an author and a booking agent. The matchbooks that were released to promote the small cast (despite what was advertised) provide an insight into the type of production it really was. While the matchbook cover promised an urban, New York–style production (▶Figures 9.1 and 9.2), the inside had an image printed on the matches themselves, making it clear that this was nothing more than a girlie show (Figure 9.3).

Another *Passing Show of 1945* was also active while the Shuberts' *Passing Show of 1945* was in preparation. Not unlike Scibilia's girlie extravaganza, this revue was small, of low quality, and localized. It was advertised for several weeks in Montreal, with performances running three times a day, including a midnight show. Some of the performers listed were The 3 Stowaways, Ted Claire, Len Howard's Orchestra, and Evelyn Taylor.⁵⁵ These were small affairs, and much like the dozens of Follies-titled shows that covered the country in the 1940s, they were the final gasps of vaudeville-style entertainments, usually appearing in either movie theaters or the small nightclubs that hosted them.

As strange as it may have been to be in such a new environment, both the Shuberts and Willie Howard continued to flourish after the Chicago closing. Willie, despite receiving a letter with such harsh criticism, continued performing in clubs even after *The Passing Show* ended. He had one last Broadway hurrah as part of the 1947 revival of *Sally*, where he was "the Duke of Czechogovinio." The new version ran just over a month, closing on June 5, 1948. Willie died in January of the following year, having been on Broadway from the time he was twenty-eight years old until he was sixty-six. As for the Shuberts, the organization they worked so hard to build during the 1900s into the 1920s continues to be one of the most successful theatrical businesses on Broadway, even in 2016. The Winter Garden Theater still prospers, most notably housing Andrew Lloyd Webber's *Cats* for eighteen years (and all

Fig. 9.3. *Scibilia's Broadway Passing Show matchbook inside, 1939. Author's Collection.*

of its 7,485 performances). Even the format of the large-scale revue had a few more shows to offer during the 1950s; the *New Faces* series had multiple editions even into the 1960s, and many non-series revues managed to score long runs. Eventually, the revue would splinter into a number of different types (composer-driven shows, small cast shows, and a multitude of non-linear or non-narrative shows), with most finding a home off-Broadway.

But there is no question that whatever the revue became, it had once been an enormous production, employing dozens (if not hundreds) of people during its Broadway and touring runs. When *The Passing Show* was at its height, it was one of the most impressive productions made in New York, and audiences came to the Winter Garden in droves to see it. The revues featured excellent music, fresh dances, huge scenery and effects, and they consistently made a profit and received excellent notices. After four or five months in Manhattan, trains carried stars like the Howard Brothers, Trixie Friganza, Fred Astaire, Marilynn Miller, and so many others to theaters nationwide, offering the height of live entertainment to audiences. Year after year, as the curtain went up on Winter Garden revues, Harold Atteridge and his colleagues probably watched anxiously from the wings as girls rushed past into the footlights and onto the runway. Staging *The Passing Show* was a way of life for dozens of creative people, and it was produced at a pace that matched the speed of modernity; the "rapid-fire" construction of an Oriental garden or the quick rewriting of a catchy chorus happened at a rate that made the new century (appropriately) seem like a world that had left the past behind. At one moment, a hula girl would dance by, while in the next, Ed Wynn could be blowing up a tire for a car that didn't work. One year, a patron might see the burning of San Francisco, while in another, a cavalry charge might come booming toward the audience from the stage. It is true that Ziegfeld and his *Follies* were fundamental to the history of theater, but, unlike their posthumous legend, they were not the only game in town. *The Passing Shows* had their own spirit, and the giddiness Charlotte Greenwood, Fred Allen, and others felt at joining the cast attests to that. Every year, the new production was glamorous and dazzling. It was breathtaking and it was shocking. It was sensational and it was memorable. And, of course, *The Passing Shows* changed constantly. Although they may be forgotten today, *The Passing Shows* were some of the most important entertainments of their time. For the theatergoer who loved revues, it was never to be missed. When they arrived at the Winter Garden during the hot summer months, the first-nighters were always thrilled. To them, each annual edition of *The Passing Show* was an event—"as new, bright, and welcome as the morning sun" (see Figure 9.4).

Fig. 9.4. *Advertisement for* The Passing Show *of 1924. Author's Collection.*

NOTES

1. See chapter 8 for a sample of these comments.

2. "Coffey Fights Shuberts Over Ziegfeld Name," *Yonkers Herald Statesmen*, March 21, 1934, 5.

3. This time in Burke's life is covered in great depth in Grant Hayter-Menzies, *Mrs. Ziegfeld: The Public and Private Lives of Billie Burke* (Jefferson, NC, and London: McFarland & Company, Inc., 2009).

4. Ibid., 143.

5. Contract in *Ziegfeld Follies* show file, Shubert Archive, box 88, folder S17.

6. "Shubert Departs for Coast Tryout," *New York Times*, July 29, 1933, 14. The telegrams are located in *Ziegfeld Follies* show file, Shubert Archive, box 88 (numerous folders).

7. Art Arthur, "Roving Reporter Reviews Rambles," *Brooklyn Daily Eagle*, January 9, 1934, 23.

8. Telegram from Billie Burke to Lee Shubert, Ziegfeld Follies show file, January 12, 1934, Shubert Archive, box 88, folder S17.

9. "Curves 'Out' for 1934 Beauties, Experts Say; Willowy Types Rule," *Syracuse American*, January 14, 1934, 5.

10. Advertisement of Hudson Music Hall, *Saratogian*, October 2, 1934, 12.

11. "Swimming Exhibition by Y.W.C.A. Attracts Large Crowd," *Niagara Falls Gazette*, April 23, 1934, 7.

12. "In Home Concert," *Buffalo Courier-Express*, April 12, 1936, 6.

13. "Durante Continues Labor on Craziest of Follies," *Buffalo Courier-Express*, June 3, 1934, 9.

14. "Shuberts Face Lawsuit Over 'Ziegfeld Follies,'" *Syracuse Journal*, March 21, 1934, 3.

15. "Former Aide Testifies in Ziegfeld Case," *Rochester Daily Record*, June 7, 1934, 1.

16. "Shubert Claims Right to Use Ziegfeld Name," *Yonkers Herald Statesman*, March 24, 1934, 4.

17. "Ziegfeld Debts Not to Be Paid by Famous Film," *Yonkers Herald Statesman*, July 15, 1936, 9.

18. Some think the debts were eventually paid by longtime associates of Burke, according to Hayter-Menzies, *Mrs. Ziegfeld*.

19. Cynthia Brideson and Sara Brideson, *Ziegfeld and His Follies*, 415.

20. Hayter-Menzies, *Mrs. Ziegfeld*, 162.

21. Coincidentally, the movie *Yiddle with His Fiddle* was also released in 1936, and it was the most successful Yiddish-language film ever made.

22. Cynthia Brideson and Sara Brideson, *Ziegfeld and His Follies*, 416.

23. Ann Ommen van der Merwe, *The Ziegfeld Follies: A History in Song* (Lanham, MD: Scarecrow Press, 2009), 16.

24. Some of the other numbers included in the sequence are listed in Ken Bloom, *Hollywood Song: The Complete Film Musical Companion* (New York: Facts on File, Inc., 1995), 356–57.

25. Cynthia Brideson and Sara Brideson, *Ziegfeld and His Follies*, 410.

26. Letter from J. J. Shubert to Billie Burke Ziegfeld, April 10, 1939, *Ziegfeld Follies* show file, Shubert Archive, box 88, folder S-189.

27. Letter from J. J. Shubert to Billie Burke Ziegfeld, May 4, 1939, *Ziegfeld Follies* show file, Shubert Archive, box 88, folder S-189.

28. This is interesting because the "Sweepstakes" sketch starring Fanny Brice and Hume Cronyn was taken from the *Ziegfeld Follies of 1936*.

29. Cynthia Brideson and Sara Brideson, *Ziegfeld and his Follies*, 422.

30. Ibid., 421.

31. William A. Everett, *Sigmund Romberg*, 10.

32. "Rialto Gossip," *New York Times*, November 22, 1931, 129.

33. "Gossip of the Rialto," *New York Times*, July 31, 1932, X1.

34. At first, vaudeville continued in the same locations, with live entertainment offered in between the showings of movies. This practice lasted about fifteen years, with movies predominating after 1945.

35. Walter Hawley, "What's Going On in Chicago," *Vaudeville News*, September 24, 1926, 8.

36. By the early 1940s, these locations were being reviewed in *Billboard* on a page entitled "Night Clubs—Vaudeville." *Variety* also eventually allocated reviewers to attend and report on these shows. The earlier decades, though, remain quite opaque and await further study.

37. It is important to note that the revue was one of the most popular genres in early sound film, with some very important movies released in the late 1920s and early 1930s that employed the nonlinear device to keep audiences entertained. *The Show of Shows* (1929) and the *Hollywood Revue of 1929* were of particular interest, but one of the most interesting, in my opinion, was *King of Jazz* (1930). These movies used many techniques that had been invented in stage shows of the past, but *King of Jazz* was the first to seriously play with film as a different medium.

38. Arthur Pollock, "Just Because of 'Oklahoma!' We'll Have Better Musical Comedies Hereafter," *Brooklyn Eagle*, April 4, 1943, 31.

39. Letter from Will "Mac" Morrissey to J. J. Shubert , August 27 1945, *Passing Show of 1945/6* show file, Shubert Archive, box 100.

40. Bill Smith, "Diamond Horseshoe, New York," *Billboard*, September 1, 1945, 32.

41. Bill Smith, "Roxy," *Billboard*, August 18, 1945, 27. The column also mentions that Ravazza would lead sing-alongs with the club by using a giant screen above him that would project the lyrics above so all could read them and join in.

42. There were shades of this in the past, with the trumpet players asked to also use cornet, and clarinet players asked to use instruments in different keys, but the doubling mentioned here was new.

43. *Passing Show of 1945/6* show file, Shubert Archive, box 100.

44. Thank you to George Ferencz for pointing to the connection to dance bands of the 1940s.

45. "Dream Ballet" partitur by Irving Actman, Passing Show of 1945/6 show series, Shubert Archive, box 456, package 1.

46. Kamarova had been active throughout Europe in the 1930s, and was for a time the director of the Folies Bergere. She continued to work in New York (mostly in night clubs) throughout the 1940s. Randall had been working on Broadway, including in the *Follies* and other revues, since the 1910s.

47. Letter from Bill Bunt to J. J. Shubert, October 10, 1945, *Passing Show of 1945/6* show file, Shubert Archive, box 9, folder 16. Other correspondence between the two parties is located in the same folder.

48. *Passing Show of 1945/6* show file, Shubert Archive.

49. *Passing Show of 1945/6* show file, Shubert Archive, box 100.

50. The partners had written the song, "America! Love It or Leave It," in 1941, and were very interested in patriotic songs, becoming part of the USO effort during the war. O'Hara believed that music was a source of untapped potential to transform people's lives, be it through patriotism or as an aid to mental or physical health. For more, see Arthur B. Sederquist, "Geoffrey O'Hara: Composer with a Cause," *The Rotarian*, September 1961, 17.

51. Mack had been a Broadway performer since the 1920s, often working for the Shuberts, but he had gone to Hollywood during the early 1930s, directing and screenwriting.

52. Passing Show of 1945/6 show file, Shubert Archive, box 100. It appears from the documents that Mack stopped trying to alter Howard's work after this, resigned to the fact that the older performer was not going to change.

53. For documents concerning these shows, see *Ziegfeld Follies* show file, Shubert Archive, box 88B, folder 5.

54. Mailgram from Mitzi Briggs to Fredric Gershon, *Ziegfeld Follies* show file, April 2, 1975, Shubert Archive, Box 88B, folder 7.

55. Advertisement, *The Montreal Gazette*, February 26, 1945, 3.

POSTSCRIPT

My purposes in writing this book were twofold. First, I wanted to tell some of the stories surrounding *The Passing Shows* and their world, with an emphasis on why they have been erased from the larger narratives of Broadway history. But secondly, I wanted to develop the foundation for a much larger investigation of this period in Broadway studies. The reader will note that many of my endnotes contain information about possible paths for new research, with some of these indicating the locations where a scholar might look for archival materials. I truly hope this book acts as a gateway for many other valuable and underrepresented topics in musical theater history.

With that said, I want to make a few points concerning the methodologies and topics I chose to cover. I considered several methodologies for the approach to the material, but the most immediate need seemed to be to simply consider the historical record. I have a strong belief that documents (be they written, visual, sound, or other) are the best place to start for developing our notions of historical events. There are many scholars who are more interested in interpreting what they see before developing the full context for the object of study, and I wanted to make sure that I had a grasp on what *The Passing Shows* meant to the time period in which they were created. Thus, there is little in the way of examinations that center on race, gender, sexuality, modernity, or performativity in this book. The difference between Ziegfeld's Anglo perspective and the Shuberts' Jewish viewpoint would also be an interesting subject to explore. While there is clearly a great deal to say on those important issues, I feel the details of the time and place need to be established before we try to understand how they relate to our own experience.

One of the historical areas I touch upon is World War I, but again, there is so much that relates directly to the war that is part of the content of the revues that it would take an entire chapter to do it justice. Small issues, such as Oscar Radin's inclusion of European national anthems in 1914, and larger ones, like the Howard Brothers' changing the content of their jokes during the years of American involvement, all could find a place in the discourse. *The Passing Shows* and many other musical productions (both book shows as well as revues) have connections to the war that could be discussed in more depth, but the topic is deserving of a monograph of its own.

One contextual issue that I want to mention is that I have chosen to maintain the heteronormative language used during the time, especially when dealing with sexual stimulation. Simplicity of language makes it easier to write, but should not be mistaken for the lack of acknowledgment that homosexual desire would certainly have been present. I do mention sexuality with the chorus boys as one of the reasons they were dismissed after World War I, but the topic awaits more thorough treatment.

APPENDICES

APPENDIX 1

THE PASSING SHOW OF 1915
BY HAROLD ATTERIDGE

SCENE SIX: LION SCENE
Scene: A drop in "1." Before the Arena. [Enter R. J. and Sammy].

R. J.: Now, I want you to work for the moving pictures.

SAMMY: That's my job every time we move.

R. J.: What's your job every time we move?

SAMMY: Moving pictures.

R. J.: I want you to play a scene from Androcles and the Lion. You're supposed to be Androcles the Christian tailor.

SAMMY: Impossible. Who ever heard of a Christian tailor?

R. J.: It's a play by Bernard Shaw.

SAMMY: Oh p-shaw.

R. J.: Now, here's the story. Androcles took a burr out of the lion's foot and became very friendly with him. Every place the lion went you were sure to find Androcles.

SAMMY: Sure. In the lion's stomach.

R. J.: No, no, no. Androcles was a Christian, so Caesar condemned him to death and had him thrown in the lion's cage to be killed.

SAMMY: I saw that same show.

R. J.: What show?

SAMMY: *Inside the Lines.*

R. J.: When the lion came to eat Androcles, Androcles was saved, for what do you think happened?

SAMMY: That's some lyin'.

R. J.: Were you ever locked in a cage with lions?

SAMMY: Sure, I married one.

R. J.: But there's no danger. When you go into the cage, the lion is sure to recognize you.

SAMMY: You're sure, but is the lion sure? Say, can't you put me in a cage with kittens or rabbits?

R. J.: But think. This lion knows you. He'll be glad to eat off your hand.

SAMMY: Sure, my head, or my hand, or my feet.

R. J.: Well, there will be no trouble. The lion will remember you immediately.

SAMMY: Couldn't you give me a card or letter of introduction to the lion in case he should forget me?

[Roar]

R. J.: There's the lion now. They're just feeding him meat for an appetizer.

SAMMY: So I'm to be the entrée.

R. J.: When the lion starts after you, you mustn't show fear. You've got to stand squarely before him, be firm, glare at him. [Roar]. And whatever you do, keep cool.

SAMMY: I'm so cold, now I'm shivering.

R. J.: Now remember you're locked in this place. You can see that these [pulls on rubber bars] are iron bars and you cannot get out.

SAMMY: Well, I had an appointment with the lion, but if he can't keep it, I guess I'll go home. [Lion enters]. Oh, there he is, if he ever loses his memory, my folks will never know me. You're a nice lion. You're a pretty lion. You're a dandy lion. Don't you remember me? I'm Androcles the podiatrist. Don't you remember I took a splinter out of your foot? [Lion turns his head away.] [To R. J.] He's stuck up. He wants to see you.

R. J.: Goodbye, Sammy. Don't be worried, you've got one chance in a million.

SAMMY: Well, that's an even break. [Rushes to iron bars.] I can't get out. [Lion starts towards him.] Now Leo, keep your temper. You're always so wild. You'll be the death of me yet. Listen, let's talk business. I don't want to cheat you. If you ate me, you wouldn't enjoy me at all. I'll get you a nice, fat boy. Look how skinny I am. [Lion shakes his head "no."] It's all over but the flowers and the cheers. [Lion draws closer.] I've got to turn my eyes away. It's rude to watch anybody when they're eating. What strong breath he's got. He must have been eating Italians. Sleep Trilby [3 Times.] [Puts finger in lion's mouth.] I've got him hypnotized. [Slaps his face.] You dirty crook. [Lion starts at him.]

R. J.: Sammy, I've made a mistake!

SAMMY: What do you mean?

R.J.: I sent in the wrong lion!

SAMMY: This is a hell of a time to tell me!

[Close of Scene]

APPENDIX 2

LISTS, NOTES, AND SCENARIOS FOR *THE PASSING SHOW OF 1914*

SONG LIST 1

ACT 1

SCENE 1:
    Moving Picture Studio owned by QUEEN OF THE MOVIES

Numbers: 1. Opening Chorus
              2. Midnight Girl Number
              3. Boy and Girl Number
              4. Crinoline Girl Number
              5. Sari Number
              6. Moving Picture Glide

SCENE 2:
    Private office of the QUEEN OF THE MOVIES

        7. Duet

SCENE 3:
    Persian Garden

        8. A Thousand Years Ago
        9. Oh, Oh, Omar!
        10. Persian Cabaret

SCENE 3:
    Scene in one—Broadway

        11. Manhattan Mad.
        12. Whiting and Bert [*sic*]

SCENE 4:
    AIRSHIP EFFECT

ACT 2

SCENE 1: Grand Central Station—Washington.
SCENE 2:
TRAIN EFFECT
SCENE 3:
Drop in One.
SCENE 4: Scene at the San Francisco Fair

SONG LIST 2
W/SCENARIO 4

SONG NUMBERS
SCENE 1

1. Opening Number—"A Persian Night."
2. Waltz Theme Song—"A Thousand Years Ago."
3. Big Cabaret Number—"Oh, Oh, Omar!"

- : -

4. Big Scotch Number—"Kitty MacKay"
5. "Manhattan Mad"
6. "My Crinoline Girl"—Number with Crinoline Girls.
7. "The Tango Wedding"—Wedding Business done to Tango.
8. Girls with Different Colored Wigs—"I love the girl with the hair do pink; hair of blue, etc. etc. but the one girl is the good old fashioned girl with her own hair."
9. Big Hungarian Rag Song—"That Haunting Hungarian Tune" or & c., built on the "Hazaazaa Number" from "Sari."
10. "The Moving Pictures Glide"—Dance with that hurried business of moving pictures
11. "Meet Me in the Little Café"
12. "Along Came Ruth"
13. "Any Night"—Number built on the type of "In the Night" from "The Queen of the Movies"
14. "Queen of the Movies"
15. "The Whirl of the World"
16. Big Rag Number—"When Claudia Smiles."
17. "Me for a Midnight Girl"

SONG LIST 3

Act 2.   Lay-out.

SCENE 1 - Gymnasium Scene.
   " 2 - Railroad Drop in "One." Scene, and Freeman and Dunham's Specialty
   " 3 - Railroad Scene.
   " 4 - Drop in "One." "Salvation" Number, Muriel [Window]. T. Roy Barnes – "gun" business, etc.
   " 5 - The Sloping Path (Kelly)
   " 6 - Drop in "One." Number—Keane and "Bohemian Rag"—Collins
   " 7 - Opening Number "San Francisco Town"—Demarest

     Short Dialogue, and
     "Silence & Fun" Number—Hughes
     Short burlesque, and
     "Eagle Rock"—Granville.
     Burning Effect, and
     Transition.
     "California"

SCENARIO 1

SCENARIO FOR PASSING SHOW OF 1914.

The curtain to rise on an elaborate Persian Garden with the embellishments and environments of "A Thousand Years Ago" and "Omar the Tentmaker."

At the rise of the curtain, the stage to be absolutely empty, with the accompaniment of the oboe and the harp, until the appearance of the leading female character.

Then the appearance of "Omar," the vagabond musician, embodying the parts of "Omar the Tentmaker" and Dixey's part in "A Thousand Years Ago."

There should be a pretty love scene, and then the Waltz Song, which shall be the theme all through the entire play.

After that, the various characters in both plays aforementioned are introduced, until the scene becomes a Persian Cabaret, which shall be a very good number with all the color of the Orient, balloons, confetti, lanterns, and make it a sort of a carnival.

After this big carnival scene, Omar is arrested as a heretic for professing that there shall be a Broadway a thousand years from now; also that the man shall see the women's faces, and that there shall be Tango dancing, turkey-trotting, Zepplin [sic] airships, and all the funny sayings of the present period. He is taken and put into the stocks. He is told that he will be given his freedom if he answers correctly three riddles a la "Thousand Years Ago." He fails in the last riddle, which must be made very funny, and he is again put in the stocks the same as in "Omar the Tentmaker." As they are about to beat him, LIGHTS OUT.

The next time you see him, he is floating over the heads of the audience on a crane, and there he tells what will happen in the future. This scene to be about 3 or 4 minutes long, until the scene can be set on the stage for the Napoleonic Period, the directoire, in which the character of the crazy man from "The Misleading Lady" playing the part of Napoleon. This scene to run for about 15 minutes.

Then a scene in "one" where we are brought to the Gambling Palace at Monte Carlo. This is where we want to show semi-modern dances, the kan-kan [sic]. This is to be entirely French.

From there we take the Zepplin [sic] airship and sail across the Atlantic with the Thomas Effect.

The opening of the second act to be some big scene in New York City, either an idealized restaurant, dance palace, or a locale which will lend itself to dress and color.

From there we want a scene in "1," which shall be the railroad station where they get on the train—the New York Central, showing three cars instead of one car as they do at the Princess Theatre. They are going to the Exposition in San Francisco. After that scene, a scene in "1," a semi-oriental scene, like the modern Chinatown of San Francisco, or some scene which will lend itself to environments and atmosphere, and then to the Presidio overlooking the Panama Exposition in San Francisco and the Golden Gate.

SCENARIO 2

Scenario "A" Passing Show of 1914.

Drop in "One" showing Baldpate Inn in the distance, where the Tired Business Woman—"The Queen of the Movies"—has her moving picture studio.

A novelist (a la "Seven Keys of Baldpate") is on his way to write a novel in 24 hours in Baldpate Inn, which he believes to be a secluded spot. It is disclosed that the Queen of the Movies is rehearsing a new film, dramatizing all of the plays of the season.

The Novelist finds himself in many queer adventures, believing them to be real, a la "Seven Keys to Baldpate," although everything is being performed for the film company, which the Queen of the Movies controls. He attempts to rescue Kitty MacKay from the Russian secret police, the Gypsy band, etc., etc., etc.

Scenario "B"

First scene and prologue, a Persian Garden a thousand years ago, introducing Omar and combining the best things of "A Thousand Years Ago" and "Omar Khayyam," Broadway prophecy, etc. etc. as in original scenario.

Scene 2. The Office of "The Queen of the Movies" the Tired Business Woman, who controls the moving picture industry. This is to be an idealized office of the Modern Woman. She examines three or four men applicants for stenographers, making love to them all, and reversing the situation in "Help Wanted."

The reincarnated "Omar," now the modern novelist (a la "Seven Keys of Baldpate") applies for a position. She makes desperate love to him, tempts him with wine, etc. etc., a la "1999" and reversing the second act situation of "The Yellow Ticket." Omar is engaged to play Napoleon, the new film picture.

Scene 3. Moving Pictures Studio, the scene to be Directoire Garden, or etc. with the escaped lunatic, the other Napoleon, spoiling the film, etc.

Subsequent film to be the adventures of Kitty MacKay and Napoleon, Kitty MacKay being kidnapped by a Gypsy Band at the instigation of the Secret Police, etc etc., etc.

Scenario "C"

First scene a Persian Cabaret, where Omar Khayyam is employed, and where everything is done as in "A Thousand Years Ago." Omar is in love with Kitty MacKay, who is being hounded by the Russian Secret Police, at the instigation of the Queen of the Movies, who is in love with Omar. The entire story to be modern with all the characters of the plays used.

SCENARIO 3

Opening chorus of scene 1. Discovered stenographers—clerks—and camera men. After Opening—McGee the Novelist tells of hiring all the prominent actresses and actors for a new film to be made called "From a Thousand Years Ago to Today." He has scene with King Bagot and Mary Pickford telling them that he can't use the regular moving picture people any more, only the prominent actresses and actors. He tells of hiring THE MIDNIGHT GIRL—THE CRINOLINE GIRL—SARI etc., to pose for the pictures. Enter MIDNIGHT GIRL with nurses. As the office clock strikes twelve they change to Cabaret girls. After Number enter Adele who is engaged to act and fact brought out that McGee is in love with Kitty MacKay. Possible number McGee and Adele (duet and dance). After this enter Kitty MacKay pursued by the Baron, who is in love with her, and who is determined to put every obstacle in the way of McGee writing a successful film picture; because the Baron knows that McGee is in love with Kitty. The Baron has great influence with the Russian Secret Police. Number— Kitty MacKay and Scotch Girls. 2 (Kitty MacKay is the daughter of the Queen of the Movies). QUEEN OF THE MOVIES has a scene with Roosevelt and Huerta in which they are set off to work for the pictures. Roosevelt makes arrangements to be lost in Brazil. After this enter CRINOLINE GIRL, scene with Camera Man, then enter Sari and Gypsy Fiddlers. Sari Number. After this McGee holds a rehearsal scene ending with the Moving Picture Glide and close of scene.

SCENE 2: Scene is written with the exception that QUEEN OF THE MOVIES tries to make love to McGee. She discharges her daughter, Kitty MacKay, from the firm but reinstates her.

SCENE 3: PERSIAN GARDEN. At finish Omar's spirit departs and he lands on Broadway.

SCENE 4: A BROADWAY STREET. Here is the Baron, who realizes that Kitty MacKay who is absolutely necessary for McGee's picture to be a success, is made away with the Baron and the Russian Secret Police who take her away in an airship.

SCENARIO 4
"PASSING SHOW OF 1914"

ACT I—SCENE I: A Persian Garden A Thousand Years Ago.

Omar Khayyam, a vagabond player, comes in quest of the hand of Shireen. The conditions are that he must answer three riddles successfully. This he does, but delivers the prophecy of a Broadway a thousand years in the future, and is put in stocks by her father. A Spirit, leaving the mortal body, delivers the Rubiat in the Prophecy of a Broadway.

Song Numbers –   1. "A Persian Night"
                  2. "A Thousand Years Ago"
                  3. "Oh, oh, Omar"

SCENE II: The Moving Picture Studios of "The Queen of the Movies."

Mrs. Shireen, of the firm of "Mrs. Shireen and Daughter."

Mrs. Shireen rent the studios of Baldpate Inn to take her moving pictures. She commissions Moving Picture Novelist, William Hallowell MaGee, to write a new scenario film, "The Adventures of Kitty MacKay."

Her daughter, Shireen, is to be cast for the part of "Kitty MacKay." Mrs. Shireen, contrary to the advice of her lawyer, makes love to the White Slaves employed by the firm.

Here, also, is introduced "The Misleading Nut," who believes he is Napoleon, who escapes from his keepers at the lunatic asylum. Mr. Omar, who was Omar Khayyam a thousand years ago, comes to the studios, and Mrs. Shireen makes love to him.

Shireen enters in time to save Mr. Omar from her mother, and Omar discovers in Shireen his lover of a thousand years ago.

Mrs. Shireen, after disinheriting her daughter from the firm, reconsiders and forbids Mr. Omar from ever meeting Shireen again. At her signal, her gang of White Slavers take Mr. Omar away, and Shireen is kept and forced to work as Kitty MacKay in the new film being made.

Song Numbers–   4. Opening Number
                 5. Number to split the scene or finish the scene.

SCENE III: One of the Studios at Baldpate Inn, owned by the Queen of the Movies.

Locale—?

Song Number:—"The Moving Picture Glide" No. 6

William Hallowell McGee (The hero of "Seven Keys to Baldpate") outlines to the assistant camera man the wonderful scenario he has drawn up of "The Adventures of Kitty MacKay," which Shireen is to be featured in, and which scenario is to be played that day.

The scenario tell how Kitty MacKay, who is in love with Napoleon, steals the Mona Lisa picture, and is bringing it to Napoleon so that he may have funds enough to equip a new army. She is to meet Napoleon, but is pursued by his enemies, a band of Hungarian Gypsies and the Russian Secret Police, the Okrana ("The Yellow Ticket").

Kitty arrives ill, in charge of a nurse, "The Midnight Girl," who deserts her when the clock strikes 12 for the cabarets, and her friend "Adele," who comes to help her, is taken away by Baron Stephan Andrey of the Russian Police. Kitty is kidnapped by the Hungarian Gypsy band, and is rescued by Napoleon, and they both escape in an

Airship. This is the first half of the picture. Magee, the novelist, says that he himself is going to play Napoleon in the picture.

The assistants tell him the story is terrible, improbably and silly, but the Novelist declares, "It is as George Cohan says, what the public wants."

Magee, the Queen of the Movies, and the Camera Man start to take the picture.

THE PICTURE AS PLAYED

During the following, all characters except Omar, who believes Kitty to be in real trouble, the Queen of the Movies, Magee are playing for the camera.

Kitty MacKay arrives with the Mona Lisa picture, accompanied by her Scotch friends.

No. 7—Big Scotch Number "Kitty MacKay."

The Midnight Girl comes with Nurses, to take care of Kitty MacKay, who is ill, but hearing a clock strike twelve, cannot resist the call of the cabaret, and they change to "Midnight Girls."

No. 8—"Number for the Midnight Girls."

Sari comes with the Hungarian Gypsy Band to kidnap Kitty. At this juncture, Omar breaks in on the picture, saying that Shireen is here and in trouble. He has argument with the Queen of the Movies and breaks up temporarily the taking of the picture. They put him out, and continue the action of Sari and the Gypsy Band.

The Crinoline Girl, a detective female impersonator, comes in search of the Mona Lisa picture, and follows on the trail of the Gypsy Band.

No. 9—"Crinoline Girl Number."

The Movie Men and the Queen of the Movies announce a five minute wait for changing reels.

The Misleading Nut comes in, dressed as Napoleon, and has burlesque scene a la "Misleading Lady," directing his army, etc. He says he may be crazy but his is more sane than the women who wear pink hair, blue hair, etc. etc. (The Nut exits on the number)

No. 10—"I Love the girl with the hair do pink; hair of blue, etc. etc."

Omar returns, has scene with the Queen of the Movies, burlesque love scene, built on some play, possibly "The Secret." Omar overhears the Camera Man say that Shireen (Kitty) is to meet Napoleon, and determines, unknown to the others, to appear before her as Napoleon. Omar leaves, and the Moving Picture men start on—

THE SECOND REEL

Adele, Kitty MacKay's friend, comes in search of her, but is met by the Russian Secret Police, the Okana.

No. 11—Song Number for Adele

Baron Stefan Andrey and the Police make away with Adele.

Magee now enters playing Napoleon. He exits and the Misleading Nut enters as Napoleon, mixing up all the business for the Camera. The Hungarian Gypsies return with Kitty MacKay, but at the this juncture Magee Napoleon comes to save her, closely followed by the Misleading Nut Napoleon and finally by Omar Napoleon— the situation of the three Napoleons.

The Queen of the Movies interferes at this juncture and once more has Omar taken away, and the Magee Napoleon announces to Kitty that they must fly away in the airship.

No. 12—Closing Number of the Scene.

SCENE IV: Drop in "one," showing another locale of the Queen of the Movies' Studios at Baldpate.

(This could be a rehearsal given by Magee of one of the moving picture actresses, and would be an ideal scene of Whiting and Burt as Whiting could easily do the Magee, Novelist.)

SCENE V: The Airship Effect, with Napoleon leading Kitty MacKay and if possible showing Omar trying to reach his sweetheart, Shireen (Kitty) whom he believes to be in trouble.

CAST LIST 2
W/SCENARIO 4

SCENE 1: Shireen
Omar, a vagabond player
Maxixe
Turkey-Trot
Tango
Imam Allafake
First Priest
Second Priest

SCENE 2. Magee, the novelist from "Baldpate"
The Queen of the Movies
Omar
Shireen
Panthea, lawyer for the Queen of the Movies
The Misleading Nut
Bertie the Lamb
Cyril Grumpy

SCENE 3. Queen of the Movies
Omar
Shireen, now "Kitty MacKay"
The Midnight Girl
The Crinoline Girl (Played by the Misleading Nut)
Adele
Sari
Magee
The Misleading Nut
First Camera Operator
Second Camera Operator

SCENE 3. Cont.
Baron Stefan Andrey

SCENE 4. Magee, the novelist
Mary Pickinghard

Many of these characters double, and other incidental characters introduced.

BIBLIOGRAPHY

Adickes, Sandra E. *To Be Young Was Very Heaven: Women in New York before the First World War*. New York: Palgrave Macmillan, 2000.

Allen, Fred. *Much Ado About Me*. Boston: Little, Brown, and Co., 1956.

Arnold, Elliot. *Deep in My Heart*. New York: Duell, Sloan, and Pierce, 1949.

Aronson, Rudolph. *Theatrical and Musical Memoirs*. New York: McBride, Nast, and Co., 1913.

Astaire, Fred. *Steps in Time*. New York: Harper Collins, 1959 and 1981.

Baral, Robert. *Revue: A Nostalgic Reprise of the Great Broadway Period*. New York: Fleet Publishing, 1962.

Barrios, Richard. *A Song in the Dark: The Birth of the Musical Film*. New York and Oxford: Oxford University Press, 1995.

Bloom, Ken. *Hollywood Song: The Complete Film Musical Companion*. New York: Facts on File, Inc., 1995.

Bordman, Gerald. *American Musical Revue: From the Passing Show to Sugar Babies*. New York and Oxford: Oxford University Press, 1985.

Bordman, Gerald. *American Musical Theatre, A Chronicle*. 3rd ed. New York and Oxford: Oxford University Press, 2001.

Brideson, Cynthia, and Sara Brideson. *Ziegfeld and His Follies: A Biography of Broadway's Greatest Producer*. Lexington: University Press of Kentucky, 2015.

Chach, Maryann, Reagan Fletcher, Mark E. Swartz, and Sylvia Wang. *The Shuberts Present: 100 Years of American Theater* (Shubert Archive). New York: Harry N. Abrams, 2001.

Charyn, Jerome. *Gangsters and Gold Diggers: Old New York, the Jazz Age, and the Birth of Broadway*. Emeryville, CA: Thunder's Mouth Press, 2003.

Clum, John M. *Something for the Boys: Musical Theater and Gay Culture*. New York: Palgrave, 1999.

Damase, Jacques. *Les Folies du Music Hall: A History of the Music-Hall in Paris*. London and New York: Spring Books, 1962.

Davis, Lee. *Scandals and Follies: The Rise of the Great Broadway Revue*. New York: Limelight Editions, 2000.

Depue, Oscar B., and C. Francis Jenkins. *Handbook for Motion Picture and Stereopticon Operators*. Washington, DC: The Knega Company, 1908.

Drutman, Brian. "The Birth of the Passing Show" in *The Passing Show: The Newsletter of the Shubert Archives*, vol. 11, no.1 (Summer 1987), 1–3.

Everett, William. *Sigmund Romberg*. New Haven, CT: Yale University Press, 2007.

Ferencz, George J., ed. *"The Broadway Sound": The Autobiography and Selected Essays of Robert Russell Bennett*. Rochester, NY: University of Rochester Press, 1999.

Fields, Armond, and L. Marc Fields. *From the Bowery to Broadway: Lew Fields and the Roots of American Popular Theater*. New York and Oxford: Oxford University Press, 1993.

Gardner, Edward Foote. *Popular Songs of the Twentieth Century: Volume I—Chart Detail and Encyclopedia (1900–1949)*. St. Paul, MN: Paragon House, 2000.

Grant, Mark N. *The Rise and Fall of the Broadway Musical*. Boston: Northeastern University Press, 2004.

Green, Martin, and John Swan. *The Triumph of Pierrot: The Commedia dell'arte and the Modern Imagination*. University Park: Pennsylvania State University Press, 1993.

Hamberlin, Larry. *Tin Pan Opera: Operatic Novelty Songs in the Ragtime Era*. New York and Oxford: Oxford University Press, 2011.

Hamm, Charles. *Irving Berlin: Songs from the Melting Pot—The Formative Years (1907–1914)*. New York and Oxford: Oxford University Press, 1997.

Harding, Alfred. *The Revolt of the Actors*. New York: William Morrow & Company, 1929.

Harris, Warren G. *The Other Marilyn*. New York: Arbor House, 1985.

Hayter-Menzies, Grant. *Charlotte Greenwood: The Life and Career of the Comic Star of Vaudeville, Radio, and Film*. Jefferson, NC, and London: McFarland and Co., 2007.

Hayter-Menzies, Grant. *Mrs. Ziegfeld: The Public and Private Lives of Billie Burke*. Jefferson, NC, and London: McFarland & Company, Inc., 2009.

Henderson, Mary C. *The New Amsterdam: The Biography of a Broadway Theatre*. New York: Hyperion, 1997.

Hiroshi Garrett, Charles. *Struggling to Define a Nation: American Music and the Twentieth Century*. Berkeley and Los Angeles: University of California Press, 2008).

Hirsch, Foster. *The Boys from Syracuse: The Shuberts' Theatrical Empire*. Carbondale and Edwardsville: Southern Illinois University Press, 1998.

Holman, Michael. "Breaking: The History." In *That's The Joint: The Hip-Hop Studies Reader*, edited by Murray Forman and Mark Anthony Neal. New York: Routledge, 2004.

Jablonski, Edward. *Gershwin: A Biography*. New York: Doubleday, 1988.

Koegel, John. *Music in German Immigrant Theater: New York, 1840–1940*. Rochester, NY: Boydell and Brewer, Ltd., 2009.

Langer, Susanne K. *Feeling and Form: A Theory of Art*. New York: Charles Scribner's Sons, 1953.

Lawrence, David Haldane. "Chorus boys: words, music, and queerness (c.1900–c.1936)," *Studies in Musical Theatre*, 3:2 (2009), 157–69.

Lees, Gene. *Portrait of Johnny: The Life of John Herndon Mercer*. Milwaukee, WI: Hal Leonard, 2004.

Levinson, Peter. *Puttin' On the Ritz: Fred Astaire and the Fine Art of Panache*. New York: St. Martin's Press, 2009.

Lightweis-Goff, Jennie. "'Long Time I Trabble on de Way': Stephen Foster's Conversion Narrative," *Journal of Popular Music Studies*, 20:2, 150–65.

Lowrey, Carolyn. *The First One Hundred Noted Men and Women of the Screen*. New York: Moffat, Yard, and Co., 1920.

Mander, Raymond, and Joe Mitchenson, *Revue: A Story in Pictures*. New York: Taplinger Publishing Co., 1971.

mcclung, bruce d. *Lady in The Dark: Biography of a Musical*. New York and Oxford: Oxford University Press, 2007.

McNamara, Brooks. *The Shuberts of Broadway*. New York and Oxford: Oxford University Press, 1990.

Mizejewski, Linda. *Ziegfeld Girl: Image and Icon in Culture and Cinema*. Durham, NC: Duke University Press, 1999.

Mordden, Ethan. *Ziegfeld: The Man Who Invented Show Business*. New York: St. Martin's Press, 2008.

Ommen van der Merwe, Ann. *The Ziegfeld Follies: A History in Song*. Lanham, MD: Scarecrow Press, 2009.

Rodger, Gillian, and Jonas Westover, "American Revue." In *Encyclopedia of Popular Music of the World*, vol. 6: *Genres*, edited by John Shepherd. London: Continuum Press, 2013.

Senelick, Laurence. "Transvestitism 2." In *Encyclopedia of Homosexuality*, edited by Wayne R. Dynes. New York: Garland Publishing, 1990.

Shtier, Rachel. *Striptease: The Untold History of the Girlie Show*. New York and Oxford: Oxford University Press, 2004.

Simonson, Mary. *Body Knowledge*. New York and Oxford: Oxford University Press, 2013.

Singer, Barry. *Black and Blue: The Life and Lyrics of Andy Razaf*. New York: Schirmer, 1992.

Spoto, Donald. *Possessed: The Life of Joan Crawford*. New York: Harper Collins, 2010.

Stempel, Larry. *Showtime: A History of the Broadway Musical Theater*. New York: Norton, 2010.

Stratyner, Barbara. *Ned Wayburn and the Dance Routine: From Vaudeville to the Ziegfeld Follies*. Madison, WI: A-R Editions, 1996.

Stufft, Monica Eugenia. "Chorus Girl Collective: Twentieth Century American Performance Communities and Urban Networking." Ph.D. diss., University of California, Berkeley, 2008.

Suskin, Steve. *The Sound of Broadway Music: A Book of Orchestrators and Orchestrations*. New York and Oxford: Oxford, 2009.

Van Aken, Kellee. "Race and Gender in the Broadway Chorus." PhD diss., University of Pittsburgh, 2006.

Vannatter, Loy. *And Then It Was Winter*, vol. 2. Tucson, AZ: Wheatmark, 2010.

Westover, Jonas. "Louis Hirsch." In *The Grove Dictionary of American Music*, 2nd ed., edited by Charles Hiroshi Garrett. New York and Oxford: Oxford University Press, 2013.

Westover, Jonas. "Orchestrations for *The Passing Show of 1914*: An Analysis of the Techniques of Frank Saddler and Sol Levy." In *Music, American Made: Essays in Honor of John Graziano*, edited by John Koegel. Sterling Heights, MI: Harmonie Park Press, 2011.

Westover, Jonas. "Shaping a Song for the Stage: How the Early Revue Cultivated Hits," *Studies in Musical Theatre* 6:2 (2012), 153–71.

Westover, Jonas. "Shubert (family)." In *The Grove Dictionary of American Music*, 2nd ed., edited by Charles Hiroshi Garrett. New York and Oxford: Oxford University Press, 2013.

Westover, Jonas. "A Study and Reconstruction of *The Passing Show of 1914*: The American Musical Revue and its Development in the Early Twentieth Century." Ph.D. diss., Graduate Center of the City University of New York, 2010.

Witmark, Isidore, and Isaac Goldberg. *From Ragtime to Swingtime: The Story of the House of Witmark*. New York: Lee Furman, Inc., 1939.

Zwilling, Leonard. *A TAD Lexicon*. Etymology and Linguistic Principles, vol. 3. Rolla, MO: G. Cohen, 1993.

INDEX

Red Pepper (magazine), 100, *101*
Reed, James, 149n51
Reed, Jessie, 218
Reinhardt, Max, 96
Reisner, C. Francis, 20
Remick Music Publishing, 126–8,
 130, 210
Remick, Jerome, 126–7, 222
Renault, Francis (Antonio Auriemma),
 xxi, 44–5, 52, 57, 58nn20–6,
 138–40, 198
Return of Peter Grimm, The, 71
Revue of Revues, The, 9–10, 204
Ring, Blanche, xxi, 38–9, 45, 215
Rio Rita, 222
Rising, William, 24
Rittman, Trude, 121
Roberts, Bobbie, 102–4
Roberts, Lee S., xxv
Robertson, John, 107
Robinson Crusoe, Jr., 10, 80
Rodgers, Richard, 121, 129, 223n6, 240
Rodriguez, Isabel, xxi, 135, 137,
 140, 142
Rogers Brothers, 69
Rogers, Will, 52, 211
Rogerson, Clarence, 22
Rollins, Rowena, 239, 241
Romberg, Sigmund, xxi, 17–18, 55, 77,
 102, 121–3, 146n4, 146n13, 183,
 186, 193–7, 222, 235
Roosevelt, Teddy, 16, 182, 192
Rose, Billy, 239
Rose, Fred, 78
"Rose of the Morning," 146n13
Rose, Vincent, 210
Rosenblatt, Cantor Josef, 83
Rosenfeld, Sydney, 8
"Rosie Rosenblott," 77
Roth, Herb, 97
"Royal Wedding," 95
Rugel, Yvette, 25
Ruggles, Charles, xxii, 55
Rush, Barbara, 231
Russell, Bob, 240
Russell, Lillian, 44
Ryan, Sue, 237, 239, 241

Saddler, Frank, xxii, 21, *22*, 123–4, 129
"Sadie, You Won't Say Nay," 64
St. Helier, Ivy, 79
Sally, 214, 221–2, 232, 244
Salome, 38, 57n7, 135
Salvation Nell (play), 184–5
"Salvation Nell" (song), 184–5,
 185, 199n9
Sandow, Eugene, 202, 231
Sands Hotel and Casino, 243
Sari, 141, 193–4
"Sari Dance," 141, 171
Saturday Evening Post, 22
Savoy and Brennan (Bert and Jay),
 212–3, 218
Schaetzlein, Larry, 79
Scheherezade, 17
Schirmer (publisher), 18, 126
Schlageter, Ernest, 24
School Days (Gus Edwards), 58n20
Schrader, Marie B. ("Madame Critic"), 97,
 101–2, 112, 176
Schubert, Franz, 33n63
Schulz, William, 21
Schwartz, Jean, xxii, 17, 55, 79, 126,
 129–30, 193
Scibilia, Anton, 244–5, *245*
Selden, Edgar, 191
Selwyn, Arch, 229
Seven Keys to Baldpate (play), 156, 183
"Shakespearean Rag, The," 77
Shannon, Bessie, 107
Shapiro, Bernstein, and Co., 31n43, 125
Shay, Morris, 64
Sherman, Al, 79
"She's the Mother of Broadway
 Rose," 78, 81
"She Taught Me to Dance the
 Fandango," 20
"Shine On Harvest Moon," 232
Show Boat, 129, 222
Show Is On, The, 84
Show of Shows, The (film), 115n2, 248n37
Show of Wonders, The, 10, 46, 80,
 127, 213
Shubert-Colonial Theater (Cleveland), 110
Shubert Gaieties of 1919, 86, 221